Mark

Mark

MARY ANN BEAVIS

Baker Academic

a division of Baker Publishing Group
Grand Rapids, Michigan

Published by Baker Academic
a division of Baker Publishing Group
PO Box 6287, Grand Rapids, MI 49516-6287
www.bakeracademic.com

Printed in the United States of America

Library of Congress Cataloging-in-Publication Data
Beavis, Mary Ann.
    Mark / Mary Ann Beavis.
        p.   cm. — (Paideia: commentaries on the New Testament)
    Includes bibliographical references and index.
    ISBN 978-0-8010-3437-4 (pbk.)
    1. Bible. N.T. Mark—Commentaries. I. Title.
BS2585.53.B43 2011
226.3′07—dc23   2011019244

To Daisy and Willow (Bar. 6:21 NAB)

Contents

Figures

Foreword

Paideia: Commentaries on the New Testament is a series that sets out to comment on the final form of the New Testament text in a way that pays due attention both to the cultural, literary, and theological settings in which the text took form and to the interests of the contemporary readers to whom the commentaries are addressed. This series is aimed squarely at students—including MA students in religious and theological studies programs, seminarians, and upper-division undergraduates—who have theological interests in the biblical text. Thus, the didactic aim of the series is to enable students to understand each book of the New Testament as a literary whole rooted in a particular ancient setting and related to its context within the New Testament.

The name "Paideia" (Greek for "education") reflects (1) the instructional aim of the series—giving contemporary students a basic grounding in academic New Testament studies by guiding their engagement with New Testament texts; (2) the fact that the New Testament texts as literary unities are shaped by the educational categories and ideas (rhetorical, narratological, etc.) of their ancient writers and readers; and (3) the pedagogical aims of the texts themselves—their central aim being not simply to impart information but to form the theological convictions and moral habits of their readers.

Each commentary deals with the text in terms of larger rhetorical units; these are not verse-by-verse commentaries. This series thus stands within the stream of recent commentaries that attend to the final form of the text. Such reader-centered literary approaches are inherently more accessible to liberal arts students without extensive linguistic and historical-critical preparation than older exegetical approaches, but within the reader-centered world the sanest practitioners have paid careful attention to the extratext of the original readers, including not only these readers' knowledge of the geography, history, and other contextual elements reflected in the text but also their ability to respond correctly to the literary and rhetorical conventions used in the text. Paideia commentaries pay deliberate attention to this extratextual repertoire in order to highlight the ways in which the text is designed to persuade and move its readers. Each rhetorical unit is explored from three angles: (1) introductory matters; (2) tracing the train of thought or narrative or rhetorical flow of the argument; and (3) theological issues raised by the text that are of interest to the contemporary Christian. Thus, the primary focus remains on the text and not its historical context or its interpretation in the secondary literature.

Our authors represent a variety of confessional points of view: Protestant, Catholic, and Orthodox. What they share, beyond being New Testament scholars of national and international repute, is a commitment to reading the biblical text as theological documents within their ancient contexts. Working within the broad parameters described here, each author brings his or her own considerable exegetical talents and deep theological commitments to the task of laying bare the interpretation of Scripture for the faith and practice of God's people everywhere.

Mikeal C. Parsons
Charles H. Talbert

Preface

My interest in the Gospel of Mark began with my doctoral dissertation on Mark 4:11–12, written at the University of Cambridge between 1984 and 1987 and published in 1989 as *Mark's Audience: The Literary and Social Context of Mark 4.11–12*. My interest has endured from then until now, as reflected in my subsequent journal articles on various aspects of the Gospel (Beavis 1987; 1988; 1998; 2008; 2010). These have included reader response, feminist, disability rights, and tradition critical perspectives. During this time, my research has been enriched by my years of teaching courses on the New Testament and the Bible and Western culture at St. Thomas More College and elsewhere and through graduate student supervision.

In view of my enduring interest in Mark, I was delighted to be invited by Baker Academic to write this volume for the Paideia series. While this commentary reflects some of the perspectives mentioned above, I have focused on the historical and literary-critical aspects of the text relevant to the intended audience of the series: "MA students in religious and theological studies programs, seminarians, and upper-divisional undergraduates—who have theological interests in the biblical text" (see foreword). My experience with students and church Bible study groups has taught me that many readers thirst for more than the impressions of the Gospels they have imbibed through family, church, and popular culture. Rather, they want to understand the Gospels for themselves as historical, literary, and theological documents with ongoing relevance for the individual, church, and society. This commentary is offered not as a definitive interpretation of Mark but as an aid and encouragement to further critical inquiry and new understandings on the part of the reader.

Many thanks to the series editors, Mikeal Parsons and Charles Talbert, for their patience and encouragement and to the anonymous peer reviewers who raised many challenging questions in their comments on the first draft of this volume. I am also grateful to James Ernest and the editorial team at Baker Academic for their patient assistance and attention to detail. Finally, I would express my gratitude to my employer, St. Thomas More College, for providing me a supportive environment for the project.

Mary Ann Beavis

Abbreviations

General

alt.	altered	lit.	literally
b.	Babylonian Talmud	*m.*	Mishnah
ca.	*circa*, approximately	MT	Masoretic Text, Hebrew OT
cent.	century	NT	New Testament
cf.	compare	OT	Old Testament
chap(s).	chapter(s)	par.	parallel
col(s).	column(s)	pl.	plural
e.g.	*exempli gratia,* for example	rev.	revised
esp.	especially	*t.*	Tosefta
ET	English translation	trans.	translator
et al.	*et alii,* and others	vol(s).	volume(s)
fig.	figurative	x	following a numeral = times, number of occurrences
i.e.	*id est,* that is		
Lat.	Latin	*y.*	Jerusalem Talmud

Bible Texts and Versions

ASV	American Standard Version		E. Nestle and] B. Aland et al. 27th rev. ed. Stuttgart: Deutsche Bibelgesellschaft, 1993.
KJV	King James Version		
LXX	Septuagint		
NA[27]	*Novum Testamentum Graece.* Edited by [E. and	NAB	New American Bible

NASB	New American Standard Bible	NIV	New International Version
NETS	*A New English Translation of the Septuagint*. Edited by A. Pietersma and B. G. Wright. New York: Oxford University Press, 2007.	NLT	New Living Translation
		NRSV	New Revised Standard Version
		RSV	Revised Standard Version

Ancient Corpora

OLD TESTAMENT

Gen.	Genesis
Exod.	Exodus
Lev.	Leviticus
Num.	Numbers
Deut.	Deuteronomy
Josh.	Joshua
Judg.	Judges
Ruth	Ruth
1–2 Sam.	1–2 Samuel
1–2 Kings	1–2 Kings
1–2 Chron.	1–2 Chronicles
Ezra	Ezra
Neh.	Nehemiah
Esther	Esther
Job	Job
Ps./Pss.	Psalm/Psalms
Prov.	Proverbs
Eccles.	Ecclesiastes
Song	Song of Songs
Isa.	Isaiah
Jer.	Jeremiah
Lam.	Lamentations
Ezek.	Ezekiel
Dan.	Daniel
Hosea	Hosea
Joel	Joel
Amos	Amos
Obad.	Obadiah
Jon.	Jonah
Mic.	Micah
Nah.	Nahum
Hab.	Habakkuk

Zeph.	Zephaniah
Hag.	Haggai
Zech.	Zechariah
Mal.	Malachi

DEUTEROCANONICAL BOOKS

1–2 Esd.	1–2 Esdras
Jdt.	Judith
1–4 Macc.	1–4 Maccabees
Sir.	Sirach
Tob.	Tobit
Wis.	Wisdom of Solomon

NEW TESTAMENT

Matt.	Matthew
Mark	Mark
Luke	Luke
John	John
Acts	Acts
Rom.	Romans
1–2 Cor.	1–2 Corinthians
Gal.	Galatians
Eph.	Ephesians
Phil.	Philippians
Col.	Colossians
1–2 Thess.	1–2 Thessalonians
1–2 Tim.	1–2 Timothy
Titus	Titus
Philem.	Philemon
Heb.	Hebrews
James	James
1–2 Pet.	1–2 Peter
1–3 John	1–3 John
Jude	Jude
Rev.	Revelation

DEAD SEA SCROLLS

CD	Damascus Document
1QH	Thanksgiving Hymns
1QpHab	Pesher on Habakkuk
1QS	Community Rule
11QT	Temple Scroll

RABBINIC LITERATURE

'Abod. Zar.	'Abodah Zarah
Bek.	Bekorot
Ber.	Berakot
B. Qam.	Baba Qamma
Giṭ.	Giṭṭin
Mak.	Makkot
Mek.	Mekilta
Midr. Esther	Midrash on Esther
Ned.	Nedarim
Pesaḥ.	Pesaḥim
Rab.	Rabbah
Šabb.	Šabbat
Sanh.	Sanhedrin
Ta'an.	Ta'anit
Ṭohar.	Ṭoharot
Yebam.	Yebamot

OLD TESTAMENT PSEUDEPIGRAPHA

Apoc. Ab.	Apocalypse of Abraham
Apoc. El.	Apocalypse of Elijah
Apoc. Zeph.	Apocalypse of Zephaniah
2 Bar.	2 Baruch (Syriac Apocalypse)
1 En.	1 Enoch (Ethiopic Apocalypse)
Jub.	Jubilees
L.A.B.	Liber antiquitatum biblicarum (Pseudo-Philo)
Liv. Pro.	Lives of the Prophets
Pss. Sol.	Psalms of Solomon
Sib. Or.	Sibylline Oracles
T. Ben.	Testament of Benjamin
T. Dan	Testament of Dan
T. Iss.	Testament of Issachar
T. Jud.	Testament of Judah
T. Levi	Testament of Levi
T. Mos.	Testament of Moses
T. Naph.	Testament of Naphtali
T. Sol.	Testament of Solomon

APOSTOLIC FATHERS

1–2 Clem.	1–2 Clement
Did.	Didache
Herm. Sim.	Shepherd of Hermas, Similitude

NEW TESTAMENT APOCRYPHA AND PSEUDEPIGRAPHA

Prot. Jas.	Protevangelium of James

NAG HAMMADI CODICES

Gos. Phil.	Gospel of Philip
Gos. Thom.	Gospel of Thomas

Ancient Authors

AMBROSE

Spir.	De Spiritu Sancto

ARISTOTLE

Poet.	Poetics
Pol.	Politics
Rhet.	Rhetoric

ATHANASIUS

Hom. sem.	Homilia de semente

CICERO

Off.	De officiis

DEMETRIUS

Eloc.	De elocutione

DIO CHRYSOSTOM

Or.	Orations

DIOGENES LAERTIUS

Liv. Phil.	Lives of Eminent Philosophers

EPIPHANIUS
Ancor.	Ancoratus
Pan.	Panarion

EUSEBIUS
Hist. eccl.	Historia ecclesiastica

HIPPOLYTUS
Antichr.	De antichristo

IRENAEUS
Haer.	Adversus haereses

JOHN CHRYSOSTOM
Hom. Matt.	Homiliae in Matthaeum

JOSEPHUS
Ag. Ap.	Against Apion
Ant.	Jewish Antiquities
J.W.	Jewish War
Life	The Life

JUSTIN MARTYR
1 Apol.	First Apology
Dial.	Dialogue with Trypho

JUVENAL
Sat.	Satirae

LIVY
Hist.	Historiae

ORIGEN
Comm. Matt.	Commentary on Matthew
Fr. Matt.	Fragments on Matthew

PHILO OF ALEXANDRIA
Contempl. Life	On the Contemplative Life
Embassy	On the Embassy to Gaius
Good Person	That Every Good Person Is Free
Names	On the Change of Names
Spec. Laws	On the Special Laws
Virtues	On the Virtues

PHILOSTRATUS
Vit. Apoll.	Vita Apollonii

PLINY THE ELDER
Nat.	Naturalis historia

PLUTARCH
Exil.	De exilio
Rom.	Romulus

TACITUS
Ann.	Annals
Hist.	Histories

TERENCE
Phorm.	Phormio

VALERIUS MAXIMUS
Fact.	Facta et dicta memorabilia

VIRGIL
Georg.	Georgics

Anonymous Works

Alex. Rom.	Alexander Romance	Ep. Diog.	Epistles of Diogenes

Modern Works, Editions, and Collections

BDAG	A Greek-English Lexicon of the New Testament and Other Early Christian Literature. By W. Bauer, F. W. Danker, W. F. Arndt, and F. W. Gingrich. 3rd ed. Chicago: University of Chicago Press, 2000.

DBI	*Dictionary of Biblical Imagery.* Edited by Leland Ryken, James C. Wilhoit, and Tremper Longman III. Downers Grove, IL, and Leicester, UK: Inter-Varsity, 1998.
OTP	*The Old Testament Pseudepigrapha.* Edited by James H. Charlesworth. 2 vols. Garden City, NY: Doubleday, 1983–85.
P.Oxy.	*The Oxyrhynchus Papyri.* Edited by B. P. Grenfell et al. 73 vols. London: Egypt Exploration Society, 1898–2009.
Str-B	Hermann L. Strack and Paul Billerbeck. *Kommentar zum Neuen Testament aus Talmud und Midrasch.* 6 vols. Munich: Beck, 1922–61.
TDNT	*Theological Dictionary of the New Testament.* Edited by Gerhard Kittel and Gerhard Friedrich. Translated by Geoffrey W. Bromiley. 10 vols. Grand Rapids: Eerdmans, 1964–76.
WDCH	*The Westminster Dictionary of Church History.* Edited by Jerald C. Brauer. Philadelphia: Westminster, 1971.

Mark

Introduction

For most of Christian history, the Gospel of Mark has been neglected by church leaders and theologians because, following the opinion of Augustine of Hippo, it was thought to be an abridged version of Matthew:

> For Matthew is understood to have taken it in hand to construct the record of the incarnation of the Lord according to royal lineage, and to give an account of a great deal of his deeds and words as they stood in relation to this present life of men. Mark follows him closely, and looks like his associate and epitomizer. For in Mark's narrative he gives nothing in concert with John apart from the others. . . . Taken by himself, Mark has relatively little exclusively to record, and taken in conjunction with Luke, even less. In concurrence with Matthew, Mark has a great number of passages. Frequently he narrates in words almost numerically and identically the same as those used by Matthew. (*Harmony of the Gospels* 1.2.4, in Oden and Hall 1998, xxvii)

Furthermore, Mark, like Luke, was believed to have been written not by one of the apostles, as were Matthew and John, but by a second-generation Christian who had never met Jesus. Nobody seems to have bothered to write a commentary on Mark until the seventh century; the first was written by an anonymous Irish monk (Cahill 1998), closely followed by the British chronicler and theologian Bede (AD 673–735). Nonetheless, the so-called Second Gospel (because of its customary placement after Matthew) was recognized as Scripture from an early date, due to an early church tradition that connected Mark with Peter (see Schildgen 1998, 37).

The relative disinterest in Mark began to shift radically in the eighteenth century with the rise of the historical criticism of the Bible. Scholars began to question the traditional accounts of Gospel origins, and Christian Hermann Weisse (1801–66) marshaled evidence to demonstrate that Mark could

---

Ancient Commentaries on Mark

Although, as mentioned in the main text, no full-length Christian commentary on Mark is extant from before the seventh century, there are numerous references to Markan passages in early Christian writers. Unlike modern historical-critical biblical scholars, the ancient interpreters regarded the Scriptures as divine revelation, a seamless whole, a source of truth to be put into practice by believers. While the biblical stories were regarded as historically valid, the literal sense of the text was regarded as conveying only one level of meaning, to be supplemented by other forms of interpretation. In the Western world, theologians eventually recognized a "fourfold sense of scripture": literal (or historical), allegorical (or symbolic), tropological (or moral), and anagogical (having to do with the afterlife), summarized by a Latin verse, translated here by Robert M. Grant: "The letter shows us what God and our ancestors did; the allegory shows us where our faith is hid; the moral meaning gives us rules of daily life; the anagogy shows us where we end our strife" (quoted in Scobie 2003, 11, adapted). The rabbis developed a similar fourfold scheme for the interpretation of Jewish scripture, summed up by the acronym PARDES ("Paradise"): *peshat*, the literal meaning; *remez*, the symbolic meaning; *drash*, the midrashic or homiletic meaning; and *sod*, the mystical or secret meaning (see Unterman 1991, 152). Although this commentary does not share all the assumptions of the ancient writers, their comments are cited throughout in order to illustrate the range and quality of interpretations of Mark throughout Christian history.

---

not be an abbreviation of Matthew, as Augustine had held. Rather, Matthew and Luke must have used Mark as their source, since both Gospels integrate large portions of Mark, follow Mark's ordering of events, and seldom agree against Mark. Heinrich Holtzmann (1832–1910) accounted for the material shared by Matthew and Luke but missing from Mark by postulating a sayings collection "Q" (after the German word *Quelle*, meaning "source") used by both Matthew and Luke in addition to Mark. This "Two Source Hypothesis," accepted by the majority of NT scholars today, holds that Mark is not merely a digest of material that is more fully covered in the other Gospels, but rather the oldest of all, the source of Matthew and Luke (together with Mark, called "Synoptic Gospels," from the Greek *synoptikos*, "seen together"), and the model for all four.

Initially the insight that Mark was very probably the earliest written account of the life of Jesus excited scholars because if Mark was the oldest Gospel, this made it the closest to the historical Jesus. This conclusion was challenged with the publication in 1901 of William Wrede's *Messianic Secret* (ET, 1971), which argued that the evangelist's purpose was theological, not historical—that Mark was written not to record eyewitness accounts of the life of Jesus but to explain that Jesus was not recognized as the messiah in his lifetime because he deliberately suppressed his messianic identity. At the same time, scholars like Martin Dibelius (ET, 1934; lived 1883–1947) and Rudolf Bultmann (ET, 1963; lived 1884–1976) were dissecting the Gospels into their constituent "forms"—pre-Gospel materials such as parables, sayings, and legends—which had circulated orally among believers before they were compiled into Gospels by Mark and the other evangelists. The method of "form criticism," which regarded the social settings of the pre-Gospel units of tradition as windows into the needs and concerns of the early church rather than as historical evidence about Jesus, dominated Gospel scholarship for the first half of the twentieth century. Consequently there was little interest in Mark in and of itself; rather, the Gospel was seen as a collection of sources to be dissected and analyzed.

In the decades since the publication of Willi Marxsen's *Der Evangelist Markus* (1956; ET, 1969), scholars returned to the consideration of the Gospels as literarily unified works rather than as compendia of source materials. This began with the method of Gospel interpretation pioneered by Marxsen and other German scholars known as *Redaktionsgeschichte*, usually translated as "redaction criticism." This method assumes the validity of form criticism but seeks to understand the use made of the forms (early Christian traditions) by the Gospel writers in order to uncover their distinctive theological outlooks and concerns. Initially the focus of redaction criticism was on distinguishing between editorial input and pre-Gospel material, but it soon became apparent that the evangelists were not just transmitters of tradition but also authors in their own right. Thus it became necessary to consider the Gospels as wholes and shaped by their authors' aims and the needs of their respective communities, leading to more explicitly literary critical interpretations (cf. Perrin and Duling 1982, 236). More recently, redaction criticism has been superseded by a plethora of specialized methodological approaches, some literary (e.g., narrative criticism, reader response, deconstruction, reception history, rhetorical criticism), some ideological (e.g., feminist, liberation theological, Marxist), and some social scientific (for an overview of some of the methods that have been applied to Mark, see J. Anderson and Moore 1992).

The methods of source, form, and redaction criticism have undermined the argument that since Mark is the first Gospel to have been written, it is the most likely to contain eyewitness accounts of the words and deeds of Jesus. Nevertheless, scholars continue to use the materials preserved in the Gospels, other NT writings, and extracanonical works to reconstruct the career of the historical Jesus, albeit with widely differing results (for a survey of some of these, see Witherington 1997). This commentary recognizes that Mark contains some traditions that may go back to Jesus himself and will point out some of these, but the historical Jesus is not the main subject of the pages that follow. Rather, the focus is on the redaction-critical insight that the Gospels were written by the evangelists not so much to convey historical information as to address the issues facing their own Christian communities—in the case of Mark, probably a small house church in a city somewhere in the Roman Empire. For Mark's community, Jesus was not merely a revered historical figure but truly a living presence who instructed, encouraged, and challenged them through the medium of the Gospel.

Authorship, Date, Setting

While several scholars have argued that Mark was not written for a single church in a given locale but rather for Greek-speaking believers throughout the Roman world (e.g., Bauckham 1998; Peterson 2000, 200–201; Shiner 2003, 26–27), most regard the Gospel as addressed to a community whose location, geographically and temporally, is highly relevant to its meaning. It is certainly true that within decades of its composition, Mark began to be regarded as Scripture by Christians in various locales, but the evangelist wrote at a specific place and time for reasons relevant to local needs.

Unfortunately, the author gives us no explicit information about his identity, location, or circumstances. Like the other Gospels, Mark is anonymous in that the author does not identify himself in the body of the text; in this commentary, the name "Mark" (and the assumption that the author was male) will be used by convention—although as Virginia Woolf quipped, in literary history, "anonymous" has often been a woman. The titles of the Gospels are dated to the second century, when early Christian authors begin to mention Gospels "according to" Matthew, Mark, Luke, and John. The term "gospel" or "good news" (*euangelion*) to refer to these books was no doubt derived from Mark 1:1, which announces the "gospel/good news of Jesus Christ, Son of God."

The name Mark (*Markos*), a common name in the Roman Empire, appears several times in the NT, but never in the Gospels. Mark is not listed as one of the twelve apostles. Notably, Paul mentions a "fellow worker" by the name of Mark (Philem. 24; cf. Col. 4:10; 2 Tim. 4:11, both regarded as deutero-Pauline), and Acts refers to a "John Mark" as the son of Mary of Jerusalem (12:12) and a companion of Paul and Barnabas (12:25; 15:37, 39). The late and pseudonymous 1 Pet. 5:13 ends with a greeting from the chief apostle and "my son Mark" from the church in "Babylon" (an early Christian code word for Rome). Early Christian tradition regards all these "Marks" as the same figure, the John Mark of Jerusalem who initially accompanied Paul, Silas, and Barnabas but who, along with Barnabas, parted ways with the others after an argument over the young man's perceived unreliability: "Barnabas wanted to take with them John called Mark. But Paul decided not to take with them one who had deserted them in Pamphylia and had not accompanied them in the work. The disagreement became so sharp that they parted company;

Barnabas took Mark with him and sailed away to Cyprus" (Acts 15:37–39). Whether or not all these Marks were the same person, it is noteworthy that Acts, the first "church history," contains this rather unflattering portrayal of a man later identified as the writer of an authoritative Gospel.

The first author to speak of Mark as a Gospel writer was Papias, bishop of Hierapolis in Asia Minor, who wrote in the first half of the second century. Although Papias is said to have written five books of *Expositions of the Sayings of the Lord* (Eusebius, *Hist. eccl.* 3.39), all that is left of them are scattered fragments in ancient ecclesiastical authors (see Holmes 2006, 302–18). Among them are two references to the authorship and composition of Mark, both quoted by the historian Eusebius (fourth cent.):

> And the elder used to say this: "Mark, having become Peter's interpreter, wrote down accurately everything he remembered, though not in order, of the things either said or done by Christ. For he neither heard the Lord nor followed him, but afterward, as I said, followed Peter, who adapted his teachings as needed but had no intention of giving an ordered account of the Lord's sayings." Consequently Mark did nothing wrong in writing down some things as he remembered them, for he made it his one concern not to omit anything that he heard or to make any false statement in them. (Eusebius, *Hist. eccl.* 3.39.14–15, in Holmes 2006, 310)

The "elder" referred to as the source of the tradition is "the Elder John," thought by Eusebius to be a figure distinct from John the apostle (*Hist. eccl.* 3.39.4). Papias's other reference to Mark is cited as one of the sources for a tradition about the circumstances behind the writing of the Gospel:

> But so great a light of godliness shone upon the minds of Peter's listeners that they were not satisfied with a single hearing or with the oral teaching of the divine proclamation. So, with all kinds of exhortations they begged Mark (whose Gospel is extant), since he was Peter's follower, to leave behind a written record of the teaching given to them verbally, and did not quit until they had persuaded the man, and thus they became the immediate cause of the scripture called "The Gospel according to Saint Mark." And they say that the apostle, aware of what had occurred because the Spirit had revealed to him, was pleased with their zeal and sanctioned the writing for study in the churches. Clement quotes the story in the sixth book of the *Hypotyposes* [*Institutions*], and the Bishop of Hierapolis, named Papias, corroborates him. He also says that Peter mentions Mark in his first epistle, which they say he composed in Rome itself, as he himself indicates, referring to the city metaphorically as Babylon in these words: "She who is in Babylon, who is likewise chosen, sends you greetings, as does Mark, my son." (*Hist. eccl.* 2.15, in Holmes 2006, 317)

Taken together, these early references to the Gospel's authorship associate Mark (although not necessarily John Mark of Jerusalem) with both Peter and

Rome, a triangulation repeated throughout church history, as ably summarized by Brenda Deen Schildgen (1998, 35–36):

> The Papias tradition was repeated in a variety of ways by Justin Martyr, who, in his *Dialogue with Trypho* (ca. 135) refers to the *apomnēmoneumata* ["memoirs"] of Peter as the source of the "sons of Thunder" designation for James and John, a phrase unique to Mark (Mark 3:17). Irenaeus of Lyons (130–200) claimed Mark was Peter's interpreter and disciple ([*Haer.*] 3.1.1). The *Anti-Marcionite Prologue* (ca. 4th cent.) and the *Evv. Prologi Vetustissimi* likewise refer to Mark as the interpreter of Peter and describe him as "*colobodactylus*" (stumpy-fingered), a description used by Hippolytus in the third century. Irenaeus of Lyons, Clement of Alexandria (ca. 180), and Origen (ca. 200)—according to Eusebius (260–339)—Tertullian (ca. 160–ca. 220) in *Adversus Marcionem* IV, 5, and Eusebius in *Ecclesiastical History* (323) connected Mark to Peter once again (II, XV:1–2), as did John Chrysostom (ca. 386–398) in his homilies on Matthew. Jerome, in his *Commentary on Matthew* and *On Famous Men* (392), repeated the by then well-established tradition that Mark was Peter's interpreter who recorded what he had heard Peter preach in Rome. This association of Mark and Peter held such authority that it echoed through the Middle Ages and even showed up with the Reformers, such as John Hus, for example—"Mark was ordained by God to write the gospel of the true deeds of Christ, and instructed by Peter, with whom he was intimate"—and John Wyclif's *Concordia evangeliorum super Mattheum*.

Although the volume of witnesses to the traditional triad of Mark-Peter-Rome is impressive, their historical value is questionable. Some early Christian writers (Papias, Tertullian, John Chrysostom) link Mark with Peter but do not mention Rome; others refer to Mark but link him with neither Peter nor Rome (Hippolytus, Adamantius, *Apostolic Constitutions*, Augustine; cf. C. Black 1993, 36). The ancient sources never link Mark with Rome independently of

The Death of Judas according to Papias

Papias relates a highly legendary tradition that after Judas delivered Jesus to his enemies, he became so bloated with corruption that "he was not able to pass through a place where a wagon passes easily, not even his bloated head by itself." His eyelids swelled up so much that his eyes were invisible; and his genitals became loathsome, and he began to pass pus and worms when he relieved himself. After much suffering, he finally died "in his own place, and because of the stench the area is deserted and uninhabitable even now; in fact, to this day one cannot pass that place without holding one's nose, so great was the discharge from his body, and so far did it spread over the ground" (Apollinaris of Laodicea quoting Papias, in Holmes 2006, 316; cf. Acts 1:16–20).

Emmanuel Tzanes, Wikimedia Commons

Figure 1. Icon of St. Mark the Evangelist, by Emmanuel Tzanes, 1657.

Peter, an association that seems to have originated with 1 Pet. 5:13, an epistle regarded by most contemporary scholars as written not by the apostle but by an admirer in the late first or early second century. Also, the Papias fragments contain some traditions that are obviously apocryphal, such as the fantastic tale of the death of Judas (see sidebar).

Moreover, Rome is not the only location associated with Mark in early Christian tradition; some third- and fourth-century Eastern writers place him in Alexandria, notably John Chrysostom (*Hom. Matt.* 1.7), who remarked that Mark composed his Gospel in Egypt at the entreaty of his disciples (see C. Black 2005, 238).

There are also features of the Gospel itself that cast doubt on the tradition that it was written by an associate of Peter. If the evangelist based his Gospel on the reminiscences of the apostle, why does he not mention his reliance on such an authoritative source? Why would a writing based on the teachings of Peter contain such unflattering stories about him (cf. Mark 8:32–33; 14:37, 66–72)? Although Mark is not written in sophisticated Greek, it is not "translation Greek," militating against the notion that Mark was the "interpreter of Peter"; since John Mark was from Jerusalem, his first language, like Peter's, would have been Aramaic (Juel 1990, 17; cf. Grant 1943, 89–124). Form and redaction criticism have demonstrated that, like the other Gospels, Mark is not a transcript of apostolic memoirs but a mosaic of pre-Gospel traditions from various sources, artfully edited together into a connected narrative.

9

Pre-Markan Sources

In addition to the individual traditions (e.g., parables, miracle stories, sayings) used by Mark, scholars have speculated that the evangelist integrated some larger collections of material into the Gospel. Most notably, many scholars have argued that the Passion Narrative (14:1–16:8) is based on an earlier, connected account of the arrest, trial, and execution of Jesus, although this hypothesis has been challenged in recent years (e.g., Crossan 1995). Other possible pre-Markan collections include the parables in Mark 4:1–34, the controversies in Mark 2, the cycles of miracle stories in Mark 5 and 7 (see Achtemeier 1970; 1972), and the apocalyptic discourse (Mark 13). In addition, Mark contains two sequences—where Jesus feeds a multitude (6:30–44; 8:1–10), crosses the sea of Galilee with his disciples (6:45–56; 8:10), enters into a dispute with Pharisees (7:1–13; 8:11–13), and delivers a discourse concerning food (7:14–23; 8:14–21)—that may reflect two versions of a common tradition. (For a discussion of other possible pre-Markan collections, see Verhey 1984, 51–53.)

Despite the many problems with the traditional account of Mark's authorship, many contemporary scholars continue to argue for the Roman provenance of the Gospel (e.g., Lane 1974, 21–25; Pesch 1976–77, 1:112–13; Ernst 1981, 21–11; Hengel 1985, 1–30; Senior 1987; Gnilka 1998–99, 1; Donahue 1995; Donahue and Harrington 2002, 38–46; Moloney 2002, 11–12; Incigneri 2003; C. Black 2005, 237–38; Culpepper 2007, 26–29). However, those scholars who regard Mark as a "Roman Gospel" do not necessarily hold the view that the author was Peter's associate (John) Mark (for a recent exception, see Stein 2008, 5–9) but identify him more cautiously as an anonymous leader addressing the members of a Roman house church. The author's use and occasional explanations of Aramaic terms to his audience (5:41; 7:34; 9:5 [rabbi]; 11:21 [rabbi]; 14:36; 15:34) bespeaks a possible Eastern, Jewish background, although knowledge of the meanings of a few Aramaic words is no indicator of fluency. The evangelist's apparent confusion over the details of Palestinian geography is often cited as evidence that he could not have been John Mark of Jerusalem—or anyone from that region—but the supposition that someone living in a given area would necessarily be well informed about local geography is highly questionable (cf. Stein 2008, 5–6).

In general terms, it can be cogently argued that references in the Gospel correspond well to what is known of Roman Christianity between the Claudian expulsion of Jews from the city "at the instigation of Chrestus" in AD 49 (Suetonius, *Claudius* 25.4; see Rutgers 1998, 105–6) and the Roman defeat of Jerusalem in AD 70. From Romans (1:8–15), we know that the church in Rome was not founded by Paul; scholars speculate that Christianity was brought there by Hellenistic Jewish-Christians from the East, and that the Christ-faith in Rome began in the synagogues. If indeed disputes over "Chrestus"—possibly a (Latinized) misspelling of *Christos*—were what prompted Claudius to expel the Jewish population (or at least part of it) from Rome, their numbers would have included followers of Christ (cf. Acts 18:2). It is likely that even after the emperor's edict had lapsed, tensions between the synagogues and their Jewish-Christian members would have escalated, leading to the formation of independent house churches and their incorporation of non-Jewish members.

Nero's famous persecution of Roman Christians after the great fire (AD 64) would have driven a deeper wedge between synagogue and church as Jews tried to disassociate themselves from the "deadly superstition" that had erupted in Rome and had caused the horrible deaths of so many followers of Christ (Tacitus, *Ann.* 44.2–5). The eruption of the rebellion in Judea (AD 66–70), the "year of four emperors" after Nero's suicide in 68, and the accession to the imperial throne of Vespasian, the general responsible for crushing the Jewish revolt, would have been alarming to both Jews and Christians throughout the Roman Empire, but especially in Rome. The impression made by the capture of Jerusalem on the Romans "is shown by the fact that the triumph of Vespasian and Titus celebrated in Rome in 71 was . . . the 'only Roman triumph ever to celebrate the subjugation of the population of an existing province'" (Walters 1998, 184, citing Millar 1993, 79). The text of Mark reflects a fearful community (e.g., 4:40; 6:51; 9:32; 10:32; 16:8), where adherence to Jewish practices was controversial (e.g., 2:1–11, 15–28; 3:1–6; 7:1–23), and gentile members were accepted (e.g., 5:1–20; 7:24–30, 31–37). The prophetic discourse is designed to assuage anxieties over the war in Judea (13:14–23), and the destruction of the temple is expected, if not explicitly described, in 13:2 (cf. 11:11–23; 13:14). The apocalyptic outlook of the author and his audience (cf. Mark 13) can be

---

Mark and Apocalyptic Literature

The term "apocalyptic" ("revelation" or "unveiling"), from the Greek name of the book of Revelation (*Apokalypsis*), refers to both the worldview that anticipates the end times in the near future ("imminent eschatology") and to a body of visionary/prophetic literature that expresses that worldview. Apocalyptic speculation was popular in some Jewish, and eventually Christian, circles between 250 BC and AD 250. In the Christian canon, the only two full-blown examples of apocalyptic literature are Dan. 7–12 and Revelation, but there are many extrabiblical examples, such as *1 Enoch*, *2 Baruch*, and *4 Ezra* (= 2 Esdras). Mark 13:1–37, known as the "little apocalypse," and other references in Mark (e.g., 8:38; 9:1; 14:62), suggests that the evangelist and his audience shared an apocalyptic outlook, although it is an overstatement to call the Gospel an example of apocalyptic literature (e.g., Kee 1977; cf. Horsley 2001, 122–25).

explained with reference to the shocking prospect of the despoilation of the holy land, city, and temple in the East.

The members of the Markan community anticipated persecution (13:9–13; cf. 4:17). The only human character in Mark to pronounce Jesus "Son of God"—an identification that aligns with God's (and the narrator's) view—is a Roman centurion (15:39; cf. 1:1, 11; 9:7). Although Mark, like the other writings of the NT, is written in Greek, it contains a number of Latinisms: denarius, *quadrans* (both Roman units of currency), centurion, census, *krabattos* ("cot"), legion, *modios* (a measure of grain), *xestēs* (a liquid measure), praetorium, *spekoulatōr* ("executioner"), and *phragelloō* ("to flagellate"). Mark also occasionally uses a Latin word to explain a Greek term (12:42; 15:16; see Harrison 1971, 183). Although these loanwords are suggestive of a Western provenance for the Gospel, they are common Latinisms that could be found in any Greek-speaking locale in the Roman Empire and do not necessarily point to Rome itself as the place of composition.

The main alternative to the Roman Gospel hypothesis locates the writing of Mark either in Galilee (Marxsen 1969) or nearby southern Syria (e.g., Kee 1977; Theissen 1991; cf. Marcus 1992a; Rohrbaugh 1993). Christians living in these areas would certainly have been acutely aware of the war in Judea, and their proximity to the cataclysmic events taking place in the Holy Land might well have given rise to the apocalyptic prophecies of Mark 13. Indeed, much of the internal evidence cited above could be marshaled to support Syrian or even Palestinian provenance, with the important exception of the author's many explanations of Aramaic words and phrases, which would be needless in an area (like Syria or Galilee) where Aramaic was widely spoken (see Mac-Mullen 1966, 4–5). However, unlike the Roman hypothesis, the only ancient traditions that link the Gospel with the Eastern Empire are the surmise that "Mark" was John Mark of Jerusalem and the association of the evangelist with Alexandria. Thus, while the weight of the evidence tips the balance in favor of Roman (or at least Western) provenance, it is not compelling enough to assign Mark to Rome or any other location, although the fact that most early Christian communities were founded in cities makes an urban setting likely. The dating of the Gospel is less difficult. The reference to the Jewish rebellion (13:14–23)—and possibly to the destruction of the temple (13:2; cf. 11:11–23; 13:14)—points to a date near the Roman defeat of Jerusalem (AD 70).

Audience

Since the 1980s, a number of scholars have applied methods from literary criticism that focus more on the reader or audience of Mark than on the author (e.g., Fowler 1981; 1991; 1992; Beavis 1987; 1989; Tolbert 1989; Heil 1992; Hester 1995; Dowd 2000; Bolt 2003; Driggers 2007). As illustrated above, more information about the audience of the Gospel can be inferred from its contents than about its author. The term "audience" is used here in preference to the term "reader" because in antiquity the written word was meant to be read aloud and heard, not read silently for the edification of the individual reader (Beavis 1989, 19). Thus the "reader" of a document like Mark would have been a literate person with the ability to declaim the Gospel aloud to the audience, "the intermediary between the written and the spoken word, text and audience" (Beavis 1989, 19). The ancient rhetorician Quintilian describes the benefits of experiencing an oral performance:

> The advantages conferred by reading and listening are not identical. The speaker stimulates us by the animation of his delivery, and kindles the imagination, not by presenting us with an elaborate picture, but by bringing us into actual touch with the things themselves. Then all is life and movement, and we receive the new-born offspring of his imagination with enthusiastic approval. We are moved not merely by the actual issue . . . , but by all that the orator himself has at stake. Moreover his voice, the grace of his gestures, the adaptation of his delivery (which is of supreme importance in oratory), and, in a word, all his excellences in combination, have their educative effect. (*Institutio oratoria* 10.1.16–17a, trans. Butler 1933)

In this sense, the first "reader" or oral performer of the Gospel was probably the evangelist himself, presenting his work to the members of his community, perhaps adding explanations and even answering questions as he went along (cf. Malbon 2002; Shiner 2003).

The audience presupposed by Mark already has some knowledge of the story they are about to hear. The God they worship is the God of the Jewish scriptures, attested to by prophets like Isaiah (Mark 1:2; 7:6) and Elijah (6:15; 8:28; 9:4–5, 11–13; 15:35–36). They are familiar with the law of Moses (1:44; 7:10; 9:4–5; 10:3–5; 12:19, 26), and they know who King David was and that the messiah is believed to be his descendant (2:25; 10:47–48; 11:10; 12:35–37). They respect the Jewish scriptures (12:10, 24; 14:49) and believe in angels (1:13; 8:38; 12:25; 13:27, 32) and Satan (1:13; 3:23, 26; 4:15; cf. 8:33). They know what synagogues are (1:21, 23, 29, 39; 3:1; 5:22, 35–38; 6:2; 12:39) and may have occasion to enter them (13:9). They are familiar with Jewish Sabbath observance (1:21; 2:23–24, 27–28; 3:2, 4; 6:2; 16:1), and they know of Jerusalem and its temple, at least by reputation (1:5; 3:8, 22; 7:1; 10:32; 11:1, 11–16, 27; 12:35, 41; 13:1, 3; 14:58; 15:29, 38, 41). However, they need explanations for Aramaic expressions (5:41; 7:11, 34; 14:36; 15:22, 34) and certain Jewish practices and beliefs, especially those pertaining to Palestinian groups like Pharisees and Sadducees (e.g., 7:3–4, 11; 12:18; 14:12; 15:42). This does not necessarily rule out the possibility that some members of the Markan community were of Jewish ethnicity, since Greek-speaking Jews would not necessarily understand Aramaic or be familiar with the Jewish sects of

---

Jewish and Gentile Christians

To call believers "Christians," whether Jewish or gentile, in Mark's time is anachronistic since this is a term found only in the later books of the NT as a designation for followers of Christ (Acts 11:26; 26:28; 1 Pet. 4:16); in this commentary it will be used for purposes of convenience. The contents of Mark indicate that the community was made up of members of both Jewish and gentile ethnicity. Possibly some of the gentile members of the community were attracted to aspects of the Jewish way of life, or they were being criticized for not adopting Jewish practices pertaining to Sabbath observance (e.g., 2:23–28; 2:1–6), separation from non-Torah-observant "sinners" (e.g., 2:15–17), fasting (e.g., 2:18–22), and ritual purity (e.g., 7:1–23). The same evidence could be interpreted to suggest that Jewish believers were being condemned by other members of the Markan community for being too lax in their practice of the law.

Jesus's time, some thirty years earlier. The members of Mark's audience anticipated a worldwide mission (13:10a; 14:9), and some of them were probably missionaries who feared persecution and even martyrdom (13:9–13; cf. 4:17). They had a vivid apocalyptic hope and expected the decisive manifestation of the kingdom of God imminently (9:1; 13:30).

The use of reader/audience response provides the interpreter with a helpful repertoire of perspectives on the Gospel. On the literary plane, they help us to distinguish between the various "audiences" that figure in and behind the text. At one level, the author of Mark, the narrator of the Gospel, addresses an audience made up of members of his church community. He does this not only directly, through explanations and addresses to "the reader" (13:14) or to "all" (13:37; cf. 4:9, 23–24), but also through the characters in the story: through Jesus, whose words are always reliable, and through the disciples and other characters, who, like the different kinds of soil in the parable of the sower (4:3–8, 14–20), "hear the word" in more or less satisfactory ways. The focus on the reader/audience also raises the question of what kinds of expectations the first-century hearers would have brought to bear on the Gospel—what kind of a book is it, and how would this affect the way it was heard and interpreted?

Genre

Although Christians have long referred to Matthew, Mark, Luke, and John as "Gospels," this designation for writings about the words and deeds of Jesus was not current until the second century, when the term *euangelion* began to be used in the plural (*euangelia*, "Gospels") (*2 Clem.* 8.5; Justin Martyr, *1 Apol.* 66.3; *Dial.* 10.2; 100.1). Mark, like Paul, uses the term *euangelion* to refer to the proclamation of God's saving work (1:14–15; 8:35; 10:29; 13:10; 14:9; Bryan 1993, 33). Thus Mark's superscription, which refers to the "gospel" of Jesus Christ, Son of God (1:1), does not refer to the genre of the book but to its content, the saving message ("good news") of the reign of God. Although Mark did not consciously set out to create a distinctive genre of writings about the life and works of Jesus, he did set a literary precedent followed by the other NT evangelists. As France (2002, 5) observes,

> Once the term had become established as a designation for the four canonical versions of the one εὐαγγέλιον (so that τὸ εὐαγγέλιον κατὰ Μᾶρκον is properly translated not "the gospel[-book] by Mark" but "the [one] gospel in Mark's version") it became available as a literary label for other works about Jesus which came to be written from the second century onwards, however different in character they may have been from the narrative "gospels" of the first century. Hence the *Gospel of Thomas, Gospel of Peter, Gospel of Philip, Gospel of Truth, Gospel according to the Hebrews*, and the like. The term which for Mark had designated the (hitherto oral) message of the first-century churches had thus come to mean something like "a church book about Jesus."

Thus Mark holds a distinguished place in the history of Christian literature, and of Western literature as a whole (see also my comments on Mark 1:1). Although the evangelist did not regard his book as belonging to the literary genre of "gospel," for ease of expression, it will be referred to as such throughout this commentary.

If Mark did not set out to create a new "gospel" genre (for scholars who have taken this view, see the discussion in Collins 2007, 19–22; see also Beavis 1989, 38), what kind of a book did he intend to write? This question has important implications for interpretation. If Mark was written as history or biography, for example, we would understand it very differently than if it were meant to be fiction or poetry. Several Greco-Roman literary genres have been proposed as the models for the Gospel. Mark has obvious affinities with Hellenistic biography (*bios, vita*), a classification made as early as the second century, when Justin Martyr (*1 Apol.* 66–67) called the Gospels the *apomnēmoneumata* ("memorabilia") of the apostles. Many contemporary scholars have interpreted Mark as having been influenced by Hellenistic *bios* ("life") literature (e.g., Talbert 1970; Standaert 1978, 433–40; Shuler 1982; Robbins 1984; Beavis 1989, 37–39; Bryan 1993; Burridge 2004). Charles Talbert's (1970, 17) description of ancient biography—"prose narrative about a person's life, presenting supposedly historical facts which are selected to reveal the character or essence of the individual, often with the purpose of affecting the behavior of the reader"—approximates the contents and purpose of the Gospel well enough to justify imagining that its first-century hearers would have understood it as a kind of "life" of Jesus. The range of Greco-Roman biographies of philosophers (Diogenes Laertius), sophists (Philostratus), religious figures and miracle workers (Philo, Philostratus), and public figures (Plutarch, Suetonius), some written for apologetic purposes (Xenophon of Ephesus, Philodemus, Philostratus, Porphyry), is diverse enough to allow an identification of Mark as an early Christian biographical narrative about Jesus (cf. Beavis 1989, 39). Among other ancient genres suggested as influences on Mark are the Hellenistic novel (e.g., Tolbert 1989), the Homeric epic (e.g., MacDonald 2000), and what Adela Yarbro Collins (2007, 42–52) calls the "eschatological historical monograph." Many scholars have seen similarities between Mark and ancient drama—a topic to which I will return below.

One eminently plausible suggestion regarding the genre of Mark is the observation that the Gospel is most at home in the domain of biblical narrative: "Both in its simple but vivid language and in its style of rapid narrative with frequent changes of scene it resonates with the Old Testament cycles of prophetic narratives and with the stories of the lives of biblical heroes like Moses and David. . . . Mark's 'pre-texts' are the Jewish Scriptures, which he generally cites in Greek" (Donahue and Harrington 2002, 16). Mark's Jesus functions within a narrative world ruled by the God of Israel, where prophets like John the Baptist, Isaiah, and Elijah are revered; angels appear to minister to the Son of God (1:13); figures like Moses, Abraham, Isaac, Jacob (12:26), David, and Abiathar (2:25–26) are respected; miracles and exorcisms are possible; and prophecy is fulfilled. If Mark modeled the Gospel on the Jewish scriptures, an intriguing question is whether this means that he meant to write Scripture. In Mark's time, although there was a concept of sacred, authoritative writings generally classed as Law, Prophets, and Writings (see the prologue to Sirach), there was no closed Jewish "canon" of Scripture. Hellenistic Jewish writings include many works modeled on the ancient scriptures (see *OTP*), which were probably regarded as quasi-scriptural by some ancient Jews. Some of these books—such as Sirach, the Wisdom of Solomon, 1–2 Maccabees, Judith, Tobit, and even (for Ethiopia and Eritrea) *1 Enoch*—are included in Catholic and Orthodox Christian Bibles. Possibly Mark was familiar with such writings and composed his book about Jesus in this tradition.

A generic influence on Mark that may seem much more far-fetched to the modern reader is the suggestion that the Gospel resembles a Greek tragedy. Nonetheless, as noted above, many contemporary scholars see Mark as modeled on ancient drama (e.g., Bilezikian 1977; Standaert 1978; Stock 1982, 16–30; Beavis 1989, 31–35; S. Smith 1995; Lescow 2005). Many others describe the Gospel more generally as having a dramatic quality (e.g., Perrin and Duling 1982, 237–39; Hengel 1985, 137; France 2002, 11–15; Burridge 2004, 239–40; Collins 2007, 91–93; for further references, see Beavis 1989, 192n134). Since Greek tragedy was very much a part of Greco-Roman education in the first century, it is plausible that Mark and the educated members of his audience would have had some familiarity with dramatic works, even if they had never attended a play, although attending theater was not confined to the upper classes in antiquity. Moreover, in Mark's time the "closet drama," a play written for private presentation rather than for public performance, was popular, at least among the social elite: all of the plays of Seneca belong to this genre. As Stephen H. Smith (1995, 229) remarks, "Mark's Gospel was written with just this kind of situation in mind—to be read expressively by a lector before a closed circle of Christians in the setting of a private house" (cf. Beavis 1989, 33–35). As I have noted elsewhere,

> If the author were a Jewish-Christian from Palestine, as the tradition asserts, there is no reason to rule out the influence of the theatre; Herod the Great built theatres in Jerusalem, Caesarea Maritima, Sepphoris, Damascus, and Sidon. There are records of Roman Jewish actors, and hellenistic Jews, like their Gentile neighbours, were avid theatre-goers. It has been argued that Job, Judith, *4 Maccabees*, and the Apocalypse were modelled on Greek tragedy; the Alexandrian Jewish dramatist Ezekiel wrote a play based on the Exodus story. (Beavis 1989, 35)

In fact, Ezekiel the Tragedian's *Exagōgē*, a drama about the Exodus written sometime between the second century BC and the first century AD by an Egyptian Jew, is the most complete surviving example of a Hellenistic tragedy (R. Robinson 1985, 805). Unlike the *Exagōgē*, Mark is not a play, but a Scripture-like narrative; however, as Collins (2007, 91) puts it, Mark is "written in the tragic mode," and the Gospel's plotting and structure show dramatic influence (see the section on structure below).

Literary Features

Mark's Greek style is not polished but resembles the language of a Hellenistic popular novel (see Tolbert 1989, 59–78; Beavis 1989, 35–37). Despite its lack of literary sophistication, the Gospel is noted for its vivid and engaging quality. Mark's usual way of constructing sentences is to connect clauses with the Greek conjunction *kai* ("and"), a device characteristic of popular literature and reminiscent of Jewish scriptural narratives (see Donahue and Harrington 2002, 17). This is combined with the frequent use of the adverb *euthys* ("immediately," 42x), lending a quality of breathless urgency to the narrative, as here:

> John appeared in the desert baptizing and preaching a baptism of repentance for the forgiveness of sins. *And* there went out to him all the country of Judea and all the Jerusalemites, *and* they were being baptized by him in the Jordan, confessing their sins. *And* John was clothed in camel's hair *and* a leather belt around his waist *and* was eating locusts and wild honey. *And* he preached saying, "The man stronger than I comes after me, of whom I am not worthy to loosen

17

the straps of his sandals. I have baptized you with water, but he will baptize you with Holy Spirit." (Mark 1:4–8)

Mark's frequent use of the historic present—using the present tense of verbs to refer to past events—adds to the immediacy and excitement of the story: for example, "And passing by he saw Levi, son of Alphaeus, sitting by the toll office, *and he says* to him, 'Follow me!'" (2:14). Mark often uses hyperbole (exaggeration) to emphasize the impact of the events he relates, and he repeats words and phrases to add to the drama of the scene: *"In the evening, when the sun set,* they were bringing to him *all those having illnesses and possessed by demons.* And *the whole city* was gathering at the door" (1:32–33). Like a Greek play, the Gospel is punctuated by choral outbursts in which groups of characters comment on the events they are witnessing in unison: "and they marveled exceedingly, saying, 'He has done all things well; he both makes the deaf hear and the mute speak!'" (7:37b). Mark often uses colorful details to bring the story to life: in the feeding of the five thousand, the crowd is instructed to sit down on the "green grass"; in the tale of the blessing of the children, Jesus takes one of the children in his arms (9:36; cf. 10:13–16); in the story of the stilling of the storm, Jesus is asleep on a cushion as the wind and the waves

The Greek Novel

As noted in the main text, the Greco-Roman novel or "romance" has been suggested as a possible literary influence on Mark (e.g., Tolbert 1989, 59–83; Beavis 1989, 35–37). Many extant ancient novels are popular fiction, melodramatic stories about the adventures of two young lovers who are separated, undergo thrilling trials and tribulations, and are happily reunited in the end, as in Chariton's *Chaereas and Callirhoe*, Xenophon of Ephesus's *Ephesian Tale*, Longus's *Daphnis and Chloe*, Achilles Tatius's *Leucippe and Clitophon*, and Heliodorus's *Ethiopian Tale (Aethiopica)*. A famous example of a comic novel by a Latin author is Apuleius's *The Golden Ass (Metamorphoses)*, where the hero is turned into a donkey and, after a series of embarrassing exploits, is restored by the goddess Isis. Some novels focus on the career of a famous person, such as Xenophon of Athens's *The Education of Cyrus* and the anonymous *Alexander Romance*. Many early Jewish and Christian writings resembling romance literature in vocabulary, style, and plotting survive, such as *Joseph and Aseneth*, *3 Maccabees*, *Acts of Paul and Thecla* (see Wills 1994, 223–38; Pervo 1994, 239–54). Some of these are considered Scripture (e.g., Dan. 1–6, Esther, Tobit, Judith). Richard Pervo (1987) has argued that the NT book of Acts shows strong parallels with the ancient novel. This is to say not that books like Acts or the Gospel of Mark were written *as* novels but that their authors composed them in a way that would be entertaining and appealing to their audiences, much as contemporary religious leaders use popular media to convey their message.

beat on the boat (4:38). Similarly, the explanations of Aramaic expressions add a touch of local flavor for the Greek-speaking audience of the Gospel.

Mark is famous for the use of intercalation, the sandwiching of one story within another (e.g., 3:20–35; 4:1–20; 5:21–43; 6:7–30; 11:12–21; 14:1–11; 14:17–31; 14:53–72; 15:40–16:8). This device signals the reader/audience that the intercalated stories are related in some way. Thus the story of Peter's denial (14:53–54, 66–72) frames the account of the trial of Jesus before the Sanhedrin (14:55–65), adding a layer of bitter irony to the Passion Narrative: as Jesus is being interrogated and abused, Peter is comfortably warming himself by the fire (14:54) and disavowing any relationship to Jesus, despite the disciple's oath that he would rather die than defect (14:31). The story of the mission of the Twelve (6:7–13, 30) brackets the account of the execution of John the Baptist (6:14–29), both informing the reader/audience of the death of John and offering a chilling vignette of the cost of discipleship. On a larger scale, Mark often repeats similar stories in order to underline important themes: Mark contains two stories of the healing of blind men (8:22–26; 10:46–52) and two stories about the healing of the deaf (7:32–37; 9:14–27), which relate to metaphorical blindness and deafness of the various characters in the narrative. The two feeding narratives (6:30–44; 8:1–10) take place respectively in Jewish and gentile territory, reflecting Jesus's mission to both Jews and gentiles. The theme of the disciples' misunderstanding of the significance of Jesus's words and deeds is highlighted in three scenes that take place in a boat on the Sea of Galilee (4:35–41; 6:45–51; 8:14–21), where Jesus rebukes the disciples for their incomprehension and lack of faith. Mark contains three Passion predictions (8:31; 9:31; 10:33–34) and three parousia predictions (8:38–9:1; 13:26–27; 14:62), which relate to both the suffering and vindication of Jesus, the son of man. The theme of discipleship is emphasized by three calls/commissionings of the disciples (1:16–20; 3:13–19; 6:7–13). Mark's use of the "rule of three"— the propensity of storytellers to build narratives around groups of three (see Booker 2004, 229–35)—also surfaces in individual pericopes: Bartimaeus's sight is restored after his third request (10:46–52); Jesus finds the disciples sleeping in Gethsemane three times (14:32–42); Peter famously denies Jesus thrice before the rooster crows twice (14:66–72).

Mark is an omniscient narrator, who has full knowledge of the events he relates and even of the thoughts and internal dispositions of the various characters, including Jesus. From his all-knowing perspective, he can describe events happening simultaneously in different places (e.g., 6:7–16; 14:53–72). Mark tantalizes the reader/audience by foreshadowing significant events that will happen later in the story; he briefly refers to the plot to kill Jesus in the first main section of the Gospel (3:6; cf. 6:29). Throughout the Gospel, Jesus is portrayed as a prophet with the ability to read the thoughts of others and to discern the truth (e.g., 2:8; 6:30, 39), and whose prophecies consistently come to pass (e.g., 8:31; 9:31; 10:31–32), thus establishing the reliability of his words, even when he prophesies events outside the narrative of the Gospel (e.g., 13:4–37; 14:62). The omniscient perspective of the author is authenticated by divine utterances: "and a voice came out of the heavens, 'You are my son the beloved; in you I am delighted'" (1:11; cf. 9:7). God's presence behind events is often indicated by the use of the divine passive: "Child, your sins *are forgiven* [by God]" (2:5); "You seek Jesus the Nazarene who was crucified; he *has been raised* [by God]; he isn't here" (16:6). As Ira Brent Driggers (2007, 11) has perceptively noted, while Jesus is the main character of the Gospel, God is the main actor. Although Jesus is the character in Mark who aligns most closely with the will of God (3:35), even he finds the demands placed on him by divine destiny hard to bear (e.g., 14:35–36).

In addition to Jesus and God, Mark's dramatic narrative features a host of characters, both individual and collective. Most of these belong to the latter category: groups of characters who stand in different kinds of relationship to Jesus and his mission. In addition to the Twelve, who are appointed specifically to participate in Jesus's mission (3:13–19; 6:7–13, 30), the evangelist portrays Jesus as accompanied by a larger group of disciples (e.g., 2:13–14; 4:10; 15:40–41). Of the Twelve, Jesus singles out Peter, James, and John as an "inner circle" of followers who accompany him at significant points in the story (5:37; 9:2; 14:33; cf. 13:3). Simon Peter, the first disciple to heed the call of Jesus (1:16–18), is listed first among the Twelve (3:16); he is the first human character to recognize that Jesus is the messiah (8:29). Despite his prominence, he is a flawed and fickle disciple, who rebukes Jesus when he begins to speak of suffering (8:32), speaks out foolishly at the transfiguration (9:5–6), falls asleep at Gethsemane (14:37), and cannot live up to his promise never to desert Jesus (14:29–31, 66–72). Of the Twelve, the only other named disciple of prominence is Judas, who hands Jesus over to his enemies after greeting him with a kiss (3:19; 14:10, 43, 45).

Other collective characters who appear in the narrative are the throngs of people who pursue Jesus so he can teach, heal, and exorcize them; the demons ("unclean spirits"), who dread Jesus's powers to expel them; Jewish authority figures, who generally test and oppose Jesus (Pharisees, Herodians, scribes, Sadducees, chief priests); and members of Jesus's family, who fail to honor his calling (3:21, 31–35; cf. 6:1–4). Some prominent religious and political figures are named: John "the baptizer," who heralds the arrival of Jesus; Jairus, a ruler of the synagogue (5:22); Herod Antipas, responsible for the execution of the prophet; Pilate, the Roman official who sentences Jesus to death. Most of the characters who interact positively with Jesus are not named but are designated by their afflictions (a leper; a blind man; a deaf man; the demoniac "Legion, for we are many"; a woman with a hemorrhage; a centurion), their relationships to others (Peter's mother-in-law, the daughter of Jairus, the son of a man in the crowd), their ethnicity (a Syro-Phoenician woman), or their socioreligious status (a rich man, a scribe). An exception is

Bartimaeus, "the son of Timaeus," whose faith is rewarded by the restoration of his vision (10:46–52); yet so is Barabbas, the brigand set free by Pilate at the demand of the crowd (cf. 6:3; 14:3; 15:21, 43). Whether named or unnamed, individual or collective, Mark's characters usually function as "types" who display varying levels of comprehension of Jesus's identity and mission. The two figures who meet with the Markan Jesus's unqualified approval are anonymous: a poor widow (12:41–44) and the woman who prophetically anoints Jesus for burial (14:1–9).

In Mark, Jesus's journey from the baptism to the cross begins at the Jordan, where the Israelites crossed into the land of promise in the time of Joshua; goes to Galilee, where he carries on the bulk of his ministry of preaching, teaching, and healing; and then to Judea and Jerusalem, where he meets his destiny. His mission is not confined to Jewish regions but fans out into gentile territory: the Decapolis (5:1–20; 7:31); the region of Tyre and Sidon (7:24–30); the villages of Caesarea Philippi (8:27–30). His reputation attracts people from afar: "from Jerusalem and from Idumea and from beyond the Jordan and the region of Tyre and Sidon" (3:8). On a smaller scale, some of Mark's physical settings have special significance. Donahue and Harrington (2002, 22) note that "the house" (e.g., 1:29; 2:15; 3:19–20; 5:19; 7:17; 9:33; 14:3, 14–15; cf. 4:10–12) contrasts with the synagogue, where Jesus "most often meets opposition, reflecting perhaps the emerging conflict between the Markan 'house churches' and the synagogues" (1:21, 28, 29, 39; 3:1; 12:39; 13:9). Similarly, Mark contains several scenes where Jesus has significant

Notes on Translation

This commentary is based on my own translation of the Greek text of Mark from NA[27]. In general, I have tried to capture the colloquial and vivid quality of Mark's style, rather than smoothing over the rough spots. I have departed from the familiar translation of terms like "kingdom of God" (*basileia tou theou*) because the noun *basileia* has the dynamic sense of "rule" or "reign" as well as the territorial sense of "kingdom" or "realm." Similarly, *euangelion*, often translated as "gospel," is rendered in its ancient Greco-Roman sense as "good news." However, I have translated the phrase *ho huios tou anthrōpou* conventionally as "the son of man," which in English sounds like a christological title. Yet, to the hearers of Mark, it would have meant something more like "human one" or "human being." I have used gender-inclusive language as often as the context allows; readers should remember that Mark's references to groups of people, including disciples, usually include both women and men. Although the Greek word used for "God" (*theos*) is masculine, the Gospel seldom refers to God as "he," preferring to repeat the substantive (e.g., "With human beings it is not possible, but not with God; for all things are possible with God," 10:27). Unless otherwise indicated, biblical quotations from books other than Mark are based on the NRSV.

exchanges with the disciples in a boat (4:35–41; 6:45–51; 8:14–21; cf. 4:1), an ancient symbol of the church (Daniélou 1961, 58–70; Goodenough 1958, 159). The Gospel begins with the prophetic announcement of the "way of the Lord" (1:2–3), and the motif of the way (*hodos*) to Jerusalem dominates the Gospel from the recognition scene at Caesarea Philippi (8:27–30) to the "triumphal entry" (11:1–10). The temple, Jesus's first destination on entering Jerusalem, meets with his most vigorous prophetic condemnation (11:12–23; 12:1–11; 13:1–2).

Major Themes

Mark is a complex document, containing a multitude of characters, themes, and messages. It is not possible to reduce the "message of Mark" to one over-arching concern, but several stand out. As stated above, Jesus is the predominant figure in the narrative, designated by a variety of titles, most prominently: messiah (*christos*; 1:1; 8:29; 9:41; 14:61; 15:32; cf. 12:35–37; 10:46–52); Son of God (1:1, 11; 3:11; 5:7; 9:7; 15:39; cf. 14:61–62); and prophet (6:4, 15; 8:28; cf. 1:24). Jesus's preferred self-designation is "son of man" or "human one" (*ho huios tou anthrōpou*; cf. 2:10, 28), with connotations of suffering (8:31; 9:31; 10:33–34; cf. 9:9, 12), service (10:45), and eschatological judgment (8:38; 13:26; 14:62; cf. 14:21, 41; Dan. 7:13–14). However, Mark's Jesus is revealed as much or more by the way his character is portrayed throughout the Gospel narrative: in his words, deeds, and relationships. In Mark, Jesus does not proclaim a message about himself, but about God (1:14; 3:35; 7:8–9, 13; 8:33; 10:6, 9, 27; 11:22; 12:17, 24–27, 28–34; 13:19; cf. 15:39) and the reign of God (1:15; 4:11, 26, 30; 9:1, 47; 10:14–15, 23–25; 12:34; 14:25; 15:43). Although he has prophetic and miraculous powers, Mark's Jesus is a very human figure, capable of intense emotions of anger (1:41; 11:15–18), compassion (6:34; 8:2), love (10:21), and anguish (14:34; 15:34, 37). The essence of his preaching, as summarized in 1:14–15, is "the good news of God"; the family of Jesus consists of those who do the will of God (3:35); his prayer in Gethsemane is "not my will, but yours" (14:36).

Mark's portrait of the disciples—especially the Twelve—is paradoxical. On the one hand, they are called by Jesus to accompany him and to share in his work (3:13–19; 6:7–13, 30). They respond enthusiastically to his call (1:16–20; cf. 2:14); the women follow and care for him to the very end (15:40–41; 15:47–16:8). It is Peter who recognizes that Jesus is the messiah (8:29). On the other hand, throughout the Gospel, the disciples—especially members of the Twelve—frequently fail to understand the words and deeds of Jesus (e.g., 4:13, 40; 6:50–52; 7:18; 8:14–21; 10:13–14, 35–45), even though he offers them private instruction (e.g., 4:10–13, 33–34; 7:17–18; 9:28–29; 10:11–12; 13:3–37). Ultimately they all desert him (14:50; 14:72; cf. 16:8). The readers/audience, like the disciples, are left with the question of whether they can live up to the demands of doing the will of God (3:35; 14:36).

Mark's depiction of Jews and Judaism is similarly nuanced. Although Mark's Jesus occasionally visits non-Jewish regions, he is a Jew among Jews; his mission is focused on Galilee and Judea, where he attends synagogues on the Sabbath (1:21–29; 3:1–5; 6:2), visits the temple (11:11, 15–17, 27–33; 12:1–44), and celebrates Passover (14:12–26). His disagreements with scribes, Pharisees, and Sadducees question not the authority of the Jewish law (Torah) but rather its interpretation and application (e.g., 2:1–12, 15–17, 18–22, 23–28; 3:1–6; 7:1–22; 10:1–12; 12:13–40). Jesus's critique of the temple concerns the shortcomings of its human administrators not of the institution itself (11:15–18; 12:1–11), and his warning against "the scribes" (12:38–40) is not a blanket condemnation (cf. 12:28–34) but a censure of the hypocrites among them. Likewise, individual members of "authority" groups—Jairus, a synagogue ruler; the "good scribe"; Joseph of Arimathea, a member of the Sanhedrin— are portrayed sympathetically.

Mark's portrayal of the Jewish authorities (scribes, Pharisees, Sadducees, chief priests) belongs to the larger theme of response to Jesus and his prophetic message. Mark's Jesus speaks in parables, and all things come to pass "in parables" (4:11, 33–34a). The "mystery of God's reign" is "given" to the disciples, but the parables veil the significance of the words and deeds of Jesus from outsiders: "in order that 'Seeing they might see and not perceive, hearing they might hear and not understand, lest they repent and be forgiven'" (4:12; cf. Isa 6:9–10). Ironically, those who should be most receptive—religious authorities, disciples, even Jesus's family and neighbors (3:21, 31–35; 6:1–6)—respond with varying degrees of incomprehension and even hostility (however, cf. 5:22; 10:17–22; 12:28–34; 15:43). Marginal figures—a frightened woman (5:25–34), an insistent blind man (10:46–52), a persistent gentile mother (7:24–30)—do much better. Mark is permeated with the language of seeing, hearing, perceiving, and understanding, both literal and metaphorical (e.g., 4:1–34; 8:14–21; 13:3–37; 7:31–37; 8:22–26; 10:46–52; 9:25). Faith, not fear or unbelief, is the key to insight, healing, and miraculous power (1:15; 2:5; 4:40; 5:35–36; 9:24; 10:52; 11:22–24). Even Jesus requires those around him to have faith in God's power to work through him (6:5–6; cf. 9:14–27). The vision imparted by faith constitutes a sort of "apocalyptic epistemology"—a special way of knowing about the true meaning of events through divine revelation—that Markan characters display to varying degrees (Marcus 1984; Garrett 1998, 63–66).

The theme of suffering looms large in the second half of the Gospel, introduced by the first Passion prediction: "And he began to teach them that it was necessary for the son of man to suffer many things and to be rejected by the elders and by the scribes and by the chief priests and to be killed and after three days to rise up" (8:31). The notion of a suffering messiah would have seemed strange to Jewish members of Mark's audience, and the prospect of a crucified hero would have been shocking to any ancient listener, since crucifixion was a form of execution reserved for those considered to be the lowest of criminals; as Paul observed, "Christ crucified" was "a stumbling block to Jews and foolishness to Gentiles" (1 Cor. 1:23). Modern-day readers are invited to consider how joining a sect that worshiped a recently executed criminal from an obscure corner of the globe would strike family and friends—even with the convert's sincere belief that the "savior" had been raised from the dead! While suffering heroes are not absent from the Greek tradition (see MacDonald 2000, 15–19, 135–47), Mark's primary archetypes for Jesus are Jewish: the righteous sufferer (e.g., Job [12:2–3; 16:20; 19:14], Jeremiah [20:6–11], the psalmist [Pss. 27:11–12; 31:21–22]; the Servant [Isa. 52:13–53:12]); the Maccabean martyrs (2 Macc. 6:10–11, 18–31; 7:1–42); the rejected prophet (cf. Mark 6:4; cf. 12:1–11). The motif of divine vindication of the suffering one is integral to these traditions: "The stone that the builders rejected has become the cornerstone; this is from the Lord, and it is marvelous in our eyes" (Mark 12:10–11; cf. Ps. 118:22–23). In Mark, Jesus models not just his own suffering and vindication but also that of his followers—including the disciples of Mark's time, who must take up their own cross and risk their own lives for the sake of the good news if they want to share in his resurrection (8:34–35; cf. 13:9–13). The one who endures to the end will be saved (13:13).

As stated above, one of Mark's primary literary models is the Jewish scriptures, which are used in many ways throughout the Gospel. The prologue begins with a citation of "Isaiah the prophet" (1:2–3), whose words are fulfilled in the appearance of John and, more important, Jesus. Throughout Mark, the Scriptures are fulfilled in the words, deeds, and mission of Jesus (e.g., 4:11–12; 7:6–7, 37; 9:9–13; 12:10–11; 14:27, 49; cf. 1:15). The biblical archetypes of the prophets, especially Elijah and Elisha, inform the portrayal of John and Jesus (e.g., 1:6; cf. 2 Kings 1:8; Mark 6:15; 8:28; 9:11–13; cf. 15:35–36). Jesus communes on the mountain with the great prophets Moses and Elijah (9:2–8); he speaks of himself as a prophet, and others identify him as such (6:4, 15; 8:28). Jesus engages with other Jewish scripture experts on points of interpretation (e.g., 7:5–13; 9:10–13; 10:2–9; 12:18–27, 28–33, 35–37) and uses a scriptural precedent to defend his disciples' unorthodox praxis (2:25–26). His teachings are bolstered by scriptural references: the cleansing of the temple is accompanied by prophetic quotations: "'My house shall be called a house of prayer for all the nations,' but you have made it into 'a cave of bandits'" (11:17; cf. Isa. 56:7; Jer. 7:11). The parable of the tenants is followed by a quotation of Ps. 118:22–23: "The stone that the builders rejected has become the cornerstone; this is from the Lord and it is marvelous in our eyes" (Mark 12:10). Mark's Passion Narrative is so dense with scriptural allusions that it has been called "prophecy historicized" (Crossan 1995; cf. Goodacre 2006; see the sidebar "Prophecy Historicized or History Remembered?" in the chapter on Mark 14:1–15:47).

Structure

Nearly twenty years ago, Joanna Dewey (1991, 221) quipped that "of making outlines of the Gospel of Mark there is no end, nor do scholars seem to be wearying of it." The situation remains similar today, although most contemporary commentators concur that the Gospel is divided into a Galilean section (1:1–8:21) and a Jerusalem section, including the Passion Narrative (11:1–16:8), which frame a journey to Jerusalem that features three Passion predictions (8:22–10:51; cf. Donahue and Harrington 2002, 47). Dewey's own proposal takes seriously the insight that the Gospel was composed for oral performance. Thus she denies that Mark has a clear linear structure but says rather that it "consists of forecasts and echoes, variation within repetition, for a listening audience" (Dewey 1991, 234). Dewey's approach is a useful reminder that the evangelist probably did not sit down and map out an elaborate outline into which he slotted the traditional materials he wanted to present. He may not have "written" the Gospel at all but, like Paul, dictated his book to a scribe (cf. Rom. 16:22; cf. 1 Cor. 16:21; 2 Thess. 3:17; Col. 4:18), a common practice in antiquity. Also similarly to Paul, Mark intended his book to be read aloud to an audience.

My proposal regarding the structure of Mark distinguishes between Mark's plotting, which reflects the plot structure of ancient dramas, and the physical structure of the book, which—despite the Gospel's complex interplay of incidents, themes, foreshadowings, and retrospections—is quite simple: Mark repeatedly alternates between lengthy narrative sections and major blocks of teaching material. Like an ancient drama, Mark begins and ends with a well-defined prologue (1:1–13) and epilogue (16:1–8). The first half of the narrative corresponds to the *desis* ("complication") of a Greek tragedy, "the part from the beginning up to the point which immediately preceded the occurrence of a change from bad to good fortune or from good fortune to bad" (Aristotle, *Poet.* 18.2, trans. Halliwell 1927). In Mark, this corresponds with the Galilean mission (1:14–8:26), where Jesus teaches, preaches, and performs healings, miracles, and exorcisms with great success. This section of the Gospel is punctuated by choral outbursts from the crowds and the disciples, such as "What is this? A new teaching with authority! He even commands the unclean spirits, and they obey him!" (1:27; 2:12b; 4:41; 7:37). Peter's confession at Caesarea Philippi (8:27–29) is a classic recognition scene (*anagnōrisis*), the discovery of an identity previously concealed—Jesus is the messiah (see Aristotle, *Poet.* 11, 16). This incident marks a "change of fortune" ("reversal," *peripeteia*); immediately after Peter's confession, for the first time, Jesus prophesies the suffering, death, and resurrection of the son of man (8:31–33). According to Aristotle, a recognition scene "is most effective when it coincides with reversals, such as that involved by the discovery [that the hero has inadvertently killed his father and married his own mother] in the *Oedipus*" (*Poet.* 10.5). The Markan denouement (*lysis*, "unraveling"), "from the beginning of the change down to the end" (*Poet.* 18.3), comprises the second half of the Gospel: the journey to Jerusalem, where Jesus continues to prophesy his fate (9:31; 10:33–34) as he teaches his disciples on the way (9:30–10:52); his miraculous activity declines, he passes judgment on Jerusalem, and his prophecies are fulfilled. Mark's plot structure can thus be summarized as follows:

Complication (*desis*, 1:1–8:26)
Recognition (*anagnōrisis*, 8:27–30)
Reversal (*peripeteia*, 8:31–33)
Denouement (*lysis*, 9:1–16:8)

Within this plot structure, Mark organizes his material in alternating sections of narrative and teaching material, bracketed by a prologue and an epilogue:

Prologue: Jesus is heralded by John the Baptist and proclaimed Son of God (1:1–13)
Transition: Summary of the good news (1:14–15)
Narrative: Jesus preaches, teaches, and performs miracles in Galilee (1:16–3:35)
Teaching: Parables discourse (4:1–34)
Narrative: Jesus's ministry continues in and beyond Galilee (4:35–6:56)
Teaching: Jesus teaches on matters of ritual and moral purity (7:1–23)
Narrative: Jesus's ministry continues in gentile regions; Peter's confession at Caesarea Philippi marks a reversal in the plot (7:24–9:29)
Teaching: Jesus teaches the disciples on the way to Jerusalem (9:30–10:52)
Narrative: Jesus prophesies against the temple and meets with opposition in Jerusalem (11:1–12:44)
Teaching: Apocalyptic discourse (13:1–37)
Narrative: Passion Narrative (14:1–15:47)
Epilogue: Women at the empty tomb (16:1–8)

In the accompanying outline of the book as a whole, the central narrative sections are labeled Act 1, Act 2, and so on; the intervening sections of teaching material are called interludes. The first and last teaching sections, Mark's "parables discourse" (4:1–34) and the "apocalyptic discourse" (13:1–37), underline two important Markan themes: listening/understanding (4:3, 12, 15, 18, 20, 23, 24, 33) and seeing/keeping alert (13:5, 9, 14, 21, 23, 26, 33, 35, 37). As I have noted elsewhere, whether the author intended it or not, the physical layout of the Gospel "resembles that of a five-act Hellenistic play, with the place of the four choruses taken by teaching scenes" (Beavis 1989, 163). This

An Outline of Mark

Prologue: John and Jesus (1:1–13)

The beginning of the good news (1:1)

John the messenger (1:2–8)

Jesus the Son (1:9–13)

Transition: Summary of the good news (1:14–15)

Act 1: Jesus in Galilee (1:16–3:35)

The first disciples called (1:16–20)

First synagogue visit: Teaching and an exorcism (1:21–28)

Simon's mother-in-law and others healed (1:29–34)

Retreat and continuing ministry (1:35–39)

A man with leprosy cleansed (1:40–45)

Controversy stories (2:1–3:6)

The spread of Jesus's fame (3:7–12)

The appointment of the Twelve (3:13–19)

Postscript and transition (3:20–35)

Interlude: Teaching in parables (4:1–34)

Introduction (4:1–2)

The parable of the sower (4:3–9)

Why parables? (4:10–13)

Interpreting the parable of the sower (4:14–20)

Additional sayings and parables (4:21–32)

Conclusion (4:33–34)

Act 2: Beyond Galilee (4:35–6:56)

Jesus calms the wind and the waves (4:35–41)

Jesus exorcises the Gerasene demoniac (5:1–20)

A dead girl is raised, a hemorrhage stopped (5:21–43)

Jesus is dishonored in his hometown (6:1–6a)

The Twelve and the Baptist (6:6b–33)

The feeding of the five thousand (6:34–44)

Jesus walks upon the sea (6:45–52)

Conclusion (6:53–56)

Interlude: Teaching on ritual and moral purity (7:1–23)

Jesus's opponents (7:1–13)

The crowd (7:14–16)

The disciples (17:17–23)

Act 3: Mission in gentile regions (7:24–9:29)

Exorcism of a Syro-Phoenician woman's daughter (7:24–30)

Healing of a deaf man in the Decapolis (7:31–37)

Feeding of the four thousand (8:1–9)

The Pharisees ask Jesus for a sign (8:10–13)

Jesus rebukes the disciples on a boat voyage (8:14–21)

In gentile cities (8:22–30)

First Passion prediction; Peter and Jesus trade rebukes (8:31–33)

The suffering of the son of man; first parousia prediction (8:34–9:1)

Jesus's transfiguration (9:2–8)

Elijah and the son of man; second Passion prediction (9:9–13)

A boy with a deaf and mute demon (9:14–29)

Interlude: Teaching on the way to Jerusalem (9:30–10:52)

Teaching in Galilee (9:30–50)

Teaching in Judea (10:1–45)

Transition to Jerusalem: A blind man at Jericho (10:46–52)

Continued

commentary follows the outline suggested above; more-detailed suggested outlines of each section are included under Introductory Matters.

About This Commentary

As part of the Paideia series, this commentary is meant to address the needs of scholars and pastors, but above all, of undergraduate and graduate students in religious studies programs, theological colleges, and seminaries. With this in mind, I have used my experience as a teacher and as a student as one of the resources brought to bear on the task; I have tried to include information and perspectives of pedagogical interest and value. The focus of the commentary is on the text in its current form, rather than on the prehistory of the Gospel, the history of the text, or the historical Jesus, although I may briefly comment on such matters if they are of particular interest or relevance to the understanding of the text. It does not presuppose any particular set of doctrines or denominational milieu but recognizes that many of its readers will be interested

Mark and Modern Drama

Biblical scholars are not the only ones to have noticed the dramatic quality of Mark. In 1977, the British actor Alec McCowen first performed *St. Mark's Gospel* as a one-man play, based on the King James Version of Mark, in a church basement in Newcastle, England. This production was performed to much acclaim soon afterward in major venues in London and New York. A video version was recorded in 1990. The NT scholar David Rhoads has also performed a "Dramatic Presentation of the Gospel of Mark," likewise available on video (for other recordings, see Malbon 2002, 107–9; Shiner 2003, 9n6). A postmodern spin on the Gospel tradition is *The Gospel at Colonus*, a recasting of the tragedy by Sophocles in African-American gospel style, first performed in Philadelphia in 1985 and available on DVD (New Video NYC, 2008).

in theological as well as historical-critical and literary questions. The methodology is eclectic but uses elements from several of the subdisciplines of NT studies (e.g., source, form, redaction, reader/audience response, rhetorical, social scientific, feminist) in order to illumine some of the many facets of the Gospel. While I have benefited enormously from the wealth of commentaries and other secondary resources on Mark and engage with them frequently on the following pages, the primary focus is on the Gospel and what it meant to its earliest hearers. (Two recent commentaries that were unavailable to me until very late in the writing of this volume are Culpepper 2007 and Marcus 2009; both are listed in the bibliography.) Like other commentaries, this one reflects my own contextual, exegetical, and theological choices, preferences, and biases—as Canadian, academic, Anglican, liberal, feminist, social-justice oriented—both consciously and unconsciously. Above all, it is an invitation for present-day readers to appreciate the many messages, challenges, and rewards of reading and interpreting Mark today as they undertake their own effort to see, hear, and understand the Gospel.

Mark 1:1–13

Prologue: John and Jesus

Introductory Matters

Mark 1:1–13 is often described as Mark's prologue. In Greek literature, a *prologos* is the part of a play before the entry of the chorus, often in the form of a monologue narrating facts that introduce the main action (see, e.g., Aristotle, *Poet.* 12.4). For example, in Euripides's *Hecuba* (fifth cent. BC), the phantom of Polydorus, the son of Priam of Troy, recaps the events of the Trojan War that led to the captivity of his mother, Hecuba, and the other women of the city. After this, Hecuba and the chorus of Trojan women enter, and the narrative proper begins. According to Aristotle's *Rhetoric*, other cultural forms, including speeches and musical compositions, should begin with introductions (*prooimia*) or preludes (*proaulia*) corresponding to the dramatic prologue (*Rhet.* 3.14).

Biblical authors other than Mark make use of prologues. The deutero-canonical book of Sirach, for instance, contains a prologue written by the grandson of the sage after whom the book is named, explaining the history of the text before its translation into Greek in Egypt. The Gospel of John's famous prologue (John 1:1–18) describes Jesus as the preexistent Word (*logos*) of God testified to by the Jewish scriptures and by John the Baptist (see Perkins 1990, 951–52). Mark 1:1–13 functions like the *prologoi* of many ancient plays and other literary works by informing the reader/audience of the events leading up to the ministry of Jesus. The omniscient narrator cites a prophetic witness to the events that are about to be related, summarizes the career of John the Baptist, and introduces Jesus as the "man more powerful" than the prophet. Mark recounts how Jesus was baptized and experienced a heavenly vision, then was driven by the Spirit into the desert, tested by Satan for forty days, and sustained by angels. Up to this point in the narrative, Jesus does not speak—he is only spoken about.

The prologue shows many characteristics of Mark's style: *kai* parataxis, or the sequential linking of sentences and clauses with the conjunction "and" (*kai*; this word appears fourteen times in 1:4–13); the use of the adverb *euthys* ("immediately"; vv. 10, 12—a word that appears forty-two times in the Gospel). The passage is packed with the kinds of Markan "traits of vivid detail" noted by Westcott (1860, 366), such as the description of John's attire and diet (v. 5), the prophet's assertion that he is unfit to loosen the straps of Jesus's sandals (v. 7), the description of Jesus's vision of the heavens being torn apart and the Spirit descending "like a dove" (v. 10). The evangelist's notice that "*all* the country of Judea and *all* the Jerusalemites" (v. 5) went out to John is a typical Markan exaggeration that lends the narrative a sense of vividness and excitement. The terse narration, with its hurried pace and intriguing details, gives the prologue a vibrant and dramatic quality.

Scholarly opinion is divided as to the extent of Mark's prologue. Frank J. Matera (1988, 4) notes that at the beginning of the twentieth century, it was common to assume that the prologue ended at 1:8 since John the Baptist's preaching was the prelude to Jesus's ministry (e.g., the Westcott-Hort text of the Greek NT [1881] placed v. 8 at the end of the first paragraph). In midcentury, Robert H. Lightfoot (1950, 15–20) influentially argued that the prologue was comprised of Mark 1:1–13 since vv. 9–13 supply the vital background information that Jesus is from Nazareth in Galilee and that he is the unique Son of God. In 1965–66, Leander E. Keck argued that the prologue should also include vv. 14–15 since the use of the term *euangelion* ("gospel") in vv. 1 and 15 forms an *inclusio* (the use of the same or similar words at the beginning and the end of a sense unit): "vv. 14f. are a climactic statement that fulfills the word of John about Jesus, while at the same time it rounds out the over-arching interest in εὐαγγέλιον" (Keck 1965–66, 361). Today commentators remain divided as to whether the prologue ends at v. 13 or v. 15 (for ending at v. 13, e.g., see Hooker 1997, 1–22; Moloney 2002, 27–30; Donahue and Harrington 2002, 59–69; for ending at v. 15, e.g., see Mann 1986, 193–94; Harrington 1990, 598–99; Boring 1991). Matera's (1988, 5) reasons for preferring v. 13 for the prologue's end are persuasive:

1. 1:1–13 is set apart from the following verses by its location in the desert and by its references to the Spirit (vv. 8, 10, 12), which plays a relatively minor role elsewhere in the Gospel (cf. 3:29; 12:36; 13:11).
2. John's preaching refers to something that will happen in the future, while Jesus's preaching (1:14–15) refers to something that has happened.

**Mark 1:1–13
in the Narrative Flow**

▶Prologue: John and Jesus
(1:1–13)

The beginning of the good
news (1:1)

John the messenger
(1:2–8)

Jesus the Son (1:9–13)

3. In 1:1–13, the narrator imparts privileged and vital information to the reader/audience: "that John the Baptist is to be understood in the light of the quotation attributed to Isaiah (1:2–3), that the Spirit has come upon Jesus (1:10), that the Father identifies Jesus as his beloved Son (1:11), and that Jesus has confronted Satan in the wilderness (1:12–13)" (Matera 1988, 5).

To these observations, it should be added that only John and the voice from heaven speak in this section; Jesus, whose words predominate in the remainder of the Gospel, does not speak until vv. 14–15, marking off these verses as distinct from the prologue.

Tracing the Narrative Flow

The Beginning of the Good News (1:1)

Strictly speaking, Mark 1:1 (**Beginning of the good news of Jesus Christ, Son of God**) is a sense unit in itself, since scholars often describe it as a title or superscription to the Gospel or even as a scribal gloss (Croy 2001). For this reason, it could be treated as distinct from the prologue. However, since the mandate of this commentary is to interpret the text as it stands, this initial verse will be considered as integral both to the prologue and to the Gospel.

Although the Greek text of v. 1 contains only seven words (*archē tou euangeliou Iēsou Christou huiou theou*), it is extremely important both for the interpretation of Mark and for the history of Western literature. It contains one of seven usages of the term *euangelion* ("gospel" or "good news") in Mark (1:14, 15; 8:35; 10:29; 13:10; 14:9; cf. 16:15). By way of comparison, the noun occurs "only four times in Matthew (never absolutely, though always so in Mark except for the title), never in Q, M, L, or John" (Boring 1990, 66; however, cf. Mark 1:14, where the phrase **the good news of God** is a nonabsolute usage). Apart from Paul, for whom "gospel" refers to missionary preaching, the word seldom appears in the NT (see Carrington 1960, 31–32). Willi Marxsen argues that Mark both introduced the Pauline term *euangelion* into the Synoptic tradition and that he deliberately applied it to his entire book (1969, 125). In Mark, he asserts, Jesus is made present in the Gospel, and at the same time the proclaimed Gospel represents Jesus (128–29).

In Mark 1:1, the *euangelion* is **the good news of Jesus Christ, Son of God**. The question whether this phrase is objective or subjective—does it refer to the message *about* Jesus Christ or about *belonging to* Jesus Christ?—is moot; the evangelist does not distinguish between the preaching of Jesus and that of the early church. From **the beginning** (*archē*), the evangelist reveals to the reader/audience what many of them already know: that Jesus is messiah (here the designation **Jesus Christ** is used almost as a proper name, a usage familiar to early Christians). While it should be noted that the phrase **Son of God** is missing from some ancient manuscripts of Mark and may be the result of scribal expansion (Metzger 1994, 62; 1975, 73; for a complete list of the nine variants of this verse, see Croy 2001, 107–8), in the canonical text it foreshadows three proclamations of Jesus's divine sonship that punctuate the Gospel at significant points: Jesus's baptism, transfiguration, and death (1:11; 9:7; 15:39). Like Christ, "Son of God" is a title that early Christians would have been accustomed to hearing applied to Jesus.

As mentioned earlier, v. 1 is viewed by most scholars as a title—or an encapsulation of the content—of the entire Gospel. This does not mean that Mark used *euangelion* to describe a literary genre of works that tell the story of Jesus's life and teachings, as the term is often used today. The term *euangelion* applies to the *purpose* of the Gospel—the proclamation of the good news—not to its literary genre (cf. Phil. 4:15). However, the custom of designating literary narratives of the life of Jesus as Gospels has been traced back as early as the second century (see Gundry 1996). This makes Mark's titular use of the term a significant event not just for Christianity but also for literary history.

John the Messenger (1:2–8)

If Mark 1:1 designates the contents of the entire document, then the prologue proper is made up of vv. 2–13. As discussed above, the prologue is, as Dennis Nineham (1963, 55) put it, "a sort of curtain-raiser, in which the reader is made aware of the true theological situation." However, several scholars have argued that the prologue does not simply supply background information but also functions as an "interpretive key" to the entire Gospel (Matera 1988; Boring 1990; Hooker 1997). It opens with a formula citation of **Isaiah the prophet** (vv. 2–3), actually made up of phrases from Exod. 23:20; Mal. 3:1; and Isa. 40:3 (an "error" corrected by both Matthew and Luke; see Matt. 3:3; Luke 3:3–6). Whether or not the evangelist knew this was a mixed citation, it conveys to the reader/audience some very important information about three of the main characters of the Gospel: God, John, and Jesus. God is the invisible actor who sends his **messenger** (*angelos*) **before *your*** face. The messenger referred to in Exod. 23:20 is an angel whom God will send to guard *Israel* on the way to the promised land; in Mark, the *angelos* is the messenger John the Baptist, and the "you" addressed by God is Jesus. In its original context, Mal. 3:1 refers to an eschatological "messenger" whom God will send to prepare for the day of *God's own* arrival in judgment; in Mark, the messenger is sent to prepare the way for *Jesus*, whom God addresses in the prophecy with the second-person pronoun (**who shall prepare** *your* **way**, not "my way" as in Malachi). The quotation of Isa. 40:3 (**A voice crying in the desert, Prepare the way of the Lord, Make straight his paths**) originally referred to the "new exodus" of Israel from Babylonian exile back to Judea; in Mark, the voice is John's, and the Lord of the verse is not God but the Messiah Jesus (cf. Mark 12:36–37), for whom the prophet is divinely commissioned to pave the way. The prophetic citation both grounds John and Jesus within the sacred history of Israel and places them in an eschatological framework—the promises of the ancient scriptures are about to be fulfilled; the arrival of the Lord-Messiah is imminent. The repetition of terms that describe the function of the messenger as one who *prepares* (*kataskeuasei, hetoimasete, eutheias poieite*) for the arrival of the Lord makes it clear that John is a significant but secondary figure: the emphasis is on Jesus. Similarly, the repetition of terms referring to the road/way/paths (*hodos, tribous*) points to the theme of "the way" in the Gospel (2:23; 4:4, 15; 6:8; 8:27; 9:33; 10:52), especially as it pertains to discipleship: "Jesus is about to go 'on the way' which is prepared by John the Baptizer and which ends in Jerusalem. His disciples are to follow him in this 'way'" (Best 1981, 15–16).

Following the **just as it is written** (*kathōs gegraptai*) that introduces the prophecy, 1:4–8 demonstrate its fulfillment in the appearance of the messenger, John, baptizing and preaching **in the desert,** and in the arrival of Jesus, the **Lord** (*kyrios*) of the prophecy (vv. 9–11). John is dressed like Elijah (2 Kings 1:8; cf. Zech. 13:4), **clothed in camel's hair and a belt around his waist** (Mark 1:6; in Mal. 4:5 [3:23 MT], the "angel" of the prophecy quoted in Mark 1:2 is specified as Elijah), an identification of John that is made explicit in 9:13. Matera notes that in rabbinic exegesis, Exod. 23:20 and Mal. 3:1 identified the coming "messenger" with Elijah (Matera 1988, 7; citing Str-B 1:591), an association that Mark also makes. The **baptism of repentance for the forgiveness of sins** is akin to the ritual bath (*miqveh/miqweh*) required of gentile coverts to Judaism; in John's ritual, the *miqveh* has become a sign of repentance not for outsiders but for Jews (Stookey 2000, 147). The location of the baptism at the Jordan River is loaded with significance in the sacred history: it is the site of Israel's crossing from the wilderness into the promised land (Josh. 3:14–17; 4:23–24; cf. Ps. 114:3, 5; Deut. 4:22), and where Elijah was translated into heaven (2 Kings 2:7–12). Mark's notice that **all Judea** and **all the Jerusalemites** went out to John is, as John Drury (1973, 31) perceptively observed, a sort of running of Israel's history backward: the people of Judea flock back to the river where they had crossed into the promised land in the time of Joshua. For Mark, the baptism offered by John is a new turning point for Israel, an event as portentous as the crossing of the Jordan.

If John is the eschatological Elijah, then the reader/audience is primed to expect that the **stronger man** (*ho ischyroteros*) whose **sandal straps** John is **unworthy to untie** will share some characteristics with Elijah's disciple and

The Eschatological Elijah

According to 2 Kings 2:11–12, Elijah did not die but was taken up into heaven in a flaming chariot borne on a whirlwind by fiery horses (cf. 1 Macc. 2:58; Sir. 48:9). The tradition of the eschatological Elijah in Mal. 4:5 (3:23 MT) seems to presuppose his heavenly existence; if he was taken up by God, he can be sent back to herald the day of the Lord. Because of the story of Elijah's translation, many Jewish legends developed about him. In heaven, transformed into the angel Sandalfon, he records the deeds of humans and guides the souls of the dead to paradise. As God's messenger, he returns to earth in human form to assist people in times of need. One of his functions is to announce the messianic age, so the songs that end the Sabbath express the hope that Elijah will return in the week ahead (Unterman 1991, 69). The tradition of the cup of Elijah—a special cup of wine poured out at the Passover Seder—"represents the Messianic redemption" (Unterman 1991, 70). Mark's equation of John and Elijah (9:13) seems to reflect an early form of such traditions with which not all NT authors agree (cf. John 1:21, 25).

successor Elisha, who received a "double share" of the Spirit of his predecessor (2 Kings 2:9).

According to Jewish tradition, Elisha's double share of Elijah's spirit gave him double the miracle-working power of Elijah (R. Brown 1971, 89; Ginzberg 1913, 239). In an important article, Raymond E. Brown enumerates many similarities in the Gospels' portrayal of Jesus and the pattern of Elisha's career: like Jesus, Elisha is a prophet who moves among the people, helping the poor and needy; Elisha travels around locations in Northern Israel (Shunem, Gilgal, Jericho, Dothan) as Jesus travels around Galilee; Elisha and Jesus are prodigious wonder-workers, even to the extent that after Elisha dies, a dead man is revived when his corpse touches the prophet's bones (2 Kings 13:20–21; Brown 1971, 89–90). In the book of Sirach, Elisha is remembered as a supremely powerful prophet: "He performed twice as many signs, and marvels with every utterance of his mouth. Never in his lifetime did he tremble before any ruler, nor could anyone intimidate him at all. Nothing was too hard for him, and when he was dead, his body prophesied. In his life he did wonders, and in death his deeds were marvelous" (Sir. 48:12b–14). The Baptist's proclamation that the coming one will **baptize you with Holy Spirit** (Mark 1:8) echoes the tradition that Elisha inherited double the prophetic spirit (2 Kings 2:9). However, in the light of the Malachi prophecy, which anticipates the coming of the day of the Lord in the wake of the eschatological Elijah, Mark's emphasis on the vast superiority of John's successor exceeds any known Jewish traditions about even Elisha; the one who comes after John will be a mighty agent of God who will inaugurate the end times.

Jesus the Son (1:9–13)

The first usage in Mark of the phrase *kai egeneto*—translated in the KJV as "and it came to pass"—immediately precedes the appearance of Jesus. This formula occurs only a few times in the Gospel (Mark 2:15, 23; 4:4), but it appears hundreds of times in the Jewish scriptures. Here, in combination with the similarly portentous **in those days**, the arrival on the scene of the Lord (cf. Mark 1:3) is cast in deliberately scriptural-sounding language, conveying the impression to the reader/audience that Jesus is a figure of "biblical" significance (cf. Donahue and Harrington 2002, 16, 64; Moloney 2002, 36). He comes from **Nazareth of Galilee**, a regional origin that sets him apart from the Judeans who flock to John for baptism (v. 5). However, even Jesus is **baptized in the Jordan by John** (v. 9), implying *metanoia* ("repentance" or "conversion") on his part (the other evangelists revise this scene to mitigate the embarrassment of a repentant Jesus; Matt. 3:13–15; Luke 3:21; cf. John 1:29–34; 3:22–23). Jesus's vision of **the heavens being split apart** and **the Spirit** descending on him **like a dove** as he is **coming out of the water** (Mark 1:10) is reminiscent of mystical narratives where the heavens open up to impart a great revelation to an exalted seer (e.g., Acts 7:56; 10:11; *T. Levi* 2.6; 5.1; 18.6; *T. Jud.* 24.2; *2 Bar.* 22.1; cf. Rev. 4:1). Again, the influence of 2 Kings 2:9–12 is apparent, with the association of a prophetic succession, a heavenly vision, and the descent of the spirit (cf. 2 Kings 2:15). In Jewish apocalyptic literature, the coming of the spirit is associated with the messianic age (*1 En.* 49.3; 62.2; *Pss. Sol.* 17.42; *T. Levi* 18.7; *T. Jud.* 24.2).

It is difficult to identify the source of the scriptural allusion in the utterance of the heavenly voice, **You are my Son the beloved; in you I am delighted** (Mark 1:11). As Matera (1988, 18n31) observes, "The text can allude to Genesis 22:2, Psalm 2:7, or Isaiah 42:1. The choice made here is crucial since it can result in understanding Jesus's sonship in terms of Isaac imagery (Gen. 22:2), royal imagery (Ps. 2:7), or servant imagery (Isa. 42:1)." He judiciously concedes that the evangelist may expect the reader/audience to recognize all of these allusions: "Jesus is the royal Son of God who comes as the Lord's Servant to surrender his life" (Matera 1988, 18n31). The likening of the spirit to a dove (*hōs peristeran*) is notoriously obscure (Gero 1976, 17; Mann 1986, 200). It may intensify the royal dimension of the imagery since the descent of a dove or other bird upon an elect person is a feature of ancient Near Eastern legend (Gero 1976, 19); Ps. 2:7 is an enthronement psalm, where God's anointed king is elected to rule over the nations: "You are my son; today I have begotten you." The dove image may also reflect the ancient interpretation of the dove as a soul-bird, closely associated with divine presence and protection (Goodenough 1958, 30–31); Philo of Alexandria (*Spec. Laws* 4.22 §117) identified the dove with divine Wisdom (*Sophia*). Mark 1:11 is sometimes offered as evidence of Mark's "adoptionist Christology" since it implies that Jesus first *becomes* Son of God with the descent of the God's Spirit and divine ratification (see

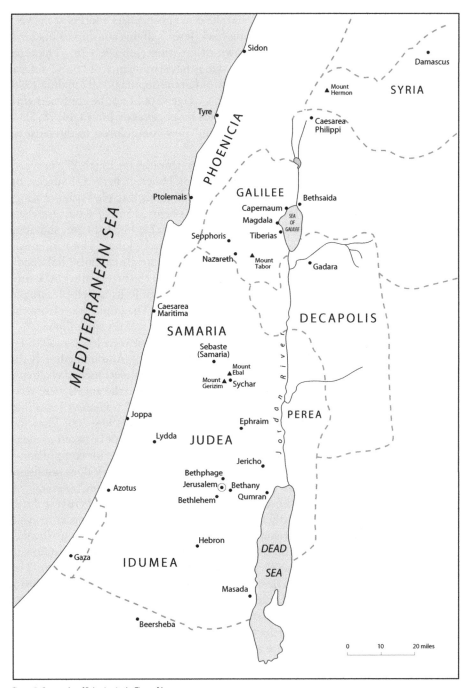

Figure 2. Geography of Palestine in the Time of Jesus.

Dunn 1980, 47)—an implication that the other evangelists address at the very beginning of their Gospels, pressing back Jesus's divine sonship to his birth (Matt. 1–2; Luke 1–2) or to the dawn of creation (John 1:1–18). The term translated here as "beloved" (*agapētos*) may have the nuance of "only" since it is often used to translate the Hebrew *yāḥîd* in the Septuagint (Donahue 1988, 592, citing V. Taylor 1966, 161–62). This usage should not be confused with the Johannine "only-begotten Son" (*huios monogenēs* of John 1:14, 18; 3:16, 18). The translation "dearest" or "darling" may come closest to the sense of the adjective as it applies to Mark's Jesus.

The descent of the Spirit upon Jesus carries through the Elijah-Elisha typology at work in the narrative (cf. 2 Kings 2:9, 15). However, in the OT succession narrative (Carroll 1969), Elijah is the "Father" to his disciple Elisha (2 Kings 2:12), whereas in Mark, Jesus is proclaimed as beloved Son *of God*, elsewhere in Mark referred to as Father (*patēr*; cf. Mark 11:25; 13:32; 14:36), signaling the superiority of the disciple (Jesus) to the master (John). The Father-Son relationship between God and Jesus established here also entails filial obedience, for, as Morna Hooker (1997, 16) observes, in the first century AD, sons were expected to be obedient to their fathers: "since Jesus is well-pleasing to God, we know that he is in fact obedient to him." The implication from the outset is that Jesus's relationship with God is intimate, yet subordinate.

The obedience implied by the filial relationship between Jesus and God is illustrated by the conclusion of the prologue (1:12–13): **And immediately the Spirit cast him out into the desert. And he was in the desert forty days, being tested by the Adversary, and he was with the beasts, and the angels were serving him.** Here, language of the Spirit of God "casting" (*ekballei*) Jesus into the desert seems to contradict Christopher S. Mann's (1986, 200) assertion that the Spirit's descent "into" Jesus (*eis auton*) should not be taken to mean that "his subsequent ministry was simply the result of interior compulsion." However, apart from propelling him into the desert, the Spirit does not figure actively in the brief account of Jesus's "temptation," or "testing" (*peirazō*; cf. 8:11; 10:2), where Jesus withstands forty days with *ho satana*, here translated literally as **the Adversary** rather than the more usual "Satan," in order to avoid the lavish postbiblical Christian demonology that the proper name invokes (see H. Kelly 2006; Wray and Mobley 2005). Throughout Mark, references to "the Satan" can be interpreted consistently with the OT view of *hasatan* (Hebrew) as one who tests and obstructs the mission of Jesus (Job 1–2; 1 Chron. 21:1; Zech. 3:1–2; Mark 3:23, 26; 4:15; 8:33; see H. Kelly 2006, 13–31, 80–84). Jesus's ability to resist the Adversary establishes his faithfulness to God and demonstrates that he is worthy of divine approval.

The **forty days** of testing are a conventional symbol of times of trial (e.g., the forty years of Israel's wilderness wandering; the forty days and forty nights of the flood; Elijah's forty-day flight to Mount Horeb [1 Kings 19:8]). The number forty is also associated with the beginning of new epochs in salvation history, such as the covenant with Noah (Gen. 7:17; 8:6; 9:8–17), Moses's sojourn on Mount Sinai (Exod. 24:18; 34:28), the entry into the promised land (16:35), and Jesus's appearances after the resurrection (Acts 1:3; Gunner 1962, 845). In the light of the Elijah-Elisha typology, Jesus's desert sojourn especially echoes Elijah's journey to Horeb, with the shared motifs of forty days, the wilderness, and the angelic ministry to the prophet (1 Kings 19:1–18; cf. 19:19–21, where the call of Elisha immediately follows the theophany at Horeb). The note that Jesus was **with the beasts** (*thēria*) has been interpreted either as the portrayal of Christ as a "new Adam" living in Edenic harmony with wild animals (e.g., Bauckham 1994b), or as part of the "menacing wilderness" associated with the testing motif (Heil 2006). In view of the range of meanings of the word *thērion*, which can mean "any living creature, excluding humans" (BDAG 455), there may be an echo of the story of the ministry of the ravens to Elijah in 1 Kings 17:2–6 (though the meaning of the term *thēria* [**animals**] does not usually extend to birds).

Although there are discernable parallels between Elijah's wilderness sojourn and Jesus's forty days in the desert, there are significant contrasts. Elijah flees in fear from the fury of Jezebel, but Jesus is prompted by the Spirit of God. Elijah is despondent and prays for death; Jesus withstands the tests of the Adversary, witnessing to his superiority to the first Elijah, as well as to the second (Mark 1:7–8). Elijah is succeeded by Elisha, but it is Jesus who is the mighty successor to John, the hoped-for eschatological Elijah. The reference to angels in v. 13 not only reinforces the typology (cf. 1 Kings 19:5, 7), but it also forms an *inclusio* with the quotation of Mal. 3:1 in Mark 1:2, where the word *angelos* also occurs, a framing that further defines vv. 2–13 as a prologue.

As noticed earlier, several scholars have suggested that the Markan prologue not only supplies the readers/audience with vital background information but also functions as an "interpretive key" to the entire Gospel (Matera 1988; Boring 1990). Matera asserts that the prologue introduces the Markan themes of the messiahship of Jesus (1:14–8:30); the necessity of listening to the beloved Son, even when he speaks of his suffering (8:31–10:52); the "testing" of Jesus in Jerusalem (11:1–13:37); and the recognition that Jesus is the Son of God (14:1–16:8; Matera 1988, 9–15). Boring (1990, 63–68) finds five main Gospel themes in the prologue:

1. The power of the Christ as a manifestation of God's power.
2. The story of the Christ as the key to God's mighty acts in history.
3. The weakness of the Christ, which represents "the weakness and victimization of humanity, and is thus the true power of God."
4. The secrecy of the Christ as a literary-theological device that ties together human weakness and divine power.
5. The disciples of the Christ as God's messianic people.

All these themes certainly are found in Mark, but it is questionable whether the prologue was designed by the evangelist to be as programmatic as these modern scholars suggest. However, modern readers with "eyes to see and ears to hear" (cf. Mark 4:11–12) will find echoes of the prologue throughout the Gospel, especially the theme of the way (path, journey, road, roadside, all translating the Greek *hodos*, which occurs sixteen times; Boring 1990, 66), the issue of the identity of Jesus, his relationship with God, and his faithfulness in times of testing.

Theological Issues

The word *archē* that abruptly announces the beginning of Mark, has a range of meanings that include "first cause," "ruler," and "rule" in the abstract sense of office and function: "If 1:1 is a title for the whole document, then the whole document ought to be considered the ἀρχή" (Boring 1990, 53). This statement points to the great significance of Mark for Christian belief and practice. As the oldest Gospel, it is not only the foundation and model for the other Synoptic Gospels (and possibly for John; see D. Smith 1992); it is also the source of much of our knowledge of Jesus's life. For example, without Mark, we might not know that Jesus was a Galilean, that his mother's name was Mary, that he was an artisan, and that he had sisters as well as brothers (6:3). Jesus's relationship with John the Baptist would not be documented, and we would not know the names of the Twelve or of Mary Magdalene. Jesus's teaching in parables, the stories of miracles and exorcisms, the trial and execution narratives, are all part of Mark's legacy to the church and to the world. In a very significant way, Mark is the *archē* of the "fourfold Gospel" of the church (Irenaeus, *Haer.* 3.11.8).

Although the identity of Jesus—in technical terms, Christology—is very much an issue throughout Mark, *theology* in the strict sense of understanding God is at the heart of the Gospel (Donahue 1988). In Mark, Jesus does not typically preach about himself, or about his identity as messiah, but proclaims God and the reign of God (*hē basileia tou theou*). As Francis Moloney (2002, 30) observes, the theocentrism of the Gospel is apparent throughout the prologue:

> God dominates this prologue, mentioned by name in 1:1 and present in direct speech in vv. 2–3. In vv. 4–5 and 6–8 the Baptist is the subject of most of the verbs, but his activity fulfills what God had promised in vv. 2–3. . . . God and the Spirit are the main actors in Jesus's initial experiences until, at the close of vv. 1–13, Jesus is *with* the wild beasts and served by the angels. This prologue establishes an important truth for the reader: *the chief agent in the action that follows is God.*

The stage is set for Jesus's initial proclamation of the good news of God in 1:14–15.

Nicaea and Chalcedon

The Council of Nicaea (AD 325), the first ecumenical council of the church, promulgated the doctrine that Christ is "of the same being" (*homoousios*) with God the Father—not a creature, as Arius believed, and not merely "of similar being" (*homoiousios*), as some later fourth-century figures proposed. The Council of Chalcedon (AD 451), the fourth ecumenical council, promulgated a definition regarding the unity of the divine and human natures of Christ (the Chalcedonian Decree) as "truly God and truly [hu]man, . . . acknowledged in two natures without confusion, without change, without division, without separation" (*WDCH* 176). These trinitarian and christological doctrines are ultimately based on the Christian Scriptures, but it would be anachronistic to claim that they inform NT understandings of Jesus.

In contemporary Christian proclamation, Mark 1:1–8 is a lectionary reading for the second Sunday in Advent. Mark's portrayal of John the Baptist as the messenger sent by God to "prepare the way" for Jesus reminds us of the deep roots of Christian faith in Judaism and the Jewish scriptures. John is a Jewish prophet who fulfills the Jewish scriptures, the eschatological Elijah who "prepared the way" for the messiah. While Mark assumes continuity between the ministries of John and Jesus, and clearly portrays Jesus as a figure of greater stature than John in salvation history, John is not portrayed as a disciple of Jesus. Rather, Jesus heeds John's preaching of a baptism of repentance for the forgiveness of sins (1:4, 9) and strikes out on his own ministry (1:14–15). Mark's depiction of a *human* Jesus who seeks baptism and is proclaimed the dearest Son of God, so much at variance with Christian expectations of a flawless Christ (cf. Heb. 4:15; 2 Cor. 5:21), illustrates that this Gospel, like the other NT Scriptures, embodies "Christology in the making" (Dunn 1980) and invites reflection on the relationship between the NT Scriptures and the classic christological doctrines of Nicaea and Chalcedon, taken for granted by Christians today.

Mark 1:14–15

Transition: Summary of the Good News

Introductory Matters

As noted above, some scholars regard 1:14–15 as part of Mark's prologue; others see these verses as the introduction to and as part of the next main section of the Gospel (e.g., V. Taylor 1966, 107, 165). Another approach is to conceptualize their function as a transitional summary between the prologue and the body of the Gospel, referring back to the previous section and introducing a new section. Similar "summary statements" (*Sammelberichte*) are found throughout Mark (for a complete list, see Donahue and Harrington 2002, 71–72). However, this initial summary is especially significant. It not only marks the transition from the preparation for the good news onward to its initial proclamation by Jesus in Galilee; it also encapsulates some of the main themes of Jesus's ministry: "The time is fulfilled, the reign of God is near; repent and believe in the good news" (v. 15). The repetition of the term *euangelion* in both verses links them with the title in 1:1 and points to the distinctively Markan emphasis on this term.

Tracing the Narrative Flow

Mark 1:14 begins with the adversative **but** (*de*), breaking the *kai* parataxis of vv. 5–13, thus marking a significant change. In Mark, Jesus's public career begins where John's ends; there is no overlap between the ministries of the two prophets, as there is in John 3:22–24, where John, Jesus, and their disciples baptize together. The reference to the arrest of John (lit., the "handing over," *paradidōmi*) is so terse that it seems to presuppose that the reader/audience already has some previous knowledge of this event; the circumstances of John's imprisonment and execution are recounted in Mark 6:17–29. The notice that John **was handed over** sounds an ominous note and foreshadows Mark's many references to the "handing over" of Jesus/the son of man (3:19; 9:31; 10:33; 14:10–11, 18, 21, 41, 42, 44; cf. 13:9,

> **Prologue: John and Jesus (1:1–13)**
>
> **The beginning of the good news (1:1)**
>
> **John the messenger (1:2–8)**
>
> **Jesus the Son (1:9–13)**
>
> ▶**Transition: Summary of the good news (1:14–15)**

12). Jesus returns to his native region of **Galilee** to begin his ministry, and it is in and around Galilee that his mission of preaching, healing, and teaching mostly takes place (Mark 1:14–9:50; see Freyne 1988, 32–68).

The message that Jesus proclaims (*kēryssō*) is **the good news of God** (*to euangelion tou theou*), a phrase found nowhere else in the Gospels but which occurs several times in Paul's Letters (Rom. 1:1; 15:16; 2 Cor. 11:7; 1 Thess. 2:2, 8, 9; cf. 1 Pet. 4:17). Apart from the title, this is the only nonabsolute usage of the term *euangelion* in Mark: in the other references, the "gospel" is simply preached; here Jesus's message is specified as "of God." As with 1:1, the question whether the genitive is objective or subjective—the good news *about* God or the good news *coming from* God—is unresolvable; no doubt the evangelist would have concurred with both senses. The identification of God as the source and content of the good news in this summary of Jesus's preaching points to the theological focus of this Gospel.

Jesus speaks for the first time in 1:15, further specifying the nature of the good news: **The time is fulfilled, the reign of God is near; repent and believe in the good news.** The theme of prophecy and fulfillment introduced in the prologue is carried forward by Jesus (cf. 13:4; 14:49; 15:28); the use of the Greek word *kairos*, referring to a specific opportune time as opposed to *chronos*, usually referring to an indefinite period of time (however, see BDAG 1092), underlines the eschatological import of the message (cf. Mark 13:33). Joel Marcus (1989, 53) suggests that the expression "the time is fulfilled" (*peplērōtai ho kairos*) reflects "the Jewish apocalyptic concept of the eschatological measure; . . . when the measure of time allotted to the old age is full, the new age will come." The phrase translated here as **the reign of God** (*hē basileia tou theou*)—often translated as "kingdom of God"—announces one of the main themes of the Gospel (4:11, 26, 30; 9:1, 47; 10:14, 15, 23, 24; 12:34; 14:25; 15:43). In English, **reign** captures the meaning of *basileia* better than "kingdom": "The word 'kingdom' is static and evokes a *place* where a king (or queen) rules. Greek *basileia* is more active and dynamic, with the nuance of the 'reigning' of God as well as a setting for that reign" (Donahue and Harrington 2002, 71). The notion that God reigns over Israel and over the world has a long biblical pedigree (Exod. 19:5–6; cf. Deut. 14:2; 26:18–19; see Beavis 2006, 48–52). However, the idea that the reign of God was the content of the preaching of Jesus is a Markan contribution to the Gospel tradition (Paul uses the phrase only six times and never connects it with Jesus's preaching; Gal. 5:21; 1 Cor. 4:20; 6:9–10; 15:24, 50; Rom. 14:17; cf. 1 Thess. 2:12; Col. 4:11; 2 Thess. 1:5), and the meaning of the term must be inferred with reference to its usages within the Gospel (e.g., Kelber 1974). Jesus's call for repentance/conversion and faith (*metanoeite kai pisteuete*) both shows continuity with John's **baptism of repentance** (v. 4) and introduces the new and characteristically Markan theme of faith/belief in the good news of God that Jesus proclaims.

Theological Issues

Theological reflection on Mark 1:14–15 often pertains to the theme of preaching, since Jesus's first public act in the Gospel is to proclaim the good news of the reign of God (e.g., Mays 1972; Alsup 1979; Gutiérrez 1991). As noted above, Marxsen (1969, 128–29) asserts that for Mark, the Gospel represents Jesus to the believing community: the good news as proclaimed throughout Mark makes Jesus present to the reader/audience. However, it must be remembered that the good news proclaimed by Jesus is the nearness of the reign of God, a reality that both preceded him (cf. Pss. 10:16; 24:8; 29:10; 47:2–4; 84:3; 95:3–5) and that would come into fruition after him: "the kingdom was preexistent, since God had ruled the world since its creation; it was a present reality, since God's kingship was eternal; it would be manifested perfectly in the future, as the prophets had foretold" (Beavis 2006, 99). God's rule was exercised over the entire earth but especially over Israel, God's chosen people. Mary Rose D'Angelo (1992, 206) makes the startling suggestion that in imagining the context of Jesus's life, theologians need to make a shift "from the person of Jesus to the community in which his career was located," a movement focused on the reign of God. This was not simply a hope for better things to come but specifically a movement of oppressed people from imperial rule to God's reign. D'Angelo's comments regarding the historical Jesus are also germane to the interpretation of Mark, in that the good news mediated through the words and deeds of Jesus in the Gospel challenges "imperial orders"—be they political, colonial, institutional, or religious—experienced by the people of God throughout history.

Mark 1:16–3:35

Act 1: Jesus in Galilee

Introductory Matters

Many scholars see the next main section of Mark as ending at 3:6, where the Pharisees and Herodians conspire to destroy Jesus (e.g., Nineham 1963, 110; Tolbert 1989, 132; Donahue and Harrington 2002, 47; Moloney 2002, 45–48). Mark 3:6 is the culmination of a series of challenges to Jesus's authority that begins with the healing of a paralyzed man (2:1–12; see 2:6–7, 16, 18, 24; 3:2), and it is an important foreshadowing of the events of the second half of the Gospel. However, as noted above, the mention of the arrest of John (1:14) has already hinted that Jesus will meet with similar treatment, and people (including Jewish leaders, the disciples, and Jesus's relatives and neighbors) continue to question his teachings and activities throughout the Gospel (e.g., 3:20–21, 22; 6:1–5, 11; 7:1–5; 8:15, 32–33; 9:14, 19, 38; 10:2, 13; 11:27–33; 12:13–17, 18–27, 35–37; 14:1–2, 4–5). Thus Mark 3:6 marks a decisive turn in the *plot* of the Gospel but not in its organization of material (cf. Dewey 1991, 226–28). Rather than positing a major break in the narrative at 3:6, I prefer to focus on the theme of discipleship as it is developed in 1:16–3:35, beginning with the call of the first disciples in 1:16–20, and ending with Jesus's words about his true family in 3:31–35.

As the first main section or "act" of the Markan drama, 1:16–3:35 introduces many of the main characters and themes of the first half of the Gospel. Jesus calls and gathers disciples, culminating in the naming of the Twelve (1:16–20; 2:13–17; 3:13–19). Jesus is repeatedly shown engaging in his characteristic activities of teaching, healing, and exorcism with great success

(1:21–28, 29–31, 32–34, 39, 40–44; 2:1–12; 3:1–6, 10–11), and his reputation spreads throughout Galilee and beyond (1:28, 32–34, 37, 45; 3:7–12). The issue of Jesus's identity is raised several times (1:24, 27; 3:11, 22). However, despite his authoritative teaching and his skill as a healer and exorcist, there is opposition to his activities, by authority figures (2:6–7, 16, 18, 24; 3:2, 6, 22), and even by members of his own family (3:21). Throughout this section, Jesus is on the move, from Capernaum to the countryside and back, to and fro from the shore of the Sea of Galilee, into the desert, up a mountain, in and out of synagogues, houses, and the first of several boats. As noted above, the plot of the Pharisees and Herodians to have him executed is introduced in 3:6; furthermore, the culmination of the appointment of the Twelve is a notice of Judas's future role in the conspiracy (3:19). Jesus foretells that there will be a time when "the bridegroom" will be taken away (2:20).

In the light of Mark 1:1–15, there are some surprising omissions in the section. The central theme of Jesus's proclamation, the reign of God (v. 15), is not mentioned, and neither is the term "gospel." While Jesus is portrayed as a teacher (1:21–22, 27; 2:13) and preacher (1:38; 3:14), the content of his teaching and proclamation is not developed in much detail. Apart from the observation about Judas, it seems unlikely that the other newly minted disciples will prove to be inadequate in their comprehension of Jesus and even loyalty to him. As a capable storyteller, Mark prepares the reader/audience for major developments in the narrative and also creates suspense—How will the plot against Jesus unfold?—while leaving room for the unexpected.

In addition to the theme of disciple gathering, Mark 1:16–3:35 is permeated with Jewish religious questions and settings. Two incidents take place in synagogues, on the Sabbath (1:21–28; 3:1–6; cf. 1:39). Jesus's behavior on the Sabbath is scrutinized by religious experts (2:24; 3:2). Issues of ritual purity (1:44), the forgiveness of sins (2:5–11), association with sinners (2:15–16), fasting (2:18–20), and blasphemy (2:7; 3:20–30) arise. Throughout the section, Jesus handles every situation adroitly: disciples leave their livelihoods to follow him; people are astounded by his teaching; unclean spirits flee at his command; the sick are healed; he decisively responds to even the most serious challenges to his credibility, including suspected blasphemy (2:7). Jesus lives up to John's promise of his successor's greatness (1:7–8) and illustrates through his words and deeds what it is to be God's beloved Son. At the same time, the section is full of dramatic irony: the demons expelled by Jesus recognize him as God's agent (1:24, 34; 3:11), but religious authorities and even his own family do not.

Although (as noted in the introduction to the commentary) Mark defies neat attempts at structuring, a roughly concentric outline of the major incidents in this section can be discerned. First, it is bracketed by narratives of the call of disciples (1:16–19; 3:13–19). The call of another disciple, Levi (2:13–17), appears at the approximate midpoint between them. The section is further bracketed by two incidents on the Sabbath in a synagogue (1:21–28; 3:1–6).

The initial synagogue visit is followed by two major healings (1:40–45; 2:1–7). The second synagogue scene is preceded by two challenges to Jesus's authority (2:18–22, 23–28). The incidents in the central section (2:1–3:6) are also stories where Jesus's authority is challenged. The final sequence of incidents (3:20–35), which follows the naming of the Twelve, can be considered as a postscript to the section or, like 1:14–15, as a transition to the next section (4:1–34). The scribes' accusation that Jesus expels demons by the power of Beelzebul (3:22–30) echoes and intensifies the controversies of 2:1–3:6; this charge is bracketed by Jesus's relatives' attempt to seize him (3:21) and Jesus's statement that his true family consists not of his biological relations, but "whoever does the will of God" (3:31–35)—an implicit commentary on the demands of discipleship (cf. 10:29–30).

Tracing the Narrative Flow

The First Disciples Called (1:16–20)

This section of Mark begins with a brief but highly portentous narrative of the call of the first disciples: Simon, Andrew, James, and John (1:16–20). On his return to his native region of Galilee (1:9), Jesus does not initially go to Nazareth, where presumably his family lives (1:9; cf. 6:1–6), but to the western shore of the Sea of Galilee, where he calls two pairs of brothers. For an ancient reader/audience, this omission might have been noteworthy: a loyal son would be expected to visit his family before embarking on a prophetic career, like Elisha, who returns to his parents to kiss them good-bye before setting out with Elijah (1 Kings 19:20).

Although historically it is possible that Jesus knew some of the disciples prior to his prophetic ministry, which might explain their eagerness to follow him, the Gospel gives the impression that this is the first encounter between Jesus and the four men. The repetition of the adverb *euthys* ("immediately,"

Prologue: John and Jesus (1:1–13)

Transition: Summary of the good news (1:14–15)

▶**Act 1: Jesus in Galilee (1:16–3:35)**

The first disciples called (1:16–20)

First synagogue visit: Teaching and an exorcism (1:21–28)

Simon's mother-in-law and others healed (1:29–34)

Retreat and continuing ministry (1:35–39)

A man with leprosy cleansed (1:40–45)

Controversy stories (2:1–3:6)

The healing of a paralyzed man (2:1–12)

The call of Levi (2:13–17)

The question about fasting (2:18–22)

The question about the Sabbath (2:23–28)

Second synagogue visit: Healing a man with a withered hand (3:1–6)

The spread of Jesus's fame (3:7–12)

The appointment of the Twelve (3:13–19)

Postscript and transition (3:20–35)

Jesus's relatives and true discipleship (3:20–21)

Controversy with the scribes (3:22–30)

Jesus's true family (3:31–35)

Figure 3. The Sea of Galilee (Lake Tiberias).

1:18, 20) enhances the sense that the first disciples follow Jesus instantaneously, without asking questions or considering the consequences for their families or livelihoods. The note that the two sons of Zebedee left their father in the boat with the hired men (v. 20) would have been particularly shocking to an ancient audience, whose cultural values included a strong sense of familial loyalty and respect, especially for parents (Donahue and Harrington 2002, 75; Moloney 2002, 53; cf. Exod. 20:12; Deut. 5:16; Prov. 22:22–25; Tob. 5:1; Sir. 3:1–16). The rapid pace of the call narrative, and the fishers' immediate willingness to leave their nets and follow Jesus, underlines the sense of eschatological urgency in Jesus's initial message: "The time is fulfilled!" (Mark 1:15).

Mark's focus on the occupation of the first disciples—they are **fishers** (1:16, *halieis*)—conveys some information about their socioeconomic status. The first two brothers, Simon and Andrew, are portrayed as casting their weighted nets from the shore; James and John are in a boat with their father and hired men (*misthōtōn*), preparing their dragnets, which would yield a much larger catch (Donahue and Harrington 2002, 76). The two different fishing methods used indicate that the sons of Zebedee were more prosperous than Simon and his brother. Both sets of brothers are said to leave (*aphentes*) their occupation behind (along with nets, boats, servants, and family members) and follow (*ēkolouthēsan*) Jesus (cf. the summary of the demands of discipleship in 10:29–30). Jesus's promise to make Simon and Andrew **fishers of human beings** (1:17b) is jarring; although the KJV's phrase "fishers of men" has become famous, Best observes that the fishing metaphor "never became important as a description of the activity of the ministry of the whole church; . . . the fisherman's first encounter with his fish is when he kills it for food for himself or others" (Best 1981, 172–73). In the Jewish scriptures, the fishing metaphor often refers to the wrathful judgment of God, upon both individuals and nations (Eccles. 9:12; Amos 4:2; Hab. 1:14–17; Ezek. 26:5; 29:3–5; 32:3–4; Jer. 16:16). The usage here is more benign, conveying the theme of the eschatological harvest begun by Jesus and the disciples (cf. *DBI* 290) and emphasizing the urgency of their mission.

This passage introduces two settings that recur throughout the first half of Mark: the Sea of Galilee and the boat (Mark 1:16, 19–20). Many commentators have noted that this "sea" is actually a freshwater lake, more correctly called the "Lake of Gennesaret" by Luke (5:1), and referred to as the "Sea of Tiberias" by John (21:1). Mark's usage of the term sea (*thalassa*) rather than lake (*limnē*) is sometimes seen as deliberately evocative of a supposed fear of the sea suffered by ancient Israelites as a nonmaritime people (e.g., *DBI* 290; Malbon 1984, 375–76). Prior to Mark's Gospel, there is no previous reference to a "Sea of Galilee" in ancient literature (Clark 1962, 348), but the designation of it as a sea is consistent with Semitic usage (M. Black 1967, 133); in the OT it is called the "Sea of Chinnereth/Chinneroth" (Num. 34:11; Josh. 12:3), and in modern Hebrew it is called Yam Kinneret ("Sea of Kinneret"). Its shores were heavily populated due to the fishing industry on both its western (Jewish) and eastern (gentile) sides (Donahue and Harrington 2002, 73–74; cf. Josephus, *J.W.* 3.506), which shows that Jews of Jesus's time were not intimidated by

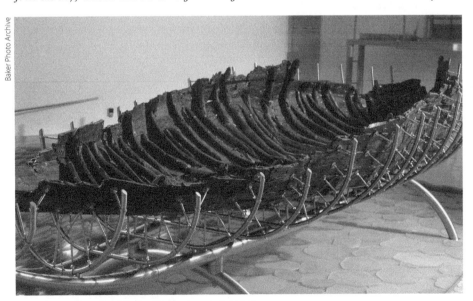

Figure 4. Remains of an ancient fishing boat discovered near the Sea of Galilee.

this "sea," described by Josephus as notable for the purity of its water, its unique varieties of fish, and the beauty of the surrounding country. However, the usage of the term "sea" as opposed to "lake" does enhance the symbolic possibilities of the Markan stories where Jesus and the disciples are alone in a boat on the water (esp. in the stories of calming the storm [4:35–41] and the walking on water [6:45–52]; Malbon 1984, 375–77).

The identity and order of the first disciples called are significant. Simon (renamed Peter in 3:16) is always named first in NT lists of the Twelve (Mark 3:16–19; Matt. 10:2–4; Luke 6:14–16; Acts 1:13), perhaps reflecting his historical status as a leader of the earliest church in Jerusalem (Gal. 1:18; 2:9; Acts 15:6–11). Simon's brother Andrew is included among the Twelve (3:18), and later in Mark, he, along with Peter, James, and John question Jesus about the coming destruction of the temple (13:3–4); according to John's Gospel, it is Andrew who brought his brother to Jesus (John 1:41–42). James (in Greek *Iakōbos*, or Jacob) is one of three significant figures in the early church by this name; the others are James son of Alphaeus (also one of the Twelve, 3:18) and James the brother of Jesus (6:3; Matt. 13:55), an important leader of the earliest church in Jerusalem (Gal. 1:19; 2:9, 12; Acts 12:17; 15:13; 21:18). It is James "the brother of the Lord"—not the disciple mentioned here—whom Paul, perhaps sarcastically, refers to as one of the "pillars" of the Jerusalem church, along with Simon Peter and John son of Zebedee (Gal. 2:9).

First Synagogue Visit: Teaching and an Exorcism (1:21–28)

The next incident takes place on the Sabbath in a synagogue at Capernaum, where Jesus both teaches and cures a man with an unclean spirit (1:21–28).

Capernaum

The Gospels represent Capernaum as the home base of Jesus's mission (cf. Mark. 2:1; Matt. 4:13). Located on the northwestern shore of the Sea of Galilee, the town is identified with modern-day Tell Ḥum. In the first century it was a fishing village with a population of no more than 1,500, with modest houses, unpaved roads, a crude harbor, and a lack of Greco-Roman architecture. The famous "Jesus boat" was found by archaeologists nearby and illustrates the kind of vessel used by Galilean fishers. Coming from the southwest, a major road passed through Capernaum and headed northeast to Syria. A Q saying (Matt. 11:23; Luke 10:15) passionately denounces Capernaum for not attending to Jesus's teachings. However, a rabbinic reference associates Capernaum with *minim*, a group of Jews considered to be heretical, possibly Jewish-Christians (*Eccles. Rab.* 1.86; see Reed 2000, 220–21).

Synagogue

The synagogue is not to be confused with the temple (*hieron, beit ha-mikdash* [*bayit ha-miqdāš*], "house of the sanctuary") in Jerusalem, the center of the Jewish sacrificial cult. The term synagogue is from the Greek *synagōgē*, referring to a place of assembly; the term *proseuchē* ("house of prayer") is also used in some ancient sources to refer to a Jewish place of worship (cf. Acts 16:13). There is no pre-Hellenistic evidence of Jews worshiping in synagogues, but the NT frequently refers to synagogues in Galilee and Judea (e.g., Mark 1:21; Matt. 4:23; Luke 4:16–30; 7:5; Acts 13:5, 14–15, 43; 14:1; 15:21; cf. Josephus, *Life* 54 §280; *J.W.* 2.14.4–5 §§285–91), indicating that the synagogue was a well-known institution in Palestine by the first century AD. Three pre–AD 70 synagogues have been excavated in Israel: at Gamla, Masada, and Herodium. There are no undisputed remains of the first-century AD synagogue at Capernaum mentioned in Mark, but a large synagogue dated to the fourth century and a nearby fifth-century octagonal church, traditionally known as St. Peter's House, are the most imposing archaeological remains at the site (see Atkinson 2000, 1260–62; Reed 2000, 220).

Form-critically, the pericope appears to be a conflation of two stories: one in which Jesus teaches and astonishes the people (Mark 1:21–22, 27a), and an exorcism (vv. 23–26, 27b). From a redactional perspective, the passage contains a story within a story: the account of Jesus's authoritative teaching frames the cure of the possessed man, similar to the "Markan sandwiches" found throughout the Gospel (e.g., 3:20–35; 4:1–20; 5:21–43; 6:7–30; 11:12–21; 14:1–11; 14:17–31; 14:53–72; 15:40–16:8; Edwards 1989; Rhoads and Michie 1982, 51). Unlike many other instances of this technique in Mark, both stories take place in the same setting, but the effect is similar: "The two related stories illuminate and enrich each other, commenting on and clarifying the meaning, one of the other" (Rhoads and Michie 1982, 51).

The narrative begins by establishing Jesus's (and the disciples') Jewish piety: on reaching Capernaum, they "immediately" enter the synagogue on the Sabbath, and Jesus teaches (the first of seventeen Markan usages of the verb "teach" [*didaskō*]). Possibly, the scene depicts the Jewish practice of asking a visitor to comment on the weekly Torah portion (*parashat hashavuah*). The content of Jesus's teaching is not recounted, but the reaction of the hearers is dramatic; the verb *ekplēssomai* (cf. Mark 6:2; 7:37; 10:26; 11:18) denotes extreme astonishment: the colloquial "they were blown away" would be a modern equivalent. Mark explains the reason for this reaction: **He was teaching them as one having authority, and not as the scribes** (1:22b). The scribes (*grammateis*) were a class of expert interpreters of Torah (Sir. 38:24–39:11; 1 Macc. 7:12; 2 Macc. 6:18–20; 7:12; cf. Mark 12:28–34; Matt. 23:2–3); the contrast that astounds the congregation may be between Jesus's teaching—the proclamation of eschatological fulfillment (cf. 1:15)—and the kind of jurisprudence enshrined in the Mishnah (ca. AD 200), a compilation of rabbinic opinions on the interpretation of the law (see Neusner 1989). Jesus speaks as one with the right to make his own pronouncements on the meaning of Torah rather than appealing, like the scribes, to authoritative texts or teachers (cf. Fredriksen 1999, 103).

Interpolated into this scene is the story of a man with an **unclean spirit** (Mark 1:23–26) who **was immediately in their synagogue** (v. 23), crying, **"What have you to do with us, Jesus of Nazareth? I know you, you have come to destroy us—you are the holy man of God!"** The term "unclean spirit" (*pneuma akatharton*) is unattested in extrabiblical Greek literature (Bolt 2003, 53); in the NT it is found mostly in Mark and parallel passages in the Synoptic Gospels (9x in Mark; 2x in Matt.; 6x in Luke; cf. Acts 5:16; 8:7; Rev. 16:13; 18:2). The only usage of the phrase in the Jewish scriptures is in Zech. 13:2, which speaks of removal of false prophets and "the unclean spirit" (*to pneuma to akatharton*, LXX) from Israel on the day of the Lord. If the evangelist had this prophecy in mind, the use of the phrase would emphasize the eschatological import of the exorcisms performed by Jesus; as the prophet foretold, "unclean spirits" are being purged from the land (Mark 1:32–34; 3:11–12, 22; 5:1–20; 7:24–30; 9:14–29). Throughout Mark, "unclean spirit" is used synonymously with "demon" (*daimonion*; e.g., in the story of the Gerasene exorcism, the man is said to have an unclean spirit [5:2, 8, 13]; in the same story, he is described as demon-possessed [*daimonistheis*, 5:18; cf. 3:22, 30; 5:16]). Demons (*daimonia, daimones*) were popularly regarded not as fallen heavenly beings but as ghosts of the dead, which could be manipulated by magic to attack the living (see Bolt 2003, 56–64).

The wording of 1:23 implies that the man burst into the midst of the synagogue service. The "us" of the man's question ("What have you to do with us?") refers to the unclean spirits, to whom Jesus is a threat. The man's use of the title **holy man of God** (usually translated as "Holy One of God," e.g., NAB, RSV, NRSV, NIV, KJV, NASB) is sometimes interpreted as an acclamation of Jesus's true identity (e.g., Hurtado 1983, 14), as a statement of Jesus's messianic status (e.g., Nineham 1963, 79, although, as Nineham admits, there is no evidence that this was a messianic title among Jews of Jesus's time), or even as demonic recognition of Jesus as a preexistent supernatural entity manifested on earth (Gathercole 2006, 152). In the Bible, the precise phrase *hagios tou theou* appears only in this verse and its parallel in Luke 4:34. However, Elijah is described in similar terms in 2 Kings 4:9 (*anthrōpos tou theou hagios*; cf. Judg. 16:17 [Samson]; Ps. 106:16 [Aaron]); and the phrase "man of God" (*'îš ha'ĕlohîm, anthrōpos tou theou*) is used frequently in the Jewish scriptures to refer to both human and angelic figures (e.g., Moses [Deut. 33:1; Josh. 14:6; 1 Chron. 23:14; Ezra 3:2]; angelic messengers [Judg. 13:6, 8; 1 Sam. 2:27];

prophets [1 Sam. 9:6–10; 1 Kings 12:22; 13:1–32]; Elijah [1 Kings 17:18, 24; 2 Kings 1:9–13]; Elisha [2 Kings 4:42; 5:8–15, 20]; and David [2 Chron. 8:14; Neh. 12:36]). The intent of the man's outcry is not confessional but defensive; by showing that they know Jesus's identity as a "holy man of God," the spirits (note the use of the first-person plural in Mark 1:24) are trying "to gain the upper hand and thus control him" (Bolt 2003, 68; Donahue and Harrington 2002, 80; cf. Stern 1992, 88). This reverses the usual situation in confrontations between magicians and spirits, where the human adept tries to manipulate the demon through knowledge of its name; here Jesus is unaffected by the spirit's recognition of his identity (Bolt 2003, 69).

Jesus's response to the challenge is a simple rebuke: **Be silent and come out of him!** (v. 24). The vivid depiction of the effect of the exorcism on the man—the spirit convulses him and cries out in a loud voice—adds a final note of drama. The congregation's expression of amazement (v. 27) connects the two events in the synagogue: **And all were amazed so that they questioned among themselves, saying, "What is this? A new teaching with authority! He even commands the unclean spirits and they obey him!"** The Markan summary in v. 28 is the first of several notices of the spread of Jesus's reputation throughout the region (cf. 1:45; 3:7; 5:20; 6:54–56; 7:36–37).

Simon's Mother-in-Law and Others Healed (1:29–34)

The story of the healing of Simon's mother-in-law (1:29–31) is terse and fast paced; Jesus and the four new disciples "immediately" leave the synagogue; they enter the house of Simon and Andrew, where the woman is lying ill with a fever. The brothers "immediately" tell Jesus of her condition; he goes to her and raises her by the hand (cf. 1:31; 5:41; 6:5; 7:32–33; 8:23, 25; 9:27): **and the fever left her, and she was serving them** (1:31). It is tempting to interpret the mother-in-law's service to Jesus and the disciples (*kai diēkonei autois*) after the healing as a model of Christian ministry, since elsewhere in Mark, Jesus extols "serving" (*diakoneō*) as a hallmark of discipleship (10:42–45), and Jesus's women followers are said to have "ministered to" (*diēkonoun*) him (15:41). As Deborah Krause observes, several prominent feminist interpreters "argue that Simon Peter's mother-in-law's service to Jesus and the disciples is part of a comprehensive narrative message from Mark about the importance of women as models of faith, or as part of a tradition that bears witness to the centrality of women disciples within the service (διακονέω) of the Jesus movement and the early church. Simon Peter's mother-in-law is thus heralded as the 'woman who *ministers* to Jesus, and as an example of an early disciple'" (Krause 2001, 41, citing Tolbert 1992, 263–74; and Schottroff 1993, 80–118; cf. Donahue and Harrington 2002, 85). In its immediate context, however, the woman's resumption of her household duties demonstrates that she is truly healed (cf. 1:43; 5:43), and illustrates her gratitude; it is also an expression of the hospitality due to an honored guest (cf. Heb. 13:2; 1 Pet. 4:9; Rom. 12:13;

1 Tim. 5:10), as mandated by her status as an elder woman in the family (on the role of women in household management, see Osiek and MacDonald 2006, 144–52). This initial healing is the first of four Markan "acts of power" to the benefit of women (cf. 5:21–24, 35–43; 5:25–34; 7:24–30; Donahue and Harrington 2002, 85). Like the exorcism in the synagogue, the healing of Simon's mother-in-law takes place on the Sabbath.

Only **in the evening, when the sun had set** (1:32), so that the Sabbath is over, do the townspeople gather at the door, bringing their sick and demon-possessed friends to be healed (1:32–34; cf. Stern 1992, 88). However, the fact that Jesus's first two acts of power take place on the Sabbath and are publicly acclaimed foreshadows the controversies about the Sabbath that recur in this section of the Gospel (2:23–28; 3:1–6).

Retreat and Continuing Ministry (1:35–39)

Jesus's busy night of ministering to the sick and oppressed is followed by a predawn retreat to **a desert place** (1:35, *erēmon*) for prayer, indicating Jesus's reliance on God as the source of his power and authority. Like the crowd, Simon and the other disciples pursue him because **everyone** is looking for him (v. 37). The expansion of the mission is announced in v. 38: **Let's go into the nearby villages in order that I might preach there; for this I have come.** Simon Gathercole (2006, 84) regards the phrase **for this I have come** (*eis touto gar exēlthon*) as a formula indicative of a Markan preexistence Christology (cf. 1:24; 2:17; 10:45). However, the saying is better interpreted as harking back to 1:14, where Jesus arrives in Galilee and preaches the good news of God. The notice that Jesus preaches in synagogues *and* casts out demons suggests that his controversial practice of healing/exorcism on the Sabbath is habitual (see note on 3:1–6 below).

A Man with Leprosy Cleansed (1:40–45)

The location of the next incident, the cleansing of a man with leprosy (1:40–45), is not identified, but its placement implies that it is a typical incident from Jesus's Galilean mission, possibly even in one of the synagogues mentioned in the summary statement that immediately precedes it (v. 39). This time Jesus is approached by the "leper" (*lepros*)—a person whose identity has been submerged by the disease from which he suffers—who both pleads with him (*parakalōn auton*) and poses a challenge: **If you want to, you have the power to cleanse me** (v. 40). Commentators often explain that the "leprosy" of the Bible is probably not Hansen's disease but a variety of skin conditions (Lev. 13:1–44) and that the levitical legislation includes even discolorations of clothing and of the walls of houses (e.g., Avalos 2000; cf. Lev. 13:47–59; 14:34–57). Whatever the precise symptoms, Torah requires that a person diagnosed by a priest as having a leprous disease "shall wear torn clothes and let the hair of his head be disheveled; and he shall cover his upper lip and cry out 'Unclean, unclean.' He shall remain unclean as long as he has the disease; he is unclean. He shall live alone; his dwelling shall be outside the camp" (Lev. 13:45–46). Leviticus 14:2–32 describes the complex ritual by which a person healed of leprosy may be declared free of disease by a priest and restored to a state of ritual purity, and thus to participation in the community. This is why the man implores Jesus to "cleanse" (*katharisai*) him rather than to heal him of the condition; his disease has made him a religious and social outcast.

The manuscript tradition is divided regarding Jesus's reaction to the man's entreaty. While the majority of witnesses agree that Jesus was **moved with pity** (*splanchnistheis*), according to several ancient texts, he **was angered** (*orgistheis*). The former wording is reflected in most modern translations, but many scholars have been intrigued by the latter: as the more difficult reading, it is more likely to have been changed by an early scribe to harmonize it with the notion of Jesus as a compassionate savior (e.g., G. Telford 1982; Loader 1996, 53–58; Ehrman 2005, 133–35). Matthew and Luke both include this story in their Gospels (Matt. 8:2–4; Luke 5:12–16), but neither mentions Jesus's emotional reaction, perhaps due to the other evangelists' discomfort with Mark's attribution of anger to Jesus (cf. Mark 3:5; Matt. 12:11; Luke 6:8; also, cf. Mark 10:14; Matt. 19:14; Luke 18:16). Mark's reference to Jesus's reaching out his hand and touching the man before affirming his wish to heal him (**I do want to; be cleansed!**) seems to support the "compassionate" reading, but in v. 43, Jesus is said to have "snorted with anger" at the man (*embrimēsamenos*)—or "sternly charged him," as in many translations—and **cast him out** (*exebalen auton*—of the synagogue?), which coheres with the minority reading of v. 41: **and moved with anger, reaching out his hand, he touched him.** The usual translation is unproblematic; it is easy to imagine why Jesus would feel pity for someone afflicted with a debilitating disease. As Ehrman (2005, 137; cf. Loader 1996, 54–55) reports, interpreters have speculated as to why Mark would portray Jesus as angered by the man's request:

> One commentator, for example, argues that Jesus is angry with the state of the world that is full of disease; in other words, he loves the sick but hates the sickness. There is no textual basis for this interpretation, but it does have the virtue of making Jesus look good. Another interpreter argues that Jesus is angry because this leprous person had been alienated from society, overlooking the facts that the text says nothing about the man being an outsider and that, even if it assumes he was, it would not have been the fault of Jesus's society but of the Law of God (specifically the book of Leviticus). Another argues that, in fact, *that* is what Jesus was angry about, that the Law of Moses forces this kind of alienation. This interpretation ignores the fact that at the conclusion of the passage (v. 44) Jesus affirms the Law of Moses and urges the former leper to observe it.

An interpretation that is more cognizant of the Jewish context of the story is William Loader's (1996, 55–56) suggestion that Jesus is infuriated by the man's disrespect for the law, since he is walking around in public rather than isolating himself. Thus the story demonstrates Jesus's power to cleanse the man but acknowledges the indignation that Mark and his audience would have felt at the man's flouting of Torah (cf. Mark 7:9–13), especially if, as suggested above, the healing is envisioned as taking place in a synagogue. Jesus's concern for the law is demonstrated by his instruction to the man: **Tell no one anything, but go and show yourself to the priest and offer for your cleansing that which Moses has stipulated, as a witness to them** (1:44). The injunction to silence seems to be at variance with the rest of Jesus's instructions; it would entail a journey to the temple in Jerusalem (the functional equivalent of the tent of meeting; Lev. 14:11, 23), a physical examination by a priest to verify the cure, and the offering of certain sacrifices and other rituals during an eight-day period (14:1–32). Interpreters are divided as to the referent of the final phrase **as a witness to them** (*eis martyrion autois*, Mark 1:44b). For example, Donahue and Harrington (2002, 90) comments that in "the levitical legislation . . . the cleansing itself is for the examining priest evidence of the cure, while the sacrifice is a public sign of the cure." Christopher S. Mann (1986, 220) suggests that "the proof in question appears to be that of the healer's allegiance to the Law." Another possibility is that the phrase is not part of Jesus's admonition but a Markan explanation of Jesus's reason for sending the man to partake in the verification ritual; Jesus does this **as a witness to** his own—and the cleansed man's—fidelity to the law to the people who view the miracle. The injunction to silence, then, would underline the urgency of the command to the man to appear before a priest, to fulfill his legal obligations, and be officially declared clean.

In view of the typological linkages between Mark's portrayal of Jesus and the Elijah/Elisha cycles, the possibility of a relationship between this anecdote and the only story of the healing of a leper in the Hebrew Bible, the cure of Naaman by Elisha (2 Kings 5:1–27), is worth considering. There are many obvious differences between the two narratives: Naaman is a Syrian "man of valor" who hears of Elisha's healing power from his wife's Israelite maid. The prophet sends a messenger to the hero with instructions to wash himself seven times in the Jordan, which he at first refuses to do because he is insulted that the prophet has not attended him personally. He relents when his servants urge him to follow Elisha's instructions, and his flesh is restored to health. However, reminiscent of the Markan story, there are two notable displays of anger in the Naaman narrative: the king of Israel "rends his clothes" when he receives a letter from the king of Syria mistakenly requesting *him* to heal Naaman (2 Kings 5:7; here the tearing of the king's garment is best interpreted as a sign of anger and frustration; cf. Isa. 37:1; Mark 14:63; Matt. 26:65; Acts 14:14; *DBI* 319); and Naaman himself is angry (*ethymōthē*) because he had expected the prophet to personally wave his hand (*epithēsei tēn cheira*) over the leprous skin (2 Kings 5:11–12; cf. Mark 1:41: *ekteinas tēn cheira autou hēpsato*) rather than sending a messenger. There are also two displays of disobedience to the prophet's command: Naaman's initial refusal to follow his instructions and the servant Gehazi's demand that the Syrian pay a reward for the miracle, although Elisha has expressly refused to accept anything (2 Kings 5:15–24), after which the prophet is so displeased that he curses the servant and his descendants with leprosy forever (vv. 25–27). Jesus's angry demeanor may echo the stormy tone of the Elisha tale. Like Gehazi (who becomes leprous), the cleansed man is disobedient, because rather than following Jesus's stern admonitions, he leaves and begins to proclaim the word so that Jesus **was no longer able to enter into a city openly, but he was outside in desert places; and they came to him from everywhere** (v. 45). As in the Elisha narrative, the cure of the man with leprosy spreads the news "that there is a prophet in Israel" (2 Kings 5:8; cf. Swete 1908, 31).

Controversy Stories (2:1–3:6)

Mark 2:1–3:6 constitutes a series of controversy stories that introduce the theme of escalating opposition to Jesus by various authority figures: scribes (2:6, 16); Pharisees (2:16, 18, 24; 3:6); disciples of John (2:18); and Herodians (3:6; see Dewey 1973; Boring 2006, 73–74; V. Taylor 1966, 91–92; Dibelius 1934, 210; Albertz 1919, 5–16). This subsection of Mark shows a modified chiastic structure (A, B, C, B', A') in which A and B are linked by the theme of forgiveness of sin, and B' and A' are linked by the theme of Sabbath observance. Line C, the question about fasting, stands as the central focus of the arrangement (Boring 2006, 74).

    A Healing of a paralytic; accusation of blasphemy over forgiveness of sin (2:1–12)
      B Call of Levi; controversy over dining with sinners (2:3–17)
        C Question about fasting (2:18–22)
      B' Controversy over keeping the Sabbath (2:23–28)
    A' Controversy over healing on the Sabbath (3:1–6)

Within the larger framework of 1:16–3:35, these stories introduce the theme of escalating opposition to Jesus, beginning with the unspoken questioning of some scribes (2:6) and culminating in the plot of the Pharisees and Herodians to destroy him (3:6).

2:1–12. The conflict stories begin (2:1–12) with a healing (vv. 1–5, 11–12) that brackets a response by Jesus to scribal criticism (vv. 6–10; cf. 1:21–28). The cure of a paralyzed man takes place in a house at Capernaum, where Jesus has returned to be **at home** (*en oikō*), possibly the house of Simon and Andrew, the site of the first healing miracle (Mann 1986, 223; Donahue and Harrington

2002, 93). Jesus's reputation as a powerful man of God, spread far and wide by the man cleansed of leprosy, has followed him; as soon as his where-abouts are discovered, **many gathered together so that there was no room, not even at the door, and he was speaking the word to them** (v. 2). The story abounds in the kinds of vivid details characteris-tic of Mark. The disabled man is carried by four bearers on a pallet or mat, and due to the crowd around Jesus, they resort to opening up the roof (*apestegasan*) and lowering the man into the room (vv. 3–4). Mann (1986, 223) notes that the scene depicts "a flat roof with an earth covering," charac-teristic of a modest dwelling (cf. Matt. 9:2 and Luke 5:18–19, where the poor man's pallet [*krabatton*] is upgraded to a bed or couch [*klinē*] and the roofing of the house is specified as tile [*keramos*]). Jesus, in response to the four litter-bearers' faith—and possibly the afflicted man's faith (*tēn pistin autōn*)—does not immediately perform the cure but makes a surprising pronouncement: **Child, your sins are forgiven!** (v. 5). This is the first of many usages of faith language (*pistis, pisteuō*) in Mark (cf. 4:40; 5:21–24, 35–43; 5:25–34; 6:5–6; 9:14–29; 10:46–52; 11:22–23), where faith/belief/trust are inextricably bound up with the ability to do miracles. Jesus's unexpected declaration may presuppose "the commonly accepted view of his own time that there was a strong and even decisive con-nection between sin and bodily sickness" (Mann 1986, 224; cf. John 9:2; esp. Luke 13:1–5; see also John 5:14; James 5:14–16; *DBI* 209–10).

More germane to the theme of this section of Mark, Jesus's words provoke **certain scribes** to consider whether they amount to blasphemy: **Who has the power to forgive sins but God?** (Mark 2:7). The scribes' internal dialogue (**pon-dering in their hearts**, v. 6) distorts Jesus's words; he does not personally forgive the man's sins but pronounces them **forgiven** by God, the assumed subject of the passive verb (as Mann notes, there is no instance in the Gospels of Jesus saying "I forgive" [1986, 224]; cf. 2 Sam 12:13). Up to this point in the Gospel, the healings and exorcisms have been received with unqualified enthusiasm, but here the unspoken charge against Jesus, which will be repeated in the trial before the Sanhedrin (Mark 14:64; cf. 3:28–30), is very serious. Blasphemy, the act of slandering or cursing God, is a violation of Torah punishable by stoning (Lev. 24:10–16), a method of execution that, according to other NT documents, was occasionally used by groups of zealous vigilantes (e.g., John 8:1–11; Acts 6:8–8:1; 14:19–20; 2 Cor. 11:25). Here Jesus intuits the scribes' thoughts (*epignous . . . tō pneumati autou*) and retorts using a variation on the rabbinic device of *qal wa-ḥomer* ("easy and hard"), an a fortiori argument (if *A* is true, then *B* is much more true). In this saying, Jesus reverses the order, making it from hard to easy: **What is easier, to say to the paralyzed man "Your sins are forgiven," or to say, "Arise and take up your pallet and walk?"** (Mark 1:9). In a Jewish context, forgiveness of sin (violations of Torah) was effected through repentance and atonement available through the sacrificial system (as stipulated by Torah; Lev. 4:1–5:13; 16:29–34; 23:27–32). Thus God's forgiveness was accessible to any repentant Jew. If something as serious as offenses against Torah can be forgiven by God, how hard can it be for mere physical healing to be effected through faith in God's power? As with forgiveness, healing of the lame is a divine power (Isa. 35:6; Jer. 31:8; Mic. 4:6; Zeph. 3:19).

The next sentence reiterates the connection between forgiveness of sins and healing: **"But in order that you might see that the son of man has authority upon the earth to forgive sins,"** he said to the paralyzed man, **"Arise, take your pallet and go home"** (Mark 2:10–11). Some translators see the saying about the son of man's authority as part of Jesus's reply to the scribes, asserting his own prerogative as God's chosen agent (cf. 1:1, 11). Others see it as an editorial aside to Mark's audience (cf. 7:19; 13:14), affirming their belief that Jesus is the eschatological son of man (*ho huios tou anthrōpou*), who will preside at the right hand of God over the gathering of the elect (14:62; 13:26–27).

The man is **raised up** (*ēgerthē*) and, like Simon's mother-in-law, **immediately** demonstrates that he is cured by taking up his mat and leaving, to the acclaim

---

Son of Man

In Mark and the other Gospels, the term "the son of man" (*ho huios tou anthrōpou*) is frequently used as a self-designation of Jesus (e.g., Mark 2:10, 28; 8:31, 38; 9:9, 12, 31; 10:33, 45; 13:26; 14:21, 41, 62); however, the phrase is seldom used elsewhere in the NT (cf. Acts 7:56; Heb. 2:6; Rev. 1:13; cf. 14:14). It appears to be a translation of the Hebrew *ben ʾādām* (Aramaic *bar ʾĕnāš*), which can refer to a human being or to humanity as a collective (e.g., Num. 23:19; Job 25:6; Pss. 8:4; 80:17; 144:3; Ezek. 2:1; Dan. 7:13; 8:17). Scholars disagree as to whether the reference to "one like a son of man" in Dan. 7:13–14 is titular or simply a description of the eschatological Israel as a human figure in contrast to the bestial figures of Daniel's vision (7:1–8). The Jewish Parables of Enoch (*1 En.* 37–71) lend some support to the usage of "son of man" to refer to an eschatological redeemer figure in Jewish apocalyptic circles. In Mark, Jesus refers to himself as the son of man in three major contexts: (1) with reference to his authority as son of man (2:10, 28); (2) in predictions of his suffering, death, and resurrection (8:31; 9:9, 12, 31; 10:45; 14:21, 41); and (3) in parousia predictions (8:38; 13:26; 14:62). Possibly, the term son of man was used as a self-designation (as a modest circumlocution for "I," reflecting contemporary Aramaic idiom) by the historical Jesus (see, e.g., Vermès 1973, 188–91).

of the crowd: **everyone was astonished and glorified God, saying, "We've never seen anything like this!"** (Mark 2:12).

2:13–17. The next episode, 2:13–17, is a conflation of three separate units of pre-Markan tradition, edited together into a brief but complex narrative involving elements of call, controversy, and pronouncement. Verse 13 is a typical Markan editorial seam (**And again he went by the sea; and the whole crowd came to him, and he was teaching them**), which precedes the call of **Levi son of Alphaeus** (cf. 3:18, where the disciple James is also called "son of Alphaeus"), whose profession of toll collector (*telōnēs*) is indicated by his location, **sitting by the toll office** (v. 14). The call of Levi follows the pattern of the initial call of Simon, Andrew, James, and John (1:16–20): Jesus sees a potential disciple in the midst of his work, he issues an invitation to follow him (*akolouthei moi*), and the disciple accepts the call without questions or delay. Levi is not included in the list of the Twelve in Mark 3:13–19 (the Matthean version of the call narrative names the toll collector as "Matthew" [9:9]). Since Mark envisions Jesus as having a circle of disciples wider than the Twelve (e.g., 3:34; 4:10; 9:38–40; 10:29, 52; 14:16–18; 15:40–41), it is not surprising that the call of a "disciple" (cf. 2:16) other than the Twelve is featured.

A related incident follows, in which Jesus and his disciples (presumably including Levi), in Greco-Roman style, are **reclining at table** (*katakeisthai*) in **his house**, together with **many toll collectors and sinners**. The setting is presumably the house of Levi, but it could conceivably be a house in Capernaum where Jesus resides, possibly the home of Simon and Andrew. In 2:15 is Mark's first use of the term disciple (*mathētēs*), a Greek term meaning a pupil or apprentice (BDAG 609), perhaps reflecting the Hebrew *talmîd*, a disciple wholeheartedly dedicated to a teacher (Stern 1992, 23; cf. 10:24–25). Toll collectors (*telōnai*) in the Galilee of Jesus's time were minor Herodian employees who collected "the myriad of minor taxes, sales taxes, customs taxes, taxes on transport" (Donahue 1971, 42). Both Greek and Jewish sources regard them as disreputable (e.g., Cicero, *Off.* 15–21; Dio Chrysostom, *Or.* 4.14; *m. Țohar.* 7.6; *m. B. Qam.* 10.2; *m. Ned.* 3.4), and in the NT they are mentioned together with sinners (Matt. 9:10; 11:19; Luke 7:34; 15:1), fornicators (*pornai*; Matt. 21:31; Luke 18:11), and gentiles (Matt. 5:46–47; 18:17), probably because the taxation system involved corruption and unduly high tariffs (Donahue 1971, 49). Mark 2:15–16 contains the earliest NT usage of the stock phrase **toll collectors and sinners**; the term sinners or "sinful people" (*hamartōloi*) in its early Jewish context probably refers to persons who habitually violated Torah (cf. Prov. 1:10; 11:31; 13:6, 21, 22; 23:17) or who lived outside the law like gentiles (Gal. 2:15), rather than occasional transgressors.

The banquet is the setting for Mark's second controversy story: **the scribes of the Pharisees** ask the disciples why their master eats with toll collectors and sinners (2:16). These scribes would be Torah scholars belonging to the Pharisaic movement within Judaism, an influential, legally rigorous sect that

stressed both oral tradition and written law; matters of ritual purity and tith-
ing; and belief in "afterlife, judgment, and a densely populated, organized
spirit world" (Mason 2000a, 1043; cf. Josephus, *J.W.* 2.8.12–14 §§159–66; *Ant.*
13.5.9 §§171–73; 13.10.6 §§297–98; 18.1.2–3 §§11–15). Throughout Mark, the
Pharisees are always portrayed as in conflict with Jesus over his teachings and
lifestyle (2:24; 3:6; 7:1, 3, 5; 8:11, 15; 10:2; 12:13). This time the criticism of
Jesus is spoken, but addressed not to him but his disciples. Nonetheless, Jesus
hears it and replies directly to the scribes with a proverbial saying that would
be apt in a variety of contexts; here it decisively refutes the scribal critique:
**The strong do not have need of a doctor, but the sick do; I haven't come to call
righteous people but sinners!** (2:17). The term "righteous people" (*dikaious*)
here has a technical Jewish meaning of persons who live in accordance with
Torah; "sinners" are those who routinely violate it.

2:18–22. The location of the third controversy is unspecified (2:18–22); presumably it takes place in or near Capernaum. More significantly, it is placed
immediately after the accusation that Jesus dines with legally unobservant
people. For the first time, the opponents address Jesus directly, but about his
disciples' conduct, not his own: **And the disciples of John and the Pharisees
were fasting. And they came and said to him, "Why are the disciples of John
and the disciples of the Pharisees fasting, but your disciples are not fasting?"**
(v. 18). The periphrastic imperfect *ēsan nēsteuontes* implies a habitual state of
fasting, perhaps indicating that John's disciples followed the austere lifestyle
of their leader (cf. 1:6) by fasting at times other than the Day of Atonement
(Lev. 16); the legal strictness of the Pharisees implies that fasting beyond the
requirements of Torah was also part of their practice. The Jewish scriptures
refer to fasting in the context of mourning (2 Sam. 1:12; 3:35; 1 Chron. 10:12;
Jdt. 8:6), prayer (1 Kings 21:27–29; Jon. 3:5), and preparation for visionary experiences (Exod. 34:28; 1 Kings 19:8; cf. *2 Bar.* 12.5; 21.1–3; *Apoc. El.* 1.20–22),
or for facing danger (Ezra 8:21–22, 31; Esther 4:15–16; Dan. 6:17–25; 9:3; Jdt.
4:9, 13; see Smith-Christopher 2000, 456). In Mark 9:29, Jesus recommends
fasting to his disciples as a preparation for undertaking an exorcism. Here,
however, Jesus's disciples—and Jesus himself—are implicitly criticized by
the questioners for lack of spiritual discipline (on the understanding in the
ancient world that the master is responsible for the actions of his disciples;
see Daube 1972–73).

Jesus answers with a series of parabolic sayings, beginning with a question
that echoes the words of the critics: **Are the sons of the wedding hall able
to fast [*nēsteuein*] when the bridegroom is with them?** (2:19). The answer is
clearly no: the wedding guests (or bridegroom's attendants; cf. BDAG 681) are
expected to feast along with the family: **For the time the bridegroom is with
them, they are not able to fast** (on wedding customs in first-century Palestine,
see Balabanski 2002, 82–84). The next sentence strikes a prophetic note: a day
will come when the bridegroom will have been **taken away** (*aparthē*) and the

attendants will fast (v. 20). In the Markan context, these sayings are clearly allegorical and amount to an implicit Passion prediction: the bridegroom is Jesus, the disciples are the attendants, and the day of fasting will take place when Jesus is handed over to his executioners. The eschatologically loaded phrases **the days will come** and **on that day** frame the saying (e.g., Jer. 7:32; 9:25; 39:17; Amos 2:16; 8:11; 9:13; Isa. 22:12; Ezek. 20:6; 24:26; Zeph. 1:9–10; 3:11, 16; Hag. 2:23; Zech. 9:16; 11:11; 12:3–11). The motif of fasting after the removal of the bridegroom is reminiscent of Jeremiah's warnings: "And I will bring an end to the sound of mirth and gladness, the voice of the bride and bridegroom in the cities of Judah and in the streets of Jerusalem; for the land shall become a waste" (Jer. 7:34; see also 16:9; 25:10; cf. 33:11; Joel 2:16).

At first glance, the parables of the patch (Mark 2:21) and the wineskins (v. 22) seem to have little bearing on the question about fasting (cf. Luke 5:36, where these sayings are identified as "parables"). For this reason, some scholars think that these were simply secular proverbs added to the Jesus tradition (e.g., Carlston 1975, 128; against this view, see Perkins 2002, 127–28). As Perkins states, the images of patching old garments with whatever cloth is available and using old containers to hold new wine reflect "the needs and activities of the poor, not the rich." Thus the resulting loss of clothing and drink would be especially severe: "A mistake means more than punishing a young or inept slave, apprentice or wife. The family might lose something necessary to its survival once the cloak is more torn than before, the wine spilt and the skins burst" (Perkins 2002, 130–32). These parables reiterate the theme of newness in Jesus's ministry (cf. Mark 1:27), as summed up by the final clause: **but new wine is for fresh skins** (2:22), which uses two Greek terms for "new," *neos* and *kainos*. The eschatological context of fulfillment announced in 1:15 demands new ways of doing things; any other course of action would result in destruction and loss. The tragic note sounded by the saying on the removal of the bridegroom (2:20) is echoed here; Jesus's "new" teaching and practice will not conform to the expectations of his critics. From the perspective of the evangelist and his audience, this will lead to disaster for both: the bridegroom will be taken away and his attendants will fast; the disciples of John and the Pharisees will miss the opportunity to enjoy the wedding banquet (cf. Matt. 25:10).

2:23–28. Mark 2:23–28 is another Sabbath dispute (cf. 2:1–12; 3:1–6). This pericope stands out among the other debates about Sabbath observance in the Gospels; it is not connected with a miraculous healing or exorcism, and it is not occasioned by anything that Jesus says or does (Meier 2004, 563). As in the previous two controversy stories, it is the behavior of the disciples that is directly criticized, this time by Pharisees: **And it happened that he was passing through the grainfields on the Sabbath, and his disciples began to make a path, picking the heads of grain. And the Pharisees said to him, "Look, why are they doing what is not lawful on the Sabbath?"** (vv. 23–24). The issue here is not that the disciples are taking grain that does not belong to them (Deut.

23:25) but that they are working by picking the grain rather than observing the Sabbath rest (Gen. 2:2; Exod. 20:8–11; 31:12–17; 35:2; Deut. 5:12–15; Num. 15:32–36). Jesus's answer, rather than using Torah to refute the accusation, alludes to an incident in the life of King David (1 Sam. 21:1–6 [21:2–7 LXX]): **Haven't you read what David did when he was in need and he and those with him were hungry—how he went into the house of God when Abiathar was high priest and he ate the bread of the presence, which it was not lawful to eat except for the priests, and he shared it with those with him?** (vv. 25–26). As many scholars have noted, however, the version cited here differs in many respects from the original story: David is alone, not with his men; he is on the run from Saul and lies to the priest in order to obtain the holy bread; the priest in the story is Ahimelech, not his father, Abiathar; there is no mention of David's actually eating the bread or sharing it with anyone (see Meier 2004, 575–79). Furthermore, there is no indication that the showbread incident took place on the Sabbath, which makes it a less-than-apt precedent with which to defend the disciples. The main point of comparison between the scriptural story and the disciples' behavior is that both David and presumably the disciples are in need (though in Mark's account there is no explicit mention of their eating the grain) and that their hunger makes it permissible to set aside the demands of the law. Jesus concludes with a proverb that concurs with other ancient Jewish legal opinions: **The Sabbath was made for the sake of human beings, not human beings for the sake of the Sabbath** (2:27; cf. *b. Yoma* 85b; *Mekilta*; *m. Šabb.* 1.1—cited in Stern 1992, 89; cf. 1 Macc. 2:34–41, where Mattathias and his followers resolve to fight on the Sabbath rather than die). However, the attitude to Sabbath observance reflected here is undoubtedly more casual than would have been typical among Jews of Jesus's time (see Donahue and Harrington 2002, 111) and probably reflects disputes about Sabbath observance in Mark's community (see Meier 2004, 578–79). The final saying in the pericope—**Thus the son of man is lord even of the Sabbath** (2:28)—is often considered as part of Jesus's argument (e.g., NAB, NRSV, NIV), but like the reference to the son of man in 2:10, it is better interpreted as an editorial aside to the audience, asserting the prerogatives of Jesus, whom they believe to be "the son of man sitting at the right hand of the Mighty One" (14:62).

3:1–6. The next incident takes place on the Sabbath in a synagogue (3:1–6), like the first exorcism story (1:23–28; cf. 1:29–31). Jesus's opponents from the last pericope, the Pharisees, are apparently the ones who are **watching him to see if he would heal . . . on the Sabbath, in order that they might accuse him** (cf. 3:6), as they have accused the disciples of working on the Sabbath. Conveniently for the critics, **a man with a withered hand** is there (v. 1b); the perfect participial phrase *exērammenēn echōn tēn cheira* indicates that the man suffers from a long-term disability. A suspicious reader might surmise that the man has been planted there in order to trap Jesus, or that the Pharisees know that the man will be there, and that Jesus will heal him, thus violating the Sabbath rest. However, even in this culminating incident of the controversy cycle, Jesus's opponents do not address him directly (cf. 2:8); rather, they are observing (*paretēroun*) while Jesus instructs the man to **rise up in the midst** and asks a rhetorical question: **Is it lawful to do good on the Sabbath or to do evil, to save life or to kill?** At one level, the answer is obvious: in general terms, it's lawful to do good, and unlawful to do evil at any time. However, the question from a Jewish perspective is whether healing on the Sabbath constitutes a good and lawful deed, or whether an act that would be laudable on any other day of the week is sinful when committed on Shabbat. The Mishnah does not list medical treatment as a Sabbath violation (*m. Šabb.* 7.2), and *m. Yoma* 8.2 stipulates that life-threatening illnesses and other threats to life supersede the prohibitions against working on the Sabbath. As in the previous story, where the disciples pick grain on the Sabbath even though they are in no imminent danger of starvation, the man, whose condition is chronic, does not have a life-threatening illness; the healing could wait until sundown (cf. 1:32–34). Again, Jesus's question implies a lenient attitude to Sabbath observance: of course the healing of this man is permissible and constitutes a good deed; to refuse to heal the man immediately would be unmercifully scrupulous.

Jesus's critics do not answer him (*hoi de esiōpōn*, 3:4). As in the story of the healing of the paralyzed man (2:8), Jesus is able to discern the unspoken thoughts of the onlookers: **And looking around with anger, grieved at their hard-heartedness, he says to the man, "Hold out your hand." And he held his hand out, and it was restored** (3:5). This time the reason for Jesus's anger (*met' orgēs*) and sorrow is clear (cf. 1:41); the term "hard-heartedness" (*pōrōsis tēs kardias*) recalls the many uses of this terminology in the Hebrew scriptures, where it refers to cruelty, disobedience, and the refusal to heed God's word (Josh. 11:20; 1 Sam. 6:6; 2 Chron. 36:13; Ps. 95:8; Prov. 28:14; Isa. 63:17; Dan. 5:20; Zech. 7:12; cf. Ezek. 3:7). In the most famous of examples, the Pharaoh of the exodus is repeatedly described as hardening his heart against the divine will (Exod. 8:15, 32; 9:34; cf. 7:13, 14, 22; 8:19; 9:7, 35), or as being hardened against the Israelites by God (4:21; 7:3; 9:12; 10:1, 20, 27; 11:10; 14:4, 8, 17). In Mark, the disciples are described as hard-hearted (6:52; 8:17) when they fail to understand the import of Jesus's miracles. An early Christian homily (falsely attributed to the fourth-century Christian theologian Athanasius of Alexandria) makes a perceptive exegetical parallel between the man's disability and the moral state of Jesus's critics: "If he was withered in his hand, the ones who stood by were withered in their minds" (*Hom. sem.* 28; cited in Oden and Hall 1998, 35). According to Vermès (1973, 25), a healing by word alone would not constitute a Sabbath violation, but in this instance, the healing is effected without a word or action other than the instruction to the man to extend his hand, thus implicitly leaving the credit for the miracle to God alone. Ironically, this miracle is followed not by enthusiastic acclaim but by a notice that the Pharisees immediately went out and **plotted with the Herodians** [supporters

of the Galilean tetrarch Antipas] **to destroy him** (3:6; cf. 12:13; 8:15; 6:14–29).
This is the first unambiguous announcement of Jesus's impending execution
(cf. 11:18; 12:12; 14:1).

The Spread of Jesus's Fame (3:7–12)

The five conflict stories are followed by an expanded summary statement
of the spread of Jesus's fame as a healer and exorcist (3:7–12; cf. 1:28, 32–34,
39, 45; 2:1–2). After the healing in the synagogue, Jesus and the disciples return to the sea (3:7; cf. 2:13), a site where he has taught before. He is followed
(*ēkolouthēsen*) by a great crowd (*poly plēthos*), perhaps indicating that he
has picked up new disciples/followers along the way—like the toll-collector
Levi—despite the controversies attending his mission. The geographical scope
of Jesus's fame is emphasized: the crowds flock from both Galilee and Judea
(3:7); Jerusalem, Idumea, the area **beyond the Jordan,** and **the region of Tyre
and Sidon** (v. 8) are mentioned, indicating that both Jews and gentiles are attracted by his deeds (*hosa epoiei*). This time the crowd is so dense that Jesus
enlists the disciples to prepare a boat **in order that they might not crush him**
(v. 9). In 4:1, Jesus is depicted as teaching from a boat, but here the vessel
may simply be a means of escape from the throng. Verses 10–11 elaborate on
the miraculous deeds that have attracted the crowds; the sick prostrate themselves before Jesus to be healed by his touch; unclean spirits fall at his feet,
emphatically proclaiming that *he* is **the Son of God** (*sy ei ho huios tou theou*).
The scene is reminiscent of 1:1–10, where crowds from Judea and Jerusalem
flock to be baptized by John, and Jesus is acclaimed by God as beloved Son.
John's prophecy that Jesus would be mightier than himself is attested by the
broader geographical range of Jesus's fame and by the reaction he evokes:
John's followers flock to the Jordan to be baptized; Jesus's followers prostrate
themselves before him, seeking healing. Once again, the unclean spirits—the
opposite of the Holy Spirit (1:8, 10)—try to gain control over him by crying out (*ekrazon legontes*) his God-given title. As in the previous exorcisms,
Jesus is unaffected by the demons' recognition and enjoins them to silence
(**he warned them sternly not to make him known,** 3:12; cf. 1:25, 34). Like his
prophetic archetype Elisha, Jesus has been granted a larger share of spiritual
power than even his great predecessor.

The Appointment of the Twelve (3:13–19)

Mark 3:13–19 is the Gospel's third call narrative (cf. 1:16–19; 2:13–14; cf.
6:7–13). Unlike the previous calls of the four fishers and of Levi, which take
place as Jesus is **passing by** their places of work (*paragōn,* 1:16; 2:14), this
call is deliberate and symbolic. Jesus goes up a mountain and calls for himself
those whom *he* wishes (*ēthelen autos*), and they go up *to him* (*apēlthon pros
auton,* 3:13). The setting on the mountain recalls the revelation at Sinai and

Moses's solemn blessing of Israel (Exod. 19:3–6, 16–25; Deut. 32:48–34:9; cf. 1 Kings 19:8; Mark 9:2; 13:3). From among this select group (see Marcus 2000, 266), Jesus "makes" (*epoiēsen*) the Twelve, in the scriptural sense of appointing or designating persons for a task (3:14, 16; cf. 1 Sam. 2:6; 1 Kings 13:33; 2 Chron. 2:18), **in order that they might be with him and that he might send them to preach and to have authority to cast out demons** (v. 14). The significance of the number twelve (*dōdeka*) seems obvious: the number recalls the twelve tribes of Israel, and the twelve disciples symbolize a new (or renewed) Israel being initiated by Jesus (Funk 1998, 71). However, although they are singled out as a special group throughout the Gospel (4:10; 6:7; 9:35; 10:32; 11:11; 14:10, 17, 20, 43), the Twelve are never explicitly identified with a renewed Israel (the term "Israel" is used only twice in Mark, once on the lips of Jesus's opponents [12:29; 15:32]; Matthew and Luke refer to Israel twelve times apiece). The suggestion that they represent an eschatological people of God who bear Jesus's mission to proclaim the reign of God to both Jews and gentiles (cf. 3:7–18) is more persuasive in the Markan context (see Moloney 2002, 78; Marcus 2000, 267). The phrase **whom he also named apostles** (v. 14) is missing from some manuscripts and may have been added by a scribe influenced by the wording of Luke 6:13 (cf. Matt. 10:1–2). However, the only other use of the term "apostles" in Mark, in the context of the return of the Twelve from their ministry of preaching and healing (6:7–13, 30), supports the Markan identification of the Twelve as *apostoloi*, those who will be "sent" to undertake a task.

In the text as it stands, the phrase **and he made the Twelve** (3:16) echoes the earlier **and he made twelve** (v. 14). The second reference to the Twelve is missing from some ancient manuscripts, but as Metzger (1994, 69) argues, "the clause seems to be needed in order to pick up the thread of ver. 14 after the parenthesis ἵνα ... δαιμόνια [*hina ... daimonia*]." In the list that follows, the names of the disciples are given without reference to their occupations, as in the earlier call narratives. The first three disciples mentioned are given new names by Jesus: **Simon, to whom he gave the name Peter, and Jacob the son of Zebedee and John the brother of James, and he gave to them the name Boanerges, that is, Sons of Thunder** (vv. 16–17). The significance of the title *Petros* (Aramaic *Kepha*), "Rock," is unknown (see Nineham 1963, 116). However, in the Hebrew scriptures "the word *rock* is used ... with a wide variety of meanings, almost all associated with God, either as a secure foundation or stronghold, or as an obstacle to evildoers" (*DBI* 733), suggesting that the new name has a positive connotation. From this point in the narrative, with the exception of 14:37, the name Peter is consistently used instead of Simon. The brothers James and John are given the nickname **Boanerges** (*Boanērges*), translated by Mark as **Sons of Thunder**. Nineham (1963, 116) notes that "*Boanerges* is not the natural Hebrew for 'sons of Thunder'; possibly the word represents an obscure Hebrew or Aramaic form with that meaning, or perhaps the original was already corrupt by Mark's day and 'sons of thunder' was the best he could make of it." Dennis R. MacDonald (2000, 24–32) links them with the Greek mythological figures of Castor and Polydeuces, sons of the thunder-god Zeus. As with the name Peter, the significance of the title Sons of Thunder is obscure. Marcus (2000, 269) speculates that it may refer to the stormy temperaments of the two brothers (cf. 9:38; Luke 9:54). In scriptural terms, the renaming of the three disciples signifies a change in their status and indicates that they will play a role in salvation history as significant as Abram/ Abraham (Gen. 17:5), Sarai/Sarah (Gen. 17:15), and Jacob/Israel (Gen. 32:28). The nine other members of the Twelve are Andrew (here separated from his more-prominent brother, Peter; cf. Mark 1:16–17, 29), Philip, Bartholomew, Matthew, Thomas, James son of Alphaeus, Thaddaeus, Simon the Cananaean, and Judas Iscariot (3:18–19). Of these nine, only Andrew (1:16, 29; 13:3) and Judas (14:10, 43, 45) are mentioned elsewhere in the Gospel. Judas son of James is listed instead of Thaddaeus in the Lukan writings (Luke 6:16; Acts 1:13). James son of Alphaeus is possibly a brother of Levi (cf. Mark 2:14). The epithet "Cananaean" is best explained with reference to the Aramaic *qan'ān* ("zealous" or "zealot"); thus in Acts 1:13 *Kananaion* is replaced by *zēlōtēs*. The significance of the surname "Iscariot" is unclear: suggested interpretations include "'the assassin' (from the band of Judean Zealots who carried daggers and terrorized the Romans and their sympathizers in ancient Palestine; Lat. *sicarius*), 'man from Sychar,' 'man of Issachar,' 'man from Jericho,' 'carrier of the leather bag,' or 'false one, liar, hypocrite.' The most popular suggestion has been 'man of Kerioth'; however, the location of Kerioth is uncertain" (Sheeley 2000, 748). Harold Ingholt (1953, 159–60) suggests that "Iscariot" derives from the Aramaic *sāqor* ("to paint or dye red"; *m. Bek.* 9.7) and is a nickname that explains later iconography portraying Judas as red-haired. More germane to the role of Judas in Mark is the editorial explanation **who also handed him over** (Mark 3:19). The verb *paredōken* has often been translated as "betrayed" (e.g., NIV, NASB, KJV, ASV, RSV, NRSV, NAB), but as William Klassen has pointed out, the basic sense of the word is to hand over, turn over, or give up a person, for good or for ill (Klassen 1996, 41–61; cf. BDAG 762). However, elsewhere in Mark, the verb is used with the negative sense of disciples being "handed over" to councils, trial, and death (13:9, 11–12). Jayhoon Yang suggests that the inclusion of Judas in the list raises the question of whether the other members of the Twelve will fail, "just like Judas Iscariot who handed Jesus over" (Yang 2004, 254).

Postscript and Transition (3:20–35)

The structure of Mark 3:20–35 replicates the structure of the larger section, which it concludes (1:16–3:19), in that it brackets a controversy (3:22–30) within an incident bearing on the nature of discipleship (vv. 20–21, 31–35).

3:20–21. In 3:20–21, Jesus leaves the mountaintop and goes home (or into a house), and as in the previous scene where Jesus is "at home" (2:1–2), a crowd gathers, so that they were not even able to eat bread (v. 20). For the first time since Jesus's return to Galilee (1:14–15), his family (*hoi par' autou*; see Moule 1953, 52; Marcus 2000, 270) appear to take hold of him; for they were saying that he was beside himself (v. 21). The term *exestē* (he was beside himself) is used elsewhere in Mark (2:12; 5:42; 6:51; cf. 16:8) to refer to amazement at the works of Jesus, but here it refers to Jesus's own state and implies the family's belief that Jesus was out of his mind, a state often ascribed to demonic influence in the ancient world (cf. John 10:20; Marcus 2000, 271).

3:22–30. Into this chaotic scene is interposed a complex controversy narrative (3:22–30), in which scribes who had come down from Jerusalem are accusing Jesus of being in league with demons: He has Beelzebul. . . . By the ruler of the demons he casts out demons (v. 22). As in the previous controversy narratives, the scribes do not directly confront Jesus; in v. 23, Jesus summons *them* (*proskalesamenos autous*) in order to answer their criticism. As Bolt (2003, 124) notes, this is probably an accusation that Jesus is practicing magic, since sorcery was effected through the manipulation of demons, and the scribes accuse him of controlling a demonic prince. For the scribes, such activity violates Torah's prohibitions against magic (Exod. 22:18; Deut. 18:10), adding to the list of violations of religious law leveled at Jesus in Mark 2:1–3:6. Outside the NT, the name Beelzebul (probably a corrupted form of Baal-zebub, god of Ekron; 2 Kings 1:2, 3, 6, 16), used synonymously with Satan (or "an Adversary"), is not attested (cf. Matt. 12:25–26; Luke 11:18). However, the name frequently appears in the *Testament of Solomon* (dated between the first and third centuries AD), a Jewish/Christian demonological work that identifies Beelzebul as the "prince" or "king" of demons (mentioned thirteen times in the *Testament of Solomon*; see Duling 1983, 941–43).

Jesus refutes the scribes with a series of parables (Mark 3:23–27), the first usage of the important term *parabolai* in the Gospel (cf. 4:1–34). The first three parabolic sayings express the same principle: if Satan/Beelzebul, the ruler of demons, is turning on his own kind, then his kingdom (*basileia*) is falling apart (3:23–24); if his household (*oikia*) is internally divided, then it will surely fall (v. 25), and the Adversary's power will come to an end (v. 26). If, as Duling (1983, 942) argues, "much of the testament [*Testament of Solomon*] reflects first-century Judaism in Palestine," perhaps the kinds of demonological manipulations attributed to Solomon are relevant: empowered by God through the archangel Michael (*T. Sol.* 1.6–7), he uses Beelzebul and other demonic spirits to thwart their own kind. Like the man of the parable in v. 27 who binds the strong man in order to plunder his house, Solomon uses the powers bestowed on him by God and various angels to manipulate and incapacitate an array of malevolent demons (see Duling 1983, 935–37). Jesus is able to exorcise demons ("plunder the house" of Beelzebul) because, as the reader/audience knows, he has been baptized with the Holy Spirit as God's beloved Son (1:10, 12). The parable of the strong man is followed by the famous saying about the "sin against the Holy Spirit": **Amen I say to you that all the sins will be forgiven human beings and all the blasphemies which they blaspheme. But whoever blasphemes against the Holy Spirit, that person will not ever be forgiven, but is guilty of an eternal sin** (3:29), followed by an editorial explanation: **because they were saying that he has an unclean spirit** (v. 30). The *amēn* ("truly") saying may arise from accusations that members of the Markan community cast out spirits by demonic agency; in the text as it stands, the saying implies that it is the scribes, not Jesus, who are guilty of serious sin by attributing divine activity to demons (cf. Exod. 20:7).

3:31–35. Technically, 3:31–35 is a "mixed *chreia*," a brief anecdote that attributes both a saying and an action to a specific person (Hock and O'Neil 1986, 85–89). Initially the scene shifts back to Jesus's family—**his mother and his brothers**—standing outside the house, calling him (v. 31). Jesus's answer to **the crowd** that informs him that his family is looking for him is shocking. The first part of his answer is a rhetorical question: **Who is my mother and my brother?** (v. 33). The second part is an action: Jesus looks around those seated about him in a circle (v. 34a). Jesus then answers his own question with an authoritative pronouncement: **Behold my mother and my brothers; for whoever does the will of God, that one is my brother and sister and mother** (vv. 34b–35). Here Jesus's family (*hoi par' autou*, v. 21) are contrasted with the crowd gathered around him (*tous peri auton*; cf. the description of the function of the Twelve to be with him [*met' autou*]; 3:14). This explicit repudiation of biological ties would have rung harshly in the ears of an ancient audience (cf. 1:20), especially combined with the implication that Jesus's relatives, who want to seize him because they suspect he is under demonic influence (3:21), are, like the scribes, guilty of blasphemy. As Donahue and Harrington (2002, 135) note, this incident intensifies the theme of discipleship introduced in 1:16–20: "Jesus forms a new family that will be constituted by those whom he explicitly calls (the disciples) as well as those who are gathered around him to hear his teaching and are summoned to do the will of God." The definition of Jesus's true family in theological terms echoes the announcement of the good news of God in 1:14; the Markan audience is challenged to do the will of God as embodied by Jesus, whose words and deeds epitomize what this commitment to God entails. The contrast between those outside (3:31–32) and those sitting around him (v. 34) will be echoed in the next major section of the Gospel.

The Sin against the Holy Spirit

The brief but famous saying about the "unforgivable sin" against the Holy Spirit, which is uttered in the context of Mark 3:28–29 (cf. Matt. 12:31–32; Luke 12:10), has given rise to much speculation and consternation throughout Christian history. Baird Tipson (1984, 302) recounts the cases of a certain Mr. Benson, a fellow of St. John's College, Cambridge (ca. 1600), who convinced himself that "the Devil would needs persuade him that he was reprobate, and would drive him to desperation for that he had sinned against the Holy Ghost," and of Mrs. Joan Drake, a Calvinist who was so afraid she had committed the unforgivable sin that it took years of pastoral counseling from some dozen ministers to assure her of her salvation shortly before she died in 1625.

Early Christian interpreters of the saying, like Ambrose of Milan (ca. 339–397), stayed close to the literal sense of the text:

> "If anyone indeed denies the dignity, majesty, and eternal power of the Holy Spirit, and thinks that demons are cast out not in the Spirit of God but in Beelzebub, there can be no entreaty for pardon there where is the fullness of sacrilege." (*Spir.* 1.3.54, trans. Tipson 1984, 305)

However, Ambrose's student Augustine of Hippo (ca. 354–430) extended the scope of the blasphemy to "a state of permanent enmity against God, a general condition of impenitence which could arise from almost any sin" (Tipson 1984, 307). For Augustine, these persistent opponents of God were the heretical Donatists, who, by shunning the Catholic church and continuing in their erroneous doctrines, would sin unforgivably if they persisted until death. Thomas Aquinas (ca. 1225–74) expanded the range of the sin

Continued

Theological Issues

Mark's Christology—theological interpretation of the person and meaning of Jesus—is often described as a "low" Christology, one that emphasizes Jesus's humanity. Mark 1:16–3:35 introduces the "stormy and mysterious personage" of Mark's Jesus, as famously described by F. C. Burkitt (1910, xx). The Markan Jesus summarily calls disciples in the midst of their daily activities, and they follow him; he provokes criticism by healing on the Sabbath and defends his disciples when they are accused of misbehavior; he becomes enraged with a man who asks him for healing; he engages in activities that provoke suspicions of illicit magic; he rejects his biological relatives in favor of his "true family" of disciples. At the same time, he speaks and acts with decisiveness and authority that spark both astonishment and criticism: he is a powerful exorcist and healer; he audaciously appoints twelve disciples to symbolize the renewal of the theocratic ideal of ancient Israel; he forcefully against the Spirit to include "malicious thought, speech, or action" resulting from any of six states of mind: "despair, presumption, impenitence, obstinacy, resisting the known truth, and the envy of another's good" (Tipson 1984, 308–9).

Both Augustine and Aquinas envisioned the blasphemy against the Holy Spirit as a sin of "outsiders" to the Christian faith—heretics and heathens not benefiting from the ministry of the church. John Calvin (1509–64), however, interpreted the sin as apostasy committed by Christians who know the divine truth but who "with settled malice" impugn and repudiate it. For Calvin, then, the unforgivable sin provided a warning that not all members of the church would be saved (Tipson 1984, 310). Teachings like this led Robert Burton, in his famous *Anatomy of Melancholy*, to advise those who feared they had committed the unforgivable sin to avoid "this furious curiosity, needless speculation, fruitless meditation about election, reprobation, free-will, grace" and "let thy sinne bee what it will, doe but repent it is sufficient" (Burton 1638, quoted in Tipson 1984, 325).

Opponents of the Calvinist position wisely returned to the literalistic readings typical of pre-Augustinian interpreters. In the seventeenth century, the Arminian theologian John Hales noted that no one could have committed the ultimate blasphemy but "the Scribes and Pharisees, and their confederates" (Hales 1667, quoted in Tipson 1984, 325). The Markan interpretation of the saying is even more restrictive, confining the accusation of blasphemy to those who have just accused Jesus of having an unclean spirit (Mark 3:30). C. E. B. Cranfield (1959, 143) insightfully noted that the warning of the verse today applies especially to theologians and church leaders, who, like the scribes, are charged with the leadership of God's people. The warning against the "unforgivable sin" might also be applied to religious leaders who are resistant to new ways of doing things (cf. 2:21–22).

refutes his critics with clever and incisive words and deeds. As Stephen Neill and [N.] Tom Wright (1988, 124) comment:

What has this Jesus to do with the mild Galilean peasant of Renan's fancy? Here is a man of more than Napoleonic stature, who spreads around him astonishment and dismay; whose words are perplexing in the extreme; who goes on puzzling his disciples to the very end; who flouts the conventional piety of his day; and yet who all through remains human, without a single trait characteristic of the Greek hero, the θεῖος ἀνήρ [divine man]. Here are problems galore, if at any time we should venture to take it in hand to write a life of Jesus; and we may be certain that what we write will be wholly unacceptable to those who like their Jesus tamed and conventionalized, and are not willing to be led away to the bleak uplands on which he moves in the Gospel according to St. Mark.

This Jesus is both powerful and human, personally authoritative yet devoted to doing the will of God, a loyal Jew whose interpretation of Torah is often at variance with the teachings of his contemporaries. Nonetheless, the legal debates between Jesus and other religious teachers do not imply rejection or indifference to the law but "mutual engagement, common concern, shared values, religious passion" (Fredriksen 1999, 107).

The humanity of Mark's depiction of Jesus is poignantly conveyed by the evidence of strained relations between Jesus and the members of his biological family here and elsewhere in the Gospels (e.g., 3:21, 31–35; 6:1–6; Luke 2:48–49; 11:27–28; John 2:1–11; 7:3–5; 19:26–27), which seems to fly in the face of contemporary notions of Christian family values (see D. Petersen 2005). It is helpful to see the "relativization" of family relations in Jesus's teachings (cf. Mark 10:35–37; 13:12–13; Luke 14:26; Matt. 8:21–22; 10:37; 19:29; 23:9) in the broader historical context of ancient philosophical movements such as Cynicism, and the Jewish utopian communities of Essenes and Therapeutai, all of which eschewed normal family ties in the pursuit of the good or blessed life together with like-minded persons analogous to the "new family" of disciples (see Barton 1994; Ahearne-Kroll 2001; Beavis 2006, 54–68). As Ahearne-Kroll (2001, 1) observes, "Mark challenges ancient notions of traditional family ties and uses the metaphor of family to construct his notion of what it means to live the life that Jesus advocates, presumably a 'good' life." However, Mark's Jesus later criticizes those who use tradition to circumvent the commandment to honor one's parents (7:10–13; cf. Exod. 20:12; 21:17; Deut. 5:16; Lev. 20:9), and the house of Simon and Andrew (Mark 1:29–31), presumably accommodating other family members such as Simon's mother-in-law, seems to serve as Jesus's "home base" in Galilee (cf. 2:1; 3:19b). Peter's wife is not mentioned in the Gospels, but 1 Cor. 9:5 implies that she travelled with him on missionary journeys, as did the wives of other disciples. According to Catholic legend, the early Christian martyr Petronilla was Peter's daughter (Lev 2007).

In addition to introducing Jesus, the theme of discipleship pervades this section of Mark, from the initial call narrative (1:16–20) to the making of the Twelve (3:13–19) and to the pronouncement story where Jesus defines his true family (3:31–34). It may be significant that three of the controversy narratives (2:15–17, 18–22, 23–28) involve criticism of the disciples, rather than direct criticism of Jesus. If, as suggested above, these stories reflect the principle that the behavior of the disciples reflects on their master, not only do these controversies bear on the overarching theme of the section; they also echo situations in which members of the Markan audience find themselves facing opposition to their efforts to follow their controversial teacher. If the Twelve, who are chosen "to be with him and in order that he might send them to preach and to have authority to cast out demons" (3:14), epitomize the disciples of Mark's day, perhaps the twelve tribes/twelve disciples typology is double-edged, since the Jewish scriptures depict the ancient Israelites as frequently fearful and disobedient to God's will, as the disciples turn out to be as the plot develops. The disciples, like Israel of old, are, to quote Elizabeth Struthers Malbon, "fallible followers" who convey a twofold message to the audience: "anyone can be a follower, no one finds it easy" (Malbon 1983, 46; cf. Best 1981, 205–6).

Mark 4:1–34

Interlude: Teaching in Parables

Introductory Matters

If Mark 1:1–13 functions as a prologue to the Gospel, and if Mark 1:16–3:35 is the first act, introducing the powerful words and deeds of Jesus, then Mark 4:1–34 can be likened to a the chorus of a Greek drama, elaborating on the narrative as it develops. Although Jesus has already been identified as a teacher (1:21–22; 2:13), this is the first of four extended passages of his teaching that punctuate Mark (cf. 7:1–23; 10:1–45; 13:1–37). It is also the location of most of the Markan parables: the parable of the sower (or the soils) and its interpretation (4:3–8, 13–20); the parables of the lamp and the measure (4:21–25); the parable of the patient farmer (4:26–29); and the parable of the mustard seed (4:30–32). The final verse in this "parable chapter" says that "he did not speak to them without a parable" (4:34), implying that all of Jesus's teaching was parabolic, so it is important to understand what the term parable (*parabolē*) means in the Markan context.

Joachim Jeremias (1972, 11) remarked that "the parables are a fragment of the bedrock of tradition," meaning that there is a high degree of scholarly consensus that Jesus of Nazareth characteristically taught in parables. Aristotle (*Rhet.* 2.20) defined the parable as an illustrative fictional story that might have happened, and the fable (*mythos*) as a fictional illustration that could not have happened. Such stories were recommended to ancient rhetoricians because they are adaptable and easy to invent (cf. Demetrius, *Eloc.* 3.158). In the LXX and Hellenistic Jewish writings, however, the term *parabolē* is frequently used to translate the Hebrew *māšāl* (Aramaic *mathla'*), which has a much broader semantic range: "parable, similitude, allegory, fable, proverb, apocalyptic revelation, riddle, symbol, pseudonym, fictitious person, example, theme, argument, apology, refutation, jest" (Jeremias 1972, 20). In Mark 4:1–34, the term appears eight times (vv. 2, 10–11, 13 [2x], 30, 33–34), and only five times elsewhere in the Gospel (3:23; 7:17; 12:1, 12; 13:28). In Mark 4, the designation "parable" refers to a short narrative fiction (vv. 3–8), a series of proverbial sayings and exhortations (vv. 21–25), and two similitudes: comparisons of the reign of God to examples from rural life (vv. 26–28, 30–32). The other Markan references are to a narrative parable (12:1–12), a teaching contrasting ritual and moral defilement (7:15–16), and an example or lesson: "from the fig tree learn the parable" (13:28). While Mark contains only two parables as defined by the Greek rhetoricians (4:3–8; 12:1–8), the majority reflect the broader Jewish sense of *māšāl*: "I will open my mouth in a parable; I will utter dark sayings from of old" (Ps. 78:2); "to understand a proverb [*māšāl*] and a figure, the words of the wise and their riddles" (Prov. 1:6).

Throughout most of Christian history, the narrative parables have been interpreted as allegories, as narratives that bear a second level of meaning corresponding to the surface story. Mark 4:13–20 is an example of an allegorical interpretation of the parable of the sower, where each element in the story is interpreted as something else: the seed is the word, the various soils are different types of hearers. Other early Christian writers saw other allegorical meanings in the parable. For example, *1 Clem.* 24.5 saw it as an allegory of the resurrection; Justin Martyr interpreted it in terms of his own mandate to seek good ground for evangelism (*Dial.* 125). Following the influential work of Adolf Jülicher (1910), twentieth-century biblical scholarship was dominated by the view expressed by Jeremias (1972, 18–19) that "fantastic and arbitrary" allegorical interpretations had inflicted "centuries of distortion and ill-usage" on the parables. In the attempt to remove the thick layer of allegorical debris that concealed the meaning of the parables, scholars have applied a wide array of interpretive methods and strategies (see, e.g., Gowler 2000), mostly with the intention of retrieving the original words and intent of Jesus.

While recent scholarship has been more open to the possibility that Jesus sometimes allegorized his own parables (e.g., Boucher 1977, 20; Blomberg 1990, 30–38; Hagner 2000, 105–6; Parris 2002), the Markan evangelist evidently regarded allegorical interpretation as key to understanding Jesus's parabolic speech. Mary Ann Tolbert (1989, 103–4) explains: "In general the major figures or elements in Mark's parables are meant to represent other characters or actions that audiences, both in the second degree and first degree narratives, ought to be able to identify." By first-degree narrative, Tolbert (1989, 97) means the viewpoint of the implied author/narrator and the implied reader/audience; Jesus and the other Gospel characters function at the level of second-degree narrative. The parables represent "third-degree narrative," in which a character in the second-degree narrative (Jesus) tells stories "with independent agents and actions" (Tolbert 1989, 103). Although, as noted above, Mark uses the term *parabolē* to refer to a range of speech forms much broader that the easily allegorized story parables, Tolbert's statement implies that at least some of the parables may be significant beyond the immediate literary contexts in which they occur.

Many scholars argue that the structure of 4:1–34 is chiastic, but there are many differences of opinion as to the details. One possible delineation (e.g., Donahue 1988, 31; Fay 1989; Cuvillier 1993, 117; Marcus 1986, 221; Moloney 2002, 86) is as follows:

A Introduction (4:1–2)
   B Sower parable (4:3–9)
      C Explanation of parabolic teaching (4:10–12)
         D Allegorical interpretation (4:13–20)
      C' Parabolic sayings (4:21–25)
   B' Seed parables (4:26–32)
A' Conclusion (4:33–34)

A simpler configuration (e.g., Stock 1989, 164; Lambrecht 1981, 86–87; Dewey 1980, 147–52) is the following:

A Introduction (4:1–2a)
   B Parable and interpretation (4:2b–20)
      C Parabolic sayings (4:21–25)
   B' Parables (4:26–32)
A' Conclusion (4:33–34)

Tolbert (1989, 149) suggests a three-part structure:

1. Introduction (4:1–2)
2. Teaching in Parables (4:3–32)
   a. Parable of the Sower (4:3–9)
   b. First interpretation (4:10–23)
   c. Second interpretation (4:24–32)
3. Close (4:33–34)

The different arrangements highlight different elements: the first emphasizes the allegorical interpretation of the sower parable; the second, the sayings material in 4:21–25. Tolbert's suggestion, which sees all of 4:10–32 as interpreting 4:3–9, is part of her larger argument that the sower parable is paradigmatic for the interpretation of the entire Gospel.

It is impossible to adjudicate among the suggestions noted above (and many others) with regard to the structure of this passage. The parables, sayings, and exhortations can be arranged in a variety of ways, in order to draw attention to one or another aspect of the discourse. Rather than focusing on structure, the comments below will focus on the leitmotif of hearing/listening that binds the material together (4:3, 9, 12, 15–20, 23, 24, 33). From this point onward in the Gospel, the language of hearing and its corollaries of seeing, perceiving, and understanding (4:11–13) recur in significant contexts that echo Jesus's exhortation to "take heed what you hear" (4:24; cf. 6:45–51; 7:14, 18; 8:14–21; 9:1; 13:1–37; 15:39).

Mark 4:1–34 in the Narrative Flow

Prologue: John and Jesus (1:1–13)

Transition: Summary of the good news (1:14–15)

Act 1: Jesus in Galilee (1:16–3:35)

▶ Interlude: Teaching in parables (4:1–34)

    Introduction (4:1–2)

    The parable of the sower (4:3–9)

    Why parables? (4:10–13)

    Interpreting the parable of the sower (4:14–20)

    Additional sayings and parables (4:21–32)

        Two proverbs (4:21–25)

        The seed growing secretly (4:26–29)

        The mustard seed (4:30–32)

    Conclusion (4:33–34)

Tracing the Narrative Flow

Introduction (4:1–2)

The phrasing that begins the introduction (in 4:1–2) to the parables is rather wordy; literally translated, the sentence reads: **And again he went to teach beside the sea, and a great crowd gathered around him so that embarking into a boat he sat upon the sea, and the whole crowd was by the sea upon the land** (4:1). It echoes previous incidents where a crowd pursues Jesus and he has to take measures to escape the crush (cf. esp. 3:7–9). In Jewish tradition, the seated posture connotes authoritative teaching (cf. 9:35; 13:3; Luke 10:39; Acts 22:3; *m. 'Abot* 1.4). The repetition of teaching vocabulary in the first two verses (*didaskein, edidasken, didachē*) signals that the contents of the parables in the maritime discourse are typical of Jesus's teaching style and underlines the importance of the instruction that follows. The reference to **many things in parables** (1:2) indicates that all the speech forms in this section are viewed by the evangelist as parables (*mĕšālîm*) in the Jewish sense.

The Parable of the Sower (4:3–9)

Many scholars regard the parable of the sower (4:3–9) as traceable back to the historical Jesus (e.g., Dodd 1961, 135–37; Jeremias 1972, 11–12). Apart from its other NT occurrences (Matt. 13:3–9; Luke 8:5–8), forms of it appear in the *Gos. Thom.* 9 and *1 Clem.* 24.5. The parable of Jesus may have been simpler than Mark's version, and most scholars hold that it was originally told without the interpretation in 4:14–20 (for a different view, see Hagner

---

A Parable from the Mishnah

The following rabbinic parable (ca. AD 200) from *Pirke Aboth* (*m. 'Abot*, "Ethics of the Fathers") compares different types of humans to trees:

> *"He used to say, Whosesoever wisdom is in excess of his works, to what is he like? To a tree whose branches are abundant, and its roots scanty; and the wind comes, and uproots it, and overturns it. And whosesoever works are in excess of his wisdom, to what is he like? To a tree whose branches are scanty, and its roots abundant; though all the winds come upon it, they stir it not from its place."* (3.18; C. Taylor 1970, 61; cf. Jer. 17:6, 8)

2000, 105). In Mark, however, the allegorical interpretation is the key to the meaning of the parable.

On the surface, the story is a simple vignette of agricultural life. A sower scatters seed on three inhospitable types of earth (*gē*): the hardened path; thin, rocky soil; and thorny ground (4:3–7). The last stage of the sowing, however, is on good soil, and the seed yields an abundant harvest: **thirtyfold and sixtyfold and a hundredfold** (4:8). Jeremias's (1972, 11–12) influential assertion that the seemingly careless scattering of the seed reflects Palestinian farming practices, where sowing precedes plowing, has been refuted by K. D. White (1964, 301–2; cf. Payne 1978–79), who quotes extensive ancient evidence that plowing normally preceded sowing. The bountiful yield of the grains planted in fertile soil is often interpreted as unrealistically lavish, symbolizing "the eschatological overflowing of the divine fullness, surpassing all human measure" (Jeremias 1972, 150; cf. V. Taylor 1966, 251, 257; Schweizer 1970, 90–91; Donahue 1988, 34). Other scholars hold that the yield is plentiful but not unrealistic (e.g., Linnemann 1966, 181n13; K. White 1964, 301–7; Scott 1989, 357–58). However, the parable is not meant to reflect normal farming practices; rather, the parable focuses on what happens to the seeds. Moreover, it is unlikely that Mark or his audience would have engaged in elaborate computations to determine whether the description of the harvest is realistic or hyperbolic; the point is that the yield is plentiful, a blessing to the sower. There may be an allusion here to Isaac: "Mark's account, or even the straightforward 'hundredfold' in Luke (8:8a), signifies an extraordinary, magnificent abundance. Furthermore the imagery is related to the story of Isaac, who sowed and reaped a hundredfold" (Hultgren 2000, 188; "the LORD blessed him," Gen. 26:12). The concluding exhortation, **"Whoever has ears to hear, let them hear!"** (Mark 4:9), reiterates the opening exhortation, "Listen!" (v. 3), underlining the importance of *this* parable to the understanding of Jesus's teaching.

Why Parables? (4:10–13)

Sandwiched between the parable and the interpretation are four verses (4:10–13) that purport to explain not just the sower parable but also Jesus's reasons for teaching in parables: **And when he was by himself, those around him with the Twelve were asking him about the parables. And he was saying to them, "To you has been given the mystery of the reign of God, but to those outside all things happen in parables, in order that 'Seeing they might see and not perceive, hearing they might hear and not understand, lest they repent and be forgiven.'" And he says to them, "Do you not know the meaning of this parable? Then how will you understand all the parables?"** The setting of the scene is similar to 3:31–32, where outsiders are contrasted with the "true family" of Jesus; here the Twelve and a larger group of disciples are contrasted with "those outside" (4:10–11). The disciples' question relates not only to the parable of the sower but also to "the parables," a point reinforced by 4:13—to understand "this parable" is to understand "all the parables."

The saying in vv. 11–12 is known by biblical scholars as Mark's "parable theory" (or "hardening theory"), and it has generated endless debate. In Greek the term "mystery" (*mystērion*) often refers to a cult in which new members were initiated through rituals and dramatic enactments of secret myths (S. Elliott 2000, 931). In early Jewish literature, however, the term is the equivalent of the Aramaic *rāz*, referring to "God's plan for the ages that will be fully disclosed only at the eschaton" (Boring 2006, 123; Dan. 2:18–47; 4:9; cf. 1QH 5.36; 1QS 3.32; CD 3.18; *1 En.* 41.1–22; 103.2; *2 Bar.* 81.4; 2 Esd. [*4 Ezra*] 12:36–37; 14:5). Mark 4:11 specifies the content of the *mystērion*: it is "the mystery of *the reign of God*," announced in 1:15 as the substance of Jesus's proclamation, and now brought to bear on parable interpretation. The imminent reign of God is the key to parable interpretation that "has been given" (*dedotai*) to the disciples. For "those outside," as for the relatives of Jesus (3:21, 31), not just the words of Jesus but "all things" happen (*ginetai*) "in parables." Knowing that "the time is fulfilled" and "the reign of God is near" (1:15) is crucial to understanding the eschatological import not only of the parables but also of the gospel events both for the disciples and for the implied audience of Mark, implicitly included by the second-person plural (*hymin, oidate, gnōsesthe*) of 4:11, 13. The Jewish apocalyptic book *1 En.* 103.1–2 (ca. first cent. BC) contains a passage that contains a similar message:

> I now swear to you, righteous ones, by the glory of the Great One and by the glory of his kingdom; and I swear to you (even) by the Great One. For I know this mystery; I have read the tablets of heaven and have seen the holy writings, and I have understood the writing in them; and they are inscribed concerning you. (trans. E. Isaac, *OTP* 1:83)

The visionary proceeds to detail the rewards that will be experienced by the righteous and the punishments to be meted out to the unjust in the last days (*1 En.* 103.3–15). In symbolic form, the parable makes a similar contrast between the sorry fates of the first three sets of seed and the abundant yield of the seed planted in good soil.

The purpose of the parabolic teaching is explained in 4:12 by means of an abridged quotation from Isa. 6:9–10: in order that **"Seeing they might see and not perceive, hearing they might hear and not understand, in order that they might not repent and be forgiven."** The prophetic text quoted here conforms most closely to the version preserved in the Aramaic *Targum of Isaiah*, rather than to the Hebrew or the LXX. Although the written targum belongs to a date much later than the first century AD, it may reflect the targumic wording current in the time of Jesus (Donahue and Harrington 2002, 141). The conjunctions *hina*, here translated "in order that," and *mēpote*, meaning "in order that not" or "lest," imply that the purpose of the parables is to render those outside impervious to their meaning. Commentators have tried to soften the severity of the prophecy in various ways, such as suggesting that *hina* can also be translated "so that," making the outsiders' failure to repent the *result* of their lack of insight, and translating *mēpote* as "unless," making insight conditional on repentance (see Evans 1989, 92–95). Mark's earliest interpreters, Matthew (13:13–15) and Luke (8:10), both deliberately ameliorate the harshness of the saying: Matt. 13:13 changes the *hina* ("in order that") to *hoti* ("because"), so that the parables *enable* comprehension; Luke eliminates the

The Messianic Secret

The "parable theory" of Mark 4:11–12 is sometimes regarded as part of a larger Markan theme known as the "messianic secret," the idea that the Gospel was written to explain why Jesus was not recognized as messiah during his lifetime (Wrede 1901). In addition to the implication that Jesus spoke in parables in order to veil his message from the crowds, the Gospel contains several themes that imply secrecy: he performs certain miracles in private (e.g., 5:40; 7:33; 8:23); he warns several recipients of healings not to tell anyone (e.g., 1:44; 7:36); he silences demons (1:25; 3:12); he delivers special teaching to the disciples privately (e.g., 4:10, 34; 7:17–23; cf. 6:31); nonetheless, the disciples often fail to understand the meaning of his mission (e.g., 4:13, 30; 7:18; 8:16–21; 9:19). Although it has been argued that these are disparate motifs that should not necessarily be interpreted as a unified theme (notably by Räisänen 1990), from a literary perspective the Gospel conveys a strong sense that there is a mystery for the reader/audience to solve: "Is a lamp brought in order to be placed under a bushel basket or under the bed, but rather to be placed on the lampstand? For there is nothing hidden that will not be revealed, nor is anything secret that will not be manifest. Anyone who has ears let them hear" (4:21–23).

phrase "lest they repent and be forgiven" (cf. Matt. 13:15). As Marcus (2000, 300) judiciously concludes, "When all is said and done, . . . *hina* in Mark 4:12 means 'in order that,' *mēpote* means 'lest,' and the passage speaks of a deliberate divine intention that some people should misunderstand and be impenitent" (cf. Evans 1989, 92–99). Mark is an apocalyptic text that envisions serious division between believers and unbelievers, even to the point of family members betraying one another (13:9–13). However, the saying should be interpreted not anachronistically, in terms of notions of free will and predestination, but as an assurance that the divine purpose will be done despite (or even by means of) human obduracy and error. With reference to the sower parable/interpretation, it reinforces the moral that while "the word" (missionary preaching, 4:15) will not always be efficacious, it will be spectacularly successful with some hearers, and the reign of God will prevail.

Interpreting the Parable of the Sower (4:14–20)

After the explanation of the purpose of parables, 4:14–20 gives the interpretation of the parable of the sower. As noted above, although the story is usually called "the sower," the emphasis of both the parable and the interpretation is on the seeds and how they fare in different types of soil. The identity of the sower is not explained, but the seed is identified as "the word" (*ho logos*), an early Christian expression referring to missionary preaching (e.g., Mark 2:2; Gal. 6:6; 1 Cor. 15:2 NIV; Rom. 10:8; James 1:21–23; Acts 6:4; 8:4; 14:25; 16:6). As Boring (2006, 132) observes, "In these verses the imagery fluctuates between 'seed' equals 'word' and 'seed' equals various kinds of believers." The various types of hearers of the word also correlate with the different types of soil and, implicitly, with the different qualities of plants that grow in each. The seed strewn along the path and eaten by birds before it can grow (Mark 4:4) symbolizes hearers from whom the word is immediately snatched away by the Adversary/Satan (4:15). Several ancient Jewish texts (*Apoc. Ab.* 13.3–8; *b. Sanh.* 107a; *Jub.* 11.11) similarly identify birds with evil spiritual entities (Azazel, Satan, Mastema). The sprouts from the seeds that fall on thin, rocky soil (Mark 4:5) are hearers who initially receive the word joyously, but the message does not take root, and when **tribulation and persecution come on account of the word, . . . they immediately fall away** (v. 17). In the biblical Wisdom literature, justice and wisdom are often said to be "rooted" in humans (e.g., Prov. 12:3, 12; Wis. 3:15; Sir. 1:6; 24:13; cf. Jer. 17:7–8), and the wicked are often said to be "rootless" (e.g., Job 5:3; 18:16; Sir. 23:25; 40:15; Wis. 4:3–4; cf. Mal. 4:1). The reference to "tribulation and persecution" (*thlipseōs kai diōgmou*) foreshadows the "tribulation" (13:19, 24) and "persecutions" (10:30) in store for the followers of Jesus.

The plants from the seeds that fall among thorns (4:7) are hearers who are distracted by **the anxieties of the world and the deceitfulness of wealth and the desires for other things** so that the message does not bear fruit (4:19). The imagery of fruitfulness/fruitlessness is ubiquitous in the Bible, with the righteous person described as bearing good fruit (e.g., Isa. 3:10; Prov. 11:30; 12:12; 31:31) and the unrighteous person as bearing bad fruit (e.g., Jer. 6:19; 21:14; Hosea 10:13; Mic. 7:13; Prov. 1:31). The plants from the seeds that fall upon good soil and bring forth grain (Mark 4:8) are those **who hear and accept the word** (v. 20). Other NT authors use the imagery of missionary preaching that renders a bountiful harvest of believers (Rom. 1:13; Matt. 9:37; Luke 10:2). The notice that the fourth set of hearers **bear fruit thirtyfold and sixtyfold and a hundredfold** (Mark 4:20) is based on the image of individual plants yielding different numbers of grains, pointing to the differing capacities of believers to actualize ("hear") the word (cf. 4:33).

Additional Sayings and Parables (4:21–32)

The remainder of the parable chapter (4:21–41) is made up of three distinct pericopes, each beginning with an introductory formula: **and he was saying to them** (4:21, 24) or simply **and he was saying** (4:26, 30). Presumably the teachings in these verses are directed to the disciples mentioned in 4:10, not to the crowd (4:1), although it has been suggested that 4:21–25 is directed to Jesus's inner circle, due to the use of the "indoor, domestic images" of the lamp and the measure as opposed to the "outdoor" seed parables of 4:26–32 (e.g., Heil 1992, 280–82; Donahue and Harrington 2002, 150). From a reader-response perspective, it makes little difference whether the teachings are directed to the disciples or to the crowd, because it is the first-degree audience (the community for whom the Gospel was written) who are exhorted to hear with their ears, look, and listen (4:23, 24).

4:21–25. The sayings in 4:21–25 replicate the structure of vv. 1–20 in that they contain two parables (in the sense of *měšālîm*), each followed by an explanation, introduced by the conjunction *gar* ("for"):

Parable: Is a lamp brought in order to be placed under a bushel basket or under the bed, but rather to be placed on the lampstand?

Explanation: For there is nothing hidden that will not be revealed, nor is anything secret that will not be manifest. Anyone who has ears let them hear.

Parable: Look and listen! In the measure with which you measure out, it will be measured out to you, and more will be added to you.

Explanation: For the one who has, it will be given to them; and the one who does not have, what they have will be taken away from them.

The first parable takes the form of a rhetorical question; of course it would be both futile and dangerous to place a burning lamp under a basket or a couch; the natural thing to do would be to place it on a lampstand. To try to conceal the lamp would be to risk a fire, and the light would flare up uncontrollably and destructively. Like the flame, the mystery of the reign of God will undoubtedly shine forth one way or the other. The second parable shifts to the second-person plural, using the economic metaphor of the measure to symbolize the rewards of the *basileia*; as a farmer who generously measures out grain is rewarded by God for his liberality (cf. Prov. 11:24), so will those who labor in the sowing of the word (cf. Prov. 22:8; Job 4:8; Sir. 7:3; *T. Levi* 13.6; 2 Cor. 9:6; Gal. 6:7–8). Marcus (2000, 321) notes that the explanation in 4:25, a version of the proverb that "the rich get richer and the poor get poorer" (cf. Terence, *Phorm.* 1.1.7–8; Juvenal, *Satires* 3.208–9), echoes the theme and structure of Mark 4:11–12: both share the contrast between insiders, who enjoy divinely "given" knowledge of the reign of God, and outsiders, who are excluded from the revelation. Arguably, the saying in 4:22 also does this, with its contrasts of hiddenness/secrecy (to some) versus revelation/manifestation (to others).

4:26–29. The parable popularly known as "the seed growing secretly" (4:26–29) is unique to Mark, although there is an echo of the final verse in the *Gos. Thom.* 21.8–9: "Let there be among you a person who understands. When the crop ripened, he came quickly carrying a sickle and harvested it" (R. Miller 1994, 309). Mark's introductory formula explicitly relates the parable to the reign of God: **the reign of God is like . . .** (Mark 4:26). This parable contains many of the same elements as the sower parable: a man who casts seed on the earth, seeds that sprout and grow, and a threefold pattern, **first a stalk, then a head, then full grain in the head** (v. 28). This parable emphasizes the earth's capacity to bear fruit **on its own** (*automatē*), through divine and not human causation (Hultgren 2000, 387; cf. Acts 12:10; Josh. 6:5 LXX), while the man sleeps and rises, **night and day** (Mark 4:27). This ordering of the farmer's activities—"night and day" rather than "day and night"—seems peculiar to the contemporary Christian reader yet reflects a Jewish context, where the new day begins at sundown. The harvest scene in v. 29 parallels the abundant yield of the seed sown on good earth in vv. 8, 20.

Using the "master parable" of the sower as the key to unlock Mark's understanding of the parable, it is legitimate to interpret the farmer as a missionary preacher of the reign of God, whose efforts, like those of the sower, inevitably lead to a harvest of believers, whether the preacher knows it or not. The account of the harvest in 4:29 implies the theme of eschatological judgment, with its echo of Joel 3:13: "Put in the sickle, for the harvest is ripe. Go in, tread, for the wine press is full. The vats overflow, for their wickedness is great" (cf. *2 Bar.* 70.2, speaking of "the time" when "the world has ripened and the harvest of the seed of the evil ones and the good ones has come"; trans. Klijn, *OTP*

1:644–45). However, agriculture is a cyclic activity—sowing and harvest are not onetime events. Though Mark's perspective on history is apocalyptic and anticipates an eschatological gathering of the elect (13:27), the preaching of the nearness of God's reign is presented as ongoing and essential.

4:30–32. The final parable is the famous similitude of the mustard seed (4:30–32; cf. Matt. 13:31–32; Luke 13:8–9; *Gos. Thom.* 20). Like the preceding parable, it begins with an introductory formula referring explicitly to the reign of God: **To what shall we compare the reign of God or make a parable for it?** (Mark 4:30). As in the other seed parables, the grain of mustard—proverbial in Hellenistic and rabbinic sources for its smallness (see Hultgren 2000, 395)—is planted in the earth, and without further human effort, **it comes up and becomes the greatest of all the shrubs and makes great branches, so that under its shadow the birds of heaven dwell** (v. 32). The reference to the birds roosting in the branches of the plant is a prophetic image of the reign of God, as in Dan. 4:12: "Its foliage was beautiful, its fruit abundant, and it provided food for all. The animals of the field found shade under it, the birds of the air nested in its branches, and from it all living beings were fed" (cf. Dan. 4:21, 25, 32, 34–35; Ezek. 17:23; 31:6).

Several scholars argue that the mustard plant was considered to be a weed in antiquity and that the parable deliberately compares the reign of God to a dangerous, pungent, and invasive shrub (e.g., Crossan 1992, 276–79; Oakman 1986, 127). The peaceful image of birds nesting beneath the branches of the plant obviates the suggestion that the parable compares God's reign to a dangerous invader. A much-cited quotation from Pliny's *Natural History* (29.54.170) comments on the mustard plant's tenacity but emphasizes its benefits as a seasoning and, especially, as a cure for many serious ailments: snakebite and scorpion stings; fungal poisoning; phlegm; toothache; and stomach, bowel, urinary, and menstrual troubles. Matthew and Luke both call the plant a "tree" (*dendron*) to emphasize the prophetic resonances of the image, but Mark's more realistic "shrub" (*lachanon*) completes the agricultural theme of the seed parables with an image of the reign of God as a sheltering canopy. Here the "birds of the heavens" symbolize not demonic beings (cf. Mark 4:4, 15), but the nations (cf. Dan. 4:21 LXX). The pairing of the final two seed parables indicates that Mark understood them as conveying the same theme: the contrast between what is hidden at present, but which will surely be revealed (cf. Hooker 2000, 97). The mustard seed parable, particularly, develops the theme of abundant growth of God's reign, introduced in Mark 4:8, 20.

Conclusion (4:33–34)

The parable chapter concludes with a paraphrase of 4:11: **And with many such parables he spoke the word to them as they were able to hear; without a parable he did not speak to them, but privately to his own disciples he was explaining everything** (vv. 33–34). The theme of hearing/understanding the

---

Early Christian Homilies on the Sower

Cyril of Alexandria (ca. 375–444) interprets the hard soil of the path as hearers with hard, unyielding minds, who will never produce holy fruit because their hearts are barren and faithless. The seed falling on rocky ground corresponds with people who go to church but then forget what they learned there, especially in times of persecution. He exhorts his audience to nurture the growth of faith and commitment, not imagining that they can grow along with the thorns of worldly distraction (*Commentary on the Gospel of St. Luke*, homily 41). In a very different vein, John Chrysostom (347–407) explains that the seed is Christian doctrine, the ground is human souls, and the sower is Christ. Like Jesus, the sower does not distinguish between different types of soil, but preaches to rich and poor, wise and foolish, brave and cowardly. While rocks, pathways, and thorny soil cannot convert themselves, humans can, since they are endowed with reason. Thus the word of Christ may flourish wherever it falls (*Hom. Matt.*, homily 44; see Royster 1996, 14–15).

---

word that is so emphatically articulated throughout this section—forms of the verb to hear (*akouein*) appear eleven times in these thirty-four verses—will be repeated in significant contexts in the rest of the Gospel.

Theological Issues

Although some twentieth-century interpreters have insisted that the original point of Jesus's parable of the sower (4:3–8) was not the fate of the seeds but the abundant yield (v. 8; e.g., Dodd 1961, 135–37; Jeremias 1972, 150), Mark's allegorical interpretation of the seed as the word and the soils as different types of hearers (4:14–20) has long been a favorite homiletical theme.

Mary Ann Tolbert maintains that the parable of the sower and its interpretation are not only the key to the interpretation of Mark's parables, but also to the entire Gospel. She argues that the different soils/hearers in the third-degree narrative (the parable) correspond with characters in the second-degree narrative (the Gospel). The seed that falls along the path and is eaten by birds corresponds with the group of characters inimical to Jesus from their first appearance: scribes, Pharisees, Herodians, Sadducees (Tolbert 1989, 154). The seed sown on rocky ground—people who commit "immediately" but who endure only "for a season" (4:17) and falter in times of trouble or persecution—corresponds to the disciples, who "immediately" follow Jesus, but who, later in the Gospel account, abandon Jesus when they see him in trouble (14:43–50). Tolbert notes that the rocky ground (*petrōdes*) ironically evokes Peter's title "The Rock" (*Petros*, 3:16; Tolbert 1989, 154–55), the disciple who abandons Jesus after promising never to fall away (14:27, 29). Tolbert

85

admits that few characters in Mark correspond to the thorny ground—people distracted from the gospel by worldly cares and wealth—but speculates that the rich man in 10:17–22, who wants to follow Jesus but balks at the command to liquidate his wealth and give it to the poor, is an example of this kind of hearer of the word. Another is Herod Antipas, who recognizes John the Baptist as righteous and holy, and who *hears* him gladly (6:20), but who is tricked by his wife into executing the prophet: "Herod values his position, his reputation, and his oath more highly than what he has been hearing gladly. Riches, worldly power, and concern about the regard of others are all noxious weeds that kill the word" (Tolbert 1989, 157–58). The characters that correspond to the seed sown on good earth are typified by those who are healed in 5:1–43: the Gerasene demoniac, Jairus's daughter and her parents, and the woman with a hemorrhage (1989, 181–82). The present-day reader, like Mark's ancient audience, is left with the question "What kind of earth am I?" (1989, 299).

Tolbert's interpretation relates primarily to the response of the characters in the second-degree narrative, but what of the first-degree "characters"—the implied author and the implied reader of Mark's own time? The commands to hear (*akouete*) and see (*blepete*) are in the second-person plural (4:3, 24), and the admonitions to listen (4:9, 23) are addressed not just to the disciples but also to the "hearers" of the Gospel, a community engaged in missionary preaching (cf. 13:10) and facing severe trials and persecutions (13:9–13). The missionaries in the audience are not only invited to ask, "What type of earth am I?" but also to envision themselves as the protagonists in the parables. *They* are the sowers of the word, who find it difficult to understand why so many of their listeners are impervious to the good news, or who give up under duress. *They* are the ones who have lit the lamp of the gospel, which will surely illumine the world. *They* are the ones who are measuring out the word and will be amply rewarded for their efforts. *They*, like the farmer, scatter the message of the reign of God, which will inevitably bear fruit. Like the tenacious and medicinal mustard plant, God's reign will spread and provide shelter for all who seek it. The question "What type of earth am I?" continues to be relevant to Christians today, both those who "sow the word" through preaching and teaching and those who receive and nurture it.

As recognized above, the "parable theory" of Mark 4:11–12 (Isa. 6:9–10) has generated a great deal of commentary throughout history. Unfortunately, much Christian interpretation of this passage has been anti-Judaic, beginning with Acts 28:25–28, where Paul uses a citation of Isa. 6:9–10 to explain to a delegation of Roman Jews why God is now offering salvation to the gentiles; unlike the Jews, they will listen to the good news (Acts 28:28). In Acts, however, this exchange is an inner-Jewish debate between Paul and other Jews, some of whom are convinced by his exposition of the Scriptures (25:24–25). Ultimately the theme is rooted in the scriptural critique of Israel's failure to repent in the face of what the prophets interpreted as divine punishment—the

Assyrian invasion of the northern kingdom, and later, the hardships of the Babylonian exile (e.g., Isa. 29:9; 42:19; 43:8; 44:9; 56:10; 59:10; 63:17; Ezek. 3:7–9; 12:1–2). Later generations of Christian writers typically interpreted the prophecy more harshly, "to explain why the Jews rejected Christ and why they continue to reject the Christian religion" (Evans 1989, 159). Some saw the "hardening" as the punishment of the Jewish people for not believing in Christ (e.g., Justin Martyr, Origen, Cyprian, Athanasius, Ambrose, Chrysostom, Cassian). Others thought that since the Jews were habitually resistant to divine truth, their rejection of Christ should not be a surprise (e.g., Eusebius, Methodius, Commodian, Jerome, Cassiodorus). Others saw the Jewish rejection of Jesus as predestined, so that the Jews were actually divinely prevented from having faith in Christ (e.g., Tertullian, Augustine, Caesarius of Arles; Evans 1989, 159–60).

In Mark, however, the quotation does *not* bear on the Jewish people. In the context of 4:1–34, "those around Jesus with the Twelve" (v. 10) and "those outside" are all Jewish—including Jesus. To the audience of Mark's Gospel, Isaiah's prophecy applies to the "hearers" of the word, Jewish or gentile, who, for one reason or another, do not accept it. As with the sower parable, the prophecy reassures the missionary audience that the message they preach will fall on good soil, and that the reign of God will grow and flourish.

Mark 4:35–6:56

Act 2: Beyond Galilee

Introductory Matters

The stories in this section are sandwiched between two extensive blocks of teaching material, Mark 4:1–34 and 7:1–2. While Jesus's ministry of healing and exorcism is sketched in 1:21–3:35, the power of Jesus over the elements (4:35–41; 6:45–52), as an exorcist (5:1–20), healer (5:21–43), and prophetic miracle worker (6:34–44) is demonstrated in a series of highly developed and dramatic episodes. Six of the most famous miracle stories in the Bible are crowded into these chapters: the stilling of the storm, the exorcism of the Gerasene demoniac, the raising of Jairus's daughter, the healing of the hemorrhaging woman, the feeding of the five thousand, Jesus's walking on the sea. As Hedrick (1993, 221) observes, "The general impression that the segment 4:35–6:56 makes is that Jesus is a highly successful worker of deeds, wondrous and beyond normal human ability."

However, Jesus is not portrayed as all-powerful or as uniformly successful. The account of his spectacular deeds is marred by the disciples' fear and lack of comprehension (4:40–41; 6:51–52). Nonetheless, they are sent out to share Jesus's ministry of exorcism, healing, preaching, and teaching (6:7–13, 30). In his hometown, Jesus meets with astonishment and skepticism, and his powers are curtailed by his neighbors' unbelief (6:1–6). The famous tale of the execution of Jesus's forerunner, John the Baptist, foreshadows the destiny of Jesus.

Throughout this section, the theme of faith (*pistis, pisteuō*), previously mentioned only twice in the Gospel (1:15; 2:5), comes to the fore. Jesus rebukes the disciples for their lack of faith (4:40), enjoins a grieving father to believe that his child will live (5:36), and commends a woman for her strong faith (5:34). Unbelief (*apistia*) and fear (*phobos*) are presented as opposite to faith, and as impediments to mighty works (4:40; 5:36; 6:6, 50). The question of Jesus's identity—or the source of his power—continues to be raised, even by the disciples (4:41; 5:7; 6:2–3, 14–16, 49–50).

This section is framed by two similar stories where Jesus astounds the disciples by showing his authority over the sea (4:35–41; 6:45–52). In 5:1–40, Jesus is able to perform works of great power even in gentile territory, but ironically, when he returns to his own village, he is "without honor" (6:1–6). The story of Jesus in the country of the Gerasenes is followed by the intercalated stories of the raising of Jairus's daughter and the healing of a woman; similarly, the story of Jesus in his hometown is followed by intercalated narratives of the mission of the Twelve (which segues into the feeding of the five thousand) and the death of John the Baptist. The pericope, roughly at the center of the section (6:1–6), asks the key question "From whence did this man get all this?" (6:2b).

Tracing the Narrative Flow

Jesus Calms the Wind and the Waves (4:35–41)

Mark 4:35–41 is the first of three Markan narratives that take place in a boat, crossing to the other side of the Sea of Galilee (cf. 6:45–52; 8:13–21). In all three stories, there is a dialogue between Jesus and the disciples; in all three, the disciples are shown as deficient in faith and/or understanding (cf. 4:12a). In each of the stories, Jesus comments on the disciples' lack of perception/fearfulness (4:40; 6:50; 8:17–21). The first two are miracle stories; the second and third reflect back on Mark's stories of the multiplication of bread (6:34–44; 8:1–10).

Mark 4:35–6:56 in the Narrative Flow

Prologue: John and Jesus (1:1–13)

Transition: Summary of the good news (1:14–15)

Act 1: Jesus in Galilee (1:16–3:35)

Interlude: Teaching in parables (4:1–34)

▶ Act 2: Beyond Galilee (4:35–6:56)

Jesus calms the wind and the waves (4:35–41)

Jesus exorcises the Gerasene demoniac (5:1–20)

A dead girl is raised, a hemorrhage stopped (5:21–43)

Jairus seeks healing for his daughter (5:21–24a)

A woman is healed of a hemorrhage (5:24b–34)

The daughter of Jairus is raised up (5:35–43)

Jesus is dishonored in his hometown (6:1–6a)

The Twelve and the Baptist (6:6b–33)

Jesus sends out the Twelve to exorcize (6:6b–13)

The execution of John the Baptist (6:14–29)

The return of the Twelve (6:30–33)

The feeding of the five thousand (6:34–44)

Jesus walks upon the sea (6:45–52)

Conclusion (6:53–56)

Commentators have seen multiple levels of symbolism in this story, which takes place on the evening of Jesus's day of parable teaching (4:35). Mark's repetition of significant encounters between Jesus and the disciples **in the boat** has led some interpreters to infer that the boat (*ploion*) represents the church (e.g., Kertelge 1970, 98; Best 1981, 320–34; Malbon 1984, 377n40; Twelftree 2007, 116–17), a commonplace image in ante-Nicene Christian literature and iconography (Daniélou 1961, 58–70; Goodenough 1958, 159). It is highly likely that the Markan boat stories form the basis of the early Christian boat/ church symbolism (Daniélou 1961, 65). Origen of Alexandria (ca. 185–ca. 254) interprets the story this way:

> For as many as are in the little ship of faith are sailing with the Lord; as many as are in the bark of the holy church will voyage with the Lord across this wave-tossed life; though the Lord himself may sleep in holy quiet, he is but watching your patience and endurance: looking forward to the repentance, and to the conversion of those who have sinned. (*Fr. Matt.* 3.3, quoted in Oden and Hall 1998, 60; cf. Hippolytus, *Antichr.* 59)

In the Jewish scriptures, the boat as a means of salvation is particularly prominent in Gen. 8, where the ark keeps Noah and his family safe from the flood that destroys all other living things (MT: *tēbâ*; LXX: *kibōtos*); the reed basket that saves the infant Moses from drowning in the Nile is also called an "ark" (Exod. 2:5 MT: *tēbâ*; 2:3–6 LXX: *thibos*). The hellenistic Jewish writer of the Wisdom of Solomon (early first cent. AD) comments on the fragility of the ships that carry voyagers safely through the sea: "Therefore people trust their lives even to the smallest piece of wood, and passing through the billows on a raft they come safely to land." This writer alludes to the salvation of the world by Noah's ark: "For even in the beginning, when arrogant giants were perishing, the hope of the world took refuge on a raft, and guided by your hand left to the world the seed of a new generation" (Wis. 14:5–6; cf. Heb. 11:7; 1 Pet. 3:20). There is a pre-Christian example of a boat being used as a symbol of Israel in *T. Naph.* 6.1–10 that bears some resemblance to the Markan story: a vessel labeled the "ship of Jacob" appears to the patriarch, and father Jacob beckons to his sons to embark. A "violent storm and a frightful hurricane" arise; Jacob and his twelve sons are separated, the ship is swamped, the sons escape on its fragments, and they are carried to the ends of the earth. Levi prays to the Lord, the storm abates, the ship reaches dry land, and the family is reunited (see Daniélou 1961, 62). From the image of the ship of Jacob/Israel, it is a short step to the symbol of the boat as church, where Jesus encounters his disciples, saving them from external perils, accompanying and instructing them.

Another biblical boat story that may inform Mark's telling of this tale is from the book of Jonah. In Jon. 1:4–6, God sends a violent tempest after the reluctant prophet, who has boarded a ship bound for faraway Tarshish, contrary to the divine command to prophesy against the Ninevites. The boat (LXX: *ploion*) is about to disintegrate, and the sailors, like the disciples, are terrified (Jon. 1:10 LXX: *kai ephobēthēsan hoi andres phobon megan*; cf. Mark 4:41: *kai ephobēthēsan phobon megan*). Despite the storm, Jonah, like Jesus in the boat, is asleep. The captain awakens the prophet (Jon. 1:6; cf. Mark 4:38) and exhorts him to pray to his God, lest they perish (LXX: *hopōs diasōsē ho theos hēmas kai mē apolōmetha*; Mark 4:38b: *ou melei soi hoti apollymetha*). Jonah admits that the storm has been sent because of him, and he begs the sailors to throw him overboard, which they reluctantly do. The storm ceases, and the men acknowledge the power of God (Jon. 1:12–16). The narrative and verbal similarities suggest a literary relationship between the two stories (cf. Cope 1976, 96–97; Marcus 2000, 337; Wheller 2003, 58–63). There is an implicit contrast between Jonah, the reluctant prophet who flees the will of God and provokes the storm, and Jesus, the faithful prophet who does the will of God (cf. Mark 3:35) and calms the waves (cf. the explicit identification of Jesus as a prophet greater than Jonah in Luke 11:29–32; Matt. 12:41). Since the next pericope (Mark 5:1–20) is the first account of Jesus in the Decapolis, this typology is particularly apt, since Jonah is the only Israelite prophet sent to a gentile nation.

The miracle wrought by Jesus's rebuke to the wind, **"Silence! Be still!"** (4:39b) provokes an awe-filled question from the disciples, **"Who is this that even the wind and the sea obey him?"** (4:41), that is left for the reader/audience to ponder. Several psalms portray power over the waves as an attribute

Figure 5. The prophet Jonah being thrown into the sea. Sandstone relief (1579) on the house Markt 16 in Pirna.

of God (Pss. 42:7–8; 65:7–8; 89:8–9). Psalm 107 is particularly evocative of the Markan story:

> Some went down to the sea in ships, doing business on the mighty waters;
> they saw the deeds of the LORD, his wondrous works in the deep.
> For he commanded and raised the stormy wind, which lifted up the waves of the sea. . . .
> Then they cried to the LORD in their trouble, and he brought them out from their distress;
> He made them be still, and the waves of the sea were hushed. (107:23–25, 28–29)

The natural tendency of the contemporary Christian reader is to assume that since the story portrays Jesus in terms usually reserved for God—as master of the sea—that the answer to the disciples' question is that Jesus is divine. It should be remembered, however, that Jesus's archetypes, Elijah and Elisha, are also capable of impressive nature miracles (e.g., 1 Kings 17:1; 18:38, 41–46; 2 Kings 1:10, 12; 2:8, 14; 3:16–20; 4:38–41; 6:4–7). Although the ancient prophets' acts of power are usually clearly attributed to God, sometimes the miracle stories show the prophets acting as if on their own authority (e.g., 1 Kings 18:41–46; 2 Kings 2:8; 4:38–41; 6:5–7; 13:21). Likewise, the faith that Jesus calls for—**"Why are you so cowardly? Do you not yet have faith?"** (Mark 4:40)—is not faith *in him*, but faith *like that of Jesus* in the power of God to subdue the sea (cf. 11:22–23).

An influential interpretation of this passage is that since Jesus uses language to still the storm found elsewhere in exorcism stories (*epitimaō*: cf. 1:25; 3:12; 9:25; cf. 8:33; *pephimōso*: cf. 1:25), the miracle is a sort of exorcism, since "in reality and in mythology, the sea represented the waters of death" (Bolt 2003, 142; cf. Twelftree 2007, 116–17; J. Robinson 1957, 40–42; Lane 1974, 174–78; H. Anderson 1981, 145; Gnilka 1978–79, 195–96). According to this line of interpretation, the wildness of the storm is attributed to demonic powers. If this is the case, then the miracle is a fitting prelude to the lengthy exorcism narrative that follows. However, the common vocabulary of 4:39 and certain exorcism tales are not decisive evidence of a common theme; 4:38 describes the disciples as "raising" (*egeirousin*) Jesus from his sleep, the same word used by the young man at the tomb to announce the resurrection (*ēgerthē*, 16:6), a word often used in referring to resurrection (5:41; 6:14, 16; 12:25–26; 14:28; but cf. 1:31; 2:12; 9:27; 13:8; 14:42). This does not imply that Jesus's rising from his sleep foreshadows his rising from the tomb. Moreover, the argument from common vocabulary would be more persuasive if the terms *epitimaō* or *pephimōso* were found in the exorcism story that follows. Unfortunately, they are not. The story demonstrates the power of Jesus's faith in God and challenges the audience to claim a confidence in God's power that exceeds that of the cowardly disciples.

Jesus Exorcises the Gerasene Demoniac (5:1–20)

This spectacular demonstration of divine power is followed by the lengthy, vivid, and rather convoluted story (5:1–20) of Jesus's confrontation with a demon-possessed man on the other side of the Sea of Galilee, in **the region of the Gerasenes** (5:1). Gerasa (modern-day Jerash in Jordan) was a prosperous hellenized city more than thirty miles from the coast, making it an unlikely location for the stampede of pigs into the lake described in 5:13. This is probably why some ancient manuscripts locate the story in Gergesa, on the eastern shore; Matt. 8:28 places it in Gadara, about five miles southeast of the lake. For Mark, the significance of the place is not the precise location of the town, but that Jesus's mission has now spread to gentile territory, since Gerasa was one of the cities of the Decapolis (5:20), distinguished by political, social, cultural, and religious affinities with Greco-Roman culture (Mare 2000, 334). On reaching foreign soil, Jesus's first act is an exorcism, paralleling his first public act in Galilee (1:21–28).

As in the Galilean exorcism, the man **with an unclean spirit** approaches Jesus (5:2). The story of the meeting is interrupted by a dramatic description of the man's condition (vv. 3–5). The detail that he lived **among the tombs** is mentioned three times (vv. 2, 3, 5) and is in keeping with the man's "demonized" (*daimonistheis*) state (v. 18), since in Greco-Roman culture, *daimones* were popularly regarded as the ghosts of the dead (Bolt 2003, 55). His preternatural strength and violence are emphasized; people have tried to bind him, but he has repeatedly torn the chains and shackles apart: **and all night and all day among the tombs and in the mountains he was crying out and bruising himself with stones** (v. 5).

The sequence of events in the following verses is elaborate: the man catches sight of Jesus from afar, runs up and bows before him, acknowledging him as **son of the Most High God**, and begging him not to torture him (vv. 6–7; cf. 1:24). In the Bible, the expression "Most High God" is a gentile usage (e.g., Gen. 14:18; Num. 24:16; Dan. 3:26; 4:2; 2 Macc. 3:31; 3 Macc. 7:9; 1 Esd. 2:3), so it is particularly fitting in a non-Jewish setting. As in Mark 1:24, the spirit's confession is meant as a defense against the exorcist, and it is ineffective. In the initial exorcism narrative, the demon is instantly expelled by Jesus's command (1:25), but in 5:7–13a, there is an extended exchange between exorcist and possessed. The use of the imperfect form of the verb in 5:8 (*elegen*) implies that Jesus has to command the spirit to depart repeatedly (**for he was saying to him, "Come out of the man, unclean spirit!"**). While the spirit claims to know who Jesus is, Jesus has to ask the demon's name; only then is it revealed that there are multiple spirits bedeviling the man: **"Legion is my name, because we are many"** (v. 9). Only after the spirits are forced to reveal their identity do they beg Jesus not to send them far away, but into a nearby herd of pigs (v. 12).

The name Legion (or "a legion"; vv. 9, 15) obviously has a Roman military connotation, since a *legio* was a division of the Roman army made up of about six thousand men, although the word could simply be used to mean "many" (Molinari 2000). As several scholars have noted, the military terminology continues throughout the account of the expulsion: the spirits beg Jesus not to "dispatch" (*aposteilē*) them away from their home region (v. 10); the term *agelē* (v. 11) means both herd (of swine) and "a local term for a band of trainees" (Derrett 1979, 5). Jesus "permits/orders" (*epitrepsen*) the spirits to enter the swine, a word that can mean to issue a military command (v. 13a). The possessed animals rush (*hōrmēsen*) into the sea (v. 13b): "the term is a natural one for troops rushing into battle, or generally, from Aeschylus up to the accounts of the Exodus by Josephus and Philo" (Derrett 1979, 5). The large number of animals (**about two thousand**, v. 13) suggests a veritable army of pigs. It has thus been suggested that Mark's use of Roman military language to describe the rout of Legion is meant as a repudiation of the imperial occupation of Palestine (e.g., Hollenbach 1981; Theissen 1983, 256; Myers 1988, 191–93). The location of the incident in the highly hellenized Decapolis (where there are huge herds of pigs, unclean by Jewish standards) rather than in Galilee vitiates this interpretation; why would a story about the liberation of the Jews from Roman occupation be located east of the Jordan (cf. Twelftree 2007, 110)? Rather, the military metaphor presents Jesus as defeating and binding the demonic horde, as the strong man of the parable is bound and plundered by one even more powerful (3:27).

The incident is followed by two kinds of responses (5:14–20). The swineherds flee and announce what has happened, both in the city and in the countryside. The people who come to see for themselves, like the disciples after the stilling of the storm, are frightened (*ephobēthēsan*, vv. 14–15), and beg Jesus to leave the district, presumably out of fear of further destruction of property (vv. 16–17). The man, however, is transformed; the sightseers find him **seated, clothed, and sane** (v. 15a); as Jesus is about to leave, he begs to **be with him** (v. 18), a phrase elsewhere referring to the Twelve (cf. 3:14). This time, Jesus does not enjoin the man to silence (cf. 1:44), but tells him to go to his own people and announce God's (*ho kyrios*) mercy, which he does to the wonderment of the entire Decapolis (5:19–20), thus becoming the first missionary to the gentiles (Boring 2006, 155–56). The contrast between the faith of the man and the fear of the onlookers recalls Jesus's question to the disciples in 4:40: "Why are you cowardly? Do you not yet have faith?" Possibly the former demoniac serves a function for the gentile phase of Jesus's mission similar to that of John the Baptist for Galilee and Judea (cf. Wefald 1996, 14).

Adding to the prophetic theme of the story are several significant echoes of the book of Isaiah. Thus Isa. 65:1–7 describes God's outreach to "those who did not seek me, . . . to a nation that did not call on my name" (65:1), who, like the people of the Decapolis, indulge in pagan practices and eat unclean foods, including pork. Like the demoniac, they "sit inside tombs, and spend the night in secret places" (65:3–4); 65:3 LXX accuses them of sacrificing to demons (*tois daimoniois*). While the original prophecy condemns Israel for engaging in illicit activities, their Gerasene antitype proclaims God's mercy to gentiles. Isaiah 49:24–25 asks: "Can the prey be taken from the mighty, or the captives of a tyrant be rescued? . . . Even the captives of the mighty shall be taken, and the prey of the tyrant be rescued." In Mark 5:1–20, God's promise to rescue captives from bondage is realized in the exorcism of the demoniac, and by his proclamation of the good news in the Decapolis.

A Dead Girl Is Raised, a Hemorrhage Stopped (5:21–43)

Mark 5:21–43 is another Markan "sandwich," in which the story of the raising of a girl from the dead (vv. 21–24a, 35–43) frames the narrative of the healing of a woman with a hemorrhage (vv. 24b–34). These two stories are so thoroughly interlinked that they may have been connected prior to the writing of the Gospel: both involve female characters in need of healing; the number twelve figures in both stories (vv. 25, 42), as does the term "daughter" (vv. 23, 34); both stories contrast the public and the private (vv. 32–33, 40–41); and in both, touching brings about healing (vv. 27–28, 41; cf. Cotter 2001, 55). In both stories, Jesus displays prophetic powers (5:30, 36, 39) and is met with skepticism (vv. 31, 39–40). Both stories take place in an unnamed location on the Jewish side of the lake (v. 21), in the aftermath of the Gerasene exorcism.

5:21–24a. Whereas the previous healings and exorcisms involve ordinary, unnamed sufferers, in 5:21–24a Jesus is approached by a prominent local personage, **one of the rulers of the synagogue** (v. 22; cf. Acts 13:15), a class of officials variously described as responsible for the financial and physical oversight of the building (Donahue and Harrington 2002, 173), or as "simply the leader of worship services" (Marcus 2000, 355). A first-century inscription from Jerusalem describes a hereditary *archisynagōgos* named

> **An Outline of Mark 5:21–43**
>
> A dead girl is raised, a hemorrhage stopped (5:21–43)
>
> > Jairus seeks healing for his daughter (5:21–24a)
> >
> > A woman is healed of a hemorrhage (5:24b–34)
> >
> > The daughter of Jairus is raised up (5:35–43)

> ### Theodotus Inscription
>
> "Theodotus, son of Vettanos, a priest and an *archisynagōgos*, son of an *archisynagōgos* grandson of an *archisynagōgos*, built the synagogue for the reading of Torah and for teaching the commandments; furthermore, the hostel, and the rooms, and the water installation for lodging needy strangers. Its foundation stone was laid by his ancestors, the elders, and Simonides." (Hanson and Oakman 1998, 79)

Theodotus as the builder of a synagogue, which served both for Torah reading and "teaching the commandments," but also as a hostel for needy strangers.

Other than Bartimaeus (10:46–52), **Jairus** is the only character named in a miracle story, indicating that the name may be significant. Marcus (2000, 356) suggests that it could be a transliteration of *Yāʾir* ("he enlightens") or *Yāʾîr* ("he awakens"): "Either name would be appropriate for Jairus, since his *seeing* of Jesus is emphasized in our verse, and Jesus 'awakens' his daughter from the sleep of death in 5:39–43"; however, it seems unlikely that the Greek audience of Mark (or of his source) would have picked up on the Hebrew wordplay.

It may be relevant to the story that Jairus shares a name with a figure from the Hebrew scriptures, the "minor judge" Jair, who judged Israel for twenty-two years, and had thirty sons (Judg. 10:3–5). He is both positively and negatively portrayed in Hellenistic Jewish literature (Josephus, *Ant.* 5.7.6 §254; *L.A.B.* 38.1–4); if he had any daughters, they are not mentioned in the extant sources. However, his immediate successor, Jephthah (Judg. 11:1–12:7) is famous (or infamous) for his relationship with his daughter, whom he sacrificed to honor a rash vow (11:29–40). Some intriguing typological connections can be made between Jairus and Jephthah: both are prominent Israelite men with unnamed daughters of marriageable age (Mark 5:42; Judg. 11:37–38); Jairus's daughter appears, like Jephthah's, to be his only child and heir (Judg. 11:35; Mark 5:23; cf. Luke 8:42, which explicitly states that the girl is *monogenēs*; cf. Num. 27:1–11); both men are distraught at the prospect of their child's death (Judg. 11:35; Mark 5:22–23). But the contrast between the two fathers could not be greater. Jephthah must kill his daughter because of his rash vow to make a burnt offering of the first creature greeting him on his return from battle (Judg. 11:31); Jairus approaches Jesus to beg for the girl's life: **My little daughter is near death; come that you might lay hands on her in order that she might be healed and live!** (Mark 5:23). Jephthah's daughter comes out to meet him joyously and is faced with death (Judg. 11:34), but Jairus is the one who runs to Jesus and prostrates himself at his feet to beg for the girl's life.

5:24b–34. The story of the woman with a hemorrhage (5:24b–34) takes place as Jesus is on the way to Jairus's house, followed by a great crowd, pressing on him. As scholars often observe, there is a huge social gulf between the community leader Jairus and the impoverished woman, who is too timid even to ask for help: **Hearing about Jesus, coming into the crowd behind him, she touched his cloak; for she said, "If I should touch even his cloak, I shall be healed"** (5:27–28; Marcus 2000, 366; cf. Powell 2005, 69). Not only is the woman afflicted with a continuous flow of blood, but she has also spent all her money on physicians, to no avail: **Having spent all that she had, nothing was helping, but she was getting worse** (5:26). Her faith in risking Jesus's disapproval by touching his cloak is rewarded by immediate healing: **The source of the blood was dried up, and she knew in her body that she was healed from her affliction** (5:29). While Jesus must encourage Jairus not to fear but **only**

believe (5:36), he commends the woman for her faith: **Daughter, your faith has healed you; go in peace, and be cured from your disease** (5:34). This is the first of four stories in which women are presented as models for Mark's audience to emulate (cf. 7:24–30; 12:41–44; 14:3–9; cf. Beavis 1988).

5:35–43. In 5:35–43 Mark resumes the story of Jairus's daughter. In the story of Jephthah, his daughter dies and is mourned by "the daughters of Israel" (Judg. 11:40), but here Jesus makes the mourning in Jairus's household unnecessary when he raises the girl from the dead with an Aramaic endearment: *"Talitha koum,"* **that is, translated, "Little girl, I say to you, rise up!"** (Mark 5:39, 41–42; see also Beavis 2010). Some scholars describe the miracle as a resuscitation from a coma rather than a resurrection (see Hedrick 1993), due to Jesus's prescient assertion that the child is not dead but only sleeping (5:39). However, there are echoes between this story and Elijah's raising of the widow's son (1 Kings 17:17–24) and Elisha's restoration of the Shunammite woman's son (2 Kings 4:18–37; cf. Cotter 2001, 66–68, 74). Both Matthew and Luke interpret the miracle as a resurrection story (Matt. 9:18; Luke 8:49–50). As part of a cohesive section of the Gospel (Mark 4:35–6:56) dominated by accounts of Jesus's mighty works, "readers are encouraged to understand that the girl has been raised from the dead. Raising the dead is a far more remarkable feat than awakening someone from illness induced sleep, and fits better with controlling the forces of nature, exorcising demons, and healing the sick" (Hedrick 1993, 221). Jesus's remark that the girl is **not dead but sleeping** (5:39) may be a euphemism for death (Moloney 2002, 110n199), a common biblical trope (e.g., Pss. 7:5 NIV; 13:3; 76:5; 90:5 NIV; Jer. 51:57; Dan. 12:2; John 11:13; 1 Cor. 15:6 NIV).

In recent scholarship, the story of Jairus's daughter and that of the woman with the hemorrhage have both been dominated by the theme of ritual purity and the breaking of taboos. For example, Charles E. Powell (2005, 69) explains: "The issue of impurity is involved in both cases. The woman's condition would make any who touched her impure (Lev. 15:25), and so would touching the dead child's body" (cf. Hurtado 1983, 75; Mann 1986, 284–85; Tolbert 1992, 268; Dewey 1994, 481; Kinukawa 1994, 29–49; Marcus 2000, 357–58, 367–68; Moloney 2002, 107, 110; Donahue and Harrington 2002, 173–74, 180–81). On this interpretation, Jesus is a boundary breaker: rather than shunning the woman and girl because they are unclean, he restores them to purity through his touch and readmits them to society. It is further suggested that Jesus's touching of the young girl's body (5:41) amounted to an improper act, since at twelve, the girl was of marriageable age and supposedly untouchable by anyone except immediate family members or her betrothed (e.g., Moloney 2002, 110).

Such interpretations are suspect, however, since neither story explicitly mentions ritual impurity (A. Levine 2004; cf. Mark 1:40–44; 7:1–20, where matters of purity and impurity are clearly of concern). The woman's problem is that she is sick and poor; Jairus is anxious for his daughter to be healed despite the supposed fact that women "were considered less clean than men and constituted a perennial threat of pollution to men" (Dewey 1994, 481). The majority of interpreters assume that the woman's discharge is vaginal and thus subject to the legislation in Lev. 15. However, Mark does not mention the nature of the hemorrhage; as Amy-Jill Levine (2004, 75) notes: "If the woman had a sore on her leg, her breast, her nose, etc.—and all these places are possible given the semantic range of 'hemorrhage'—then while she would still be ill, she would not be impure."

The biblical, Hellenistic Jewish, and rabbinic texts that are routinely cited in support of the argument that the woman would have been considered chronically unclean and would thus have suffered from social marginalization and religious exclusion refer to menstruants (Lev. 15:19–24) and women with vaginal discharges of blood other than their monthly period (Lev. 15:25–30; cf. Ezek. 36:17; CD 4.12–5.17; 11QT 48.15–17; Josephus, *J.W.* 5.5.6 §227; *Ag. Ap.* 2.8 §§103–4; *m. Niddah*, passim; and *m. Zabim* 4.1). However, the levitical legislation does not single out women as being more prone to ritual impurity than men, since the chapter also deals with men with bodily discharges and seminal emissions (Lev. 15:1–18, 32). Men who sleep with their menstruating wives incur ritual impurity for seven days, and anyone who sits on anything a menstruant (or a woman with a vaginal discharge) has sat or lain upon is considered unclean until evening (15:20–24). But there are actually more limitations on men: the bed of a man with a discharge is unclean, as is anything he sits on, and anyone who touches or sits on them is also rendered unclean, as is anyone whom he touches or spits upon, or who touches a vessel used by him (15:4–12). The cleansing rituals for those healed of such impurities are similar for men and women (15:13–15, 28–30). In Leviticus and the postbiblical documents, ritual uncleanness is not understood to be sinful or dirty, but to be a condition experienced by both men and women, a condition that can be rectified by passage of time and appropriate ceremonies. It does not incur social or religious stigma but does prohibit people from entering the sacred precincts of the tabernacle/temple (as opposed to the synagogue) while they are in an impure state. If the woman's hemorrhage was indeed vaginal, it would prohibit her from worshiping in the temple in Jerusalem, but it would not necessarily limit her socially or prevent her from entering a synagogue (people would not know of her condition unless she informed them). Similarly, Jairus begs Jesus to lay hands on his daughter (5:23), a request that he would hardly make if it were improper for Jesus to touch the girl. Nor is there anything particularly radical about Jesus's willingness to take the hand of the lifeless child (5:41), since touching a dead body is not wrong or unholy but may be a commendable act (cf. Tob. 1:17–19; 2:3–8). The point of the story is not that Jewish boundaries have been transgressed or transcended but that the sick woman is healed and the dead girl has been raised (cf. A. Levine 2004, 77).

Jesus Is Dishonored in His Hometown (6:1–6a)

After such an impressive series of miracles, the story of Jesus's rejection in his hometown (*patris*) is jarring (6:1–6a). Surprisingly, there is no direct mention of Jesus as staying with his family, or even visiting them, although they are referred to in 6:3–4. The beginning of the story echoes 1:21–22, 27: **And it came to pass that on the Sabbath he began to teach in the synagogue, and many who were hearing were astonished, saying, "Where does this man get these things, and what is the wisdom that is given to him, and what are these mighty works that come to pass through his hands?"** (6:2). However, rather than being impressed by Jesus's authoritative teaching (cf. 1:22), the congregation is critical: **"Isn't this man the craftsman, the son of Mary and brother of Jacob and Joses and Judah and Simon? And aren't his sisters here with us?" And they were scandalized by him** (6:4). The term *tektōn*, here translated as "craftsman," is usually rendered as "carpenter," but it has a much broader range of meaning: "from shipbuilder to sculptor, but nearly always implies a person of considerable skill and can even be used of a physician" (Mann 1986, 289; some manuscripts identify Jesus not as "the craftsman" but as "the son of the craftsman"; cf. Matt. 13:55; Metzger 1994, 75–76). Although Paul, a former Pharisee, and several talmudic rabbis are reputed to have supported themselves by means of various occupations (e.g., the elder Hillel as a woodcutter and Shammai as a builder [*b. Šabb.* 31]; R. Joshua as a blacksmith [*b. Ber.* 28a]; R. Jose as a tanner [*b. Šabb.* 49b]; cf. 1 Cor. 4:12; 1 Thess. 2:9; Acts 18:3), there is no reference to Jesus or the Twelve continuing in their previous livelihoods. The townspeople's suspicion of the source of Jesus's wisdom (*sophia*, Mark 6:2) may echo the kind of elitism expressed in Sir. 38:24–34, where the work of diverse tradespeople (including the *tektōn*; 38:27) is respected but seen as an impediment to learning: "The wisdom of the scribe depends on the opportunity of leisure; only the one who has little business can become wise" (38:24). Jesus, from a local artisan-class family known in the village, is an unlikely purveyor of God's wisdom, and the "mighty works" (*dynameis*, lit., "powers") performed by him are known to the townsfolk only by hearsay; as Nineham (1963, 164) puts it: "If he came from a humble family in their midst, he could not come from God."

The reference to Jesus as "son of Mary" (6:3) is sometimes regarded as an implicit questioning of his legitimacy, since a Jewish man was normally designated by his father's name, even after the father's death (Marcus 2000, 374–75; cf. Nineham 1963, 166; cf. Matt. 13:55; Luke 3:23; John 1:45; 6:42). There are, however, exceptions. In the rabbinic literature, the metronymic is often used of men whose mothers are of higher social standing than their fathers (Ilan 1992). Richard Bauckham (1994a, 699–700) has observed that in the Hebrew Bible and some early Jewish literature, mothers are often named when a man has sons by more than one wife (e.g., Gen. 4:19–22; 22:20–24; 36:10–14; 46:10; Exod. 6:15; 1 Chron. 2:2–4, 18–19, 21, 24–26, 46, 48–49;

3:1–9). However, most of these examples presuppose polygyny, a rare practice among first-century Jews, and the fathers are named along with the mothers (Bauckham 1994a, 699–700). Possibly Mark was simply not conversant with Jewish naming customs (Nineham 1963, 166). It is also possible that the evangelist simply did not know the name of Jesus's father or that Mary was better known to the Markan audience (cf. Mark 15:21, where Simon of Cyrene is identified as the father of Alexander and Rufus). Mark 6:3 is the only unambiguous reference in the Gospel to Jesus's mother, but there are two mentions of a Mary (or Marys) who witness his death and burial, identified as the mother of sons with the same names as Jesus's brothers, Jacob (James) and Joses (6:3; 15:40–41, 47)—perhaps indicating that the mother of Jesus followed him to Jerusalem (John 19:25–27; Acts 1:14; cf. Matt. 27:56; Luke 24:10) and was remembered as a disciple (cf. Timothy, whose grandmother and mother are named in 2 Tim. 1:5 because of their faith). Even the slighting reference to her in Mark 3:31–35 evinces a woman anxious about her son's well-being.

Jesus's response to the skepticism of the congregation has become a popular proverb: **"A prophet is not without honor except in his own hometown, and among his relatives and in his household"** (Mark 6:4). The other Gospels all contain versions of this saying (Matt. 13:57; Luke 4:24; John 4:44; cf. *Gos. Thom.* 31; P.Oxy. 1:5), but only in Mark does the saying include "relatives" (*syngeneusin*, 6:4), thus strengthening the theme of Jesus's estrangement from his biological family (3:21, 31–35). Although there are many similar sayings from antiquity (e.g., Plutarch, *Exil.* 604D; Dio Chrysostom, *Or.* 47.6; Philostratus, *Vit. Apoll.*, letter 44), none of the Greco-Roman proverbs refer to the rejection of prophets, a prominent OT theme (2 Chron. 24:19–22; 36:16; Neh. 9:26, 30; Jer. 35:15; Ezek. 2:5; Dan. 9:6, 10; Hosea 9:7; cf. Isa. 53:3; cf. Donahue and Harrington 2002, 185). Another influence may be the Elijah/Elisha typology, since Elijah especially experiences rejection by Israel (1 Kings 19:1–4; cf. 2 Kings 2:23–25). Thus Mark situates Jesus as one of a long line of rejected Israelite prophets. The notice that Jesus **was not able to do any mighty works, except he healed a few sick people by the laying on of hands** (6:5) is shocking after the many miracles, exorcisms, and healings reported in the previous chapters; it underlines the connection between faith and access to the power of God in Mark (cf. 2:5; 4:40; 5:34, 36; 9:23–24; 10:52; 11:22–24); as 6:6a observes, **he marveled on account of their unbelief.**

The Twelve and the Baptist (6:6b–33)

Mark 6:6b–30 is another instance of Markan intercalation, where Jesus's commissioning of the Twelve (6:6b–13, 30) brackets the tale of John the Baptist's execution (6:14–29).

6:6b–13. The proximity of the commissioning (6:6b–13) to the rejection at Nazareth may be deliberately ironic; while Jesus meets with unbelief in his hometown, the disciples' mission of exorcism, healing, preaching, and teaching is successful (6:7, 13, 30). Jesus's instruction that **"if anywhere they do not receive you nor listen to you, leaving there, shake the dust off your feet as a witness against them"** (6:11) is an indirect commentary on the previous pericope, where Jesus's compatriots fail to accept his teaching (6:3). In the rabbinic literature, the act of shaking the dust off one's feet is an act performed by Jews on returning to Israel from unclean (pagan) territory (*m. Ṭohar.* 4.5).

While the disciples are present with Jesus throughout this section, the only other episode where they play a substantial role is 4:35–41, where they are represented as fearful and without faith. Here, however, they begin to fulfill the mandate of 3:14–15, where

the Twelve are authorized to preach and cast out demons. The instructions in 6:8–11 probably reflect the missionary practice of the Markan church; they resemble accounts of itinerant Cynic and Pythagorean philosophers (e.g., *Ep. Diog.* 7; Musonius Rufus, *On Clothing and Shelter* 19) and traveling Essenes. Unlike the Cynics, who wear a double cloak and carry a staff and provision bag, Jesus orders the Twelve **not to take anything with them on the way except only a staff, no bread, no bag, no money in their belts, but to wear sandals, and not to put on two tunics.** Like traveling Essenes, it is assumed that Jesus's disciples will be received into the houses of fellow sectarians, who will share their belongings with them (Mark 6:10a; cf. Acts 9:19b; 10:6, 48b; 18:1–3; 20:6–12; 21:4, 7–8, 16; *Did.* 11.1–12; Josephus, *J.W.* 2.8.4 §§124–27). The Markan practice is less stringent than that reflected in Q (Luke 9:3; Matt. 10:10; par. Luke 10:4), where carrying a staff and wearing sandals are forbidden, but still reflects a demand for trust in God and an expectation of hospitality among believers (Boring 2006, 175). The Twelve are sent out **two by two** (6:7), like early Christian missionary pairs (e.g., Peter and John, Paul and Barnabas, Paul and Silas, Priscilla and Aquila, Andronicus and Julia, Titus and "our brother"; Acts 3:1–11; 8:14–25; 13:42; 15:12, 39–40; 17:15; 18:18–19, 24–26; Rom. 16:3, 7; 2 Cor. 12:18; cf. 1 Cor. 9:5). The practice of anointing the sick with oil (Mark 6:13) is not associated with Jesus in the Gospel but probably reflects early Christian practice (James 5:14). This brief narrative thus inaugurates the missionaries' proclamation of God's reign as they go throughout the world (Mark 13:10; 14:9).

6:14–29. The filling in this Markan sandwich, the account of the execution of John the Baptist (6:14–29), seems to have little to do with the mission of the Twelve, or with Jesus, apart from the note that Herod had heard about Jesus, and that he mistook him for John the Baptist, whom he had executed, as risen from the dead (6:14; cf. 9:11–13). Some scholars see the insertion of this lengthy tale between the sending and return of the disciples merely as a device to mark the passage of time (e.g., Pesch 1976–77, 1:344; Hooker 1991, 158). However, a more-recent trend in scholarship is to seek thematic links between the frame and the insertion, providing a poignant contrast between the death of John, reported by his disciples, and the success of the Twelve, who report back to Jesus about **everything they did and taught** on their mission (6:30).

The story is unusual in that it focuses on characters other than Jesus—Herod Antipas, his wife, Herodias, and her daughter. Although the death of John is at issue, the prophet remains offstage. The story is also unique in that it is the only story where Mark portrays female characters unsympathetically. Herodias and her daughter are clearly the main actors in the plot against John; the king and the prophet are both the victims of manipulation by vengeful women. Both Matthew (14:1–12) and Luke (3:19–20) abbreviate the tale and downplay Herodias's role in the drama.

The historical inaccuracies in this passage are notorious. Herod Antipas was a tetrarch, not a king, and Herodias's first husband was not Philip (6:17) but another son of Herod the Great (called Herod II and Herod Boethus; see Gillman 2003, 16). Herodias and her first husband had a daughter named Salome, who is usually identified with the unnamed girl in the Markan tale (although there are variant readings that name her "Herodias his daughter," implying that she was Antipas's daughter, named after her mother; see Metzger 1994, 77). It was Salome, not Herodias, who married her half-uncle Philip. Antipas

Josephus on the Death of John the Baptist

"But to some of the Jews the destruction of Herod's army seemed to be divine vengeance, and certainly a just vengeance, for his treatment of John, surnamed the Baptist. For Herod had put him to death, though he was a good man and had exhorted the Jews to lead righteous lives, to practice justice toward their fellows and piety toward God, and so doing to join in baptism. In his view this was a necessary preliminary if baptism was to be acceptable to God. They must not employ it to gain pardon for whatever sins they committed, but as a consecration of the body[,] implying that the soul was already thoroughly cleansed by right behavior. When others too joined the crowds about him, because they were aroused to the highest degree by his sermons, Herod became alarmed. Eloquence that had so great an effect on [hu]mankind might lead to some form of sedition, for it looked as if they would be guided by John in everything they did. Herod decided therefore that it would be much better to strike first and be rid of him before his work led to an uprising, than to wait for an upheaval, get involved in a difficult situation, and see his mistake. Though John, because of Herod's suspicions, was brought in chains to Machaerus, the stronghold that we have previously mentioned, and there put to death, yet the verdict of the Jews was that the destruction visited upon Herod's army was a vindication of John, since God saw fit to inflict such a blow on Herod." (Ant. 18.5.2 §§116–19, trans. Feldman 1965)

divorced his first wife, a Nabatean princess, in favor of Herodias, and contrary to Jewish law, Herodias divorced her first husband in order to marry his half-brother, her own half-uncle (see Gillman 2003, 26). While Josephus shared the Baptist's disdain for Herodias's divorce and remarriage to her husband's living half-brother as a violation of "the ways of our fathers" (*Ant*. 18.5.4 §§135–36; cf. Mark 6:18), the Gospel's account of Antipas's reason for executing John differs from the historian's account. Josephus claims that Herod feared that John had too much influence over the people and that he might incite sedition, so he had the prophet executed at his fortress at Machaerus.

According to Mark, Herod imprisoned John in order to protect him from his wife's murderous anger over the prophet's accusation that their marriage was contrary to the law (Lev. 18:16), but Herod himself **feared John, knowing him to be a just and holy man, and he protected him, and hearing him he was very uncertain, and he was hearing him joyfully** (6:20). Antipas's pleasure in the daughter's dance at his birthday feast prompts him to offer her whatever she wants, up to half his kingdom (6:22). The daughter consults her mother; Herodias advises her to ask for the head of John; the daughter makes the request for John's head **on a dish**, and Herod is bound by his promise: **And becoming deeply grieved, the king, because of the vows and the guests, did not want to refuse her. And immediately the king, sending an executioner, gave orders to bring his head. And having left, he beheaded him in prison. And he brought his head on a dish and gave it to the girl, and the girl gave it to her mother** (6:26–28).

Josephus's explanation appears more historically plausible. Herod is more likely to have acted preemptively against John to forestall insurrection than to imprison the prophet for his own protection and then have him beheaded on a whim. However, some scholars hold that it is not necessary to choose between the accounts in Mark and Josephus: "The Christians chose to emphasize the moral charges that he brought against the ruler, whereas Josephus stressed the political fears that he aroused in Herod" (Feldman 1965, 38; cf. Gillman 2003, 82). Gillman argues that the actions attributed to Herodias and her daughter are consistent with the way in which aristocratic Roman women exercised power (2003, 91–93). Kathleen Corley, in contrast, regards the entire episode as fiction, noting that to dance before a roomful of men would be considered extremely shameful for an upper-class young woman (cf. Esther 1:10–12): "The scene for Herod's party is stock and stereotypical for the first century: an official performs an execution in the context of a banquet at the request of a courtesan" (Corley 1993, 94). Seneca the Elder (*Declamations* 9.2) records a similar scene: at a banquet, a prostitute asks the proconsul Flaminius for the favor of seeing a man beheaded; he obliges by sending for an executioner, who decapitates a convicted criminal (cf. Livy, *Hist*. 39.42–43; Cicero, *On Old Age* 42; Valerius Maximus, *Fact*. 2.9.3, cited by Corley 1993, 42n83). Corley (1993, 37) contrasts Herod's behavior with Cicero's description

The Yorck Project, Wikimedia Commons

Figure 6. *The Feast of Herod*, by Lucas Cranach the Elder, 1531.

of the lengths taken by the noble Philodamus to protect his virgin daughter from the advances of the governor Gaius Verres, who tries to manipulate the father into summoning the girl to join them at a dinner party so that he can violate her; the father offers to die rather than exposing his daughter to such abuse (cf. Cicero, *Against Verres* 2.1.26, 66–67). This criticism holds whether or not the daughter's dance was meant to be construed as innocent or erotic (J. Anderson 1992, 121–27; Gillman 2003, 56–58). Excavations of the fortress at Machaerus have revealed adjacent dining rooms for men and women (Freyne 1988, 37n6, citing Schwank 1983; cf. Mark 6:24–25), indicating that the Herods observed the Greek custom of men and women dining separately; for a girl of Hasmonean descent to appear in the men's space at all would have been an impropriety.

Mark's narrative echoes two biblical stories where women, deceit, banqueting, and death are connected (see J. Anderson 1992, 127–29; Gillman 2003, 85–88). The book of Esther is directly cited in Herod's offer to give the girl up to half his kingdom (6:23), the same promise made by Ahasuerus to his young queen (Esther 5:3, 6–7; 7:2–3). In the LXX, Esther and the other candidates for the king's harem are called *korasia*, the same word used to describe the dancing daughter (Mark 6:22, 28). Esther uses a banquet as a pretext for the accusation that prompts the king to order Haman's execution (Esther 7:1–10; *Midr. Esther* 1.19–21 even adds the head-on-a-platter motif). In the book of Judith, the heroine decapitates the besotted and intoxicated Holofernes at a banquet (Jdt. 12:10–13:10a) and brings it back to Bethulia, where she removes it from her food bag and proudly displays it to the men of the city (13:15). There are also intertextual echoes of Jezebel's persecution of Elijah (1 Kings 19–21; 2 Kings 9; cf. J. Anderson 1992, 129–30; Gillman 2003, 84–85). As Ahab is manipulated into killing the innocent Naboth by Jezebel, Herodias tricks Herod into ordering John's execution. Elijah is closely identified with John the Baptist in Mark (6:14–15; 9:11–13), so the implicit Jezebel/Herodias typology seems relevant (cf. Humphries-Brooks 2004, 152).

The story of the death of John suggests further thematic linkages between Mark 6:14–29 and its frame (6:7–13, 30): John's fate will be shared by Jesus and the disciples, all of whom will be "handed over" to hostile and murderous authorities (1:14; 3:19; 9:31; 10:33; 13:9, 11–12; 14:10–11, 18, 21, 41–44; 15:1, 10, 15; cf. Boring 2006, 178; Moloney 2002, 128). A further link can be made between Mark 6:7–30 and the adjacent story of the rejection at Nazareth. John, like Jesus, is a prophet "without honor," who meets with a violent fate. Jesus's directions to the Twelve to leave places where they are not received with hospitality and shake the dust from their feet might be a lifesaving measure for missionaries in the Markan audience.

6:30–33. The transitional verses in Mark 6:30–33 contrast with the brief account of John the Baptist's disciples' burying him in 6:29. Jesus's disciples (called "apostles" in 6:30, the only undisputed usage of this term in the Gospel) return to their master and report to him **everything they had done and taught.** The busy scene of people coming and going, so that the missionaries don't even have time to eat (6:31; cf. 3:20), attests to the success of their mission. Jesus's instruction to rest with him **in a solitary place** (lit., "a desert place") echoes previous instances of withdrawal to escape the crowds (1:35, 45; 4:1; cf. 1:12–13; 3:7–10, 20); this time, however, the disciples are expressly invited along after their missionary tour. The boat journey they take to find **a deserted place, by themselves** is not "to the other side," implying that they remain on the Jewish side of the lake (6:32). Once again the crowds pursue them: **And they saw them leaving and many people knew it and on foot from all the towns running together there, they went before them** (1:32–33, 45; 2:2, 4, 13; 3:7, 9–10, 13; 4:1; 5:21, 24, 27).

The Feeding of the Five Thousand (6:34–44)

The next major narrative, the feeding of the five thousand (6:34–44), stands in an inverted typological relationship to Herod's banquet:

Herod's guests form . . . groups (6:21), as do Jesus's (6:39–40), and only men attend both meals (6:21–22, 44). Both Jesus and Herod send out emissaries (6:7, 17, 27, 30), but for entirely different tasks. Furthermore, both utilize serving dishes, but again for different purposes (6:28, 43). Thus, the meals of Jesus and Herod serve as bold contrasts. (Corley 1993, 94; cf. Fowler 1981, 85–86, 199–227)

In Mark, this story is one of two where Jesus provides food for an astonishingly large crowd (cf. 8:1–10). The first feeding takes place in Jewish territory, the second in the gentile region of the Decapolis (cf. 7:31). The Jewishness of the first feeding is underlined by the exodus imagery that underlies the narrative. Like Moses, Jesus has compassion on the crowd because they are like sheep without a shepherd (cf. Num. 27:17). The phrase from Torah recalls the story of the appointment of Joshua (in Greek, *Iēsous*) as Moses's successor: someone "who shall go out before them and come in before them, . . . and at his word they shall go out, and at his word they shall come in, both he and all the Israelites with him, the whole congregation" (Num. 27:17a, 21b). The shepherd imagery is enhanced by the detail in Mark 6:39 that the people were instructed to recline on the green grass. For members of the audience familiar with the Palestinian climate, the reference to greenery situates the incident in the rainy season, October to early May. More than simply local color, this vivid detail evokes the "green pastures" of Ps. 23 and the blooming wilderness in the "way of the LORD," the new exodus (Isa. 35:1; 40:3; 51:3; Boring 2006, 186); in the context of a feeding miracle, it recalls the creation of the "green plants" for food in Genesis (1:30; 9:3). Most prominently, the provision of bread for a hungry crowd in the desert (Mark 6:35) echoes Exod. 16; as the Israelites grumble to Moses and Aaron over lack of food (16:2–3), so the disciples urge Jesus to send the people away to buy something to eat and challenge him when he tells them to feed the crowd themselves: "Shall we leave and buy two hundred denarii worth of bread and give it to them to eat?" (Mark 6:36–37). In both stories, two kinds of food (manna and quails, bread and fish) are provided, the people's hunger is satisfied, and there is extra left over (Exod. 16:18; Mark 6:42–43). The detail that five thousand men (*andres*) were fed does not necessarily mean that only males were present, but echoes reckonings of the congregation of Israel in the wilderness (Exod. 12:37; Num. 11:21; cf. Donahue and Harrington 2002, 207). The feeding takes place in the context of Jesus's *teaching* (6:34b), recalling the scriptural use of bread as a symbol of God's wisdom/word (e.g., Deut. 8:3; Job 23:12; Prov. 9:5; Sir. 15:3; cf. Philo, *Names* 44 §§259–60). The term used for "basket" in Mark 6:43 is *kophinos*, mentioned by the satirist Juvenal (*Sat.* 3.14; 6.452) as being characteristically used by poor Jews in Rome (cf. Mark 8:8, where the baskets are called *spyrides*). The number of baskets of fragments left over is twelve, possibly contrasting the twelve tribes of Israel and the seven (or seventy) nations of the world (Donahue and Harrington 2002, 207; cf. Mark 8:8; *Gen. Rab.* 37).

The feeding narratives also resonate with the Elijah-Elisha typology that underlies Mark's portrayal of Jesus. When the widow of Zarephath shares her meager bread and water with Elijah during a famine, God miraculously multiplies the remaining flour and bread until the rains return (1 Kings 17:7–16; cf. 2 Kings 4:1–7). Elisha multiplies twenty loaves of barley bread to satisfy

Stephen von Wyrick

Figure 7. Bread and fish mosaic before the altar in the church at Tabgha commemorating Jesus's feeding of the five thousand. This church to the west of Capernaum is on the opposite side of the Sea of Galilee from where Mark 6:30–44 places the feeding. This is likely due to an accommodation to later pilgrimage needs.

the hunger of a hundred men (LXX: *andrōn*), with some left over (2 Kings 4:42–44). At another level, the feedings anticipate the eschatological banquet, where "the LORD of hosts will make for all peoples a feast of rich food, a feast of well-aged wines, of rich food filled with marrow, of well-aged wines strained clear" (Isa. 25:6; cf. *1 En.* 62.12–16; *2 Bar.* 29.1–8); compare Mark 14:25, where the Last Supper is interpreted as foreshadowing a banquet in the realm of God (see Priest 1992; D. Casey 2002). The account of the distribution of the bread (6:41) is dense with liturgical language—"took," "gave thanks," "broke," and "gave" (Mann 1986, 300; cf. 8:6; Matt. 14:19; 15:36; 26:26; Luke 9:16; 22:19; John 6:11; 1 Cor. 11:23–24)—that would remind the Markan audience of their own sacred meals (Mark 14:22).

Jesus Walks upon the Sea (6:45–52)

The last major pericope in this section, Mark's second sea miracle (6:45–52), mirrors the first (4:35–41). Jesus "forces" (*ēnankasen*) the disciples to embark for Bethsaida, a gentile town at the northeast corner of the lake, and sends the crowd away while he retires to a mountaintop to pray (6:45–46), reflecting his pattern of seeking solitude after a period of intense activity (cf. 1:12–13, 35; 6:31). Commentators often puzzle over the strength of the verb used to describe Jesus's dismissal of the disciples; perhaps the motif of Jesus's *compelling* them to leave relates to the theme of faith versus fear that unites the two sea miracles. Although the disciples have been commissioned by Jesus to share in his ministry and have successfully done so on their own (6:7–13, 30), and have seen and participated in a series of powerful miracles (5:1, 37; 6:41), they are just as terrified by their second experience of danger at sea as they were the first time. Like Jesus's challenge to the disciples to give the hungry crowd something to eat (6:37), his sending them off challenges them to rely on divine power rather than his presence.

The second voyage, like the first, begins in the evening (6:47). Jesus, in prayer on the mountain, sees that the disciples **were rowing with difficulty, for the wind was against them, and around the fourth watch of the night he** came to them, **walking on the sea, and he wanted to pass by them** (6:48). The time lag between "evening" (*opsias*) and "the fourth watch" (the last of the four Roman night watches, ending at dawn), and also Jesus's plan (*ēthelen*) to pass the disciples by—both indicate that this is a test of their faith: Jesus is deliberately ignoring them. Many commentators connect the scene of Jesus treading the waves with the scriptural theme of God's power over the wind and the sea (e.g., Donahue and Harrington 2002, 213; Boring 2006, 189), especially passages where God is said to make a path through the waters (Job 9:8; Ps. 77:19; Isa. 43:16; for Greco-Roman parallels, see Boring 1995, 98–100; MacDonald 2000, 148–53). In view of the Elijah-Elisha typology evident throughout this section, the parting of the Jordan by both prophets may also be in view (2 Kings 2:8, 14). Similarly, the combination of the term "to pass by" (*parelthein*) with Jesus's greeting *egō eimi* ("it is I," 6:50) is often interpreted as indicating an epiphany: Jesus's "passing by" the disciples is compared to the glory of YHWH "passing by" Moses (Exod. 33:17–34:8) or Elijah (cf. 1 Kings 19:11–13); the *egō eimi* is connected with God's self-disclosure at Sinai (Exod. 3:13–15 LXX: *egō eimi ho ōn*; e.g., Marcus 2000, 430–32; Moloney 2002, 134; Boring 2006, 190). However, as with the first sea miracle, it is important not to project later doctrines about the divinity of Christ onto Mark's Jesus, who is shown as praying to God at the beginning of the story (6:46), and not as divine himself.

Instead of recognizing their master and emulating his supreme confidence in God, they mistake him for a phantom (*phantasma*), are once again terrified, and are astonished when the wind ceases as he approaches the boat (6:49–51; cf. 4:41). Jesus's rebuke—**"Take courage, it is I—don't be afraid"** (6:50)—echoes the earlier story: **"Why are you so cowardly? Have you no faith?"** (4:40). This time the evangelist explains the reason for the disciples' fearfulness: **they did not understand about the loaves, but their hearts were hardened** (6:52). Reference to hard-heartedness has already appeared in the description of the Pharisees who conspire against Jesus (3:4–6). This is a state of stubborn resistance to divine revelation as epitomized by Pharaoh in the plague narratives (Exod. 7:13–14, 22; 8:15, 19, 32; 9:7, 12, 34–35; 10:1, 20, 27; 11:10; 14:8; cf. Donahue and Harrington 2002, 214); here the disciples are in danger of being as oblivious to God as their opponents are. Perhaps what the disciples misunderstand about the miracle of the loaves is that just as *they* have the power to feed the crowd (6:37), *they* would have as much power over the elements as Jesus if only they shared his faith in God's power to provide for and rescue them. The cowardice of the disciples is underlined by the fact that in ancient Greco-Roman tradition, phantoms (ghosts of the dead) are either stopped short or destroyed by bodies of water; the audience would judge that the disciples are not only fearful but also rather foolish (see Combs 2008). The ability to walk on the sea is characteristic of divine men and heroes—figures like Jesus—not of ghosts (see Collins 1994).

Conclusion (6:53–56)

The section concludes with a Markan summary (6:53–56). Rather than reaching their original destination of gentile Bethsaida, they land at Gennesaret, still in Jewish territory. People throughout the region pursue Jesus for healing, whether in the towns or in the countryside. The summary ends with the earliest reference to people touching **the fringe of his garment** for healing (6:56; cf. 5:27–28). The word *kraspedon* ("fringe" or "hem") probably refers to the tassels (LXX: *kraspeda*) worn by Jewish men to remind them of God's commandments (Num. 15:38–39; Deut. 22:12; as noted by Marcus 2000, 437). The weakness of the disciples' faith contrasts with the enthusiastic response of the crowds at Gennesaret, who have not witnessed any of Jesus's miracles but have heard of his miraculous deeds and have faith that they can be healed simply by touching his cloak (cf. 5:27–29).

Theological Issues

This section is dominated by miracle stories, which invite theological reflection not just about the role of the miraculous in the Gospel, but also about the identity of Jesus, the role of faith, the situation of the Markan church, and Christian ethics. At one level these vivid and highly dramatic narratives were no doubt meant to entertain as well as to edify Mark's first-century audience. The exorcism of a violent demoniac, the beheading of John the Baptist at the behest of a dancing girl, miracles that surpass those of the ancient prophets—all are the stuff that biblical epics are made of and that are beyond the experience of most contemporary readers. In the nineteenth and early twentieth centuries, rationalizing explanations of miracles like feeding narratives were popular, such as the suggestion that the numbers of people fed may have been exaggerated, or that the meal was sacramental, and so each person received only a small piece of bread (see Nineham 1963, 179).

Some contemporary interpreters continue to question whether the feedings are meant to be interpreted supernaturally. For example, in his political interpretation of Mark, Ched Myers (1988, 206) argues that the feeding of the five thousand reports nothing supernatural; the true miracle is in the triumph of an economics of sharing in community over the ethos of autonomous consumption in an impersonal marketplace. Megan McKenna (1994, 15–16) gives the story a feminist homiletical twist, speculating that the women in the crowd brought food along with them and shared the surplus with those around them, perhaps encouraged by Jesus's sharing of his own provisions. However, in the context of 4:36–6:56, with its exorcisms, healings, and demonstrations of divine power over the wind and the sea, it is implausible to argue that the feedings can or should be read purely naturalistically. For the evangelist, faith in God has the power to work miracles (9:23–24; 11:22–23). At another level, the feedings and other miracle stories convey a christological message: Jesus is a prophet with powers that echo and surpass those of the prophets of old, a holy man with an unprecedented relationship with God. The feeding stories, especially, convey an ethical message: Mark's Jesus is concerned about both the physical and spiritual hunger of the shepherdless flock (6:34), whom he both teaches *and* feeds. Jesus's injunction "*You* give them something to eat" (6:37) extends beyond the disciples to Christians of today, an enduring challenge to contemporary people of faith to reach out to both the spiritually and physically hungry.

Another level of theological purpose inherent in these tales pertains to Mark's ecclesiology or "doctrine of the church." If, as suggested above, the boat symbolizes the church of the evangelist's time, the key to the stories in this section is in the two boat narratives that bracket it. Like the church, the boat separates the disciples from the crowds and protects them from danger. In the boat, as in the church, the community encounters Jesus, who teaches, encourages, and exhorts them to have faith. The boat/church is "a locus of salvation, where Mark's community can trust in God to keep the vessel afloat" (Wheller 2003, 114). Many early Christian writers understood these stories this way; thus Origen of Alexandria wrote:

> The Savior thus compelled the disciples to enter into the boat of testing and to go before him to the other side, so to learn victoriously to pass through difficulties. But when they got in the middle of the sea, and of the waves in the temptation, and of the contrary winds which prevented them from going away to the other side, they were not able, struggling as they were, to overcome the waves and the contrary wind and reach the other side without Jesus. In this way the Word, taking compassion on those who had done all that was in their power to reach the other side, came to them walking upon the sea, which for him had no waves or wind. (*Comm. Matt.* 11.5, quoted in Oden and Hall 1998, 88–89)

In the fourth century AD, the Roman Christian poet Prudentius (*Hymn* 6, quoted in Oden and Hall 1998, 90) recognized the theological focus of the boat narratives:

> O mighty is the power of God,
> The power that all things did create,
> That calmed the waters of the sea
> When Christ upon its surface walked,
> So that in treading on the waves,
> He moved dry-shod across the deep,
> Nor ever did He wet his soles
> As light He skimmed the surging flood.

Although the boat stories end on a reassuring note—Jesus calms the wind and the waves—in both instances the disciples are rebuked for their fearfulness and lack of understanding. At the very center of the section, Jesus is rejected by his own country, kin, and family; their question "From whence did this man get all this?" (6:2b) is echoed by the disciples (4:41; 6:52; cf. 6:37), even after they are commissioned to share in his ministry. The source of Jesus's wisdom and miraculous power is his faith in God, in contrast to the shaky faith of the disciples. Throughout the Gospel, Jesus repeatedly urges the disciples to embrace the steadfast and powerful faith in God modeled by him (e.g., 4:40; 9:18–19, 23–24; 11:22). This is a call that pertains not only to the persecuted members of the Markan community (13:9–13; cf. 4:17); it also reminds Christians today that they have access to the same source of divine empowerment as Jesus, whatever challenges they encounter. From a Christian perspective, God is ever present, yet it is within the context of community, the ancient "ship of the church," that faith is fostered and supported.

Mark 7:1–23

Interlude: Teaching on Ritual and Moral Purity

Introductory Matters

This lengthy interlude is cast in the form of a controversy between **the Pharisees and certain scribes from Jerusalem** and Jesus over the dining habits of **some of his disciples** (7:1–2). Within the structure of the Gospel, it forms a transition between two main sections: 4:35–6:56, sandwiched between two sea miracles, and 7:24–9:29, bounded by two exorcisms of gentile children. There are some similarities between this section and the discourse in parables (4:1–34): both invoke a prophecy of Isaiah (Mark 4:12; 7:6b–7); both distinguish between Jesus's teaching to the crowds and his private teaching to the disciples (4:11; 7:17); in both, Jesus rebukes the disciples for their lack of understanding (4:13; 7:18); and both discourses describe Jesus's teaching as parabolic (4:2, 10, 13, 33–34; 7:17). Some ancient manuscripts heighten the similarity between the two passages by adding the exhortation "If anyone has ears to hear, let them hear" between 7:15 and 17 (cf. Mark 4:9; 7:14; Metzger 1994, 81).

Gregory Salyer (1993) has argued that Mark 7:1–23 can be analyzed rhetorically as an elaborated *chreia*. In Greco-Roman rhetoric, a *chreia* is "a concise statement or action attributed with aptness to some specified character or to something analogous to a character" (Theon, *Progymnasmata* 3.2–3, ed. Butts 1986b). There are three basic kinds of *chreiai*: saying, action, and mixed (3.22–23). A saying-*chreia* makes a point with words and no action: for example, "Diogenes the philosopher, on being asked by someone how he could become famous, responded, 'By thinking as little as possible about fame'" (3.25–26). An action-*chreia* reveals a character's thoughts through an action, rather than through words: for example, "Diogenes the Cynic philosopher, on seeing a boy eating delicacies, struck the pedagogue with his staff" (3.74–75). A mixed-*chreia* involves both speech and action: for example, "A Laconian [i.e., Spartan], when someone asked him where the Lacedaemonians [i.e., Spartans] have the boundaries of their land, showed his spear" (3.82–83). Here the question is the saying, and the brandishing of the weapon is the action (see Butts 1986a, 132–33). Mark, like the other evangelists, was a Greek writer who frequently cast stories about Jesus in *chreia* form. For example, Mark 2:16–17 is a saying-*chreia*:

> And it happened that he reclined at table in his house, and many toll collectors and sinners sat together with Jesus and his disciples. And the scribes of the Pharisees, seeing that he eats with the sinners and toll collectors, said to his disciples, "Why does he eat with toll collectors and sinners?" And hearing them, Jesus says to them, "The strong do not have need of a doctor, but the sick do; I haven't come to call righteous people but sinners!"

Mark 2:13–14 is a mixed-*chreia*:

> And passing by he saw Levi, son of Alphaeus, sitting by the toll office, and he says to him, "Follow me!" And having risen up, he followed him.

James R. Butts (1986a, 133–37) has gathered many other examples of Gospel *chreiai*.

In Salyer's analysis, Mark 7:1–23 is constructed around the saying (*chreia*) in vv. 6b–7, a quotation of Isa. 29:13: "as it is written, 'This people honors me with their lips, but their heart they take away from me; in vain they are devout, teaching as doctrines human instructions.'" This saying is expanded through the addition of dialogue and elaborated with arguments for the constituent parts of the *chreia* (Salyer 1993, 142). The passage as a whole is thus a complex rhetorical composition, designed to challenge the Pharisees' traditions (cf. Salyer 1993, 144–45, for the fuller version of the outline I've summarized below):

Narrative introduction (7:1–2): The Pharisees see that some disciples eat with unwashed hands.

Digression (7:3–4): Explanation of Pharisaic customs regarding ritual purity.

Question (seeking rationale) (7:5): The Pharisees ask Jesus why his disciples eat with unwashed hands.

Argument (replying to the question) (7:6–16).

    Praise (7:6a): Isaiah was right.

    Chreia (7:6b–7): Quotation of Isa. 29:13.

    Paraphrase of *chreia* (7:8): Contrast between commandments of God and human traditions.

Citations of ancient authority (7:9–10): Commandments of God transmitted through Moses.

Example (7:11–12): Pharisaic custom of Korban.

Paraphrase (7:13): The Pharisees nullify the commandments of God by invoking Korban.

Contrary as counterthesis (7:14–16): Contrast between what goes into a person and what comes out of a person. Only the latter confers impurity.

Scene/setting change: Amplification of the counterthesis (7:17–22).

Interrogation (7:17): The disciples ask Jesus about the "parable."

Restatement of first part of the counterthesis as an interrogation (7:18): Nothing that enters a person from outside can make them unclean.

Rationale (7:19a): Contrast between the heart and the stomach.

Inference (7:19b): Jesus thus declares all foods clean.

Restatement of second part of counterthesis (7:20): What comes out of a person makes them unclean.

Rationale (7:21–22): Impure thoughts and actions come from the heart.

Conclusion (7:23): Impure thoughts and actions confer impurity.

On this interpretation, Mark 7:1–23 is a piece of epideictic rhetoric—rhetoric that offers praise or blame and is oriented toward the present—meant to censure the Pharisees and scribes: "They are to be blamed for erecting a tradition around the law that nullifies the law itself" (Salyer 1993, 146).

While *chreiai* conveyed traditional, time-honored wisdom and values, they often portrayed the speaker as reversing the expectations or challenging the views of the questioner, as well as of the audience (Butts 1986a, 133). This is frequently the case in Mark: in the examples cited above, Jesus challenges the assumption that a prophet should not dine with toll collectors and sinners (2:16–17), and even calls one to be his disciple (2:13–14). Mark's elaborated *chreia* in 7:1–23 conveys the values of Jesus by contradicting his opponents' assumptions about ritual purity and the role of tradition.

Although the complex construction of this section is summarized well by Salyer's outline, it contains many features that require further comment. The discourse falls naturally into three main parts, corresponding to three different audiences at the level of second-degree narrative:

1. Jesus's opponents (7:1–13)
2. The crowd (7:14–16)
3. The disciples (7:17–23)

Although the argument begins with a question about eating with unwashed hands (7:5), Jesus's lengthy answer in 7:6–13 does not relate directly either to the disciples' behavior or to the issue of ritual purity. Rather, Jesus's defense of the disciples is grounded in the distinction between the commandment of God and human tradition (7:9–13); he directly addresses the opponents' question only in his address to the crowd (7:14–16) and to the disciples (7:17–23).

Tracing the Narrative Flow

Jesus's Opponents (7:1–13)

Jesus's opponents in 7:1–13 are identified as **Pharisees and certain scribes coming from Jerusalem** (7:1, 5), two groups already identified as hostile to Jesus (2:6, 16, 24; 3:6, 22). The practice of eating with **unclean hands** is attributed to **some disciples** (7:2), leaving open the possibility that other members of Jesus's circle, including Jesus himself, did wash before eating (cf. 2:15–17, where Jesus's choice of dining partners, but not his adherence to tradition, is questioned by "scribes of the Pharisees"). The evangelist includes a lengthy explanation to the implied reader, who is assumed to be unfamiliar with Pharisaic rites, about the custom of purifying the hands before meals; eating with "common hands" (*koinais chersin*) means that the hands are **unwashed** (*aniptois*, 7:2). According to v. 3, the Pharisees **and all the Jews** eat only after washing their hands **to the wrist** (*pygmē*, lit., "with the fist"), an assertion repeated in v. 4a: **coming from the marketplace unless they wash** (lit., "baptize" or "immerse") **themselves they do not eat.** The assertion that "all the Jews" follow Pharisaic practice is probably an overgeneralization; it is unlikely that other sectarian groups like the Sadducees, or the majority population of Jewish peasants, artisans, and slaves—especially those in Diaspora—would have been so observant (cf. Boring 2006, 199). More accurately, the evangelist mentions that this hand-washing ritual belongs to **the tradition of the elders** (v. 3): it is not required in the written Torah, where ritual washing is required only of priests (Exod. 30:17–21). The Pharisees viewed Israel as "a kingdom of priests" (Exod. 19:6) and voluntarily followed the parts of the law required only of priests. The "tradition of the elders" refers to a system of rules and practices over and above the written law, meant to "build a fence around Torah," to ensure that the divine law would not be broken (*m. ʾAbot* 1.1). The mishnaic tractate *Yadayim* ("Hands") codifies the kinds of practices at issue here: **purification of cups and pitchers and bronze vessels [and pallets]** (Mark 7:4b). The listing of these practices as characteristic of "all the Jews"

**Mark 7:1–23
in the Narrative Flow**

Prologue: John and Jesus (1:1–13)

Transition: Summary of the good news (1:14–15)

Act 1: Jesus in Galilee (1:16–3:35)

Interlude: Teaching in parables (4:1–34)

Act 2: Beyond Galilee (4:35–6:56)

▶ Interlude: Teaching on ritual and moral purity (7:1–23)

Jesus's opponents (7:1–13)

The crowd (7:14–16)

The disciples (7:17–23)

---

does more than simply explain them to gentile readers; it also portrays them as strange and excessive, possibly in order to discourage interest in Jewish observances among the Markan community.

Jesus's answer to his opponents is presented in two parts (7:6–8, 9–13), neither of which directly addresses the topic of the purification of the hands. Rather, Jesus applies the prophecy of Isa. 29:13 directly to the Pharisees and scribes, whom he accuses of being **hypocrites** ("play-actors"): "'**This people honors me with their lips, but their heart they take away from me; in vain they are devout, teaching as doctrines human instructions**'" (7:6–7). To drive home the point, the prophecy is paraphrased in the second-person plural in the next verse: "**Leaving the commandment of God, you observe human tradition**" (7:8). The second part of the answer is signaled by the formula **and he said** (7:9a). As proof of the assertion that his opponents reject God's commandments in favor of human tradition (7:9b), he contrasts the strict requirements of Torah ("Moses") to honor parents (Exod. 20:12//Deut. 5:16; Exod. 21:17; Lev. 20:9) with the practice of declaring something dedicated to God ("*korban*, that is, an offering"; 7:11b) in order to evade the duty to support one's parents (7:12). As Boring (2006, 200–201) reports, "The details of this presumed arrangement are vague. No such practice in Jesus's day is known from Jewish sources, and it is likely that the purported arrangement is a matter of Christian polemics." The Mishnah (*Ned*. 9.1–2; 5.6; ca. AD 200) stipulates that the duty to support one's parents supersedes even the scripturally mandated irrevocability of a vow (Num. 30:2–4). The answer concludes with another paraphrase of Mark 7:8 (cf. v. 9) and a generalizing dismissal of the opponents' practice: "**You annul the word of God with the tradition that you hand down; and you do many similar things**" (7:13; here, the phrase "word of God" refers to the commandments of Torah).

The Crowd (7:14–16)

Jesus's address to the crowd (7:14–16) begins with an echo of the wording of the parables discourse (4:3, 9, 23, 24): "**Listen to me, all of you, and understand**" (7:14b). As with 7:6–13, the teaching is not directly related to the issue of hand washing: "**There is nothing outside the person entering into them that is able to pollute them, but that which comes out of the person is that which pollutes the person**" (7:15). This *chreia* could be taken to refer back to the ritual purification neglected by the disciples (7:2)—their failure to wash before eating is not defiling—but it seems to abrogate the very law, which includes the dietary laws of Torah (Lev. 11; Deut. 14), that Jesus upholds in his reply to the scribes and Pharisees.

The Disciples (7:17–23)

Perhaps this is the reason for the disciples' incomprehension of the "parable" in the scene of private teaching that follows (7:17–23). Again, Jesus's impatient reply echoes the similar scene in Mark 4:10–13: **"How can you be so uncomprehending?"** (7:18a). By way of explanation, Jesus paraphrases and elaborates on the *chreia*: **what enters a person** (food) does not enter **the heart** (the governing center of the human; see Walker 2000, 563) but **into the stomach, and it goes out into the toilet**, so it is not defiling (vv. 18–19). Rather, **what comes of a person** is truly defiling (v. 23): **"For out of the human heart evil imaginations come, fornications, thefts, murders, adulteries, greed, wickednesses, deceit, debauchery, the evil eye, blasphemy, pride, foolishness"** (vv. 21–22). Neyrey (1986, 120) suggests that this catalog of vices is roughly based on the Ten Commandments:

The Ten Commandments	Vices in Mark 7:21–22
1 Do not kill.	Murder
2 Do not commit adultery.	Fornication, adultery, licentiousness ("debauchery")
3 Do not steal.	Theft
4 Do not bear false witness.	Envy ("the evil eye"), slander ("blasphemy")
5 Do not defraud.	Covetousness ("greed")
6 Honor your father and mother.	(See Mark 7:9–13)

To Neyrey's list should be added a seventh parallel:

7 Do not take God's name in vain.	Blasphemy (*blasphēmia*; cf. Mark 2:7; 3:28–29; 14:64)	

It also resembles the lists of vices found in many NT writings (Rom. 1:29–31; 1 Cor. 6:9–10; 2 Cor. 12:20; Gal. 5:19–21; 1 Tim. 1:9–10; 2 Tim. 3:2–4; 1 Pet. 4:3). The distinction between moral defilement and ritual defilement does not necessarily obviate the latter; both moral and ritual legislation (and the written and oral law) were part of the same body of sacred tradition. The central message of Jesus's teaching in this section is that external religious observances are empty without moral dispositions and behaviors, a point made by the Israelite prophets (e.g., Isa. 1:10–12; 29:13; 66:3; Jer. 6:19–21; 7:21–23; Hosea 6:6).

Sandwiched between the two parts of Jesus's explanation is Mark's terse parenthetical comment: **purifying all foods** (7:19b; NRSV: "Thus he declared all foods clean"). The evangelist interprets Jesus's pronouncement as a ruling that abrogates the dietary regulations of Torah. Again, the first-degree audience—Mark's readers/hearers—are implicitly advised that they need not observe Jewish dietary law, an issue debated among generations of early Christians (see Acts 10:9–16; 15:29; Col. 2:16, 21; 1 Tim. 4:1–5; cf. Rom. 14:20–21; 1 Cor. 8:7–9; 10:27).

Theological Issues

Practices pertaining to ritual purity and impurity and the written and the oral law seem to be far removed from the concerns of contemporary Christian readers. It would be easy to dismiss this section as simply an artifact of ancient debates about whether Jewish laws and customs should be adopted by gentile Christians, of little relevance today.

The central *chreia* around which the entire passage is composed is the quotation from Isa. 29:13, which contrasts external devotion with internal apostasy: "This people honors me with their lips, but their heart they take away from me; in vain they are devout, teaching as doctrines human instructions." The prophecy does not condemn Israel's honoring God "with their lips," nor does it devalue the externals of devotion in and of themselves. Rather, it denounces the "disconnect" between the nation's declared commitment to the law of God and their lack of really understanding the purpose of the law: "Their worship [fear] of me is a human commandment learned by rote" (Isa. 29:13b; cf. 1:10–17).

There is no shortage of contemporary examples of people, institutions, and even nations that claim to be religious while ignoring or interpreting away the moral principles they purport to espouse, like the Pharisees criticized by Jesus for abusing the custom of *korban* by using it to circumvent their Torah obligations to their parents. For example, the sexual abuse scandals that have plagued the Roman Catholic Church for decades obviously violate Catholic moral teaching on sexuality and the dignity of the human person. Though such crimes are regularly condemned by Catholic leaders, they all too often have been suppressed, blamed on external factors (the media, society, feminism, homosexuals), or dealt with internally instead of being reported to public authorities, as justice for the victims demands. If *korban* was not actually practiced by the Pharisees of Jesus's time, something similar is at work today: canon law is being used to circumvent criminal law. As the German philosopher Immanuel Kant (1724–1804) observed, human beings share "a disposition, to argue against . . . [the] strict laws of duty and to question their validity, or at least their purity and strictness; and, if possible, to make them more accordant with our wishes and inclinations, that is to say, to corrupt them at their very source, and entirely to destroy their worth—a thing which even common practical reason cannot ultimately call good" (Kant 1909–14, §20). This is exactly the human tendency deplored by Jesus in his critique of *korban*: it is a loophole that allows the neglect of parents, whom the law obligates observant Jews to honor.

Another question for contemporary readers to consider is whether there is value in observances and rituals such as those attributed to the Pharisees "and all the Jews" by the evangelist. Although the Hebrew scriptures (cf. Pss. 1:2; 37:31; 40:8; 78:5; 94:12; 119:1–176; Prov. 28:4, 7, 9, 18; 31:5) condemn

Early Christians and the Law

Apart from the Decalogue, most contemporary Christians do not consider the 613 commandments of Torah binding; however, the earliest Christians, like Jesus and his disciples, were Jewish and hence Torah obedient. Initially, gentiles who joined the Jesus movement became Jews. R. Brown and Meier (1983, 1–9) have identified four different types of Jewish/gentile Christianity typified in the NT, hinging on their attitude to Torah observance:

1. Gentiles who became Jews and took on the full observance of Jewish law, including circumcision for men (cf. Acts 11:2; 15:5; Gal. 2:4; Phil. 3:2–21).
2. Gentiles within Israel, an approach that did not require gentiles to become Jewish proselytes, but assumed that they would follow some Jewish practices, such as certain dietary regulations and chastity (Acts 15:28–29; cf. Gal. 2:9).
3. Gentiles not under the law, the position of the apostle Paul, who taught that since both Jews and gentiles are saved through faith in Christ, gentile converts are not bound by Torah in any sense (e.g., Gal. 3:10–13; Rom. 10:1–4; 11:17–24; however, Rom. 9:4–5 implies that Jewish-Christians could maintain their Jewishness even though their salvation was through Christ).
4. Jesus has replaced Judaism/the law, a radical position implied by such passages as Mark 7:19; John 1:14–18; Acts 6:8–14; Heb. 7:1–10:18 but most clearly expressed by the doctrines of Marcion of Sinope (ca. 85–160), a popular early Christian theologian who taught that the God of the Hebrew scriptures was not the God of Jesus, that Jesus Christ was sent by the true God to reveal the message of salvation. He rejected the Hebrew scriptures and most of the NT apart from the Letters of Paul and an edited version of Luke. Marcion's radical supersessionist views were condemned as heresy from an early date.

Mark's community seems to be somewhere between options 2 (some Jewish practices) and 3 (not under the law). Throughout the Gospel, Jesus is portrayed as differing with other Jews regarding the interpretation and application of the law, on *how* it relates to believers, not on *whether* it does. However, Jesus's permissive attitude to Sabbath observance (e.g., Mark 2:23–24; 3:1–5), ritual washings (7:1–8), and dietary practices (7:19) suggests that the Markan community was inclined to interpret Torah with considerable latitude, or to set it aside altogether.

Although the Pauline opinion that Christians are not under the law prevailed as gentile converts proliferated, Jewish forms of Christianity endured in the early church and are exemplified by NT books such as Matthew and James and extracanonical works such as *The Gospel to the Hebrews*, *The Gospel of the Ebionites*, and *The Gospel of the Nazoreans*.

119

reliance on external observance unaccompanied by moral and compassionate conduct, obedience to the law of God is extolled:

> The law of the LORD is perfect, reviving the soul;
> the decrees of the LORD are sure, making wise the simple;
> the precepts of the LORD are right, rejoicing the heart;
> the commandment of the LORD is clear, enlightening the eyes;
> the fear of the LORD is pure, enduring for ever;
> the ordinances of the LORD are true and righteous altogether.
> More to be desired are they than gold, even much fine gold;
> sweeter also than honey, and drippings of the honeycomb. (Ps. 19:7–10)

The mother of Lemuel (Prov. 31:5–9) reminds her son the king of his duty to obey the law by standing up for the rights of the poor and destitute and acting compassionately toward them. In the Gospel of Matthew, Jesus teaches that his purpose is not to abolish the Law and the Prophets but to fulfill them: "For truly I tell you, until heaven and earth pass away, not one letter, not one stroke of a letter, will pass from the law until all is accomplished"; Christian righteousness (faithfulness to Torah) must exceed that of the Pharisees (5:18; cf. 5:19–20). From a contemporary Jewish perspective, Rabbi Hayim Halevy Donin (1972, 29–30) explains that the observance of the law (halakah) provides profound meaning to observant Jews, as it did to Jews (including Torah-observant Christians) of the first century:

> As the halaka is all-encompassing, so might it be said that the Jewish religion is all-encompassing. There are no areas in the realm of human behavior with which it does not deal or offer guidance. To the extent that every aspect of life is regarded as subject to the guidelines established by the halaka, one cannot regard the Jewish religion—when properly observed—as filling up but one of life's many compartments, or that it is separate and distinct from other areas of one's life and concern. A person's eating habits, his [or her] sex life, . . . business ethics, . . . social activities, . . . entertainment, . . . artistic expression are all under the umbrella of the religious law, of the religious values and spiritual guidelines of Judaism. Jewish religion does not disassociate itself from any aspect of life, and does not confine its concern to a supernatural world. Fully and properly observed, the Jewish religion is life itself, and provides values to guide all of life.

This modern-day Jewish perspective is not far from the teaching of the ancient Jewish rabbi Jesus, whose words in Mark 7:1–23 convey an allegiance to "the commandment of God" that does not allow easy dichotomies between public and private, personal and political, individual and social, religious and secular, law and gospel. At the same time, Jesus's warning against mistaking human customs (e.g., denominational differences in church organization, worship, attitudes to society, and so forth) for divine revelation (Mark 7:8) is a corrective to unreflective reliance on received tradition to regulate our religious, moral, and social lives.

Mark 7:24–9:29

Act 3: Mission in Gentile Regions

Introductory Matters

This lengthy narrative section, central to the Gospel, takes place mostly in gentile regions: Tyre and Sidon (Mark 7:24), the Decapolis (7:31), and Caesarea Philippi (8:27), with brief forays back into Jewish territory (8:10–13, 22–26). By-now familiar Markan themes are repeated: Jesus continues to seek privacy and secrecy (7:24, 33, 36; 8:26, 30; 9:2, 9), but the needy seek him out (7:25, 32; 8:1, 22; 9:15), and his fame spreads (7:36–37). Jesus teaches his disciples privately (8:14–21, 27–30, 31–32a; 9:2–8, 9–13; 9:28–29), although they usually fail to understand either his public or private teachings, or the significance of the events they have witnessed (8:4, 16–21, 32b–33; 9:10–11, 28). Jesus performs spectacular miracles of exorcism (7:24–30; 9:14–27), healings of the deaf, mute, and blind (7:31–35; 8:22–26; 9:25, 27), and a second multiplication of loaves and fish (8:1–10). Strikingly, after this section of the Gospel, only one further healing, of a blind man in Jericho, takes place (10:46–52).

However, new themes emerge, and familiar ones are expressed with new intensity throughout this section. Jesus explicitly prophesies the suffering, resurrection, and return in glory of the son of man (8:31, 38; 9:9, 12, 31)—the first of Mark's famous Passion and parousia predictions (cf. 10:33–34; 13:26; 14:21, 41, 62). Two pivotal episodes explicitly focus on the identity of Jesus: Peter's confession that Jesus is the messiah at Caesarea Philippi (8:27–30), and the mountaintop transfiguration scene, witnessed only by Peter, James, and John (9:2–8). As in a Greek tragedy, the recognition (*anagnōrisis*) of Jesus's identity as the messiah is a major event, which brings new information to light (to the disciples), reversing the situation of the hero (*peripeteia*), followed by the hero's suffering (*pathos*)—in Aristotle's words, "a destructive or painful action, such as public deaths, physical agony, woundings, etc." (*Poet.* 11.10, trans. Halliwell 1927). Peter's confession is followed by the first Passion prediction:

> Answering, Peter said, "You are the messiah." And he charged them that they should speak to no one about him. And he began to teach them that it was necessary for the son of man to suffer many things and to be rejected by the elders and by the scribes and by the chief priests and to be killed and after three days to rise up. And he spoke the matter plainly. (Mark 8:29–32)

The transfiguration is followed by another prophecy of the suffering of the son of man:

> And going down from the mountains, he charged them to discuss with no one what they had seen, until the son of man should rise from the dead. And they kept the matter to themselves, questioning what the rising of the dead was. And they were questioning him, saying, "Why do the scribes say 'Elijah must come first'?" And he said to them, "Elijah has come first to restore all things; and how is it written about the son of man that he must suffer many things and be despised? But I say to you, they did to him what they wanted, just as it is written about him." (9:9–13)

Jo-Ann A. Brant (2004, 51) notes that in tragedies, recognition often alienates people rather than uniting them. In Mark, Peter's confession is followed by his reproaching Jesus for teaching that "the son of man must suffer," and by Jesus's rebuke of Peter as a "satan," or adversary (8:32b–33). The epiphany on the mountain leaves Peter, James, and John in confusion over how to react, and puzzled by Jesus's subsequent teachings (9:6, 9–13). Immediately afterward, the disciples are unable to effect the exorcism of a young boy, and even Jesus must enlist the faith of the child's father in order to cast out the demon (9:14–29).

In 8:14–21 we read the last of three scenes where Jesus chastises the disciples for their obtuseness during a boat voyage (cf. 4:34–41; 6:47–52). Also important are the "recognition scenes" and related dialogues from 8:27–9:13. Both Peter's confession and the transfiguration could aptly be called failed recognition scenes, since Peter and the others, like the disciples in the boat, show only a limited understanding of Jesus and the meaning of his ministry.

Tracing the Narrative Flow

Exorcism of a Syro-Phoenician Woman's Daughter (7:24–30)

After teaching at Gennesaret (6:53), Jesus travels northwest to the Mediterranean coast, **the region of Tyre and Sidon** (7:24). The Phoenician city of Tyre, part of the Roman province of Syria, was an ancient city that was traditionally represented in the Jewish scriptures as enemy territory but that also figured in prophetic oracles of both judgment and salvation (e.g., 1 Kings 5:1; 7:13; 9:11; Pss. 83:5–10; 87:3–6; Isa. 23:1–8; Ezek. 26–28; Joel 3:4–8; Amos 1:9–10; Zech. 9:2–4). According to Josephus (*Ag. Ap.* 1.13 §70), the Tyrians were enemies of the Jews, and in the evangelist's time, northern Galilee was dominated economically by Tyre (Theissen 1991, 71).

The **Syro-Phoenician** (7:26) woman who begs Jesus to cast a demon out of her daughter (vv. 24–30) is thus, from an ancient Jewish perspective, a member of a religiously and ethnically suspect group (v. 24). A great deal of commentary, both feminist and nonfeminist, has been devoted to this story, with widely divergent results. Interpreters differ as to whether the woman is a poor, marginalized suppliant disadvantaged by both gender and race as a Greek-speaking gentile woman (e.g., Ringe 1985, 70; Tolbert 1992, 268; Dewey 1994, 484; Kinukawa 1994, 55–56; Powery 2007, 136), or a privileged, upper-class urban exploiter (e.g., Ringe 2001, 89–90; S. Miller 2004, 92; Boring 2006, 209). There is little evidence in the pericope to support either view, although the references to household furnishings bespeak relative wealth: the daughter lies on a *klinē* ("couch," v. 30) rather than a pallet (*krabatton*; cf. 2:11), and the woman refers to a *trapeza* ("table") under which house dogs can beg (Boring 2006, 210). Interpreters do agree, however, that Jesus's answer to the woman's humble plea is harsh: **"Let the children first be satisfied, for it is not good to take the children's bread and cast it to the dogs!"** (7:27), and that her sharp retort is the "punch line" of the story: **"Sir, even**

Mark 7:24–9:29 in the Narrative Flow

Prologue: John and Jesus (1:1–13)

Transition: Summary of the good news (1:14–15)

Act 1: Jesus in Galilee (1:16–3:35)

Interlude: Teaching in parables (4:1–34)

Act 2: Beyond Galilee (4:35–6:56)

Interlude: Teaching on ritual and moral purity (7:1–23)

▶ Act 3: Mission in gentile regions (7:24–9:29)

  Exorcism of a Syro-Phoenician woman's daughter (7:24–30)

  Healing of a deaf man in the Decapolis (7:31–37)

  Feeding of four thousand people (8:1–9)

  The Pharisees ask Jesus for a sign (8:10–13)

  Jesus rebukes the disciples on a boat voyage (8:14–21)

  In gentile cities (8:22–30)

    Healing of a blind man in Bethsaida (8:22–26)

    Peter's confession at Caesarea Philippi (8:27–30)

  First Passion prediction; Peter and Jesus trade rebukes (8:31–33)

  The suffering of the son of man; first parousia prediction (8:34–9:1)

  Jesus's transfiguration (9:2–8)

  Elijah and the son of man; second Passion prediction (9:9–13)

  A demon-possessed deaf and mute boy (9:14–29)

the pups under the table eat from the children's crumbs!" (v. 24b). Jesus's use of the epithet "dogs" (*kynaria*, lit., "little dogs" or "puppies") to describe the woman and her daughter is insulting; in biblical terms, dogs are regarded as unclean scavengers (cf. 1 Sam. 17:43; Ps. 22:16; Prov. 26:11; Isa. 56:10–11; however, cf. Tob. 6:2; 11:4).

Since Jesus has already healed non-Jews (Mark 5:1–13; cf. 3:7–8), it is surprising that he initially rejects the woman's request because of her ethnicity: she and her daughter are gentile "dogs," in contrast with the "children" (*tekna*), referring to Israel (Deut. 32:20, 43; Ps. 82:6; Isa. 1:2; 17:9; 63:8; Hosea 11:1), who merit the "bread" of salvation. Faced with the pleading woman at his feet, Jesus asserts *his* ethnic and religious privilege as a Jew, whose fellow Israelites have priority in salvation history (although ultimately all nations would acknowledge the true God; cf., e.g., Isa. 2:2–3//Mic. 4:1–2; Isa. 19:25; 25:6–8; 54:15 LXX, "proselytes shall approach"; Dan. 7:14; Amos 9:12; Zech. 9:10; *Sib. Or.* 3.716–27, 772–75; *T. Benj.* 9.2; *1 En.* 10.21; 48.5; 90.33). The woman's reply acknowledges Jesus's dominant status as a reputed exorcist; she is the only character in the Gospel who unequivocally addresses him as *Kyrie* ("sir," "master," or "lord," Mark 7:28; Lat. *Domine*; one Greek codex of 10:51 also contains the title). At the same time, she undermines his rather unsympathetic, theologically loaded refusal with an observation from everyday life: children drop crumbs at mealtime, and the household pets under the table snap them up. This retort (*logos*) causes Jesus to change his mind: **"For this saying, go, the demon has gone out of your daughter"** (v. 29). The woman is thus the only Gospel character who wins an argument with Jesus, an embarrassment softened by Matthew, who attributes the healing to her great faith (Matt. 15:28)—and the whole story is left out by Luke. The fourth-century Syrian poet Ephrem commemorates the woman's boldness with the lines: "Our Lord put to shame the Canaanite woman whose love bellowed out so that she asked Him" (*Hymn on Virginity* 34.7, trans. McVey 1989, 413).

Healing of a Deaf Man in the Decapolis (7:31–37)

The brief story of the healing of a deaf man with a speech impairment (7:31–37) also takes place in gentile territory, this time in the Decapolis, after a northern detour to Sidon. It has received very little scholarly attention in journal articles, perhaps because of its similarity to the healing of a blind man in 8:22–26:

Mark 7:31–37	Mark 8:22–26
Description of journey.	Description of journey.
Deaf man brought.	Blind man brought.
Jesus is begged to lay hands on him.	Jesus is begged to touch him.
Healing occurs in private.	Healing occurs outside village.

Mark 7:31–37	Mark 8:22–26
Healing involves touch and spit.	Healing involves touch and spit.
Jesus looks up.	Jesus looks up.
Deaf man is healed.	Blind man is healed.
Commanded to silence.	Man commanded not to enter village.

This story is the first of four in which hearing and sight are miraculously restored to the deaf and blind (8:22–26; 9:14–19; 10:46–52), echoing the references to metaphorical blindness and deafness in Mark 4:12 (Isa. 6:9–10). The story is unique to Mark; none of the other Gospels contain narratives of the healing of deafness, whereas Mark has two (cf. Mark 9:17, 25; in Matt. 9:31–33, Jesus exorcizes a mute, demon-possessed [but not deaf] man; cf. Matt. 15:30–31; Matt. 11:5 and Luke 7:22 allude to Isaiah's prophecy [Isa. 35:5–6] that the blind will see and the deaf will hear).

The man is brought to Jesus; without hearing and speech, he is unaware of Jesus's reputation and unable to ask him for help on his own. Aristotle (*On Sense and the Sensible* 435a.17) opined that since speech is the source of knowledge, blind people have better access to understanding than the deaf and mute. The word often translated as "dumb" or "mute" is the rare *mogilalos* ("speaking with difficulty"), found in the NT only in Mark 7:32 (cf. Isa. 35:6 LXX). The Markan secrecy theme is reinforced by the description of the healing: **Taking him away from the crowd alone, he put his fingers in his ears, and having spit, he touched his tongue, and having looked up into heaven, he groaned and he says to him, "*Ephphatha* (that is, be opened)!" And [immediately] his ears opened, and the ligament of his tongue was loosed and he spoke rightly** (7:33–35). Some commentators see this healing as resembling an exorcism, although demonic possession is not mentioned (e.g., Marcus 2000, 478; Boring 2006, 216–17); this idea has some merit, since a "deaf and mute demon" is mentioned in Mark 9:25. The meticulous account of Jesus's six actions to perform the cure is not simply an instance of Mark's fondness for vivid details, but rather actions associated with miracle workers (see John 9:6; Pliny the Elder, *Nat.* 28.4.7; Tacitus, *Hist.* 4:81; 6:18; Suetonius, *Vespasian* 7). Jesus not only places his fingers in the man's ears and touches his tongue; he also pronounces the Aramaic word *ephphatha*, "be opened," as part of the healing ritual. That God is the source of the healing is signaled by Jesus's raising his eyes to "heaven" (a Jewish circumlocution for the name of God), and the use of the divine passive: "be opened," "his ears were opened," "his tongue was loosed."

The ending of the story reiterates the secrecy theme: **And he charged them to say nothing** (7:36a), but as in other Markan healings, the warning is not heeded: **but the more he charged them, the more abundantly they proclaimed it** (7:36b). Here it is the companions who proclaim the miracle, rather than

---

Vespasian Heals a Blind Man

"During the months while Vespasian was waiting at Alexandria for the regular season of the summer winds and a settled sea, many marvels continued to mark the favour of heaven and a certain partiality of the gods toward him. One of the common people of Alexandria, well known for his loss of sight, threw himself before Vespasian's knees, praying him with groans to cure his blindness, being so directed by the god Serapis, whom this most superstitious of nations worships before all others; and he besought the emperor to deign to moisten his cheeks and eyes with his spittle. Another, whose hand was useless, prompted by the same god, begged Caesar to step and trample on it. Vespasian at first ridiculed these appeals and treated them with scorn; then, when the men persisted, he began at one moment to fear the discredit of failure, at another to be inspired with hopes of success by the appeals of the suppliants and the flattery of his courtiers: finally, he directed the physicians to give their opinion as to whether such blindness and infirmity could be overcome by human aid. Their reply treated the two cases differently: they said that in the first the power of sight had not been completely eaten away and it would return if the obstacles were removed; in the other, the joints had slipped and become displaced, but they could be restored if a healing pressure were applied to them. Such perhaps was the wish of the gods, and it might be that the emperor had been chosen for this divine service; in any case, if a cure were obtained, the glory would be Caesar's, but in the event of failure, ridicule would fall only on the poor suppliants. So Vespasian, believing that his good fortune was capable of anything and that nothing was any longer incredible, with a smiling countenance, and amid intense excitement on the part of the bystanders, did as he was asked to do. The hand was instantly restored to use, and the day again shone for the blind man. Both facts are told by eye-witnesses even now when falsehood brings no reward."
(Tacitus, *Hist.* 4.81, trans. Moore and Jackson 1931, 161)

---

the restored man (cf. 1:27; 2:12; 5:20). The tale concludes with a choral acclamation: **And they marveled exceedingly, saying, "He has done all things
well; he makes both the deaf to hear and the mute to speak!"** (7:37). Some
commentators see the phrase *kalōs panta pepoiēken* (v. 37a) as alluding to
the first creation account: "the Septuagint version of Genesis 1:31, in which
at the end of the sixth day of creation God sees all the things (*ta panta*) that
he has made (*epoiēsen*) and concludes that they are very good" (*kala lian*;
Marcus 2000, 475; cf. Boring 2006, 218; Donahue and Harrington 2002, 241;
Mann 1986, 324). The second half of the acclamation is an allusion to Isa.
35:5–6: "Then the eyes of the blind shall be opened, and the ears of the deaf
unstopped; then the lame shall leap like a deer, and the tongue of the speechless
[LXX: *mogilalōn*] sing for joy. For waters shall break forth in the wilderness,
and streams in the desert." Isaiah's prophecy of a renewed creation is being
fulfilled through the ministry of Jesus.

Feeding of Four Thousand People (8:1–9)

Mark 8:1–9 exemplifies a particularly striking Markan compositional technique: the use of two similar stories in different parts of the Gospel (e.g., 4:35–41//6:45–52; 7:31–37//9:9–29; 8:22–26//10:46–52). The feeding of the four thousand is obviously very much like the feeding miracle of 6:30–44: both involve the multiplication of loaves; in both, the disciples initially regard the task of feeding the crowd as impossible; both echo the manna in the wilderness; in both, Jesus performs the eucharistic actions of taking, giving thanks, breaking, and distributing the food. One salient difference is that the first feeding takes place in Jewish territory (cf. 6:1–45), while the second takes place in the gentile region of the Decapolis (7:31). Indeed, the story has several features that highlight the gentile focus of the miracle: Jesus remarks that some have **come from far away** (8:3), a description often applied to non-Israelite nations in the Hebrew scriptures (e.g., Deut. 28:49; 29:22; Josh. 9:6, 9; 1 Kings 8:41; Isa. 40:4–5; Ezek. 23:40; Joel 3:8). The word used for **baskets** in 8:8 is *spyrides*, a term that does not have the specifically Jewish connotations of *kophinos* (see comment on Mark 6:43). The motivation for the first feeding is based on the scriptural metaphor of shepherd and sheep (6:34; cf. Ps. 23; Ezek. 34); whereas in the second feeding, Jesus simply has compassion on the crowd because they have gone three days without food (Mark 8:1–2). Some interpreters see the seven loaves and seven baskets full of fragments (8:5, 8; cf. 6:38, 43) as symbolizing the gentile world; thus Rudolph Pesch (1976–77, 1:404) notes that in Jewish tradition, non-Jewish peoples were divided up into seventy nations (e.g., *1 En.* 83–90) and that the seven commandments of Noah were considered to be binding for gentiles (*b. Sanh.* 56a; cf. Acts 15:19, 28–29). The Noachian laws prohibit idolatry, murder, theft, sexual promiscuity, blasphemy, eating the flesh from a living animal, and require the nations to have an adequate justice system. Marcus (2000, 489) suggests that the number seven signifies eschatological completeness, a theme that could include the recognition of the true God by the gentile nations (e.g., Isa. 11:10; 42:6; 49:6; 60:3, 5; 62:2; Jer. 16:19; Mal. 1:11; cf. Luke 13:29).

Opinions are divided as to why Mark includes two feeding narratives. One possibility is that they are pre-Markan variants of the same story that the evangelist simply took over from the tradition. Robert Fowler (1981, 43–90, 95–96) argues that 8:1–10 is the traditional story and that Mark deliberately created 6:30–44 in order to emphasize the theme of the disciples' incomprehension. Karl P. Donfried (1980), in contrast, argues that 8:1–10 was modeled on the feeding of the five thousand, on the basis of several Markan duplicate expressions (for a list of parallels, see Marcus 2000, 493–95). Whatever the redaction history of the doublet, the evangelist makes it very clear that the duplication of similar stories is intentional, noting that **in those days *again*** there was a great crowd with nothing to eat (8:1). In view of the placement of the second feeding after two miracles performed on behalf of gentiles (7:24–30,

31–37), it seems clear that this is a deliberate reinforcement of the theme that Jesus brings the good news to both Jews and gentiles, who are entitled to more than "crumbs" (cf. 7:28).

Another effect of the use of the two similar stories is to highlight the obtuseness of the disciples. In this version, the disciples, whom the audience knows have already witnessed a multiplication of loaves in the desert (6:31–32, 35), ask Jesus how he can satisfy so many people **with bread in the desert (8:4)**. This time, the disciples don't even have to search around for food, since they immediately inform Jesus that they have seven loaves along with them (v. 5; **a few fish** are also mentioned in v. 7; cf. 6:38). Ironically, they have literally "seen and seen" two almost identical situations of feeding and "not perceived," "heard and heard" and "not understood" (Mark 4:11; Isa. 6:9–10). They still fail to comprehend the significance of Jesus's words and deeds (cf. Mark 4:12; 7:18).

The Pharisees Ask Jesus for a Sign (8:10–13)

Mark 8:10 marks an interlude in the gentile mission; Jesus and the disciples embark for Dalmanutha, an otherwise unknown destination identified with Magadan/Magdala in Matt. 15:39. The Jewish destination of the crossing is indicated by the presence of Pharisees, who **began to dispute with him, seeking a sign from heaven, testing him** (Mark 8:11a). Although "the Pharisees" figure in several previous controversy stories (2:15–17, 23–28; 7:1–13) and have been identified as hostile to Jesus (3:6), this is the first story where they challenge him directly. Jesus's response is brief, pointed, and solemn; it is usually translated something like the NRSV's "Why does this generation ask for a sign? Truly [*amēn*] I tell you, no sign will be given to this generation" (8:12). The latter phrase is more literally (and less grammatically) translated **"If a sign would be granted to this generation!"** and best explained as an abbreviated form of a Hebrew oath using the solemn "amen" ("so be it"), a feature of Jewish vows (Buchanan 1965, 324–26; cf. Num. 5:19–22; Deut. 27:15–26; Jer. 11:5; 28:6). In the biblical tradition, the breaking of a vow is a very serious matter and has adverse consequences for the oath taker who fails to fulfill it. Throughout Mark, amen sayings are consistently reliable, whether in the context of threat (cf. 3:28; 9:1; 13:30; 14:18, 30) or promise (9:41; 10:15, 29; 11:23; 12:43; 14:9, 25). The oath is accompanied by Jesus's **sighing deeply in his spirit** (8:12a). The verb *anastenazō* ("to sigh") is similar to the one used in the healing of the deaf man (*stenazō*; 7:34), where it may have a magical connotation (see Marcus 2000, 474), but here it is better interpreted as a sigh of "distress in an apparently hopeless situation" (BDAG 72).

Why does Jesus react so strongly to the Pharisees' challenge? One explanation is that the radical faith demanded through the words and deeds of Jesus needs no external proof of its validity (J. Gibson 1990, 37). This view has some merit, since throughout Mark, faith precedes miracles; miracles do not inspire faith (2:5; 4:40; 5:34; 6:6; 10:52; 11:21–23). But in order to understand

Jesus's exasperated response, the meaning of the phrase "a sign from heaven" (*sēmeion apo tou ouranou*) must be clarified: what kind of a sign are the Pharisees seeking? If they are asking for a miraculous sign to authenticate Jesus's prophetic status (cf. 2 Kings 20:1–11; Isa. 38:1–20), Jesus has already performed enough miracles through the power of God ("heaven"), even in the presence of Pharisees (cf. Mark 3:1–6), to persuade all but the most hardened skeptics (cf. John 2:11, 18, 23; 3:2; 4:48, 54; 6:2, 14, 26, 30; 7:31; 9:16; 10:41; 11:47; 12:18, 37; 20:30). Jeffrey Gibson (1990, 39, 47–54) suggests that the Pharisees are challenging Jesus to produce a sign like that of first-century Jewish prophets, such as Theudas, who promised to perform certain signs to support their claims that they were divinely ordained to deliver Israel from Roman bondage (cf. Josephus, *J.W.* 2.13.4–5 §§259–63; *Ant.* 20.5.1 §§97–99; 20.8.6 §§167–70; 20.8.10 §188). According to J. Gibson (1990, 50), the signs offered by such prophets invoked key events of the exodus and conquest, and they figured in the liberation of Israel from foreign oppression, as in the crossing of the Reed (or Red) Sea, the plagues of Egypt, the fall of Jericho. On this criterion, the two feeding miracles with their strong exodus resonances would surely qualify (cf. John 6:14).

In Mark, the only other (than 8:11–12) usages of *sēmeion* are found in chap. 13; these refer to the "signs" that will precede the destruction of the temple (13:2–4), and to false messiahs and prophets who will produce signs to mislead the elect (13:22). Two categories of signs are at issue here: signs used to authenticate the claims of pretenders (13:22), and historical and apocalyptic signs wrought by God (13:2-4). Some of the latter are literally "from heaven": the darkening of the sun and moon, the stars falling from the sky, the shaking of the celestial powers, the glorious arrival of the son of man, the gathering of the elect by angels (13:24–27; cf. Rev. 12:1, 3; 15:1). Perhaps it is this kind of apocalyptic sign, which can only be worked by God (Mark 13:32), that the Pharisees seek from Jesus. The near-blasphemous nature of the request is underlined by the analysis that the Pharisees meant **to test him** (8:11); the verb *peirazō* is used only with reference to the Pharisees and Satan in Mark (1:13; 8:11; 10:2; 12:15).

Jesus's reference to **this generation**'s not receiving a sign (8:12) is somewhat puzzling in the light of 13:30: **this generation will not pass away until all these things take place.** However, in the NT generally and in Mark specifically, the phrase "this generation" is laden with negativity: they are "adulterous and sinful" (8:38), and "unbelieving" (9:19), like the "evil generation" forbidden to enter Canaan because they were unfaithful (Deut. 1:35; 32:20), or the unrighteous generation of the flood (Gen. 7:1). Jesus and the other faithful, like Noah, are not considered to be a part of the wicked generation among whom they live (see Marcus 2000, 501, citing Lövestam 1995, 8, 13, 18, 22). The emphasis here is not on the chronology of the end times but on the unworthiness of "this generation."

Jesus Rebukes the Disciples on a Boat Voyage (8:14–21)

Mark 8:14–21 is the third dialogue between Jesus and the disciples in a boat (cf. 4:35–41; 6:45–52). It draws together several Markan thematic threads: the hostility of the Pharisees, the significance of the two feeding narratives, and the incomprehension ("hard-heartedness") of the disciples. In this boat story, unlike the previous two, the exchange is occasioned not by a storm at sea but by an enigmatic saying of Jesus: **And they had forgotten to bring bread, and they had only one loaf with them in the boat. And he cautioned them, saying, "Look, watch out for the leaven of the Pharisees and the leaven of Herod!" And they discussed with each other that they had no bread** (8:14–16). After Jesus's rebuke to the Pharisees in the previous pericope, the disciples' confusion over the warning against the "leaven" of the Pharisees and Herod seems foolish. Although leaven (or yeast, *zymē*) has both positive and negative connotations in the biblical tradition (e.g., Matt. 13:33; Luke 13:20–21; 1 Cor. 5:6–8; Gal. 5:9; cf. Exod. 23:18; Lev. 2:11; 7:11–14), the tone of Jesus's words is stern (Mark 8:15); the verb *diastellō* means "to define or express in no uncertain terms what one must do, *order, give orders*" (BDAG 236). The Pharisaic "leaven" is something the disciples must watch out for (*orate, blepete apo*); in its immediate context, it must refer to the brash demand for a sign from heaven. The reference to "the leaven of Herod" is more opaque; the reader/audience knows that "the Pharisees and the Herodians" are conspiring to kill Jesus (3:6), but the disciples do not; nor is it certain that they are aware of Herod's execution of the Baptist (6:27–29). However, it is clear that disciples mistake a metaphorical warning against treachery for literal advice about bread recipes, and begin to discuss their shortage of food.

Jesus's response is sharp: **"Why do you discuss that you have no bread? Do you not yet know nor understand? Has your heart been hardened? Having eyes, do you not see, and having ears, do you not hear? And don't you remember, when the five loaves were broken for the five thousand, how many baskets full of pieces did you take up?" They say to him, "Twelve." "And when the seven for the four thousand, how many baskets full of pieces did you take up?" And they say, "Seven." And he was saying to them, "You don't yet understand!"** (8:17–21). This third exchange between Jesus and the disciples in a boat marks a deterioration in the disciples' comprehension rather than an improvement: in 4:35–41, Jesus rebukes them for their lack of faith; in 6:51–52, their fear of the storm is related to "the loaves" of the first feeding miracle because "their hearts were hardened" against the import of Jesus's wonder-working powers. This time the disciples are unbelievably dense; they think that Jesus is worried about going hungry when his pointed questions remind them that they have repeatedly seen him feed thousands with a few loaves. The phrase "having eyes, do you not see, and having ears, do you not hear?" echoes several prophetic denunciations of unbelieving Israel (cf. Jer. 5:21; Ezek. 12:2). Their failure to understand the significance of the events they have witnessed even at a superficial level shows them to be as opaque as "those outside," who see without perceiving and hear without understanding (Mark 4:11–12; cf. Isa. 6:9–10). They are like the inattentive servants of God railed against by Isaiah (Isa. 42:18–20; cf. Lemcio 1978, 332):

> Hear, you that are deaf, and you that are blind look up to see! And who is blind but my servants, and deaf but those who lord it over them? Even God's slaves have become blind. You have often seen but not observed; your ears are open, but you have not heard. (NETS)

The accusation that their hearts are hardened is serious; it is the same criticism leveled at the Pharisees in Mark 3:5, immediately followed by the notice of their plot to destroy Jesus (3:6). Donahue and Harrington (2002, 252) observe that it is the collective "heart" of the disciples that is hardened, showing their "willful resistance to signs of God's presence" (cf. Exod. 10:1, 20, 27; 11:10; 14:8; Ezek. 3:7; 11:19).

Although Mark portrays the disciples as extremely obtuse, Jesus's exasperated outburst that the disciples "don't yet understand" (*oupō syniete*, Mark 8:21) seems unhelpful at the level of second-degree narrative; after all, they have already repeatedly required private instruction from Jesus despite the gift of "the mystery of the reign of God" (4:11, 34; 7:17–18). However, at the level of first-degree narrative, "The repetition of the themes of seeing, hearing, and understanding Jesus's words and deeds certainly advances Mark's plot: the perversity of the Jewish leaders, and the dullness of the disciples, becomes more obvious to the reader with each episode" (Beavis 1989, 114). Rhetorically, the disciples function as a foil for the audience of the Gospel, which is challenged to see, hear, perceive, and understand the full significance of the unfolding story.

In Gentile Cities (8:22–30)

The next two pericopes, the healing of a blind man at Bethsaida (8:22–26) and Peter's confession at Caesarea Philippi (8:27–30), are interrelated. Both scenes take place in gentile cities: Bethsaida Julias was a predominantly gentile town and under the jurisdiction of Herod Philip (Boring 2006, 233); Caesarea Philippi, near the foot of Mount Hermon, was Philip's capital and principal residence (DeVries 2000, 209). As Boring (2006, 222) notes, the return to gentile territory is part of "the overarching theme" of the "transition from Jewish beginnings to the predominantly Gentile church of Mark's time."

> **An Outline of Mark 8:22–30**
>
> **In gentile cities (8:22–30)**
>
> **Healing of a blind man in Bethsaida (8:22–26)**
>
> **Peter's confession at Caesarea Philippi (8:27–30)**

8:22–26. As argued above, there are many similarities between the healing of a deaf man (7:32–37) and the healing of the blind man of Bethsaida (8:22–26). Many scholars also find a structural similarity between the latter story and Peter's confession (e.g., Nineham 1963, 218; Moloney 2002, 163, 165n253; Boring 2006, 233), a parallel first noted by Robert H. Lightfoot (1934, 90–91). The following table highlights the similarities:

Mark 8:22–26	Mark 8:27–30
Description of journey.	Description of journey.
After healing, Jesus questions man; first attempt at healing is only partial.	Jesus questions disciples, "Who do people say that I am?" First set of answers is unsatisfactory.
Jesus touches the man's eyes again.	Jesus questions disciples, "Who do you say that I am?"
The man now sees clearly.	Peter answers, "You are the Messiah."
Command to secrecy.	Command to secrecy.

Both pericopes are about the healing of blindness: the physical blindness of the man, and the spiritual blindness of those who wrongly identify Jesus (8:28), who are like the blind man when he partially regains his sight: **"Look, I see people like trees, walking around!"** (8:24). A second level of spiritual insight recognizes, with Peter, that Jesus is not simply **one of the prophets** (8:28), but rather that he is the messiah (8:29). By making this confession, Peter shows that, like the blind man restored to full vision, he sees things clearly (8:25), at least with respect to Jesus's messianic status (Beavis 1989, 121–22; see also Richardson 1941, 86; Hawkin 1977, 104–5). Moreover, there is a narrative progression from the dialogue in the boat (8:14–21), which highlights the metaphorical blindness (and deafness) of the disciples, to the healing of literal blindness (8:22–26), to Peter's insight that Jesus is the messiah, not simply a prophet, a resurrected John the Baptist (cf. 6:14–15), or even the eschatological Elijah (whose appearance would precede the "day of the LORD" [8:38; cf. Mal. 4:5]). Like the healing of deafness (Mark 7:32–37), the bestowal of sight, both physical and spiritual, is sign of the imminence of God's reign (Isa. 35:5–6; cf. 42:6b–7 NETS: "I will take hold of your hand and strengthen you; . . . I have given you . . . as a light to the nations, to open the eyes of the blind, to bring out from bonds those who are bound and from the prison house those who sit in darkness").

8:27–30. Jesus's questions to the disciples about his identity take place while they are **on the way** (*en tē hodō*, 8:27). This marks an important shift in the plot; up to this point, the phrase has been used only once, with reference to the hungry crowd of the second feeding story (8:3). Here Jesus begins to teach the disciples "on the way" to Jerusalem, especially about the suffering of the son of man (9:33–34; cf. 10:32, 46, 52; 11:8; see also 1:3; 4:4, 15). The reader/audience knows that Peter is correct about Jesus's identity; he is the messiah (*ho christos*). This is the first time the title appears in the Gospel after the superscription in Mark 1:1 ("the good news of Jesus Christ"). After Peter's famous confession, it occurs five more times, although Jesus never uses it unambiguously with reference to himself (9:41; 12:35; 13:21; 14:61–62; 15:32).

In dramatic terms, as mentioned above, 8:27–30 is a recognition scene (*anagnōrisis*), "the discovery of an identity previously concealed" (Bilezikian 1977, 55) that signals a turn or reversal in the plot (*peripeteia*). Although Peter's recognition is accurate as far as it goes, the full scope of Jesus's messianic identity has yet to be revealed. Hence the command to secrecy (8:30).

First Passion Prediction; Peter and Jesus Trade Rebukes (8:31–33)

In 8:31–33, Jesus begins to teach the disciples something new, signaling a change of direction in the story: **that it was necessary for the son of man to suffer many things and to be rejected by the elders and by the scribes and by the chief priests and to be killed and after three days to rise up. And he spoke the matter plainly** (8:31–32a). This is the first of the so-called Passion predictions in Mark (cf. 9:31–32; 10:32–34), all of which share the same basic structure:

First Passion prediction (8:31)

Peter misunderstands, rebukes Jesus; Jesus rebukes Peter (8:32–33)

Jesus's teaching on self-denial and discipleship (8:34–9:1)

Second Passion prediction (9:31–32)

Disciples misunderstand (9:33–34)

Jesus's teaching on the cost of discipleship (9:35–50)

Third Passion prediction (10:32–34)

James and John misunderstand (10:35–40)

Jesus's teaching on discipleship as service (10:41–45)

Here Jesus speaks to the disciples "plainly" (*parrēsia*), not just in parable form (8:32a; cf. 4:13, 34; 7:17).

The first prediction of the suffering, death, and resurrection of the son of man (cf. 2:10, 28) is followed by a heated exchange with Peter: **And taking him aside, Peter began to rebuke him. But having turned and seeing his disciples, he rebuked Peter and says, "Get behind, me, adversary, because you think not the things of God but the things of humanity!"** (8:32b–33). At the level of second-degree narrative, Peter's reaction is not surprising, and Jesus's rebuke (famously translated by the KJV as "Get thee behind me, Satan!") seems unduly severe. After all, Jesus's teaching has just taken a new and disturbing direction, and although the meaning of the title "messiah" was fluid in first-century Judaism (see the introduction), it did not include a suffering, dying, and rising figure. However, at the level of Mark's first-century readers/audience, the teaching is a blunt reminder that following Jesus includes the way of the cross.

The Suffering of the Son of Man; First Parousia Prediction (8:34–9:1)

That way is the subject of 8:34–9:1: **"If anyone wants to follow after me, let him deny himself and take up his cross and follow me: for the one who wants to save his life will lose it; but he who loses his life on account of me and of the good news will save it. For what does a person profit to gain the whole world yet to lose one's life? For what does a person give in exchange for his life?"** (8:34b–37). The teaching takes an apocalyptic turn with the first of three Markan parousia predictions (8:37–9:1; cf. 13:26–27; 14:62): **"For whoever is ashamed of me and my words in this adulterous and sinful generation, also the son of man shall be ashamed of that person when he comes in the glory of his Father with the holy angels."** And he was saying to them, **"Amen I say to you that some people are standing here who will not taste death until they see the reign of God has come in power"** (8:38–9:1). The solemn amen saying reassures the reader/audience with an oath that those "standing here" who follow the example of the suffering messiah will be vindicated when God's reign is fully manifested on earth, attesting to an imminent parousia expectation on the part of the Markan community (cf. 13:30; Nardoni 1981, 370). As Enrique Nardoni (1981, 369) observes, "The saying seems to assume that the expectation of the parousia is challenged by the fact of the death of some of the first disciples; it most likely was issued to meet this threatening confrontation and to comfort and encourage the community frustrated by the delayed parousia" (for an alternate interpretation, see N. Wright 2001, 183–84, 205; France 2002, 341–43).

Jesus's Transfiguration (9:2–8)

Like the confession at Caesarea Philippi, the transfiguration (9:2–8) takes place in gentile territory (the return to Galilee is not mentioned until 9:30), with Jesus taking Peter, James, and John up **into a high mountain alone by themselves** (9:2). In Mark, the trio of Peter, James, and John constitutes an inner circle of disciples who are the first called (1:16–20; 3:16–17) and who accompany him at significant moments (5:37; 14:33). Possibly the three are meant to invoke the three Jerusalem "pillars," although the James/Jacob described as such by Paul (Gal. 2:9) is identified with James the brother of Jesus, not one of the Twelve (cf. Acts 12:2, 17; 15:13; 21:18). The notice that the incident took place **after six days** has been most satisfactorily explained as a Semitic literary device "in which an action continues for six days and then 'on the seventh day' occurs the climax of the action" (McCurley 1974, 68; cf. Gen. 1:1–2:4a; Exod. 24:15b–16; Josh. 6:14–17; Judg. 14:17–18; 1 Kings 18:43–44).

Considerable scholarly attention has been devoted to the question whether 9:2–8 fulfills the promise of 9:1 that some of Jesus's hearers will see the arrival of the reign of God "with power" (see Nardoni 1981). As Richard T. France (2002, 346) observes, the juxtaposition of the prophecy and the transfiguration story is probably not accidental, although it is questionable whether the incident was meant completely to fulfill the prophecy. Even more scholarship has sought to prove or disprove the unlikely contention that the transfiguration is a misplaced resurrection account (see Stein 1976). In the text as it stands, it is more germane to observe that this is a second recognition scene, where Jesus's identity as God's beloved Son is ratified by a heavenly voice in the presence of the three disciples (9:7). The structure of 9:2–13 is similar to that of 8:27–33:

Recognition scene (8:27–33; 9:2–8)

Command to silence (8:30; 9:9)

Misunderstanding of disciples (8:32–33; 9:5–6, 10–11)

Teaching about the suffering of the son of man (8:31–32; 9:12–13)

The three disciples see Jesus **transformed** (*metemorphōthē*), **and his garments became shining white, such that no launderer on earth is able to bleach so much** (9:2–3). In early Jewish and Christian writings, a dazzling appearance signifies closeness to the divine glory (e.g., Exod. 34:29–35; 1 *En.* 106.2–6; *Apoc. Zeph.* 9.1–5; *Liv. Pro.* 21; Philo, *Virtues* 39 §217; Rev. 3:4; 7:9). As Francis J. Moloney notes, "An important narrative strategy is at work here. The reader is aware of Jesus' relationship to God, made clear in the prologue (see esp. 1:1–3, 9–11), but none of the *characters in the story* have been given this information. It is revealed to Peter, James, and John on the mountain" (Moloney 2002, 178). Rather than a misplaced resurrection account, the transfiguration foreshadows the glorious eschatological manifestation of the son of man (cf. 8:38; 13:26; 14:62; cf. 10:37).

The setting on a "high mountain" has given rise to speculation as to the geographical location of the story (see France 2002, 350; Donahue and Harrington 2002, 268), but more to the point is the symbolism of mountains as places for communion with the divine (e.g., Exod. 3–4; 32–34; 1 Kings 20:28; Mark 3:13; 6:46). On the mountaintop, the disciples see Jesus conversing with **Elijah and Moses** (9:4); again, much has been made of the unhistorical order in which the two prophets are named (see France 2002, 351; however, cf. 9:5b, where Peter refers to Moses first). The unusual ordering, along with the fact that Elijah was not a "writing prophet," makes the suggestion that the two symbolize the Law and the Prophets unlikely (France 2002, 351; cf. Donahue and Harrington 2002, 269). More significantly, both Moses and Elijah are associated with theophanies on Mount Sinai/Horeb (Exod. 24:15b–18; Exod. 34; 1 Kings 19:8–13), and both are reputed never to have died but to have been

The Translation of Moses

"Now as soon as they were come to the mountain called Abarim (which is a very high mountain, situated over against Jericho, and one that affords, to such as are upon it, a prospect of the greatest part of the excellent land of Canaan), . . . [Moses] dismissed the senate; and as he was going to embrace Eleazar and Joshua, and was still discoursing with them, a cloud stood over him on the sudden, and he disappeared in a certain valley, although he wrote in the holy books that he died, which was done out of fear, lest they should venture to say that, because of his extraordinary virtue, he went to God." (Josephus, *Ant.* 4.8.48 §§325–26, trans. Whiston 1987, 125)

raised up to heaven by God, although in Moses's case this was a minority Jewish view (2 Kings 2:1–11; cf. Jeremias, *TDNT* 2:939n92).

Both Moses and Elijah were regarded as eschatological prophets whose appearance would herald the day of YHWH (Mal. 4:4–5; Deut. 18:15–18; cf. Mark 9:11–13), so Jesus's audience with them signals the nearness of God's reign.

The transfiguration story is laced with imagery from the descriptions of Moses on Mount Sinai in Exod. 24 and 34: the location on a mountain (cf. 24:12) and the presence of an inner circle of followers with the central figure (24:1–2), the radiant prophet (34:29–35). It could be concluded that Jesus is being portrayed as a Moses figure (e.g., Donahue and Harrington 2002, 274),

Gerard David, Wikimedia Commons

Figure 8. *Christ on Mount Tabor (The Transfiguration),* by Gerard David, 1520.

but it is more accurate to say that Mark is portraying Jesus as one who surpasses even the great prophets Moses and Elijah. Peter's awkward reaction to the vision is part of the theme of the disciples' incomprehension: **Peter says to Jesus, "Rabbi, it is good for us to be here, and let us make three tents, one for you and one for Moses and one for Elijah." For he did not know how to react, for they were frightened out of their wits** (9:5–6; cf. esp. 4:40; 6:49–50). Commentators often observe that this first Markan usage of the title Rabbi ("my master," or "my great one") in Mark (cf. 10:51; 11:21; 14:45) seems inadequate in such a numinous scene (e.g., Moloney 2002, 179n6; France 2002, 353; Boring 2006, 262). Ched Myers (1988, 250) sees the use of the title as indicating that the disciples are aligning with the "dominant Jewish ideology" against Jesus. However, as W. Dennis Tucker (2000, 1106) notes, "In Mark only the disciples call Jesus 'rabbi,' and this address typically follows a miraculous event" (cf. John 20:16, where Mary Magdalene addresses the resurrected Jesus as *Rhabbouni*). Peter's rash offer to build "tents" (*skēnas*) recalls the Jewish Feast of Tabernacles (Sukkoth), a seven-day feast commemorating God's protection of Israel during the wilderness wanderings (Lev. 23:42–43), thus reinforcing the exodus theme.

The answer to Peter's outburst is another statement of Jesus's identity, this time from a divine source: **And a cloud came, enveloping them, and a voice came out of the cloud, "This is my son, the beloved; listen to him!"** (9:7). The cloud, a metaphor for God's presence, recalls Exod. 24:15–16 LXX: "And Moses and Joshua went up into the mountain, and the cloud covered the mountain. And God's glory descended upon the mountain, Sinai, and the cloud covered it for six days, and the Lord called Moses on the seventh day from the midst of the cloud" (NETS, alt.). The first acclamation of Jesus as God's beloved Son (see comment on Mark 1:11) is addressed to Jesus himself; the second is addressed to the disciples—and to the Markan audience—in the second-person plural: **"*You* listen to him!"** Jesus is a prophet surpassing even Moses, who communed with God "face-to-face" (Exod. 33:11; Num. 12:8; 14:14; Deut. 5:4; 34:10), or Elijah, who ascended to heaven in a whirlwind (2 Kings 2:1, 11–12). The final notice that **suddenly looking around, they saw no one anymore but only Jesus with them** (9:8) attests to the visionary quality of the incident. Moses and Elijah disappear, the voice of God is silent, normal life resumes.

Elijah and the Son of Man; Second Passion Prediction (9:9–13)

As noted above, 9:9–13 repeats the pattern of the recognition scene at Caesarea Philippi: Jesus charges the three disciples to keep silent about **what they had seen,** followed by a reference to the rising of the son of man (9:9). Like Peter in 8:32, the disciples misconstrue Jesus's words: **And they kept the matter to themselves, questioning what the rising of the dead was** (9:10). A dying and rising messiah did not figure in pre-Christian Jewish eschatological expectations; perhaps this is why the three interrogate him further about the meaning of his words: **Why do the scribes say that Elijah must come first?**

(9:11b). Jesus's answer is cryptic, but comprehensible to the reader/audience who has connected the Gospel's Elijah typology with Mal. 4:5: "Lo, I will send you the prophet Elijah before the great and terrible day of the LORD comes." The second Elijah, in the person of John the Baptist, **"has come first to restore all things; and how is it written about the son of man that he must suffer many things and be despised? But I say to you, they did to him what they wanted, just as it is written about him"** (9:12–13). Like his precursor John, Jesus the Son of Man must suffer before the eschatological restoration. However, since Jesus has been manifested in company with the two "deathless ones," Moses and Elijah, his vindication is assured (cf. Thrall 1969–70, 314–15).

A Demon-Possessed Deaf and Mute Boy (9:14–29)

The last episode in this section, the healing of a possessed boy (9:14–29), mirrors the first episode, the exorcism of the Syro-Phoenician girl (7:24–30). The story has a complex redactional history, although scholars differ on the details (see Sterling 1993, 488). The present text combines two main story lines, one involving Jesus's spectacular exorcism of a particularly stubborn spirit (9:15, 17–18a, 19c, 20–27) and the other highlighting the disciples' failure to fulfill their mandate to cast out demons with authority (9:14, 16, 18b–19, 28–29; cf. 6:7, 13):

Jesus's Exorcism	The Disciples' Failure
[15]And immediately, the whole crowd having seen him were astonished and, running, greeted him. [17–18a]And one man from the crowd answered, "Teacher, I brought my son to you, having a [mute] spirit; and whenever it takes hold of him it tears him apart, and he foams at the mouth and gnashes his teeth and seizes up; [19c, 20–27]And they brought him to him. And having seen him, the spirit immediately convulsed him, and falling on the ground he rolled around foaming at the mouth. And he asked his father, "How long has this been happening to him?" And he said, "From infancy; and often it has cast him into fire and into water in order to destroy him; but if you are able to do something, help us, having compassion on us!" And Jesus said, "If you are able! All things are possible to the person who believes." Immediately the father of the child was saying, "I believe; help my unbelief!" And Jesus, seeing a crowd running up, rebuked the unclean spirit, saying to it, "[Mute and deaf spirit], I command you, come out of him and never go back into him!" And crying out and greatly convulsing him, it went out; and he became like a corpse, so that everyone was saying that he had died. But Jesus took his hand and raised him up, and he arose.	[14]And having come to the disciples, they saw a great crowd around them and scribes disputing with them. [16]And he questioned them, "What are you discussing with them?" [18b–19][And someone said] "I said to your disciples to cast [a demon] out, and they weren't able to." And answering them, he says, "O faithless generation! How long will I be with you? How long will I bear with you?" [28–29]And when he had entered the house, the disciples privately questioned him, "Why were we not able to cast it out?" And he said to them, "This kind is not able to be expelled except through prayer."

With the healing of the blind man at Bethsaida (8:22–26), this exorcism of a boy with a **mute and deaf spirit** (9:17, 22, 25)—a redactional detail inserted by the evangelist in order to underline the theme of Jesus's healing of perceptual impairments (Mark 7:31–36; 8:22–26; 10:46–52; cf. Matt. 17:14–18; Luke 9:37–43)—brackets the two recognition scenes, both of which are misunderstood by the disciples (8:27–9:1; 9:2–13). Ironically, the literal blind and deaf are healed, but the disciples continue to see and hear without full understanding.

Although the combination of the two stories has resulted in some repetition and confusion (e.g., scribes are present [9:14; cf. 9:11], although the disciples have not yet returned to Galilee [cf. 9:30]; the crowd runs up to Jesus twice [9:15, 25]; it is unclear whether it is the crowd or the disciples who are arguing with the scribes [9:14, 16]; the boy suffers both from violent seizures and is a deaf-mute [9:17–18, 20, 25]; the difficult exorcism is attributed both to lack of faith [9:19, 23–24] and insufficient prayer [9:29]), the overall effect is dramatic, resulting in a hectic and compelling narrative. Returning down to earth from the mount of the transfiguration, Jesus and his three companions rejoin the other disciples amid a scene of failure and pandemonium.

As it stands, the text further develops the Markan themes of discipleship, faith, and spiritual insight/obtuseness. The disciples have been authorized by Jesus to cast out unclean spirits (6:7, 13), but they cannot cast the demon out of the boy. The disciples, the scribes, the crowd, and the boy's father are all included in Jesus's prophetic denunciation of this **faithless generation** (9:19). Jesus's response to the father's plea—**"If *you* are able! All things are possible to the one who believes"** (9:23)—can be read either as an ironic rebuke to the man for doubting Jesus's exorcistic power (see, e.g., France 2002, 367; Donahue and Harrington 2002, 278–79), or as demanding faith from the father (e.g., Marshall 1989, 116–18). The latter construal is consistent with Jesus's challenge to Jairus to believe in the power of God to raise his daughter (5:36), and to the disciples to give the crowd something to eat (6:37; cf. 6:5–6). The father's outburst, **"I believe, help my unbelief!"** is, as Donahue and Harrington (2002, 279) observe, "one of the most memorable and beloved statements in the New Testament because it captures the mixed character of faith within the experience of most people." Here it points to the immense power of faith to "move mountains" in the Markan worldview (cf. 11:22–23; cf. 10:27). The boy is restored to health, speech, and hearing by Jesus, but the disciples still must question Jesus privately: **"Why where we not able to cast it out?"** (9:28). Jesus's answer—**"This kind cannot be expelled except through prayer"** (v. 29)— seems out of place after the strong emphasis on faith in the body of the tale. Again the appeal is to the prayer life of the Markan reader/audience, whose ability to follow the example of Jesus was likely as imperfect as that of the disciples: "Where faith fails, prayer perishes. For who prays for that in which he does not believe? . . . So then in order that we may pray, let us believe, and let us pray that this same faith by which we pray may not falter" (Augustine, *Sermons on New Testament Lessons* 65.1, cited in Oden and Hall 1998, 117).

Theological Issues

In this pivotal section of the Gospel, Mark confirms that Jesus ministers not only to Jews, but to gentiles as well. The healings, and the miraculous feeding, that take place in the non-Jewish regions of Tyre, Sidon, Caesarea Philippi, and the Decapolis indicate that the reign of God extends beyond Israel, and that Isaiah's prophecies of healing and renewal (Isa. 35:5–6) are being fulfilled before the eyes of the disciples—and of the Markan audience. The narrative is dense with key christological affirmations either made or witnessed by disciples "on the way" to Jerusalem: Jesus is the messiah (8:29), the suffering son of man who will be manifested in glory (8:31, 38), the beloved Son of God who converses on the mountain with Elijah and Moses (9:2–8). While contemporary Christian readers may take it for granted that the title Christ encompasses election, suffering, glory, and divine sonship, these multiple facets of Jesus's identity would not necessarily have been self-evident to Mark's first-century audience, as symbolized by the disciples' difficulty in putting all the pieces together.

Perhaps the insecurities and frustrations of the disciples of Mark's time are best embodied in the difficult and dramatic exorcism of 9:14–29, where the disciples are taught that only faith in God and prayer to God (9:23–24, 29) can ensure the success of their mission.

The climax of this act in the Gospel drama is the transfiguration. In the context of Christian life, the disciples' vision of the transformed Jesus together with the deathless prophets Elijah and Moses evidences the kind of awe, wonder, and sense of mystery that are experienced by believers at key turning points in their life journeys, such as conversion, baptism, marriage, childbirth, or ordination, or in the context of worship, prayer, or meditation. For most

---

Mark's Suffering Messiah

As noted in the Introduction, the idea of a suffering, crucified messiah would have been foreign to ancient readers, whether Jewish or gentile. Although the term "messiah" ("anointed") could refer to figures as disparate as Cyrus the Great (Isa. 45:1) and the emperor Vespasian (Josephus, *J.W.* 6.5.4 §§312–13), Jewish messianic hopes often envisioned a royal, military figure who would restore Israel's sovereignty among the nations (see Juel 2000, 890). Mark explicates the contradictory themes of suffering and messiahship with reference to the Hebrew scriptures; Jesus is the righteous sufferer/rejected prophet who will be vindicated by God (e.g., Job 12:2–3; 16:20; 19:14; Pss. 27:11–12; 31:22; Isa. 52:13–53:12; Jer. 20:6–11; 2 Macc. 6:10–11, 18–31; 7:1–42; cf. Mark 6:4; 12:1–11), the subject of the lament psalms (Ahearne-Kroll 2007). The suffering and vindication modeled by Jesus will be experienced by his followers as well (Mark 8:34–35; 13:9–13).

of us, however, these "mountaintop experiences" are rare and last only for a time, and like Peter, James, and John we have to return to everyday life, with its challenges, troubles, and discouragements. This is a pattern exemplified in the careers of the prophets: Moses comes down from Sinai only to find the people worshiping the golden calf (Exod. 32:1–35); Elijah still has onerous prophetic duties to fulfill after his encounter with the "still small voice" (KJV) at Horeb (1 Kings 19:1–18). Jesus, Peter, James, and John descend from the mountain to face a chaotic and confusing hubbub. Even for the beloved son, the moment of transcendence cannot be sustained once the cloud of divinity lifts. The son of man, like the second Elijah, must suffer before he can rise from the dead (9:10–13).

In a confirmation sermon delivered on April 9, 1938, Dietrich Bonhoeffer, a German Lutheran pastor and theologian executed exactly seven years later for his anti-Nazi activism, reflected eloquently on the contrast between the peak experience of public incorporation into the Christian community and the struggle inherent in the ongoing life of faith:

> You do not have your belief once and for all. Your belief, which you profess today with all your hearts, demands to be won anew tomorrow and the day after tomorrow: indeed, it demands to be won anew with every new day. God gives us always just precisely so much faith as we need for the present day. Faith is the daily bread which God gives us. You know the manna story: while the children of Israel were in the wilderness, they received it every day, but as soon as they tried to store it up for the next day, it spoiled. So it is with all God's gifts. So it is with faith too. Either we receive it anew every day, or it decays. One day is long enough to keep faith. Every morning brings a new struggle to push through all the unbelief, through all the littleness of faith, through all the vagueness and confusion, through all the faintheartedness and uncertainty, to reach faith and wrest it from God. Every morning of your lives will begin and end with the same prayer: I believe, dear Lord: help my unbelief. (G. Kelly and Nelson 1990, 310)

Even Jesus, who converses on the spiritual Sinai with Moses and Elijah, needs the wavering faith of the desperate father of an afflicted child to wrest the demon from the boy. Augustine (*Sermons on New Testament Lessons* 65) reflects on the constant tension between faith and unbelief in his comment on the father's prayer:

> In saying, "When the Son of Man shall come, shall he find faith upon the earth?" our Lord spoke of that faith which is fully matured, which is so seldom found on earth. The church's faith is full, for who would come here if there were no fullness of faith? And whose faith when fully matured would not move mountains? Look at the apostles themselves, who would not have left all they had, trodden under foot this world's hope, and followed the Lord, if they had not had proportionally great faith. And yet if they had already experienced a completely matured faith, they would not have said to the Lord, "Increase our

faith." Rather we find here an emerging faith, which is not yet full faith, in that father who when he had presented to the Lord his son to be cured of an evil spirit and was asked whether he believed, answered, "Lord, I believe, help me in my unbelief." "Lord," says he, "I believe." "I believe": therefore there was faith; but "help me in my unbelief": therefore there was not full faith. (Quoted in Oden and Hall 1998, 117)

The tension between faith and unbelief in the father's cry captures the ambiguities and challenges of Christian life yet also points to its rewards: his child is restored, his faith—and the faith of the reader of Mark—is strengthened.

Mark's distinctive outlook on faith as *preceding* miracles, not *resulting from* witnessing them, has another layer of relevance to the Christian journey. Throughout Mark, healing is facilitated by a *community* of faith; both Jesus's confidence in the power of God, and the faith of those who surround him, are preconditions for healing (2:5; 5:34, 36; 9:23–24; 10:52). In his own hometown, even Jesus is able to heal only a few sick people because of the unbelief of his friends and neighbors (6:5–6). Like Jesus and the disciples, contemporary believers need a communal context of encouragement, support, and sharing—church, Bible study, small faith community—in order to nurture their spiritual growth toward mature faith.

Mark 9:30–10:52

Interlude: Teaching on the Way to Jerusalem

Introductory Matters

Structurally, Mark 9:30–10:52 is the third of four significant blocks of teaching material (cf. 4:1–34; 7:1–23; 13:1–37) inserted between the predominantly narrative sections of the Gospel (1:1–3:35; 4:35–6:56; 7:24–9:29; 11:1–12:44; 14:1–16:8). The teaching takes place in Jewish territory (9:30; 10:1) on the way up to Jerusalem (10:32–33). The second and third Markan Passion predictions punctuate the section (9:31–32; 10:32–34) and elaborate on the pattern of 8:31–9:1, where Jesus's prophecy of the suffering of the son of man is followed by misunderstanding by a disciple or disciples and teaching on the dangers inherent in discipleship. Throughout this section, Jesus's teaching is mostly directed to the disciples in private settings (9:33–50; 10:10–12, 23–30, 32b–34, 35–45) and pertains to the conduct of disciples at the level of both first-degree and second-degree narrative. Thus, while the teaching is addressed to the disciples as Gospel characters, it raises issues of relevance for the Markan audience: status and authority, the treatment of children, marriage and divorce, attitudes to family, the disposition of property, community boundaries. The story of Jesus's healing the blind man Bartimaeus (10:46–52) provides a transition between the teaching on the way to Jerusalem and Jesus's entry into Jerusalem (11:1–11).

As a digest of teachings on the conduct of disciples in the Markan community, Mark 9:30–10:52 is analogous to the *Community Rule* (i.e., 1QS, also known as the *Manual of Discipline*) found among the Dead Sea Scrolls, insofar as it contains instruction on "initiation into the sect and its common life, organization and discipline" imparted by an authoritative teacher (Vermès 1997, 97). It is also a precursor to the church orders of the second to fourth centuries AD, such as the *Didache*, the *Didascalia Apostolorum*, and the *Apostolic Tradition* (Vermès 1997, 98; cf. Matt. 5–7; 10; 18).

Apart from the Passion predictions, the inevitable misunderstanding of the disciples, and the teachings on the costs and rewards of discipleship—recurring themes in the section include following Jesus (9:32, 38, 41; 10:21, 28, 32, 52), the reign of God (9:1, 47; 10:14, 15, 23, 24, 25), and the example of children (9:36–37; 10:13–15; cf. 9:42; 10:24), amplifying the link between discipleship, self-giving service, and salvation. Peter, James, and John are often cast as interlocutors (9:38; 10:28, 35–44), pointing to their significance in the early church (Gal. 2:9; cf. Acts 3:1–10; 4:1–23; 8:14–17; 12:2; 15:1–21; cf. Mark 9:35 and 10:32, where the Twelve are singled out for instruction). The setting of the teaching alternates between "the way" to Jerusalem (9:33–34; 10:17, 32, 46, 52) and "the house" (9:33; 10:10), where Jesus retreats to teach the disciples.

The accompanying outline indicates the geographical transition from Galilee to Judea. The Galilee section begins with the second Passion prediction (9:30–31), and the Judea section ends with the third Passion prediction and the subsequent discussion of discipleship as service. Thus, while the first prediction was given in the gentile city of Caesarea Philippi (8:31), the second and third are uttered in Jewish regions, on the way to Jerusalem (9:30–31; 10:1, 32–34).

Tracing the Narrative Flow

Teaching in Galilee (9:30–50)

This section of teaching in Galilee begins with the second Passion prediction (9:30–32), followed by an argument that occasions some teaching on discipleship (9:33–37), a word about tolerating others who are working in Jesus's name (9:38–41), and a stern warning about harming the "little ones" (9:42–50).

9:30–32. All three Passion predictions take place in private: **He did not want anyone to know it** (9:30b; cf. 10:32). This is the tersest of the three, and contains an element of Greek wordplay that is lost in most translations: **he was teaching . . . that the human being** ["son of man," *ho huios tou anthrōpou*] **would be handed into human hands** [*eis cheiras anthrōpōn*],

> ### An Outline
> ### of Mark 9:30–50
>
> **Teaching in Galilee (9:30–50)**
>
> Second Passion prediction (9:30–32)
>
> The cost of discipleship and the example of the child (9:33–37)
>
> The unknown exorcist (9:38–41)
>
> Teachings on avoiding sin (9:42–50)

and be put to death [and] after three days rise up. The practice of reserving certain teachings for disciples is reminiscent of the procedure described in the *Community Rule* of the Dead Sea Scrolls.

The disciples' lack of understanding and fearful reaction (9:32) are typical after the fateful recognition scene at Caesarea Philippi (8:27–30): **They did not understand the word, and they were afraid to ask him** (cf. 8:31–33; 9:6, 9–10).

9:33–37. The extended teaching scene in Mark 9:33–50 takes place in the house at Capernaum that functions as home base for Jesus and the disciples in Galilee (1:21; 2:1; cf. Donahue and Harrington 2002, 284). The setting "at home" also evokes the house churches of Mark's time. Jesus's initial exchange with the disciples is cast in the form of an action/saying-*chreia*. Jesus initiates the discourse with a rhetorical question: **"What were you discussing on the way?"** (9:33). Although the disciples remain silent, Jesus, like the omniscient narrator, knows that they had been discussing who was greatest among them

---

Qumran Teaching Reserved for Disciples

"He shall conceal the teaching of the Law from men of injustice, but shall impart true knowledge and righteous judgement to those who have chosen the Way. He shall guide them all in knowledge according to the spirit of each and to the rule of the age, and shall thus instruct them in the mysteries of marvelous truth, so that in the midst of the men of the Community they may walk perfectly together in all that has been revealed to them. This is the time for the preparation of the way into the wilderness, and he shall teach them to do all that is required at that time and to separate from all those who have not turned aside from all injustice." (1QS 9.20, trans. Vermès 1997, 111)

(9:34; cf. 9:10). After Jesus's two prophecies of his suffering and death, the disciples' conversation is deeply ironic: "While Jesus's eyes are fixed on martyrdom, they are preoccupied with the question of status. While Jesus is talking about rejection and death, they are apparently thinking of a continuing movement in which leadership will be an issue" (France 2002, 373). Jesus assumes the seated pose of a teacher (cf. 4:1; 13:3) and singles out the Twelve for his pronouncement: **"If anyone wants to be first, let them be last of all and slave of all"** (9:35b). This is found in several Gospel contexts (Mark 10:43–44; cf. Matt. 20:26–27//Luke 22:26; Matt. 23:11; Luke 9:48c). Here it is addressed not only to the disciples' craving for status in the realm of God but also to the ambitions of the leaders of the evangelist's time, symbolized by the Twelve.

The saying is illustrated by an action that takes full advantage of the domestic setting, followed by further elaboration: **And taking a child he sat it amid them and embracing it he said to them** (9:36). The meaning of the child in this context is contested; some interpreters see the child as an example of innocence (e.g., Herm. *Sim.* 9.29) or of receptivity (e.g., Moloney 2002, 188–89; cf. Mark 10:15), but most relate it primarily to the reversal saying: "The child represents the lowest order in the social scale, the one who is under the authority and care of others and who has not yet achieved the right of self-determination" (France 2002, 374; cf. Donahue and Harrington 2002, 285; Boring 2006, 281). The reference to the disciples of Mark's time is clear from the final pronouncement: **"Whoever receives such a child in my name, receives me. And whoever receives me, receives not me but the one who sent me"** (9:37). It is the members of the early Christian community who should extend hospitality to visiting believers ("children"; cf. 9:42; 10:24) in Jesus's name (cf. 1 Cor. 1:2, 10; 5:4; 6:11; Phil. 2:10; Col. 3:17; Eph. 5:20; 2 Thess. 1:12; 3:6; 1 John 3:23; Acts 2:38; 3:6; 5:40). However, as Juel (1990, 133) states, the literal reference to the acceptance of children within the community should not be discounted: "While the image of a child or a 'little one' may symbolize all those within the Christian family, we should not move too quickly to the symbolic. 'Receiving children'—welcoming them, caring about them—means what it says" (see Mark 10:13–16). The pursuit of mission for the sake of the gospel could lead to ruptures within the biological family but also to the adoption of new spiritual "brothers and sisters and mothers and children" (10:30; cf. 3:34–35).

9:38–41. The question of how broadly to tolerate those who labor "in Jesus's name" is elaborated in response to John's blunt declaration: **"Teacher, we saw a certain man casting out demons in your name, and we forbade him, because he does not follow you"** (9:38). At the level of first-degree narrative, the reference may simply be to believers who do not belong to the Markan community, or to non-Christian wonder-workers, who, like the sons of Sceva, used the name of Jesus to perform exorcisms (Acts 19:11–20). Again Jesus's reply expresses opposition to the kind of narrow construal of who Jesus's "followers" are,

The *Didache* on Christian Hospitality

"Now, you should welcome anyone who comes your way and teaches you all we have been saying. But if the teacher proves himself a renegade and by teaching otherwise contradicts all this, pay no attention to him. But if his teaching furthers the Lord's righteousness and knowledge, welcome him as the Lord.... Everyone who comes to you in the name of the Lord must be welcomed. Afterward, when you have tested him, you will find out about him, for you have insight into right and wrong. If it is a traveler who arrives, help him all you can. But he must not stay with you more than two days, or, if necessary, three. If he wants to settle with you and is an artisan, he must work for his living. If, however, he has no trade, use your judgment in taking steps for him to live with you as a Christian without being idle. If he refuses to do this, he is trading on Christ. You must be on your guard against such people." (Did. 11.1–2; 12.1–5, trans. Ehrman 1999, 324)

as exemplified by the Twelve: **"Do not forbid him. For no one who performs power in my name is also able to speak evil of me; for whoever is not against us is for us. For whoever gives you a cup of water in [my] name because you belong to the messiah, amen I say to you will not lose his reward"** (9:39–41). The inclusivism of Mark 9:40—"whoever is not against us is for us"—is inverted in Q: "Whoever is not with me is against me, and whoever does not gather with me scatters" (Matt. 12:30; Luke 11:23; however, cf. Luke 9:49–50, which preserves Mark's inclusivism). There is an added layer of irony in the disciples' disdain for the unknown exorcist's activities in the light of their own failure to exorcise the boy with a deaf-and-dumb demon in 9:14–29 (cf. Boring 2006, 282). The pericope is reminiscent of the instructions on how to treat Christian visitors in the *Didache*, an ancient book of church order (ca. AD 100), which contains lengthy instructions on such matters and illustrates the kinds of issues facing the traveling missionaries of Mark's time, as well as the question of how to deal with believers unfamiliar to the community.

9:42–50. The example of the unknown exorcist is sandwiched between the *chreia* on the acceptance of children and a harsh warning against scandalizing "little ones": **"And whoever causes one of these little ones of the faithful to stumble, it would be better for them to wear a donkey's millstone around their neck and be cast into the sea"** (9:42). The phrase *tōn mikrōn tōn pisteuontōn* can be read as referring either to the literal children "of the faithful" (9:36–37) or as metaphorical for believers in "the name"—"little ones among the faithful" (cf. 10:24). Although there is no need to make a decisive choice between the two interpretations, as part of a Markan frame it should be read as referring back to the unknown exorcist, whose proclamation of the messiah must not be thwarted. The punishment envisioned for disciples who cause others to err is capital; Moloney (2002, 190n37, citing Lagrange 1929, 234–35) reports that "this form of execution is taken from Roman practice, and was not unknown among the Jews." The reference to death by drowning should be taken not literally but as an exaggeration meant to emphasize the seriousness of church leaders' (like John in 9:38) causing believers to stray through their intolerance toward "outsiders."

The sayings in 9:43–48 initially appear loosely organized, with little application to the material above. However, the three parallel sayings in these verses are structured similarly, and they are connected by the repetition of catchwords:

> And if your hand causes you to stumble, cut it off; it is better for you to enter into life maimed than having two hands to pass away into Gehenna, into the unquenchable fire.
> And if your foot causes you to stumble, cut it off; it is better for you to enter into life lame than having two feet to be cast into Gehenna.
> And if your eye causes you to stumble, cast it out; it is better to enter the realm of God with one eye than having two to be cast into Gehenna, where their worm does not die and the fire is not quenched.

Here Jesus's commands are phrased in the second-person singular and are addressed specifically to John (9:38). As in the saying about the millstone, the language is hyperbolic, offering self-mutilation as preferable to being caused to stumble by one's own sinful actions, in this case, behaving inhospitably to other believers. Entering into life (9:43, 45; possibly synonymous with "eternal life": cf. Mark 10:17, 30) is equated with entering the realm of God (9:47), the opposite of being consigned to Gehenna (9:43, 45, 47), often translated as "hell" (e.g., NIV, KJV, NASB, NLT, NRSV). The name *geenna* (derived from the Hinnom Valley, southwest of Jerusalem) and its infernal associations are from biblical history:

> This valley acquired an evil reputation because of the idolatrous practice of child sacrifices offered to Moloch there during the days of Ahaz and Manasseh, two of the most notorious kings ever to lead Judah, the southern part of the divided monarchy (2 Kings 16:3; 21:6). Later, during the reign of Josiah, this faithful king had the valley desecrated in order to prevent a recurrence of this abominable practice (2 Kings 23:10). Still later the Prophet Jeremiah announced that this valley would become a place of God's future judgment, where the Lord would recompense the kings of Judah and the people of Jerusalem for their abominable deeds. Hence the valley would no longer be called the "Valley of Ben Hinnom," but the "Valley of Slaughter" (Jer. 7:30–34; 19:1–11). (Scharen 1992, 328)

In the Jewish apocalyptic *Book of Enoch*, the "accursed valley" is portrayed as a place of eschatological judgment for the unrighteous (e.g., *1 En.* 27.2).

However, the oft-repeated notion that the valley served as a dumping ground for burning refuse originated in the medieval period and has no literary or archaeological support (Scharen 1992, 328n17). The severity of God's judgment on those who sin by causing others to stumble is emphasized with a phrase from Isa. 66:24: **"where their worm does not die and the fire is not quenched"** (Mark 9:48). This was originally an oracle concerning the fate of the rebellious nations of the prophet's time: the abhorrent sight of the dead bodies of the rebels moldering and burning will be a warning to the living. Some ancient versions of this passage quote Isaiah's words of warning as a refrain in two verses (Mark 9:44, 46) that are left out of many modern translations.

The last three sayings in this chapter (9:49–50) are linked by the catchwords "fire" and "salt" but seem otherwise to bear little relationship to the material that precedes or follows them: **For all will be salted with fire. Salt is good, but if the salt becomes unsalty, how can you season it? Have salt in yourselves and be at peace with one another.** Their meaning was probably already opaque to both Matthew and Luke, who omitted them from their versions of this discourse (Matt. 5:29–30; 18:6–9; Luke 17:1–2; however, see Matt. 5:13; Luke 14:34–35). Many interpreters see a connection with Lev. 2:13 (cf. Num. 18:19; 2 Chron. 13:5), which specifies that grain offerings should be seasoned with "the salt of the covenant," although the connection seems obscure. The geologist Eugene P. Deatrick (1962, 45, 48) makes the interesting observation that in antiquity, the value of salt as both a fertilizer and an herbicide was well known, concluding that "Jesus alluded to the growth-stimulation effect of salt, since he was interested not merely in the preservation of his way of life but much more in its continued stimulation towards ever greater growth, which comes about only if Christians do not lose their saving influence on others." The third "salt" saying ("have salt in yourselves and be at peace with one another") relates back to the teaching that disciples should treat one another with peace and hospitality (cf. Donahue and Harrington 2002, 289).

Teaching in Judea (10:1–45)

The teaching in Judea falls into six sections, beginning with some instruction on marriage and divorce (10:1–12) and concluding, after the third Passion prediction (10:32–40), with further teaching on discipleship (10:41–45).

10:1–12. Mark's notice that Jesus left for **the region of Judea [and] across the Jordan** (10:1) seems geographically garbled, since the most direct route to Jerusalem from Galilee would

---

An Outline of Mark 10:1–45

Teaching in Judea (10:1–45)

> **Debate and instruction on marriage and divorce (10:1–12)**
>
> **Jesus blesses children (10:13–16)**
>
> **Jesus and the rich man (10:17–22)**
>
> **Wealth and the rewards of discipleship (10:23–31)**
>
> **Third Passion prediction (10:32–34)**
>
> **Discipleship as service (10:35–45)**

Samaritans

Josephus says that the Samaritans were originally immigrants who were moved into the northern kingdom of Israel ("Samaria") after its defeat by the Assyrians in 721 BC (*Ant.* 9.14.3 §§288–91; cf. 2 Kings 17). The Elephantine papyri, a collection of Jewish manuscripts from the fifth century BC belonging to an Egyptian Jewish community, include letters from both Jewish and Samaritan priests requesting support for the building of their respective temples in Jerusalem and at Mount Gerizim. A remnant of the ancient Samaritan community survives today, and like their ancestors, they regard themselves as the descendants of the northern tribes of Ephraim and Manasseh. The Samaritan temple at Mount Gerizim was destroyed by the Jewish ruler and high priest John Hyrcanus (ca. 110 BC). Although they were regarded as heretics by Jews in Jesus's time, a mission to Samaria is highlighted in the book of Acts (8:4–25; cf. John 4:3–42; R. Anderson 2000).

be through Samaria; some commentators opine that in order to skirt Samaritan territory, Jesus and the disciples take a detour by crossing the Jordan into Perea (see Donahue and Harrington 2002, 292; Collins 2007, 457). The teaching in 10:1–12 replicates the pattern of public teaching (10:2–9), followed by private explanation to the disciples (10:11–12), and is especially reminiscent of the earlier debate with the Pharisees in 7:1–23. Although Jesus is initially portrayed as teaching a crowd that gathers around him, as in the earlier dialogue, some Pharisees arrive and question him on the interpretation of Torah: **"Is it lawful for a man to divorce his wife?"** (10:2). Jesus turns the question back on his interrogators: **And answering he said to them, "What has Moses commanded?" And they said, "Moses permitted to write a certificate of divorce and to divorce her"** (10:3–4). Although this answer accurately reflects Deut. 24:1, the issue of grounds for divorce was a live one among Jesus's Jewish contemporaries, as the famous disagreement among the first-century rabbis Hillel, Shammai, and Akiba illustrates:

> The School of Shammai say: A man may not divorce his wife unless he has found unchastity in her, for it is written, Because he has found in her indecency in anything (Deut. 24:1a). And the School of Hillel say, (He may divorce her) even if she spoiled a dish for him, for it is written, Because he has found indecency in anything. R. Akiba says, Even if he found another fairer than she, for it is written, And it shall be if she find no favour in his eyes. (*m. Giṭ.* 9.10, in Catchpole 1974, 93)

Collins (2007, 459–65) adduces extensive evidence that Jewish divorce practices varied widely in the Second Temple period, and that the right of men, and sometimes women (cf. Mark 10:12), to divorce was taken for granted by both

Jews and gentiles. Within the context of first-century customs regarding marriage and divorce, Jesus's answer is astonishingly strict (although the Qumran documents contain two references that forbid divorce: 11QT 57.17–19; CD 4.19–5.2; see Herron 1982, 275). Using Torah to explicate Torah, he combines Gen. 1:27, **From the beginning of creation "male and female he made them"**; and Gen. 2:24, **"A man shall leave his father and his mother and be joined to his wife, and the two shall be one flesh"**—both to demonstrate that the prior legislation **(from the beginning of creation)** is more fundamental than Moses's concession to the Pharisees' **hardness of heart** (Mark 10:5–8). This prohibition of divorce is cast as a radical return to divine intention for marriage, as stipulated in the garden of Eden: **Let not humanity separate that which God has yoked together** (v. 9); Jesus gives the reasoning: once they are married, **they are no longer two but one** (v. 8b). As with the earlier teaching, Jesus's ruling on divorce applies to the Markan audience, whose marital fidelity must reflect the primal will of God (cf. 3:35).

In view of the stringency of Jesus's pronouncement, the disciples' private request for further explanation is understandable (10:10). Jesus's private answer is even stricter than his public teaching: **"He who divorces his wife and marries another woman commits adultery with her. And if she divorces her husband and marries another man, she commits adultery"** (vv. 11–12). The casual assumption of both women's and men's option to divorce probably indicates the gentile social context of the Markan community (see Collins 2007, 465). The idea that a man could commit adultery against his wife, whether by divorcing and marrying another woman or by simply having sex with another partner, is foreign to Jewish law (Deut. 22:22–24; Lev. 20:10), and as Collins (2007, 469) points out, it is also alien to Greco-Roman cultures: "Unconditional fidelity was required of the woman alone. In Greek law, [a man's] adultery was defined as 'secret sexual intercourse with a free woman without the consent of her κύριος [lit., "lord"; here, "husband"].'" The astonishing evenhandedness with respect to the sexual rights of both wives and husbands presupposed here is evidence of a level of gender egalitarianism within Mark's community that is dismissed as wishful thinking by some contemporary biblical scholars (e.g., J. Elliott 2002; 2003). Paul, citing Jesus, instructs women not to separate from their husbands and men not to divorce their wives (1 Cor. 7:10–11, 39), but in his own name (as opposed to Jesus's) advises believers to divorce their non-Christian husbands or wives if the unbelieving spouse wishes to separate; otherwise, spouses should stay together (1 Cor. 7:12–16). This contrasts with Matthew's version, which allows divorce in the case of adultery and does not mention the possibility of a woman's initiating divorce (Matt. 19:1–9).

10:13–16. Mark 10:13–16 returns to the theme of the status of children in the community (cf. 9:36–37, 42), underlining the theme of children as paradigmatic for the reign of God. After the previous teaching, the disciples' attempt to prevent children being brought to Jesus to be touched/blessed is at once shocking and typical of the lack of spiritual insight evidenced in earlier passages. As in Mark 9:36–37, the importance of children, both as members of the community and as symbolic of the divine rule, is expressed in both word and deed: **"Let the children come to me, do not prevent them, for of such is the reign of God. Amen I say to you, unless one receives the reign of God like a child, they will not be able to enter it."** And embracing them he blessed them, laying his hands upon them (10:15–16). The casting of Jesus's words as an amen saying gives the utterance the solemnity of an oath. In view of 9:36–37, the image of receiving/entering the realm of God "like a child" refers to seeking God without expectation of status or reward. Wolfgang Roth finds an inverted Elisha-Jesus typology here: "Jesus's reaction is . . . reminiscent of the brief story of Elisha's cursing of children who had mocked him when he left the city of Jericho (2 Kings 2:23–24). Thus the gospel contrasts Jesus and Elisha, while in other texts it shows him exceeding the man from Abel-meholah" (Roth 1988, 111). This kind of inversion of problematic stories from the Jewish scriptures is found elsewhere in the Gospel; see, for example, the comments on 4:35–41 and 5:21–24, 35–43 above.

10:17–22. Jesus's easy acceptance of children contrasts starkly with the near-rebuff of the next person who approaches him "on the way": **A man running and kneeling before him asked him, "Good teacher, what shall I do to inherit eternal life?"** (10:17). The supplicant's attitude of enthusiasm and humility, and his recognition of Jesus as a "good teacher," appear to be genuine and respectful. In Mark, the expression "eternal life" appears only here and in 10:30, where *zōēn aiōnion* is the gift of the "age to come." Here it is synonymous with the reign of God (Donahue and Harrington 2002, 302; cf. 10:23). The metaphor of "inheriting" eternal life bespeaks the man's pious concern with the afterlife (Dan. 12:2; *Pss. Sol.* 14.9–10; *1 En.* 40.9; *Sib. Or.* fragment 3, lines 46–49; see Collins 2007, 476). However, Jesus counters the man's question with a rebuke: **"Why do you call me good? No one is good except the one God"** (10:18). In early Judaism, addressing a human as "good" was not impossible, but it was rare (see Collins 2007, 476–77); Jesus's refusal of the adjective flows from "the typical summons in the Psalms, 1 and 2 Chronicles, and Ezra to give thanks to God because God is good. The goodness of God is associated in these passages with God's steadfast love (חֶסֶד [*hesed*]) for Israel" (Collins 2007, 476; cf. Pss. 100:5; 106:1; 107:1; 118:1; 136:1; 1 Chron. 16:34; 2 Chron. 5:13; Ezra 3:11). In view of the citation of the commandments that follows (Mark 10:19), Jesus's reply that only "the one God" (*heis ho theos*) is good is a pointed assertion of monotheism (Exod. 20:3; Deut. 5:7; 6:4), possibly directed against christological excesses in the Markan community. Of the Ten Commandments, Jesus reminds the man of five, all of them regulating interpersonal relations: **"'Do not murder, do not commit adultery, do not steal, do not bear false witness, do not commit fraud, honor your father and your mother'"** (10:19). The reference to "defrauding" (*mē aposterēsēs*) does not appear in the Decalogue (it replaces the command against covetousness in Exod. 20:17; Deut. 5:21); in the LXX, the verb refers to the illicit deprivation of workers of their wages (Deut. 24:14–15; Mal. 3:5; Sir. 4:1). In view of the revelation at the story's end that the man is wealthy (10:22), the reason for the substitution is clarified: "the rich man had not even done what many rich people were deemed all too able to do: oppress and/or take advantage of and/or deny wages" (Crossley 2005, 398).

The man's affirmation that he has followed these commandments from his youth evokes a shift in Jesus's attitude: **And Jesus, having looked at him, loved him and said to him, "You lack one thing; go, sell what you have and give it to the poor, and you will have a treasure in heaven, and come follow me"** (10:21). The verb "to love" here is *agapaō*, "to have a warm regard for and interest in another, *cherish, have affection for, love*" (BDAG 5). The radical command that the man relinquish his belongings contrasts with the theology of proverbial wisdom, which sees wealth as a reward for righteousness (Crossley 2005, 398; cf. Deut. 28:1–14; Job 1:10; 42:10; Prov. 10:22; Isa. 3:10; Tob. 12:9; Sir. 3:1, 6; 25:7–11; 35:13; 44:10–15; 51:27–30; Bar. 4:1). The notion that wealth is an impediment to salvation is a Jewish apocalyptic motif (CD 4.15–19; 1QS 11.1–2; *Pss. Sol.* 5.16; *1 En.* 96.4; 103.5–8) that finds frequent expression in the synoptic tradition (e.g., Luke 16:13//Matt. 6:24; Luke 14:16–24//Matt. 22:1–14; Luke 12:13–21; 16:19–31; cf. Crossley 2005, 398–99). The man's reaction to the conditions of following Jesus is drastic; he becomes gloomy (*stygnasas*) and leaves sorrowfully (*lypomenos*), **for he had many possessions** (10:22). The price of discipleship is too high for him; to "inherit eternal life," the rich man must liquidate his inherited wealth and undermine the inheritance rights of his heirs.

10:23–31. The teaching on discipleship in 10:23–31 flows from the story of the rich man, much as the discourse in 9:39–50 follows the account of the unknown exorcist. The dialogue begins with Jesus's observation, **"How difficult it is for those having riches to enter into the realm of God!"** at which the disciples marvel (10:23). Jesus reiterates and intensifies the saying: **"Children, how difficult it is to enter into the realm of God; it is easier for a camel to go through the eye of a needle than for a rich man to enter the realm of God!"** (10:24–25). The harshness of the camel proverb is often ameliorated with reference to the notion that there was a narrow gate called the Needle's Eye in Jerusalem, through which a camel could navigate only with difficulty; however, this is a Christian explanation popularized in the nineteenth century (France 2002, 405). To underplay the extravagance of the image, some ancient manuscripts substitute *kamilos* ("rope") for *kamēlos* ("camel"). However, the saying is similar to a Jewish one about the impossibility of an elephant passing through the eye of a needle (*b. Ber.* 55b) and is meant to emphasize the difficulty of the feat. The disciples' confusion over Jesus's words is a typical misunderstanding scene that reflects the traditional attitude that God favors the righteous with wealth: **And they were exceedingly amazed, saying to each other, "Who then can be saved?"** (10:26). Jesus's answer escalates from difficulty to impossibility: **"With human beings it is not possible, but not with God; for all things are possible with God"** (10:27). This is a sentiment that is expressed elsewhere in Mark, in Jesus's words to the father of the possessed boy (*"all things are possible* to the one who believes"; 9:23; cf. 11:22–23). In Mark's worldview, the expulsion of an intractable demon, a rich man's leaving behind his wealth to enter the realm of God, the moving of a mountain by a word—all are humanly impossible but divinely achievable.

Peter's observation in 10:28 that he and the other disciples have, unlike the rich man, **left everything and followed you** not only contrasts with the attitude of the rich man, but also expresses the position of the reader/audience of Mark, whose entry into the divine realm is contingent upon leaving **"household or brothers or sisters or mother or father or children or fields for my sake and for the sake of the good news"** (10:29). When individuals or parts of households joined a community of believers and the rest of their household did not join, it must have happened at times that the newly converted would become estranged from nonconverted members of their household. Although such converts might not have "left" parents and siblings physically, they may have lost the approval and support of their families, who would have been embarrassed and even endangered by having Christian relatives (cf. Collins 2007, 482–83).

However, Jesus's answer to Peter is not entirely reassuring. To leave one's possessions for the sake of the gospel will **"reap a hundredfold now, in this time, houses and brothers and sisters and mothers and children and fields with persecution, and in the age to come eternal life"** (10:30). The contrast between the biological family and the "true family" of disciples (3:31–32) is powerfully reasserted; the spiritual brothers, sisters, mothers, and children of the disciples surpass the families they have forsaken (or who have forsaken them). The household of faith, unlike the natal family, does not contain fathers (cf. 10:29), whose position in the structure of the ancient household was based on rank, in the manner famously described by Aristotle:

> The science of household management has three divisions, one the relation of master to slave, of which we have spoken before, one the paternal relation, and the third the conjugal—for it is a part of the household science to rule over wife and children; . . . for the male is by nature better fitted to command than the female (except in some cases where their union has been formed contrary to nature) and the older and more fully developed person over the younger and immature. (*Pol.* 1.5.3, trans. Rackham 1932)

For Jesus, as for his followers, the only *patēr* is the "Father in heaven" (cf. 11:25). The phrase "with persecutions" (*meta diōgmōn*) may refer to the kinds of social rejection and estrangement that leaving one's family would entail

---

The Secret Gospel of Mark

In 1958, Morton Smith discovered a copy of a previously unknown manuscript attributed to Clement of Alexandria (second cent. AD) in the library of the Mar Saba monastery near Jerusalem. The letter, addressed "to Theodore," refers to an esoteric, expanded version of the Gospel of Mark being used by the Carpocratian sect to promote their beliefs. Clement quotes two excerpts from the "secret gospel" meant to be inserted between Mark 10:34 and 35, and into 10:46:

> *"They came to Bethany. There was one woman there whose brother had died. She came and prostrated herself before Jesus and spoke to him. 'Son of David, pity me!' But the disciples rebuked her. Jesus was angry and went with her into the garden where the tomb was. Immediately a great cry was heard from the tomb. And going up to it, Jesus rolled the stone away from the door of the tomb, and immediately went in where the young man was. Stretching out his hand, he lifted him up, taking hold his hand. And the youth, looking intently at him, loved him and started begging him to let him remain with him. And going out of the tomb, they went into the house of the youth, for he was rich. And after six days Jesus gave him an order and, at evening, the young man came to him wearing nothing but a linen cloth. And he stayed with him for the night, because Jesus taught him the mystery of the Kingdom of God. And then when he left he went back to the other side of the Jordan. . . .*
>
> *"Then he came into Jericho. And the sister of the young man whom Jesus loved was there with his mother and Salome, but Jesus would not receive them."* (M. Smith 1973, 16–17)

Clement warns Theodore that secret Mark is being misinterpreted by the Carpocratians, but he does not condemn the secret gospel itself. Controversy has raged as to the authenticity of the Clementine letter since Smith published his findings in 1973.

---

in the class-stratified and conventional Greco-Roman society in which the Markan community was situated. It may also refer to sharing in the kinds of suffering and martyrdom expressed in the Passion predictions. The "eternal life" sought by the rich man (10:17) will be the inheritance of "the age/world to come" (10:30), a phrase common in Jewish apocalyptic and rabbinic literature (e.g., *1 En.* 1.3–9; 5.6–9; 10.7; 10.16–11.2; 25.3–7; 48.7; 71.15; 2 Esd. [*4 Ezra*] 7:113; 8:46; *2 Bar.* 14.13; 15.7; *m. 'Abot* 4.1, 21, 22; 6.4, 7). The age to come will be free of the persecutions and renunciations of "now, this time." The reversal saying, **For many who are first will be last, and the last will be first** (10:31), summarizes the import of 10:17–30. The rich man, who ranks above the disciples in the present age, will be last in the realm of God; the disciples, who have done what their social superior could not, have the advantage.

10:32–34. The final Passion prediction is uttered to the Twelve **on the way up to Jerusalem** (10:32). The violence anticipated in the events **about to happen to him** contrasts with the joyous import of the expression to "go up to Jerusalem," which evokes a pilgrimage to the temple for a festival or sacrifice (Zech. 14:17; John 2:13; 5:1; 11:55; Acts 24:11; cf. Pss. 122; 126). The phrase is also redolent of Cyrus's edict allowing the exiles to "go up" to Jerusalem to rebuild the temple (2 Chron. 36:23; Ezra 1:3, 5; 7:7, 13), and prophetic oracles of restoration: "and many nations shall come and say: 'Come, let us go up to the mountain of the LORD, to the house of the God of Jacob; that he may teach us his ways and that we may walk in his paths.' For out of Zion shall go forth instruction, and the word of the LORD from Jerusalem" (Mic. 4:2; cf. Isa. 2:3; Zech. 14:16–17). The prediction that follows, the most detailed and explicit of the three, summarizes the events of Mark 11:1–16:8: **"The son of man will be handed over to the chief priests and the scribes, and they will sentence him to death and hand him over to the gentiles, and they will mock him and spit on him and whip him and kill [him], and after three days he will rise up"** (10:33–34). Although in the Hebrew Bible the terms "high priest" (*kōhēn haggādôl*) and "chief priest" (*kōhēn hārō'š*) are both used to refer to the primary official of the temple cult, here the plural "chief priests" (*archiereusin*) appears to refer to the priestly aristocracy of Jerusalem (cf. 8:31; 11:18).

10:35–45. The response of James and John to this third and final Passion prediction follows the pattern of the previous two. However, after such an explicit prophecy of the imminent suffering of the son of man, their request is shocking: **"Grant us that we may sit, one at your right hand and one at your left hand, in your glory"** (10:37b); it recalls and illumines the disciples' earlier argument over which of them was the greatest (9:34). The sons of Zebedee envision Jesus as the anointed king (Messiah) of a restored kingdom of Israel, in which Jesus will sit enthroned in glory (cf. *1 En.* 45.3), with his first- and second-ranked courtiers at his right and left hands (cf. 1 Kings 22:19; Ps. 110:1; 1 Esd. 4:28b–30; Sir. 12:12; Mark 12:36; Josephus, *Ant.* 6.11.9 §235; cf. Matt. 19:28; 25:31). Jesus's answer is a rebuke: **"You do not know what you are asking. Are you able to drink the cup that I will drink or be baptized by the baptism by which I will be baptized?"** (10:38). In the Hebrew scriptures, the "cup" (*potērion*) is a metaphor for suffering (e.g., Isa. 51:17, 22; Jer. 25:15; 49:12; 51:7; Lam. 4:21; Ezek. 23:31–32; Hab. 2:15; cf. Pss. 11:6; 75:8; *Pss. Sol.* 8.14). Here the term usually translated as "baptism" (*baptisma*) refers to submersion in water, a biblical metaphor for death and destruction (e.g., 2 Sam. 22:5; Pss. 42:7; 88:7; Isa. 43:2; Jer. 51:42; Ezek. 26:3; Jon. 2:3). In this light, Jesus's prophetic reply to the disciples' assurance that they are able to drink his cup and endure his "baptism" is bitterly ironic: **"The cup that I shall drink you will drink, and the baptism by which I am baptized you will be baptized by, but to sit at my right hand or at my left is not mine to give, but for those for whom it has been prepared"** (10:39–40). Early Christian tradition attests

Figure 9. *The Crucifixion of Christ*, by Albrecht Altdorfer, 1526.

that James and John suffered persecution and martyrdom (Acts 4:1–22; 12:12). However, in Mark's Passion Narrative, the ones who are elevated to Jesus's right and left hands are the two criminals crucified beside him (15:27): the seats of honor coveted by the brothers are places on the cross. The divine passive ("for whom it has been prepared") emphasizes that it is God, not Jesus, who is the main actor in the drama of salvation.

The remaining verses in this section illustrate that the other ten disciples have not understood Jesus's teachings any better than the Zebedee brothers: **And having heard, the Twelve began to be indignant about James and John** (10:41). The disciples' anger does not stem from the brothers' misunderstanding of the reign of God but arose because the two are vying for the honor they all covet (cf. 9:34). Jesus amplifies the reversal saying of 9:35 as he teaches in 10:42–45: **"You know that those who think they rule the nations dominate them, and the great among them exercise authority over them. It shall not be so among you, but whoever wants to become great among you shall be your servant, and whoever among you wants to be first shall be slave of all. For the son of man has come not to be served but to serve and to give his life as a ransom for many."** The reference to the rulers of the nations ("gentiles") refers to the experience of Jews in first-century Palestine as subject to the

157

Roman imperial power, which rules and dominates them and other peoples. For Mark, however, the Romans only "think" or "appear" (*dokountes*) to rule, because the true king of the earth is God (Pss. 10:16; 24:8; 29:10; 47:2–4; 84:3; 95:3–5; cf. Exod. 19:5–6; Deut. 7:6; 14:2; 26:18–19), whose rule is based on values opposite to those of the Romans: humility rather than exaltation, service rather than mastery.

The "ransom" saying of Mark 10:45 has generated a great deal of debate regarding its relation to the figure of the servant in Isa. 53 (see the discussion in Watts 1997, 270–84; also Beale and Carson 2007, 203–6). Particularly, the saying seems to echo Isa. 53:10b–12 LXX:

> And the Lord wished to take away from the pain of his soul, to show him light and fill him with understanding, to justify a righteous one who is well subject to many, and he himself shall bear their sins. Therefore he shall inherit many, and he shall divide the spoils of the strong, because his soul was given over to death, and he was reckoned among the lawless, and he bore the sins of many, and because of their sins he was given over. (NETS)

Like the servant of God (Isa. 52:13), Jesus the Son of Man comes to serve, a righteous man who "serves many well" (53:11). The son of man, like the servant, is "given over to death" (53:11 NETS). However, the image of the life (*psychē*) of the servant-like son of man being given as a "ransom" (*lytron*) is not native to the Isaian servant songs (Isa. 42:1–7; 49:1–7; 50:4–9; 52:13–53:12); the servant of Isaiah "bears" the "sins of many" like the scapegoat on the Day of Atonement (Lev. 16:20–22). A ransom, in contrast, is a payment in return for a life (cf. Prov. 13:8), for the freedom of a slave (Lev. 25:47–52), or for the release of war prisoners (Isa. 45:13). The conflation of the "son of man" of Dan. 7:13–14, who is exalted to glory and everlasting rule, with the Isaian servant, who suffers on behalf of many, is deliberately paradoxical. Jesus as son of man is held up as the ultimate exemplar of service to the disciples/ Markan audience, stressing his willingness to give up his own life in return for the lives of others, rather than seeking to restore Israel through customary kingly rule and domination.

Transition to Jerusalem: A Blind Man at Jericho (10:46–52)

Jesus's entry into Jerusalem, the seat of ancient Israelite kingship, is preceded by the transitional story of the healing of the blind man Bartimaeus (10:46–52), the last healing miracle in the Gospel. It is also the last of four narratives about healing deafness or blindness (7:32–37; 8:22–26; 9:14–27), which relate to the lack of the disciples' perceptiveness: they repeatedly see but do not perceive, and hear but do not understand (4:12)—in contrast with the literally deaf and blind, who are healed. It is also the only story in which the recipient of the healing is named, **the son of Timaeus, Bartimaeus, a blind beggar** (10:46).

The story begins with Bartimaeus sitting **by the way** (*para tēn hodon*), in a marginal position compared to **his disciples and a great crowd** who are leaving Jericho (10:46). Overhearing that the renowned healer from Nazareth is nearby, he cries out for help, using both Jesus's name and a messianic title: **"Son of David, Jesus, have mercy on me!"** (10:47). When **many people** (presumably including the disciples) command him to be silent, he cries out all the more: **"Son of David, have mercy on me!"** (10:48).

Most interpreters have equated Bartimaeus's blindness with lack of intellectual and spiritual insight, and associated the disciples' metaphorical blindness to the meaning of Jesus's ministry with the blind man's physical disability (Beavis 1998, 23). For example, Ernest Best argues that the title "Son of David" is placed on the lips of a *blind* person (Mark 10:47–48) because it is an *inaccurate* understanding of who Jesus is. According to Best, Mark included the incident for the positive symbolism inherent in the curing of blindness: "'to see' is to go with Jesus to the cross" (cf. v. 52b), whereas to identify Jesus as "son of David" is to be "blind." In this line of interpretation, the blindness of Bartimaeus symbolizes the misunderstanding of the disciples regarding Jesus's true identity, which is revealed in the remainder of the Gospel. Only when Bartimaeus receives his sight does he attain true understanding (of the identity of Jesus); before his cure, he represents the "blindness"—synonymous with "dull-wittedness"—of the disciples (Beavis 1998, 24, citing Best 1981, 142–43; Johnson 1978, 197).

The opinion that the acclamation of Jesus as "son of David" is a mistake on Bartimaeus's part is based on Mark 12:35–37, where Jesus appears to deny that the messiah is David's son (see the comment on this passage in the next section), and on the supposed fact that Jewish expectations did not include a miracle-working messiah (e.g., Berger 1973, 3n12). However, the late first-century *4 Ezra* (= 2 Esdras) associates the messiah with "wonders" (6:25–26; 7:26–29; 13:49–50; cf. Collins 2007, 510). Moreover, Solomon the "son of David" is renowned for his miraculous powers in Jewish tradition (see Chilton 1982; Charlesworth 1995; S. Smith 1996). Jesus does not rebuke Bartimaeus for using the title, nor does he reject it; instead, Jesus stops and has his companions call the man, who despite his blindness has no difficulty locating the messiah: **And jumping up, casting off his cloak, he went to Jesus** (10:50). Due to the centrality of the language of "calling" in the pericope (10:49), the identification of the story as a call narrative has received some acceptance (e.g., Achtemeier 1978; Kertelge 1970, 181; Steinhauser 1986; Beavis 1998, 33–35; see also Kingsbury 1983, 104n159). Several scholars have interpreted the man's blindness as indicative of his prophetic insight, since both ancient Jewish and Greek tradition recognizes that blindness may be compensated for by brighter spiritual vision (Beavis 1998, 27, 37; cf. Donahue and Harrington 2002, 318, 319; Collins 2007, 510). Rather than letting others speak for the blind man, Jesus asks the man what *he* wants: **And the blind man says to him,**

"Rabbouni, let me see!" (10:51). Instead of performing the utterances and manipulations associated with the previous healings of the deaf and blind (7:33–34; 8:23, 25; cf. 9:25), Jesus proclaims that the man's own faith has healed/saved him (*hē pistis sou sesōken se,* 10:52; cf. 5:34). The man receives physical sight *because of* his spiritual perceptiveness: **And he followed him in the way** (10:52b). Bartimaeus moves from the wayside (*para tēn hodon*) to a position on the road (*en tē hodō*) as a disciple of Jesus rather than returning to his former life like the recipients of the other healings.

Theological Issues

Discipleship is the dominant theme of this section. It contains paradigmatic stories about three would-be disciples: the unknown exorcist (9:38–41), the rich man (10:17–22), and Bartimaeus (10:46–52). Each can be interpreted as a "type" of disciple known to members of the Markan community: "outsiders" who claim to be followers of Jesus but who are unfamiliar to the Markan church; potential disciples who are unable or unwilling to accept the full consequences of proclaiming the good news; and those who, like Bartimaeus, seem unfit for discipleship but who ignore all obstacles and "follow in the way." In all cases the Markan Jesus opts for inclusiveness: "Whoever is not against us is for us" (9:40); "All things are possible with God" (10:27b); "Call him" (10:49). As with the different qualities of soil in the sower parable, Christian readers in Mark's time and ever since have been challenged by the questions implicit in these narratives. Who are the "true Christians"—members of my church, denomination, theological preference, liturgical practice? This question can be extended beyond Christianity to interfaith dialogue: what unites people of faith from across the spectrum of religions? Further, Mark's typology of

With or against Us?

Augustine of Hippo wisely negotiates the two forms of the saying (Mark 9:40; Luke 9:50; cf. Matt. 12:30a; Luke 11:23a) by interpreting both as true: "one fittingly shares in the worshipping community insofar as one stands with the whole church, and not against it. Yet those same individuals must be reproached for separating themselves from the church, wherever their gathering inadvertently becomes a scattering" (*On Baptism, against the Donatists* 1.7 [9]). Elsewhere he observes that the heretics of his time should not be condemned for partaking in the sacraments ("for in these they are with us, and they are not against us"), but since the church condemns division and separation, insofar as they do not gather "with us" ("early Catholic Christians," he means) they are "against us" (*Harmony of the Gospels* 4, trans. Oden and Hall 1998, 122–23).

discipleship invites reflection on the quality of one's own discipleship: am I like the rich man who skirts the full implications of the gospel, or am I more like Bartimaeus, who follows no matter what?

Jesus's welcoming reply to the disciples' question about the unknown disciple, "Whoever is not against us is for us" (9:40; cf. Luke 9:50), has frequently been reworded in Christian history, beginning with Q's exclusivist declaration: "Whoever is *not with me* is *against me*" (Matt. 12:30a; Luke 11:23a). United States president George W. Bush famously (or infamously) paraphrased the latter at a post-September 11 news conference in 2001: "You're either for us or against us in the fight against terror." In her study of the rhetoric used in the buildup to war, Kelly Denton-Borhaug has drawn attention to how in US history "victimage rhetoric" has been used to construct "the enemy" as "savage and uncivilized, aggressive and irrational"—contrasted with American rationality, tolerance, and love for peace and freedom, from the Revolutionary War to World War II to the invasion of Iraq (Denton-Borhaug 2007, §5). This kind of thinking is not uniquely American; it typifies an us-versus-them mentality, which is frequently invoked in political, religious, and interpersonal conflicts. It can obviate any guilt that people might feel for harming "the other," since any suffering by the enemy is justified by their alignment with those "against us." In wartime propaganda, this attitude is often accompanied by quasi-religious imagery of self-sacrifice: the sacrifices that citizens, especially the military, must make in order to save civilization; and implicitly the sacrifice that must be made of the aggressors in order to purify the world (cf. Ivie 1980, 291). It is well to remember that Mark's more-inclusive version of the saying—"If you're not against us, you're for us"—is the earliest and thus has a good claim on authenticity.

Similarly, Mark's construction of discipleship in terms of suffering, service, and "taking up the cross" can easily be subverted to purposes contrary to the message of the gospel. Many theologians, especially feminists, have drawn attention to the problematic aspects of the theological glorification of self-sacrifice. The related metaphors of "sacrifice, ransom, scapegoat, justification, and martyr, despite having positive uses in speaking about Jesus's death, all have dangerous directions" (Reid 2007, 29).

Traditional ransom theories of salvation, which picture the death of Jesus as a price paid to redeem humanity from captivity to sin (or to Satan), posit a dualistic cosmology where good and evil are construed as mutually exclusive opposites, overlooking the gray areas of everyday existence (Reid 2007, 30). Triumphalist interpretations of the cross, which understand Jesus's suffering as an overture to victory, may trivialize the barbarity of crucifixion; they can make contemporary believers interpret their own or others' suffering simply as a prelude to future vindication: "Such a stance can keep persons whose suffering arises from abuse or injustice from taking action toward stopping the abuse" (Reid 2007, 31). Overemphasis on Jesus's willing self-sacrifice as a

Christians and Martyrdom

As early as the NT, there is evidence that some Christians were persecuted and even executed for their faith, sometimes at the hands of Jewish authorities, sometimes by gentiles (e.g., Mark 13:12; cf. Mark 10:39; Acts 6:5–8:2; 12:1–2; 22:20; Rev. 2:13; 17:6; 20:4). Tacitus (*Ann.* 15.44; ca. AD 55–120) tells of the torture and killing of many Roman Christians by the emperor Nero, who blamed them for the great fire of Rome, around the year AD 64. Melito of Sardis and Tertullian report an outbreak of persecution against Christians in the reign of Domitian (AD 81–96). Many scholars think that this outbreak lies behind the imagery of Revelation (Irenaeus says that Revelation was written toward the end of Domitian's reign) and that the tribulations experienced by the seven churches of Asia Minor (including the imprisonment of John on Patmos and the martyrdom of Antipas of Pergamum [Rev. 2:13]) were related to the Christians' refusal to recognize the imperial cult. The first evidence of an official policy for suppressing Christianity occurs during the reign of Trajan (98–117), in the correspondence between Pliny the Younger and the emperor, where Pliny requests Trajan's advice about whether to execute two Christian women ("deaconesses") who had been brought before him. Although sporadic persecutions broke out in various parts of the Roman world, the great crisis periods for early Christianity occurred during the reigns of Marcus Aurelius (ca. 177), Decius and Valerian (mid-third cent.), and Diocletian (early fourth cent.). The term "martyr" (*martys*) literally means "witness" in the sense of one who bears testimony to Jesus. As the persecution of Christians accelerated before the reign of Constantine (306–337), the term came to refer to one who died in the name of Christ. Although martyrs were widely admired in the early church, some Christian teachers (e.g., Clement of Alexandria, Mensurius of Carthage) cautioned against excessive fascination with martyrdom, which should be borne only if necessary.

Unfortunately, many Christian martyrs in subsequent centuries have been executed by other Christians on charges of heresy, notably during the Reformation period, when Catholics were executed by Protestants and Protestants by Catholics. Although ecumenical dialogue and cooperation have become the norm for many contemporary churches, Christians continue to be persecuted and sometimes killed for their beliefs. In 1997, *Christian Century* (December 10) published a list of ten "modern martyrs," such as the Grand Duchess Elizabeth of Russia, killed by the Bolsheviks (1918); Maximilian Kolbe, a Franciscan priest killed by the Nazis (1941); Wang Zhiming, killed during China's Cultural Revolution (1972); and Oscar Romero, the Roman Catholic Archbishop of San Salvador, assassinated for his political views (1980).

model of Christian behavior may imply that those who endure suffering at the hands of an abuser should be more concerned about the victimizer than about themselves. Furthermore, understanding the crucifixion as a sacrifice instead of recognizing it as the consequence of Jesus's commitment to God's reign implies that Jesus's death was pleasing to God, thus "legitimating hierarchy, encouraging violent behavior, and glorifying innocent victimhood" (Dewey 2004, 159). This notion has been especially destructive to marginalized persons for whom abuse and deprivation are daily realities: it legitimates their victimization by interpreting it as a "cross to bear." It also figures in the kind of propaganda mentioned above. By constructing the nation as victim, the "sacrifices" to be endured in wartime in order to thwart the enemy take on a sacrosanct quality and subtly align the state with Christ.

Another theological issue arises out of the wording of Mark 10:44–45: "Whoever wants to become great among you shall be your servant [*diakonos*], and whoever among you wants to be first shall be slave [*doulos*] of all. For the son of man has not come to be served, but to serve and to give his life a ransom for many." While the image of disciples' engaging in mutual service in imitation of Jesus's service to humanity serves as a useful corrective in the Gospel's context, where the disciples are vying for honor in the realm of God, African American theologians have radically questioned the valorization of slavery inherent in the metaphor of disciple as servant (or more literally, as *doulos*, "slave").

Clarice L. Martin (1993, 225–26) sees such teachings as potential "texts of terror" for African Americans and concludes that slave imagery cannot express the good news of the gospel. Emerson B. Powery (2007, 142) observes: "In Mark, Jesus's redemption is not confined to the crucifixion scene. In fact, his liberation comes as much from his life(-giving activities) as it does from his death. Oftentimes, the emphasis on suffering historically has had damaging effects, as suffering (on behalf of a cause) has often become the rhetoric

Slavery in the Bible

Throughout the Bible, slavery is taken for granted as a socioeconomic reality, as it was throughout the ancient world (e.g., Gen. 12:16; 17:23; 26:25; Exod. 11:5; Job 31:13; Prov. 12:9; 22:7; 29:19; Sir. 7:20; 1 Kings 9:20–22; 2 Chron. 8:7–10; 2 Kings 4:1; Amos 2:6; 8:6; Mic. 2:9; Jer. 34:8–22; Eph. 6:5; Col. 3:22; 1 Tim. 6:2; 1 Pet. 2:18–21). This is somewhat surprising when we view the importance of Israel's liberation from Egyptian bondage, a theme echoed in accounts of the Babylonian captivity (e.g., Exod. 5:1–23; 13:3; 20:2; Lev. 25:42; Deut. 6:21; Josh. 24:17; Ezra 9:8–9; 2 Chron. 36:20). However, two first-century Jewish groups that eschewed slavery were the Essenes (Josephus, *Ant.* 18.1.5 §21; Philo, *Good Person* 12 §79) and the Therapeutae, a community of Egyptian Jewish mystics where the younger members served the elders (Philo, *Contempl. Life* 9 §70; cf. *Jub.* 11.2). Slavery is never explicitly condemned in the NT, but Paul's Letter to Philemon implies that Philemon should liberate his slave Onesimus so that he can better serve the gospel (Philem. 15–20), and John of Patmos condemns the merchants whose cargo includes "slaves, that is, human souls" (Rev. 18:13 RSV).

of the powerful—who tend to 'suffer' little." It should be remembered that in the larger context of Mark, the image of Jesus as "servant of God" is part of the "new exodus" theme that pervades this Gospel. For Mark, Jesus the Son of Man is the representative of Israel, the suffering servant of Isa. 53, whose rejection and death for many becomes God's means of Israel's deliverance (cf. Watts 1997, 287). The theme of Mark's new exodus, like that of the first, is *liberation from* slavery, suffering, and oppression. In Second Isaiah, Israel, the servant of God, "will not grow faint or be crushed until he has established justice in the earth; and the coastlands wait for his teaching" (Isa. 42:4).

Mark 11:1–12:44

Act 4: Opposition in Jerusalem

Introductory Matters

The entirety of this section, and of the discourse in Mark 13, takes place in Jerusalem, over the course of three days (11:12, 20), mostly in the vicinity of the temple or within it. From this point on, the temple, mentioned for the first time in Mark 11:11, becomes a major theme of the Gospel (cf. 11:12, 15–17, 27; 12:35, 41; 13:1, 3; 14:49, 58; 15:29, 38).

The Temple

According to 2 Sam. 7:4–17, God promised King David that his offspring (Solomon) would build a "house" (temple) for his name. The building of the temple, a project that spanned seven years (1 Kings 6:38) is described at length in 1 Kings 5:1–7:51 (cf. 2 Chron. 3:1–5:1). This temple was destroyed by the invading Babylonian army (587/586 BC), and a second and probably less-magnificent temple was built to replace it under Persian auspices after the Babylonian exile, around 515 BC (Ezra 6:15). Herod the Great undertook a major renovation of this temple in 20 BC, which took many years to complete (cf. John 2:20). The second temple was destroyed at the end of the Jewish War (AD 66–70), an event commemorated in the Jewish fast of Tisha B'Av, the ninth day of the month of Av, when the Roman general Titus decided to destroy the temple—the same day of the year when the fire was lit for the destruction of Solomon's temple (2 Kings 25:8; Jer. 52:12; b. Ta'an. 29a).

Mark's portrayal of the temple and its priesthood is negative, which the evangelist conveys to the audience both discursively and symbolically. The temple, which should be "a house of prayer for all the nations" (Mark 11:17), is like a barren fig tree (11:20–21), an impressive edifice that will nonetheless soon be destroyed (13:1–2).

With the new setting, a new cast of characters enters the stage: the chief priests, scribes, and elders of Jerusalem (11:18, 27; cf. 12:28, 38–40), who have already been identified as Jesus's opponents in the Passion predictions (8:31; 10:33), and the Sadducees, who figure only in 12:18–23. The Pharisees and Herodians, mentioned as coconspirators against Jesus in Mark 3:6, reappear "in order to entrap him with a word" (12:13). The stage is set for the arrest and crucifixion in Mark 14–15.

This section is dominated by controversy and debate between Jesus and various opponents, especially the scribes, a group whom Jesus has already encountered in Galilee (2:6, 16; 3:22; 7:1, 5; 8:31; 9:14), and whose teaching contrasts with that of Jesus in both style and content (1:22; 9:11). The harsh critique of the temple cult—as the "good scribe" admits, to love God and one's neighbor is more important than all the sacrifices offered in the temple (12:33)—and the intense debates between Jesus and his interlocutors contrast with the humble example of a poor woman whose tiny donation to the temple treasury is proclaimed by Jesus to be greater than the munificent gifts of the rich (12:41–44).

**Mark 11:1–12:44
in the Narrative Flow**

Prologue: John and Jesus (1:1–13)

Transition: Summary of the good news (1:14–15)

Act 1: Jesus in Galilee (1:16–3:35)

Interlude: Teaching in parables (4:1–34)

Act 2: Beyond Galilee (4:35–6:56)

Interlude: Teaching on ritual and moral purity (7:1–23)

Act 3: Mission in gentile regions (7:24–9:29)

Interlude: Teaching on the way to Jerusalem (9:30–10:52)

▶Act 4: Opposition in Jerusalem (11:1–12:44)

   Entry into Jerusalem (11:1–11)

   Cursing the fig tree, cleansing the temple (11:12–25)

      Jesus curses the barren fig tree (11:12–14)

      Jesus cleanses the temple (11:15–19)

      The lesson of the fig tree (11:20–25)

   Debate with the chief priests, scribes, and elders (11:27–33)

   Parable of the tenants (12:1–12)

   Debate with Pharisees and Herodians (12:13–17)

   Debate with the Sadducees (12:18–27)

   Debate with a scribe (12:28–34)

   Criticism of scribal teaching (12:35–37)

   Criticism of scribal practice (12:38–40)

   The example of a poor widow (12:41–44)

Tracing the Narrative Flow

Entry into Jerusalem (11:1–11)

Jesus and the disciples pass through both **Bethphage and Bethany** (11:1) before entering Jerusalem. Although the exact location of Bethphage ("house of figs") is unknown, it was probably closer to Jerusalem than Bethany (possibly "House of Ananiah," present-day El-Azariah), approximately two miles east of Jerusalem, on the eastern slope of the Mount of Olives (see Stein 2008, 520; Collins 2007, 516). The mention of Bethphage first is explained in a variety of ways by commentators (see France 2002, 430), but Jesus's instruction **"Go up into the village before us"** (11:2a) explains the mention of the two towns adequately: Jesus and the disciples arrive in Bethany, and he instructs them to go to the next village, Bethphage, and follow his directions: **"Immediately you will find a colt tied upon which not a single person has yet sat; untie it and bring it"** (11:2b). Throughout his Passover pilgrimage to Jerusalem, Jesus and the disciples stay in Bethany (11:11–12; 14:3), not in the ancient holy city: "expressing his continuing separation from the doomed temple and the leaders responsible for it" (Heil 1997, 93; Mark 11:15–19; 13:2).

Jesus's detailed account of the events that will unfold in Bethphage—the disciples will find the unbroken colt, someone will ask why they are untying the animal, they will reply that "the master" (*ho kyrios*) needs it, and the person will send it (11:2c–3)—corresponds so closely with what happens when they get there, **just as Jesus said** (11:4–6), that Mark either intends the audience to think that the disciples are expected in Bethphage, or that Jesus has prophetic foreknowledge of events there (cf. France 2002, 431). In view of Jesus's prophecies of his arrest, execution, and resurrection (8:31; 9:31; 10:33–34), the latter seems probable (cf. 14:12–49), although the deliberate choice of Bethany as a resting place and the enthusiastic reception of Jesus by the crowd as he nears Jerusalem (11:8–10)—both bespeak preparation for the journey and remind the audience that Jesus's reputation has already spread throughout the region (cf. 3:8; 10:1; cf. 3:22; 7:1).

The depiction of Jesus's entering Jerusalem is a tapestry woven out of scriptural allusions, especially Zech. 9:9 (cf. Gen. 49:10–11; 1 Kings 1:38–40):

> Rejoice greatly, O daughter Zion! Shout aloud, O daughter Jerusalem!
> Lo, your king comes to you; triumphant and victorious is he,
> Humble and riding on a donkey, on a colt, the foal of a donkey.

The acclamation **"Hosanna! Blessed the one who comes in the name of the Lord! Blessed the coming kingdom of our father David! Hosanna in the highest!"** (Mark 11:9–10) echoes Ps. 118:25–26, with its refrain, "O Lord, save us!" (NIV; *hosanna* means "Save us now!"); here it is quoted to greet Jesus as "the one who comes" in God's name. Psalm 118 is a psalm of praise traditionally recited at the beginning of Passover (cf. Mark 12:10–11). The description of people's casting their garments on the road along with branches cut from the fields (11:8) recalls 2 Kings 9:13, where the officers of Jehu proclaim him king after spreading their cloaks before him. The practice of strewing vegetation at Jewish festivals is more connected with Sukkoth/Tabernacles (Lev. 23:39–43) or Hanukkah (1 Macc. 13:51; 2 Macc. 10:7) than with Passover. The motif of spreading branches may derive from the Hebrew text of Ps. 118:27 (cf. Mark 11:9), which refers to the decoration of the horns of the altar with "leafy boughs" (see Dahood 1970, 155, 160), although the LXX does not use the word *stibades* (branches, leaves, etc.) but simply *pykazousin* (to cover thickly). The messianic import of the incident is underlined by the reference to the restoration of the kingdom of David, whose "son" Jesus has been proclaimed by Bartimaeus (10:47–48).

Some commentators speculate that the Davidic acclamation is meant to illustrate a "false messianic expectation" concerning the nature of Jesus's messiahship and of the nature of the kingdom of God, which involves suffering and death, rather than the restoration of the Davidic throne (e.g., Moloney 2002, 220; Boring 2006, 316). However, there is no explicit identification of Jesus as the son of David in Mark 11:10 (as there is in 10:47–48), but rather an expression of hope for a restoration of political independence under a descendant of the king. The intent of the scene is not to cast the crowd thronging around Jesus as mistaken, but to herald the entry of the messiah (cf. 1:1; 8:29; 9:41) into the city where he will meet his destiny. In dramatic terms, the scene is a *hyporchēma* (dance song),

> a joyful scene that involves the chorus and sometimes other characters; takes the form of a dance, procession, or lyrics expressing confidence and happiness; and occurs just before the catastrophic climax of the play. The hyporcheme emphasizes, by way of contrast, the crushing impact of the tragic incident. (Bilezikian 1977, 127)

Like a *hyporchēma* in a Greek tragedy, the "triumphal entry" is a joyous outburst, whose promise will be tragically dashed.

The importance of Jesus's first visit to the temple is underlined by the scene of his entering very deliberately, looking around **at everything**, and abruptly returning to Bethany (11:11).

Cursing the Fig Tree, Cleansing the Temple (11:12–25)

Mark 11:12–25 is a complex composition made up of three distinct bodies of material: a miracle story in which Jesus curses a fig tree for its failure to bear fruit (11:12–14), the incident in Jerusalem known as the "cleansing of the temple" (11:15–19), and the aftermath of the fig-tree cursing, which opens into teachings on faith and prayer (11:20–25). Thus the temple-cleansing incident is framed by the miracle story, and most scholars regard this as a typical Markan sandwich, in which the two stories are meant to be mutually illuminating (e.g., 1:21–28; 3:21–35; 5:21–43; 14:53–72).

11:12–14. The fig-tree narrative takes place over the course of two days. The morning after Jesus's initial arrival in Jerusalem, he and the disciples are on their way to the city, and Jesus, being hungry, tries to find fruit on a leafy fig tree he has seen from a distance. The search turns out to be futile, **for it was not the season for figs** (11:13d), and Jesus utters a curse on the tree: **"May nobody ever eat fruit from you!"** (11:14a). The note that **the disciples heard him** (11:14b) prepares for what will happen the following morning (11:20–21).

> **An Outline of Mark 11:12–25**
>
> **Cursing the fig tree, cleansing the temple (11:12–25)**
>
> Jesus curses the barren fig tree (11:12–14)
>
> Jesus cleanses the temple (11:15–19)
>
> The lesson of the fig tree (11:20–25)

11:15–19. The temple cleansing episode (11:15–18), framed by the fig-tree story, is an action/saying-*chreia*. Jesus and the disciples enter the temple for the second time (cf. 11:11), and according to Mark, Jesus **began to cast out those who sold and those who bought in the temple, and the tables of the money changers and the seats of the sellers of doves he overturned, and he would not allow that any vessel be carried through the temple.** The kind of commerce referred to here involved the buying and selling of sacrificial animals (like the doves) essential to the operation of temple worship; similarly, the money changers exchanged coins bearing human figures—offensive from a Jewish legal standpoint—for specially minted Tyrian coins so that Jews could pay the half-shekel temple tax (see E. Sanders 1985, 63–65). The word translated here as "vessel" (*skeuē*) has a wide range of meanings: any thing or person used for a purpose; a container of any kind (see BDAG 927). By preventing the passage of the vessels and instruments necessary for the operation of the temple, Jesus symbolically brings the activities of the temple to a standstill. The historicity of this incident is highly questionable: "That the historical Jesus was able to drive out all who served temple practice (v. 15), and then to determine what was allowed to happen or not happen within the entire temple area, strains all imagination" (Moloney 2002, 224). Jesus's action signals the end of the temple service, not in his own time, but forty years later, in the time of the evangelist and his audience.

The teaching that follows explicates Jesus's action: **"Isn't it written, 'My house shall be called a house of prayer for all the nations'? But you have made it into 'a cave of bandits'"** (11:17). In its original context, the reference to the temple as a place for all to worship (Isa. 56:7) is a prophecy of the incorporation of the gentile nations into Israel, where they will worship in a restored temple (cf. Isa. 56:1–8). The antithesis in the second half of the teaching uses a phrase from Jer. 7:11a ("cave of bandits"), where the prophet is excoriating the religious leaders of Israel for thinking that they can practice idolatry and immorality yet still expect the temple to protect them:

> "And now, because you have done these things," says the LORD, "and when I spoke to you persistently, you did not listen, and when I called you, you did not answer, therefore I will do to the house that is called by my name, in which you trust, and to the place that I gave to you and to your ancestors, just what I did to Shiloh. And I will cast you out of my sight, just as I cast out all your kinsfolk, all the offspring of Ephraim." (Jer. 7:13–15)

As the ancient sanctuary at Shiloh was destroyed by the Philistines (cf. Jer. 26:6–9), and the temple of Solomon was razed by the Babylonians, so is the temple of Jesus's time vulnerable to attack and devastation. The message is not lost on the second-degree audience: **And the chief priests and the scribes heard, and they were seeking that they might destroy him. For they were afraid of him, for all the crowd was astonished at his teaching** (11:18). Then it is evening, and Jesus and his disciples return to their lodgings at Bethany (11:19).

11:20–25. The next morning, as they are walking to Jerusalem, they see that the fig tree is **withered away to its roots** (11:20), and Peter remembers the incident of the day before: **"Rabbi, look, the fig tree which you cursed has withered!"** (11:21). In terms of genre, the story is an account of a nature miracle (e.g., 4:35–41; 6:45–52; cf. 6:32–44; 8:1–10), demonstrating Jesus's power to destroy as well as to heal.

In itself, the narrative has been problematic to generations of interpreters, who have been disturbed by the portrayal of Jesus as angrily killing a living tree, a valuable source of food, for not bearing fruit out of season at Passover (April), when ripe figs would normally not be expected until June (see Stern 1992, 96; cf. the comment on Mark 6:39). Wendy Cotter (1986, 62–66) offers a plausible explanation of Jesus's otherwise unaccountable search for figs, using Pliny the Elder's observation that only on the fig tree does fruit appear before leaves (*Nat.* 16.49). Thus a tree with leaves could reasonably be expected to be bearing immature fruit, even though it was out of season. However, as early as the fourth century, Ephrem the Syrian surmised that there must be a symbolic meaning to the story: "For, if he had sought fruit from it at the opportune time, no one would have known that there was a figurative meaning embedded there" (*Commentary on Tatian's Diatessaron*, in Oden and Hall 1998, 151). The meaning Ephrem draws from the tale is that the real target of the miracle is Jerusalem, "for he had sought love in her, but she had despised the fruit of repentance." At another level, Ephrem sees the miracle as "a sign for his friends, and a miracle to his enemies," illustrating Jesus's ability to free himself from his captors: "He showed in advance . . . by means of a living plant which he caused to wither, that he would have been able to destroy his crucifiers with a word" (Oden and Hall 1998, 151). In prophetic terms, the story is an acted-out parable, similar to the dramas enacted by Jeremiah, who bought a clay jug, only to break it as a sign against Jerusalem (Jer. 19:1–15), and Ezekiel, who built and then burned a model of Jerusalem (Ezek. 4–5; cf. Acts 21:10–11; Stern 1992, 94).

Donahue and Harrington (2002, 331) note that the fig tree has been confidently interpreted "to symbolize the Jewish crowds, the Jewish religious leaders, the Temple, the sacrificial worship enacted in the Temple, Israel as God's people, Judaism as a religious system, or even the Markan community." Many contemporary interpreters, following William Telford (1980), connect the story of the fig tree directly with the narrative that it encloses: the barren tree symbolizes the metaphorical fruitlessness of the temple (e.g., Hooker 1991, 261, 265; Moloney 2002, 226–27; Boring 2006, 319), even though this connection is not explicitly made where it would be expected, in Mark 11:22–25. Since the destruction of the temple is plainly mentioned several times in subsequent chapters (13:2; 14:58; cf. 15:38), it seems reasonable to posit that the destruction of the tree foreshadows the fall of the temple. The Jewish scriptures contain many prophetic passages where Israel is compared to an unfruitful vine or fig tree that will be withered (e.g., Jer. 8:13; Ezek. 17:24; Hosea 9:10, 16–17; Joel 1:7; Mic. 7:1; cf. Job 18:16). Although none of these refers directly to the temple, the metonymic relationship between Israel and the temple makes the fig tree/temple symbolism plausible.

Seen in this light, the temple cleansing incident takes on a deeper significance. Living in the aftermath of the Jewish War, the Markan community would have been dismayed by the disaster that had befallen Judea. Jesus, in the prophetic tradition, performs a symbolic act that bears on the destruction of the temple, in both the fig-tree episode and in the temple itself. In the recent memory of the Markan audience, the Judean rebels' expectation that God would intervene to destroy the Romans and restore Israel to national independence had been proved wrong. The fig tree/temple cleansing complex reassures them that the fall of the temple had been foretold by the prophets and by Jesus himself.

The verses that follow (11:22–25), in which Jesus draws lessons about faith and prayer from the fig-tree episode, seem incongruous and prosaic after his stern denunciation of the temple. Philip Esler (2005, 49) goes so far as to deny that Mark's primary intent in 11:12–25 is symbolically to describe "a coming judgment upon Israel." Rather, he argues, the fig tree/temple cleansing complex was part of a pre-Markan source, and the evangelist added the teachings on faith and prayer to make sense of the miracle story, which was originally an etiological legend to explain the presence of a withered fig tree on the road between Bethany and Jerusalem (Esler 2005, 62–65). For Esler, Mark's own interpretation of the story lies not in the temple cleansing, but is constructed out of three originally independent sayings on the power of faith (11:22–23), prayer (11:24), and how to pray (11:25; Esler 2005, 49–50).

Mark 11:26

Some ancient manuscripts of Mark conclude Jesus's teaching on prayer in 11:24–25 with the instruction **"But if you do not forgive, neither will your Father who is in the heavens forgive your offenses"** (Mark 11:26). Since the oldest and best manuscripts of Mark do not contain this petition, most modern translations leave it out or consign it to a footnote. The additional verse was probably inserted by an unknown copyist motivated by the similarity of 11:25 to the forgiveness petition in the Lord's Prayer (cf. Matt. 6:12).

It is certainly true that the appended verses pick up on the themes of faith and prayer that are Markan favorites (see Esler 2005, 59–60; also Dowd 1988; Marshall 1989); but if the teaching in 11:23 is taken as a reference to the Temple Mount, these verses are consistent with the theme of the imminent judgment of the temple: **"Have faith in God. Amen I say to you that whoever says to this mountain, be taken up and be cast into the sea, and does not doubt in your heart but believe that what you say will come to pass, it will be done for them"** (11:22–23; Telford 1980, 163; cf. Moloney 2002, 227; Boring 2006, 324; Stein 2008, 519). The next verse reinforces the Markan theme of confidence in the efficacy of faith, prayer, and the power of God: **"All things that you pray and ask, believe that you will get, and it shall be"** (11:24; cf. 9:23; 10:27). Esler's objection that the notion of Mount Zion being taken up and thrown into the sea contradicts Mark 13:2, where Jesus prophesies that the stones of the temple will be "thrown down," seems overly literalistic: **"And when you stand praying, if you have something against someone, forgive, in order that also your Father who is in the heavens will forgive you your offenses"** (11:25). These verses reflect the link between the destruction of the temple and the prayer life of the Markan community, which has become the new "house of prayer" for believers (cf. Dowd 1988, 43–55).

Debate with the Chief Priests, Scribes, and Elders (11:27–33)

Jesus's third day in Jerusalem begins with a challenge (11:27–33) from the chief priests, scribes, and elders, identified in the Passion predictions (8:31; 10:33) as the ones who will reject him and hand him over to be executed (cf. 14:43, 53; 15:1). This is the first of five controversy narratives in Jerusalem, corresponding to the five Galilean controversies in 2:1–3:6. First, Jesus's opponents question him concerning the **authority** (*exousia*) by which he does **these things**—referring back to the temple-cleansing incident, which, as Hellerman (2000, 219) observes, is Jesus's "most overt self-assertion of divine authority." As stated above, the demonstration in the temple amounts to a prophetic act:

In his symbolic prophetic warning of the imminent destruction of the temple—the very center of Jewish social and religious life—Jesus intentionally identified himself with Old Testament prophets who, at God's command, acted out their verbal prophecies by means of certain striking behaviors (cf. Jer. 19; 27–28). In so doing, Jesus thus pointedly claims for himself the divine authority characteristic of God's messengers in the classical prophetic tradition. (Hellerman 2000, 221–22)

If the scribes, chief priests, and elders are, as Hellerman suggests, representatives of the Sanhedrin, who will later try him and hand him over to Pilate (cf. Mark 14:53–15:1), then their question is more than a challenge to Jesus's authority: it is an attempt to incriminate him by classifying him together with political figures like Theudas and Judas the Galilean, who had rallied hundreds of followers in revolt earlier in the first century AD (Acts 5:36–37; cf. Josephus, *Ant.* 18.1.1 §§4–7). According to Josephus (*Ant.* 20.5.1 §§97–98), Theudas incited a band of Judean peasants to follow him to the banks of the Jordan, where he expected to part the waters and lead them across, recollecting the politically fraught stories of the exodus and conquest (cf. Spencer 2000). A Roman cavalry unit put a stop to the prophetically inspired march, Theudas was killed, and his head was publicly displayed in Jerusalem.

Jesus responds to the opponents' challenge with a counterquestion, a device often found in rabbinic debates (Donahue and Harrington 2002, 334): **"I will ask you one thing, and you answer me, and I will tell you by what authority I do these things. Was the baptism of John from heaven or from human beings? Answer me!"** (Mark 11:29–30; cf. 2:9–10, 19, 25–26; 3:4). In the larger context of the Gospel, John the Baptist is an Elijah-like prophet whose divine authorization is presupposed, and whose destiny has been intertwined with Jesus's from the beginning (1:2–11; 2:18–22; 6:14–29; 9:11–13). The opponents are stymied: **And they spoke to each other, saying, "If we should say, 'Of heaven,' he will ask, 'Why didn't you believe him?' But shall we say, 'From human beings?' They feared the crowd; for everyone held that John was a prophet** (11:31–32). Jesus's reply relates to more than simply John's prophetic status ("from heaven"); it relates especially to his own status, since his ministry is aligned with John's: "To acknowledge the authority of John—i.e., to 'believe him'—is to acknowledge and therefore to implicitly legitimate Jesus's action in the temple on the previous day" (Hellerman 2000, 226; 11:15–19). To deny the heavenly source of John's authority would also discredit Jesus, and so it would also alienate the crowd, who regard John as a true prophet. Afraid to respond to Jesus's counterchallenge, the opponents refuse to answer, and Jesus responds in kind, thus refusing to incriminate himself: **"Neither do *I* say to *you* by what authority I do these things!"** (11:33).

Parable of the Tenants (12:1–12)

Jesus's answer to the scribes, chief priests, and elders continues with the parable of the tenants (12:1–12), Mark's only narrative parable other than the sower (4:3–8). Considerable scholarly attention has been devoted to the question of the authenticity of the parable—whether it can be traced back to Jesus in some form (e.g., Dodd 1961, 96; Jeremias 1972, 72–73; Crossan 1971; Donahue 1988, 55). Although some aspects of the parable strain credulity (cf. 12:6–7), Martin Hengel (1968, 11–16, 19–28; cf. Collins 2007, 543, 545) has shown that the parable portrays a picture of tenant farming in ancient Palestine consistent with references to conflicts between absentee landowners and their tenants in the Zenon Papyri (third cent. BC). Here in Mark, however, the parable is patently an allegory (cf. 4:13–20), prompted by events of the author's own time, not that of the historical Jesus. It is based on Isa. 5:1b–2 LXX: "The beloved had a vineyard on a hill, on a fertile place. And I put a hedge around it and fenced it in and planted a Sorech vine, and I built a tower in the midst of it and dug out a wine vat in it, and I waited for it to produce a cluster of grapes, but it produced thorns" (NETS).

The vineyard is a common metaphor for Israel in the Jewish scriptures (cf. Ps. 80:8–18; Jer. 2:21; Hosea 10:1): "For the vineyard of the Lord of hosts is the house of Israel, and the people of Judah are his pleasant planting" (Isa. 5:7). In the parable, the vineyard with its tower (Mark 12:1)—probably symbolizing the temple—is fruitful, but the tenants to whom it has been rented refuse to turn over the owner's share of the produce when he sends a series of slaves to collect: they treat the slaves abusively and even kill some (12:5), evoking Israel's rejection of a long line of prophets (e.g., 1 Kings 18:13, 22–27; 2 Chron. 24:21; 36:15–16; Neh. 9:26; on the prophets as God's rejected "servants," see Jer. 7:25; 25:4; 26:5; 29:19; 35:15; 44:4; Ezek. 38:17; Dan. 9:6, 10; Amos 3:7; Zech. 1:6; 2 Kings 9:7; 17:13, 23; 21:10; 24:2; Ezra 9:11). The Markan audience knows that the prophet John the Baptist has been put to death by Herod, who is associated with the opponents of Jesus throughout the Gospel (Mark 3:6; 8:15; 12:13). The owner's final emissary, his **beloved son** (12:6), represents Jesus (cf. 1:11; 9:7): like the son of the parable and as the Passion predictions foretell (8:31; 9:31; 10:33–34), Jesus is destined to be killed by the "chief priests, the scribes, and the elders" (11:27)—the keepers of the vineyard of Israel, to whom Jesus addresses the parable.

In the parable, both the vineyard owner and the tenants engage in dialogue; the owner speculates (apparently to himself) that the tenants will respect his son if he sends him to them (12:6b), but when the son arrives, the tenants say **to each other, "This is the heir; if we kill him, then the inheritance will be ours!"** (12:7). The drastically different expectations of the tenants and the owner have tragic results. Donahue (1988, 55) may be correct that the owner's extreme naïveté regarding the tenants' reception of his son is an expression of the prophetic theme of "divine pathos": "the long-suffering of God, who reaches out for a human response" (Hosea 2:2, 14–20; Jer. 3:11–14; Ezek. 16:59–63). However, the "key" to the Markan parable is not the owner's forbearance but rather the tenants' foolishness, as illustrated by Jesus's question, to which he provides the answer himself: "**What will the master [kyrios] of the vineyard do? He will come and destroy the tenants and give the vineyard to others**" (12:9). The Markan audience, living in the aftermath of the destruction of Jerusalem, knew that the "beloved son" had been killed and vindicated, that the temple had been razed, and that Israel was now in Roman hands (cf. Boring 2006, 328–29). Mark 12:12 confirms that the chief priests, scribes, and elders **knew that he spoke the parable against them**; they are the foolish and corrupt "tenants" who will be wiped from the land.

In Mark, then, the parable is a sort of Passion prediction in expanded, allegorical form. For the evangelist, any God-given authority that the Jewish leaders may have had has been forfeited by their neglect of their sacred obligations and by their failure to heed the warnings of the prophets; worst of all, they are about to kill the beloved son/messiah sent by God. The meaning of the parable is so apparent that there is no need for a detailed explanation of the allegory (cf. 4:14–20). However, in good Jewish style, the parable-proper (*māšāl*) is followed by a *nimshal* (application), in this case a proof text, Ps. 118:22–23 LXX (Mark 12:10–11): "**Have you not read this scripture, 'The stone that the builders rejected has become the cornerstone; this is from the Lord, and it is marvelous in our eyes'?**" (see Stern 1991, 8). In its original context, the psalm refers to an Israelite military victory against all odds; Israel, a small nation among mighty empires, has triumphed with the help of God (see Dahood 1970, 155–60). Elsewhere in the NT, the psalm is often interpreted christologically, associating the "rejected stone" with Christ (Acts 4:11; Rom. 9:32–33; 1 Pet. 2:4, 7; cf. Eph. 2:20; 1 Pet. 2:6; cf. Boring 2006, 332). The "rejected stone" is God's ultimate agent, Jesus, who will be elevated above the failed leadership of Israel. The architectural imagery points to the replacement of the temple and its failed leadership by the rule of God.

Debate with Pharisees and Herodians (12:13–17)

In the next scene (Mark 12:13–17), the chief priests, scribes, and elders send **certain Pharisees and Herodians** to do what they cannot—**entrap him with a word** (12:13).

The astute Markan reader knows that, back in Galilee, members of these groups were already plotting to kill Jesus (3:6), so their respectful request for a ruling on a point of law (*halakah*) must be insincere: "**Teacher, we know that you are true and care for no one; for you do not see the face of a person, but you teach the way of God with truth. Is it lawful to pay the poll tax to Caesar or not? Should we pay or not?**" (12:14–15). The poll tax—literally, *kēnsos*, "census"—was a toll imposed by Rome on individuals, including women and slaves, but excluding children and the aged; Collins (2007, 553)

Four Questions in Mark 12:13–37

Several scholars (e.g., Owen-Ball 1993; Sabin 2006, 107–13; Collins 2007, 552, 558, 566) have been influenced by David Daube's (1956, 158–59) interpretation of Mark 12:13–37 as reflecting a fourfold questioning scheme that would have been known by first-century rabbis. According to Daube,

> "The first question about tribute to Caesar 'falls under ḥokhmah. It is halakhic, it has regard to a point of law.' The second question, about whose wife the seven-time widow will be at the resurrection, is one of boruth. 'It is designed to ridicule a belief held by Jesus; and significantly, the particular belief attached in this manner is that which forms the target also in the illustrations of "vulgarity" quoted by the Talmud.' The third question, about which commandment is the greatest, is a question of derekh 'ereṣ: 'It is concerned with the fundamental principles on which to base one's conduct, as opposed to detailed ritual.' Finally, the fourth question, about whether Jesus can possibly be the son of David when David had called the Messiah 'Lord' (in Ps. 110:1), is a question of haggadah." (Owen-Ball 1993, 3; quoting Daube 1956, 159–60)

Daube further observes that this fourfold scheme is similar to "The Midrash of the Four Sons" in the Passover eve liturgy: a righteous son asks a question concerning a point of Jewish law, a wicked son asks a mocking question, a pious son asks a third question, and their father instructs a fourth son, who does not know enough to ask (Daube 1956, 163–65). This kind of questioning, then, is particularly apt in the context of this section of Mark, where Jesus and the disciples are in Jerusalem at Passover.

reports that "the revenues from Judea went into the public treasury (*aerarium*) rather than the imperial treasury (*fiscus*)," but Mark 12:14 speaks as if the tax were a direct tribute to Tiberius, the Roman emperor (Caesar) of Jesus's time (cf. Matt. 22:15–22; Luke 20:19–26; *Gos. Thom.* 100.1–4; *Egerton Gospel* 3.1–6). Although seemingly deferential, the question is hostile, since from a Jewish legal perspective, Torah's warning against serving other gods with one's wealth (Deut. 8:17–19) seems to proscribe paying taxes to an emperor who was worshiped in some of his eastern provinces (Owen-Ball 1993, 5). Thus Jesus's opponents are forcing him to choose between expressing disloyalty either to Caesar or to the law of Moses. As in other passages (Mark 2:8; 3:5), Jesus is aware of the antagonism behind the superficial deference: **But seeing their hypocrisy, he said to them, "Why do you test me? Bring me a denarius in order that I might see it"** (12:15; cf. 7:6, where the Pharisees are described as "hypocrites"). A denarius is a specifically Roman coin; in Jesus's time, the coin would have borne the image of Tiberius, with the inscription "Tiberius Caesar, Son of the Divine Augustus" on the front, and "High Priest" on the back (Stein 2008, 545). In and of themselves, the image and inscription might be construed as a "provocation to Jewish sensibilities" (France 2002, 468; cf. Evans 2001, 247); if so, these reservations are not shared by the Pharisees and Herodians, who present Jesus with a coin: **And he says to them, "Whose image and superscription is this?" And they said to him, "Caesar's"** (12:16).

Figure 10. A Tiberian denarius.

Baker Photo Archive

The Jesus Seminar has described Jesus's shrewd reply—**"Give to Caesar what is Caesar's, and to God what is God's!"** (12:17)—as bearing the earmarks of historical authenticity:

> Jesus's retort to the question of taxes is a masterful bit of enigmatic repartee. He avoids the traps laid for him by the question without really resolving the issue: he doesn't advise them to pay the tax and he doesn't advise them not to pay it; he advises them to know the difference between the claims of the emperor and the claims of God. (Funk, Hoover, and the Jesus Seminar 1993, 102; cf. Collins 2007, 557)

At a more profound level, the instruction to "give to God what is God's" may be undergirded by the Torah's statement that God made humanity in the divine image and likeness (Gen. 1:26 LXX: *kat' eikona hēmeteran kai kath' homoiōsin*); if Caesar's "image" (*eikōn*) inscribed on the coin implies that it belongs to him, then God's image imprinted on humans demonstrates that humanity belongs to God (Owen-Ball 1993, 10; Sabin 2006, 108). A similar lesson was derived from the story by Tertullian of Carthage (ca. AD 160–ca. 225): "That means render the image of Caesar, which is on the coin, to Caesar, and the image of God, which is imprinted on the person, to God" (*On Idolatry* 15, in Oden and Hall 1998, 159). Although the point of the story is probably not to advise the Markan audience whether to pay their taxes, early Christians regarded it as an affirmation that they should pay Roman taxes (e.g., Justin Martyr, *1 Apol.* 17; Augustine, *On the Psalms* 58.8; cf. Rom. 13:6–7). The notice that **they marveled at him** (Mark 12:17b) is a typical Markan description of the effect of Jesus's words and deeds on his audiences (e.g., 1:27; 2:12; cf. 5:42; 10:32).

Debate with the Sadducees (12:18–27)

The next question put to Jesus is from **some Sadducees** (12:18–27), a group mentioned only here in the Gospel. Although they are not described as being sent by the opponents of Jesus (cf. 12:13), the Sadducee party was made up mostly of the priestly aristocracy of Jerusalem (Mason 2000b, 1151), so a connection with the chief priests, scribes, and elders is presupposed (cf. Acts 4:1–2). They are described by Mark and by other ancient sources as rejecting such ideas as resurrection, afterlife, angels, and spirits (Acts 23:8; Matt. 22:23; Luke 20:27; Josephus, *J.W.* 2.8.14 §§164–65; *Ant.* 18.1.4 §§16–17), beliefs taken for granted throughout the Gospel. The Sadducees' challenge is couched in the form of a legal question: "**Teacher, Moses wrote for us that 'if a brother of a man dies,' and leaves a wife 'and does not leave a child,' that 'his brother must take the wife and raise up offspring for his brother'**" (Mark 12:19; cf. Deut. 25:5); it is illustrated by a parable (or exemplary story; see Beavis 2008, 604) in which a woman is married to seven brothers in a row, in obedience to Torah's requirement of levirate marriage for widows whose husbands die without issue:

> When brothers reside together, and one of them dies and has no son, the wife of the deceased shall not be married outside the family to a stranger. Her husband's brother shall go in to her, taking her in marriage, and performing the duty of a husband's brother to her, and the firstborn whom she bears shall succeed to the name of the deceased brother, so that his name may not be blotted out of Israel. (Deut. 25:5–6)

In the case cited by the Sadducees, the first husband dies without an heir, the widow marries the second brother, who meets the same fate, and so on down the line for the five other brothers until finally the woman herself dies (Mark 12:20–22). The story is obviously exaggerated: both the woman and the brothers are extremely scrupulous in obeying the law (since there was a licit means of nullifying the levirate obligation; Deut. 25:7–10), and the family is extremely unfortunate in that all the brothers die, apparently without any offspring at all (see Beavis 2008, 608–9). The point of the parable is, from the Sadducees' standpoint, to show the absurdity of the idea of resurrection, a belief that is central to the Gospel's portrait of Jesus, and to the hopes of the Markan audience (cf. Mark 8:31; 9:9, 31; 10:34; 14:28; 16:6): "**In the resurrection, when they rise up, to which of them is she the wife? For seven had her for a wife?**" (12:23).

Jesus counters the Sadducees' facetious question with a serious answer grounded in Torah, rather than through witty deflection (cf. 12:13–17): **Jesus said to them, "Is it not because of this that you are in error, you neither know the scriptures nor the power of God? For when they are raised from the dead they neither marry nor are given in marriage, but they are like angels in the heavens"** (12:24–25). Those who are raised will be exalted to an angelic state where marriage and procreation are irrelevant (cf. 2 Bar. 51.5, 10; see also Segal 1989, 510–11). Presumably the Sadducees rejected the doctrine of resurrection because it was not found in the written law, but Jesus cleverly demonstrates that it is indeed from Moses: "**Concerning the raising of the dead, have you not read in the book of Moses about the bush, how God spoke to him, saying, 'I am the God of Abraham and the God of Isaac and the God of Jacob'?**" (Mark 12:26; cf. Exod. 3:6). In the time of Moses, Abraham, Isaac, and Jacob were long dead, and yet God speaks of his relationship with the patriarchs as a present reality, implying that they are not dead but live on in a

Levirate Marriage in the Jerusalem Talmud

The Mishnaic tractate on levirate marriage, *Yebamot (Sisters-in-law)*, contains many case studies that are similar to the exemplary story in Mark 12:20–22. Here are three examples:

"Three brothers married to three unrelated women, and one brother died—these perform the rite of halisah [ḥălîṣâ] *and do not enter into levirate marriage, since the levirate tie is to a single brother-in-law and not to two brothers-in-law."* (*y. Yebam.* 8.9, summarized in Neusner 1987, 8)

"Four brothers married to four women and they died, leaving more brothers—if the oldest surviving brother wanted to take all four widows into levirate marriage, he has the right to do so. He who was married to two women and who died—the levirate marriage or halisah *of one exempts the co-wife from further connection."* (*y. Yebam.* 4.11, summarized in Neusner 1987, 9)

"A woman whose husband and co-wife went overseas, and they came and said to her, 'your husband has died,' should not remarry without halisah *or enter into levirate marriage until she ascertains whether her co-wife is pregnant. But she does not have to wait on the pregnancy of her mother-in-law, to see whether a levir will come afterward."* (*y. Yebam.* 16.1, summarized in Neusner 1987, 17)

These are hypothetical cases; in the Mishnaic period, *ḥălîṣâ* (the rite by which the levirate obligation was annulled) was practiced more often than *yibbum* (*yibbûm*, levirate marriage; Ilan 1995, 152–57). Elsewhere I have suggested that Mark 12:20–22 is a Sadducean parody of premishnaic case law of this kind (Beavis 2008, 611).

risen state. Jesus's final pronouncement reiterates his initial observation that the Sadducees are in error (*planasthe*): **"He is not God of the dead but of the living; you are greatly mistaken!"** (Mark 12:27; cf. 12:24).

Debate with a Scribe (12:28–34)

Mark 12:28–34, the story of the "good scribe," is different from the other encounters between Jesus and his questioners in this section of the Gospel. Here Jesus is approached not by a group but by an individual, a scribe— a scholar with expertise in Torah—who has overheard the debate with the Sadducees and seen that Jesus has answered them well (12:28). Although the reader/audience might expect such a figure to be opposed to Jesus, his question is not hostile or sarcastic, but serious: **"What is the first commandment of all?"** (12:28; cf. Matt. 22:34–35 and Luke 10:25, where the encounter is more confrontational). In Jewish terms, this is a question of *derek 'ereṣ* ("the way of the land"), concerning fundamental principles of conduct (Daube 1956,

60). In this context, "first" (*prōtē*) does not refer to priority in order, but in weightiness or importance (cf. Matt. 22:36). Jesus answers with not one but two commands that epitomize the commands of Torah: **"'Hear, Israel, the Lord your God is one,' and 'You shall love the Lord your God with all your heart and all your soul and with all your mind and with all your strength.' This is the second: 'You shall love your neighbor as yourself'"** (12:29–31). The first commandment is a quotation from Deut 6:4b–5, known as the Shema ("Hear!"), a daily Jewish prayer. Like the first four commands in the Decalogue (Exod. 20:2–11), it pertains to Israel's obligation to love God. The phrase "with all your mind" is not found in the Hebrew (or LXX) text of Deut. 6:5; Donahue and Harrington (2002, 355) speculate that its addition here and in Matt. 22:37 "may reflect greater concern among Jews with the 'things of the mind' in Hellenistic times." The second commandment is from Lev. 19:18b, and it parallels the six laws in Exod. 20:12–17, governing interpersonal relations among Israelites. These two foremost commandments are linked by the catchword "you shall love" (*agapēseis*).

Jesus's summary of the law in the double love commandment is paralleled in some early Jewish texts (e.g., *T. Iss.* 5.2; *T. Dan* 5.3; *Jub.* 7.20; 20.2; 36.7–8; Philo, *Spec. Laws* 2.25 §63). The practice of epitomizing the essence of the commandments may have arisen among Jews responding to Greek philosophers who tried to distill the virtues down to two essentials, piety and justice (or kindness; Collins 2007, 569). The rabbinic tradition shows the same concern:

> Rabbi Simlai said, "Six hundred thirteen commandments were given to Moses—365 negative, equaling the number of days in the year, and 248 positive, equaling the number of a man's members. David [Ps. 15] came and reduced them to eleven. Then Isaiah [33:15–16] reduced them to six, Micah [6:8] to three, and Isaiah [56:1] again to two, as it is said, 'Keep judgment and do righteousness.' Then Amos [5:4] reduced them to one, 'Seek me and live.' Or one could say with Habakkuk [2:4]: 'The righteous shall live by his faith.'" (Stern 1992, 96, citing *b. Mak.* 23b–24, abridged)

The famous story of the pagan who asked Rabbi Hillel (died AD 10) to teach him the entire Torah while standing on one foot (*b. Šabb.* 31a) includes a famous negative statement of the Golden Rule: "What is hateful to you, do not do to your neighbor. That is the whole *Torah*. The rest is commentary. Go and learn it!" (quoted in Stern 1992, 33).

The scribe accepts Jesus's summary of the law with enthusiasm: **"Well said, Teacher; with truth you said that 'There is one God and there is no other but him'; and 'to love him with the whole heart and the whole understanding and the whole strength' and 'to love the neighbor as oneself' is more important than all of the whole burnt offerings and sacrifices"** (12:32–33). The observation that love of God and neighbor is more important than sacrifice echoes Hosea 6:6 (cf. 1 Sam. 15:22; Prov. 21:3). It is also consistent with the identification of this question as concerning *derek ereṣ*, regarding fundamental principles rather than of "detailed ritual" (Daube 1956, 160). Jesus, in turn, praises the scribe's answer: **And Jesus, seeing that he answered thoughtfully, said to him, "You are not far from the realm of God"** (12:34a). The repetition of the adverbs describing the mutual approval of the scribe and Jesus, *kalōs* ("well," 12:28, 32) and *nounechōs* ("thoughtfully," 12:34) underlines the courteous and respectful tone of the exchange. There is a similarity between this encounter and the story of the rich man in 10:17–22; although both belong to groups harshly denounced by Jesus (cf. 10:24–25; 12:38–40), individuals from these groups can nonetheless draw near to and even enter the *basileia* (cf. 10:25, 27). Jesus's conversation with the scribe brings the encounters in the temple to a close: **And no one dared to ask him anything** (12:34b).

Criticism of Scribal Teaching (12:35–37)

The silence of Jesus's interrogators provides the opportunity for him to ask his own difficult question: **"How do they say that the messiah is the son of David? David himself said in the Holy Spirit, 'The Lord said to my lord, sit at my right hand, in order that I might place your enemies beneath your feet.' David himself says he is lord, so how can he be his son?"** (12:35–37). Unlike the previous questions (12:12–34), which deal with *halakah*, issues pertaining to the interpretation of Torah, this question concerns a matter of *haggadah*, nonlegal interpretation of Scripture: whether the messiah will descend from David (Daube 1956, 160; Lohse 1964, 484–85). The Scripture cited is Ps. 110:1, a coronation hymn that in Hebrew clearly refers to the "LORD" (God), who is exalting the Davidic king ("my lord") to the throne of Israel. In early Judaism, Ps. 110 was not generally regarded as a messianic prophecy (France 2002, 486), but it is frequently interpreted this way in the NT (cf. Mark 14:62; Matt. 22:44; 26:64; Luke 20:42–43; 22:69; Acts 2:34–35; Rom. 8:34; 1 Cor. 15:25; Eph. 1:20; Col. 3:1; Heb. 1:3, 13; 8:1; 10:12). The Greek text translates the name of God (YHWH) simply as "lord" (*kyrios*): "The Lord said to my lord." If, consistent with Jewish tradition, the psalm was written by David (Mark 12:36–37), why would the great king demean himself by calling his own offspring, the messiah, "my lord"?

The implication that the messiah might not be a Davidic descendant is puzzling to the Christian reader, for whom the Davidic ancestry of Jesus is a given (cf. Matt. 1:1–17; Luke 3:23–38; cf. Rom. 1:3; 2 Tim. 2:8; Rev. 3:7; 5:5; 22:16; however, cf. John 7:42). Furthermore, Jesus has already been publicly acclaimed as David's son by Bartimaeus (Mark 10:47–48; cf. 11:9–10). However, the term "messiah" ("anointed") had a range of applications in Second Temple Judaism. Though some Jewish apocalyptic writings look forward to salvation at the hands of a messianic king from the line of David (e.g., *Pss. Sol.* 17), others underplay his role (e.g., 2 Esd. [*4 Ezra*] 7:28–29: after a 400-year reign, the messiah dies before the final reign of God is established). The Qumran scrolls speak of two messiahs, one Aaronic (priestly) and one Davidic (royal), with the former being superior (e.g., 1QS 9.9–11; cf. CD 14.19). The Samaritans had no hopes for a deliverer from the line of David, but looked forward to a *Taheb* ("restorer"), a new Moses (Deut. 18:15–20; Juel 2000). Some scholars hold that Jesus's question amounts to a refutation of the scribal view that the messiah will be from the line of David (e.g., Boobyer 1959–60, 231; Schreiber 1961, 115, 131; Bultmann 1963, 213; Kelber 1974, 95; Johnson 1978, 197; Best 1981, 140; Moloney 2002, 244). However, as I have noted elsewhere:

> Jesus's question is closest to ancient catechetical riddles that can be traced back to medieval and even patristic times—for example, "Who was born and did not die? (Enoch)." This kind of riddle is based not on comparison, but on paradox. . . . Jesus's question does not imply that David's son *cannot be* David's lord, but it challenges the reader to resolve the paradox: David's son *can* be his master if he is the Messiah, who exceeds even his renowned ancestor in the destiny of Israel. (Beavis 1998, 32; cf. A. Taylor 1970, 278)

Another possibility is that, as Mark 11:10 implies, all Jews (including the messiah) can be considered as the children of "our father David." The most commonly offered explanation of the conundrum is that while accurate as far as they go, the titles "messiah" and "son of David" are inadequate to describe the true significance of Jesus, who is also the powerful Son of God and the suffering son of man, who will be exalted in the resurrection.

Criticism of Scribal Practice (12:38–40)

Jesus's teaching to the crowd in the temple precincts (12:37b) continues with a scathing condemnation of the scribes: **"Watch out for the scribes—walking around in long robes, greeting in the marketplaces, and taking the first seats in the synagogue and seats of honor at banquets—who devour the houses of widows and make a great outward showing, praying; these people shall receive the greatest judgment"** (12:38–40). The kinds of behaviors criticized here are typical of men in societies where honor is gained by the public display of wealth and privilege: they wear expensive "robes" (*stolai*) rather than simple cloaks (*himatiai*) to the marketplace (*agora*), where they would be sure to be recognized as high-status members of society. The "first seats in the synagogue" are the seats of honor, dedicated to the elders and benefactors of the synagogue in recognition of their importance in the community. Similarly, seats at banquets were assigned by social rank, with the host taking the first position, the most honored guest seated on his right, and so on (Collins 2007, 583). The parable of the banquet (Luke 14:7–10) presupposes this practice:

> When you are invited by someone to a wedding banquet, do not sit down at the place of honor, in case someone more distinguished than you has been invited

by your host; and the host who invited both of you may come and say to you, "Give this person your place," and then in disgrace you would start to take the lowest place. But when you are invited, go and sit down at the lowest place, so that when your host comes, he may say to you, "Friend, move up higher"; then you will be honored in the presence of all who sit at the table with you.

James 2:2–4 illustrates that similar habits endured at early Christian meals: "For if a person with gold rings and in fine clothes comes into your assembly, and if a poor person in dirty clothes also comes in, and if you take notice of the one wearing the fine clothes and say, 'Have a seat here, please,' while to the one who is poor you say, 'Stand there,' or, 'Sit at my feet,' have you not made distinctions among yourselves, and become judges with evil thoughts?" Worst of all, the scribes desecrate the law that they claim to uphold by violating the rights of widows, whose advocate is God and whose protection is mandated throughout the Jewish scriptures (e.g., Exod. 22:21–24; Deut. 24:17, 19–22; 27:19; Isa. 1:17; 10:2; Jer. 7:6; 22:3; 49:11; Ezek. 22:7; Zech. 7:10; Mal. 3:5; Ps. 146:9; Prov. 15:25; cf. Jdt. 8–16). The sinful behavior imputed to the scribes contrasts with their outward show of piety (Mark 12:40a). The saying that "many that are first will be last, and the last first" (10:31) is appended as a "moral" (*epimythion*) to the Lukan parable (14:11) and applies here; the scribes who seek rank and public recognition will meet with the most severe judgment (Mark 12:40b). The prophet Isaiah denounces those who "write evil, . . . turning aside the cause of the poor, seizing the judgment of the needy among my people so that a widow may become their spoil and an orphan their plunder!" (Isa. 10:1–2 NETS). The early Jewish *Psalms of Solomon* (first cent. BC) describes the fate of hypocritical leaders who devour the households of the socially vulnerable:

> May the flesh of those who try to impress people be scattered by wild animals, and the bones of the criminals (lie) dishonored out in the sun. Let crows peck out the eyes of the hypocrites, for they disgracefully empty many people's houses and greedily scatter (them). They have not remembered God, nor have they feared God in all these things; but they have angered God, and provoked him. May he banish them from the earth, for they defrauded innocent people by pretense. (*Pss. Sol.* 4.19–22, trans. R. Wright, *OTP* 2:656)

Jesus's public teaching in the temple ends with the prophecy of judgment on the scribes: These shall receive the greatest judgment (Mark 12:40b).

The Example of a Poor Widow (12:41–44)

The final teaching in this section takes place in the Court of the Women, where the temple treasury was located, and it is directed to the disciples, not to the crowd: **And sitting across from the treasury, he beheld the whole crowd casting money into the treasury. And many rich people were giving much; and** one poor widow cast in two lepta (which is a quadrans). And having called his disciples, he said to them, "Truly I say to you that his poor widow cast by far the most of those casting into the treasury; for they gave out of their abundance, but she out of her lack gave all that she had, her entire livelihood" (12:41–44). As in the previous pericope, to which this one is connected by the catchword "widow" (*chēra*), a contrast is made between the rich and ostentatious, who publicly demonstrate their ability to "give much," and the destitute widow, who can afford to donate only two copper coins of minuscule value. The coins referred to are *lepta*, a unit of currency used in the Eastern Roman Empire, a reference that the author explains in an aside to the reader/audience as equal in value to a Roman *quadrans* (12:42). As Stein (2008, 579) explains: "A quadran equals one-quarter of the value of the next Roman coin, the assarion, or 'as,' which in turn is worth one-sixteenth of a denarius. Thus the widow's contribution was the equivalent of one sixty-fourth of a denarius; a denarius was the normal pay for a day's work (Matt. 20:1–16)." Since, for a woman, a denarius was the equivalent of *two* days' wages (Schottroff 1995, 92–95), it would take the widow twice as long as a man to earn even this tiny amount.

At one level, the widow's giving away "her entire livelihood" (lit., "her whole life," *holon ton bion autēs*) is ironic: by making a donation to a treasury meant for redistribution to the poor (Moxnes 1988, 71–73), she has further impoverished herself. However, within the value system of the Gospel, where giving one's life for the sake of many is paramount (Mark 10:45), and where selling all that one has and giving it to the poor is a condition of entry into the reign of God (10:17–22), the widow's donation aligns her with Jesus. Formally, the story is an action/saying-*chreia*, where the action is performed by the widow, and the saying is uttered by Jesus to the disciples. As I have explained elsewhere:

> The widow's act epitomizes the theme of self-sacrifice which runs through the second half of Mark (8:37–16:8). She is the only character, other than Jesus and John the Baptist, who gives "all her living/life" . . . in the service of God, in sharp contrast with the rich man, who cannot bring himself to part with his possessions (10:17–22). (Beavis 1988, 6)

Significantly, although she does not directly interact with Jesus, she is the only character (other than the disciples) in this section who does not belong to the category of "opponents of Jesus."

Theological Issues

Mark 11:1–12:44 is dominated by confrontations between Jesus and various opponents, which present an unflattering picture of the Jewish leaders and institutions of Jesus's time: the temple has diverged from the divine mandate to be a place of prayer for everyone; its custodians—the chief priests, scribes, and elders—are like the wicked tenants of the parable (12:1–8), who persecute and kill God's servants the prophets and who will murder even God's own beloved Son, Jesus. The scribes are heartless hypocrites who defraud the weakest members of society while making an outward display of piety. Like the master of the parable, God will destroy the unworthy leaders of Israel "and give the vineyard to others" (12:9b).

Adela Yarbro Collins (2007, 586) cautions that the "global attack on scribes" (and other Jewish leaders) that pervades this section of Mark (and esp. 12:38–40) is unfair, adding that "Christian exegetes and preachers should take care to correct the impression of some in their audiences that this passage represents Jews as such. Rabbinic literature is full of self-criticism, and self-criticism is the best kind of criticism." A contemporary rabbi reflects on this self-critical tradition when he observes:

> Our sages taught that the two Temples were destroyed "because of our sins." One of the reasons for the destruction of the First Temple was bloodshed, while the reason for the destruction of the Second Temple was causeless hatred. Today also, even as we feel that our cause is just, we must maintain our ability to look at ourselves critically. We must remember that there is only a hairbreadth's difference between being a victim and a victimizer, and one can even be both at the same time. (Ascherman 2006)

Like the ancient Jewish sages, Mark attributes the destruction of the temple—the tower built in the midst of the vineyard (12:1)—to the sinfulness of Israel's leaders in Jesus's time, just as the first temple was destroyed on account of the offenses of their preexilic forerunners (cf. Isa. 43:27–28; Jer. 7:1–15; 23:10–12; 26:18; 52:12–23; Ezek. 10:1–22).

The Jewish-Christian commentator David Stern (1992, 97) cautions that the translator of Mark 12:38 should not insert a comma in the phrase "Beware of the scribes, which . . . ," as does the highly influential KJV. Such a translation, he argues, is not justified by the underlying Greek construction and misunderstands the intent of the entire passage. Jesus's warning is directed not against all scribes but only against those who behave immorally: "The comma makes such a rendering antisemitic, because it prejudges a whole class of Jews where Yeshua does not. Yeshua, rather, is condemning only those *Torah*-teachers who exhibit certain objectionable behaviors" (Stern 1992, 97; cf. 12:28–34). Stern situates Jesus's condemnation of the scribes in the prophetic tradition of the Jewish scriptures, where the leaders of Israel are denounced for misguiding the nation (e.g., Isa. 5:8–10, 11–14, 18–24; 10:1–3; 28:1–4; 29:1–4, 15; 30:1–3; 31:1–4; Jer. 8:8; Amos 5:18–20; 6:1–7; Mic. 2:1–4), rather than in the shameful tradition of Christian anti-Judaism. Individual Jewish leaders—Jairus (Mark

Positive Portrayals of Scribes

Although scribes are usually portrayed negatively in Mark and the other Gospels, both Jewish and Christian Scriptures contain positive depictions of scribes, especially Sir. 38:24–39:11, where the scribe is praised as "one who devotes himself to the study of the law of the Most High" (38:34), who penetrates the mysteries of prophecies and parables, advises rulers, travels to learn about good and evil from other cultures, and who prays daily for pardon for his sins. Matthew commends the "scribe . . . trained for the kingdom of heaven" (13:52), perhaps referring to his own status within his Jewish-Christian community. In addition to the good scribe of Mark (12:28–34), scribes who admire Jesus's teachings are mentioned in Matt. 8:19 and Luke 20:39.

5:22), the "good scribe" (12:28–34), and Joseph of Arimathea, a member of the Sanhedrin (15:43–46)—are portrayed positively in the Gospel.

While the criticisms of Mark 11:1–12:44 are leveled primarily against Gospel characters—the chief priests, scribes, elders, Pharisees, Herodians, and Sadducees—the evangelist always writes with the needs of his first-century audience in mind. As noticed above, in Mark's time the war in Judea, culminating in the destruction of the temple (AD 70), would have been deeply disturbing to both Jews and Christians. Until the very end, the Zealots in Jerusalem had been confident that God would intervene to save them from Rome (Josephus, *J.W.* 6.5.2–3 §§286–89), but they were wrong. Possibly members of the Markan community had also vainly hoped that the holy city would be spared. The mainstays of Jewish (and Jewish-Christian) identity—the land, the temple, pilgrimage, and sacrifice—had been destroyed. Mark sees the Jewish leaders through the lens of the disasters that Jews and Christians were coping with in the aftermath.

If the religious and social elites of Israel could go astray, so could the followers of Jesus, who, as represented by the disciples, were beginning to manifest the same attitudes and actions as Jesus's opponents in the Gospel: seeking status in the kingdom of God (10:35–40), trying to "lord it over" one another, like the rulers of the nations (10:42). The paradigm for the Markan community is not the status-hungry disciples, or the hypocritical scribes, but the poor widow, willing to give her all to do the will of God. Thus the fourth-century Syrian poet Ephrem eulogizes her: "Let one who resembles you, O widow, praise you, for my mind is too poor to gaze at you. By your poverty is convicted and exposed the provision of our greed" (*Hymn* 26.8, trans. McVey 1989, 379). Ephrem's praise of the woman does not glorify her poverty per se—in the biblical tradition, poor widows are to be assisted, not admired or extolled (e.g., Deut. 10:18; 14:29; 16:11, 14; 24:19–21; 25:5; 26:12–13; 27:19; Pss. 68:5; 146:9; Prov. 15:25; Isa. 1:17; Jer. 7:6; 22:3; 49:11; Zech. 7:10; Mal.

3:5; cf. Acts 1:1–3; 1 Tim. 5:3–5, 16; James 1:27). Mark's juxtaposition of her story with the warning against scribes who deprive widows of their property implies that her poverty is the outcome of injustice, which should be rectified (see Malbon 1991). Rather, her extravagant generosity in offering up her life/ livelihood in the service of God personifies the qualities of an ideal disciple.

Mark 13:1–37

Interlude: Teaching on the End Times

Introductory Matters

Mark 13:1–37, the eschatological discourse (or "little apocalypse"), is the last of the four blocks of teaching material that punctuate the Gospel. In particular, it corresponds to 4:1–34, the teaching in parables. There is an especially close literary relationship between these two sections. On the one hand, the parable chapter repeatedly enjoins the audience to "hear" (*akouete*) the significance of Jesus's teaching (4:3, 9, 15–16, 18, 20, 23–24, 33; cf. 4:12); in Mark 13, on the other hand, Jesus tells his disciples to "see" (*blepete*, vv. 2, 5, 9, 23, 33) or watch out for (*agrypneite*, v. 33; *grēgoreite*, vv. 34–35, 37) the signs of the times (vv. 2, 7, 21, 26, 29). The bracketing of the Gospel by these two extended discourses suggests a functional parallel between them, for Mark 4:1–34, like Mark 13:3–37, is prophetic. That is, in the overall dramatic structure of the Gospel, Mark 4:11–12 is oracular, the delivery of a prophecy that will be fulfilled in what follows: "Seeing they might see and not perceive, hearing they might hear and not understand, lest they repent and be forgiven" (Isa. 6:9–10). From this point on, the themes of seeing, hearing, perceiving, and understanding are repeated throughout the narrative. Different characters—including the disciples—show varying degrees of "blindness" and insight into the significance of events surrounding the advent of the reign of God: "Like the oracles in Graeco-Roman plays, novels, and biographies, Mark 4:11–12 foretells early on the course of events in the rest of the narrative" (Beavis 1989, 164–65).

In addition to both discourses being prophetic, they share the motif of private instruction to the disciples, in which Jesus corrects a misunderstanding on their part (4:10–13; 13:1–4). At the level of second-degree narrative, the teaching in parables pertains to the spread of God's reign through the preaching of Jesus and his disciples, but the eschatological discourse looks forward to the future, when the disciples of the evangelist's time, faced with disturbing world events, are anxiously waiting for signs of the son of man's return (13:24–27). That the disciples represent Mark's own community is clearly indicated twice in this section, where they are addressed directly in 13:14b through the "reader" of the Gospel ("Let the reader understand") and 13:37b ("What I say to you *I say to all*: Keep watch!").

The internal structure of Mark 13 follows the two questions posed by a group of disciples as Jesus is seated on the Mount of Olives, across from the temple: "Tell us, when will these things be, and what will be the sign that all these things are about to be fulfilled?" (13:4). After a series of general warnings against being misled by worldly afflictions (13:6–8), and specific warnings about the dangers that disciples will face in preaching the good news (13:9–13), Jesus turns to the subject of tribulations in Judea (13:14–23) that will precede the shaking of the heavens, the appearance of the son of man, and the ingathering of the elect (13:24–27). The discourse concludes with two parables (13:28–31, 32–37), both on the theme of eschatological readiness. Jesus's words to the disciples begin and end with injunctions to watch (13:5, 37). The exhortations in 13:14–27 are salted with the phrase "in those days" (13:17, 24; cf. 13:20), underlying the prophetic force of the language (cf. Jer. 3:16, 18; 5:18; 31:29, 33; 33:15–16; 46:26; 50:4, 20; Ezek. 38:17; Dan. 11:6, 14; Joel 2:29; 3:1; Zech. 8:6, 9–10, 23).

As the last of the extended speeches of Jesus in the Gospel prior to the Passion Narrative, the eschatological discourse can be compared to the "last words" of the patriarchs of Israel, who reveal the events that will come to pass in the lives of their posterity (e.g., Gen. 49:1–33; Deut. 33:1–29; Josh. 23:1–24:28). In early Jewish/Christian literature, this tradition is developed in an apocalyptic direction, so that the "testaments" (or farewell discourses) of the ancient heroes reveal heavenly mysteries and end-time secrets to future generations (e.g., *Testaments of the Twelve Patriarchs*, *Testament of Moses*, *Testament of Abraham*, *Testament of Isaac*, *Testament of Jacob*), as this passage from *T. Levi* 4.1 (ca. second cent. BC) illustrates:

Know, then, that the Lord will effect judgment on the sons of men.

> For even when stones are split,
> when the sun is extinguished,
> the waters are dried up,
> fire is cowed down,
> all creation is distraught,
> invisible spirits are vanishing,
> and hell is snatching spoils by sufferance of the Most High,

men—unbelieving still—will persist in their wrongdoing.
Therefore they shall be condemned with punishment. (trans. Kee, *OTP*
1:789)

In Mark 13, Jesus similarly imparts revelations to his successors—and to the audience of Mark's time—about how the future will unfold after he has departed.

Since the discourse begins with a prophecy that the temple will be destroyed (13:2), and a war in Judea is foretold in 13:14–20, most scholars interpret it as referring to the events surrounding the destruction of the temple in AD 70, although there is vigorous debate as to whether the apocalypse was composed during the first Jewish war (AD 66–70), or shortly afterward. Either way, it belongs to a time when Jerusalem was either about to be desolated or had already been razed. On either interpretation, Jesus's prophecies concerning the horrors to befall Jerusalem constitute a *vaticinium ex eventu*—a prophecy after the event—directed to the Markan community, which is concerned by alarming events taking place in Judea and is vulnerable to being "led astray" (13:6). The intent of the discourse is not so much to convey esoteric information as to reassure the audience of Mark's time that, although events seem to be spinning out of control, God is still in charge of history (cf. Lane 1974, 446; Moloney 2002, 250–51).

Although, like the rest of the Gospel, the eschatological discourse is made up of multiple sources, in its Markan form it constitutes a lengthy continuous speech, without introductory formulas (e.g., "and he said") or interruptions by the disciples (see Boring 2006, 358, citing Lambrecht 1967). While the speech contains elements that may be traced back to the historical Jesus (Dyer 1998), it seems reasonable to surmise that it is a product of early Christian prophecy,

---

Mark 13:1–37 in the Narrative Flow

Prologue: John and Jesus (1:1–13)

Transition: Summary of the good news (1:14–15)

Act 1: Jesus in Galilee (1:16–3:35)

Interlude: Teaching in parables (4:1–34)

Act 2: Beyond Galilee (4:35–6:56)

Interlude: Teaching on ritual and moral purity (7:1–23)

Act 3: Mission in gentile regions (7:24–9:29)

Interlude: Teaching on the way to Jerusalem (9:30–10:52)

Act 4: Opposition in Jerusalem (11:1–12:44)

▶ Interlude: Teaching on the end times (13:1–37)

    Transition: Jesus and the disciples leave the temple (13:1–2)

    Four disciples question Jesus in private (13:3–4)

    Jesus's answer (13:5–37)

        General warnings (13:5–8)

        Specific warnings (13:9–13)

        Afflictions in Judea (13:14–23)

        Appearance of the son of man (13:24–27)

        Final warnings (13:28–37)

---

edited by the evangelist and placed on the lips of Jesus (see Boring 2006, 359; Gaston 1970; Grundmann 1973, 259–66). From a contemporary standpoint, it may seem strange that the utterances of an anonymous prophet would be offered as the inspired speech of Jesus, whose predictions are shown to be trustworthy throughout the Gospel (8:31; 9:31; and 10:32–34 fulfilled in chaps. 14–15; see 11:1–6; also, 14:18–21 fulfilled in 14:10–11, 43–46). However, early Christian prophets, such as Paul or John of Patmos (2 Cor. 12:1–4; Gal. 1:11–12; 2:1; Rev. 1:1–2), regarded their visionary experiences as encounters with the exalted Christ and therefore as reliable (for an alternative view, see Aune 1991, 233–45).

Tracing the Narrative Flow

Transition: Jesus and the Disciples Leave the Temple (13:1–2)

Mark 13:1–2, formally a *chreia*, or pronouncement story, signals a shift to a new location: as Jesus and the disciples are leaving the temple, an unnamed disciple praises its magnificence: **"Teacher, look at the great stones and the great buildings!"** (13:1b). After the implicit and explicit criticisms leveled by Jesus against the temple and priesthood in 11:1–12:44, the disciple's comment seems rather foolish. Jesus's prophetic reply is ominous: **"Do you see these great buildings? Not a stone upon a stone will be left that won't be destroyed!"** (13:2). As with his previous utterances against the temple, Jesus's words are in the tradition of the Israelite prophets who foretold the destruction of Solomon's temple (cf. Isa. 43:28; Jer. 7:1–15; 23:10–12; 26:18; 52:12–23; Ezek. 10:1–22). The phrase "a stone upon a stone" particularly echoes the wording of Hag. 2:15–16a LXX: "And now call to mind, from this day backward, before the placing of *a stone upon a stone* in the temple of the Lord, what sort of people were you?" (cf. Collins 2007, 602). The Markan prophecy thus envisions a *reversal* of the building of the postexilic temple, and a reversion to the desolation of Israel without a sanctuary (cf. Hag. 2:15–19). Although Mark 13:2 may not correspond to the literal reality of the Roman assault on the temple, since the general Titus left three towers and part of the Western Wall standing (Josephus, *J.W.* 7.1.1 §§1–2; cf. Collins 2007, 601), Josephus observes that "for all the rest of the wall, it was so thoroughly laid even with the ground by those that dug it up to the foundation, that there was left nothing to make those that came thither believe it had ever been inhabited" (*J.W.* 7.1.1 §3, trans. Whiston 1987, 751). The apparent discrepancy between Jesus's pronouncement and Josephus's description does not prove (or disprove) that the oracle predates the events of AD 70, since it is unlikely that the Markan author or his audience had access to firsthand accounts of the destruction of Jerusalem, and hyperbole is characteristic of prophetic speech.

Figure 11. Detail from the Arch of Titus, at Rome: Judea taken captive.

Four Disciples Question Jesus in Private (13:3–4)

In the next verse, the scene shifts to the Mount of Olives, opposite the temple, where Jesus, seated in the pose of a teacher, is asked a twofold question **privately** by a select group of disciples: Peter, Andrew, James, and John (13:3), the two sets of brothers first called to follow Jesus (1:16–19), three of whom constitute the "inner circle" who accompany Jesus at key moments (5:37; 9:2; 14:33). The question, **"Tell us, when will these things be, and what will be the sign that all these things are about to be fulfilled?"** (13:4), structures most of Jesus's lengthy discourse: "When will these things be?" (13:5–13); "What will be the sign?" (13:14–31). The question relates specifically to Jesus's prophecy of the fall of the temple, a matter that would have been of acute concern to the Markan audience, for whom the war in Judea was a living reality, and which could easily be interpreted as evidence that God's reign was about to be established definitively. Josephus refers to Jewish prophets in Jerusalem who sought signs of salvation even as the temple was being consumed by fire:

> A false prophet was the occasion of these people's destruction, who had made a public proclamation in the city that very day, that God commanded them to get upon the temple, and that there they should receive miraculous signs of their

The Jewish War

In AD 66, a revolt against the Roman occupation broke out in Judea, led by nationalistic Jews who objected to the presence of gentiles in the holy land. The Syrian governor Gallus was the first to lead an army against Jerusalem in October 66, but after his sudden withdrawal from an attack on the north wall of the Temple Mount, he lost some six thousand troops to pursuing Jewish rebels. After Gallus's defeat, a revolutionary government was set up in Jerusalem, and military leaders were chosen for the various regions of the country, including the Galilee. In Rome, the emperor Nero appointed the seasoned general Vespasian to crush the rebellion. After initial successes in Galilee and much of Judea, the Roman invasion of Jerusalem was stalled in 68 by the death of Nero and the chaotic "year of four emperors," in which three claimants to the throne rose and fell in quick succession. In July 69, Vespasian moved to seize the imperial crown, and by December of that year, he was acknowledged as emperor. Meanwhile, in Jerusalem, the radical Zealot party was spreading terror throughout the city: they seized control of the temple area, sparking resistance from the general populace. By the time Vespasian's son Titus approached to attack the city (AD 70), Jerusalem was divided into multiple warring factions. Titus inevitably captured Jerusalem, burned the temple, and destroyed the city. The Roman triumph over the Jewish revolt was complete, with the exception of the fortress of Masada, which had been occupied by rebels since 66. The Roman legate Flavius Silva initiated a successful attack on the Jewish stronghold in AD 73–74; the besieged Jews are said to have committed mass suicide. The main source of information about the Jewish War is the first-century historian Josephus, in his books *The Jewish War* and *Jewish Antiquities* (for a fuller account, see L. Levine 1992).

> deliverance. Now, there was then a great number of false prophets suborned by the tyrants to impose on the people, who denounced this to them, that they should wait for deliverance from God; and this was in order to keep them from deserting, and that they might be buoyed up above fear and care by such hopes. (*J.W.* 6.5.2 §§285–86, trans. Whiston 1987, 741–42)

Josephus's account of the "signs" that occurred preceding the war sheds some light on the kinds of occurrences anticipated by the disciples' question: at Passover, a bright light that shone around the altar in the temple by night, and lasted for about half an hour; a heifer led to the sacrifice who gave birth to a lamb; the eastern gate of the temple opening of its own accord. A few days later, "before sunsetting, chariots and troops of soldiers in their armor were seen running about among the clouds," and later, at Pentecost, the priests ministering in the temple at night experienced an earthquake and a loud noise, followed by "a sound as of a great multitude, saying, 'Let us remove hence'" (Josephus, *J.W.* 6.5.3 §§288–300). As early as four years before the war, Josephus continues, Jesus son of Ananus began to utter prophecies of doom during the feast of Tabernacles, and from then on until the onset of the war, "he every day uttered these lamentable words, as if it were his premeditated vow, 'Woe, woe, to Jerusalem!'" (*J.W.* 6.5.3 §§300–306). Josephus explains to his Roman audience that while God "by all ways possible foreshows to our race what is to our preservation," nonetheless such signs were often misconstrued or ignored to suit the preferences of their interpreters (*J.W.* 6.5.4 §§310–15). Similarly, Mark's audience is cautioned not to be swayed by exaggerated reports of the eschatological significance of the Judean war.

Jesus's Answer (13:5–37)

Jesus's answer comprises general warnings (13:5–8), specific warnings (13:9–13), a description of afflictions in Judea (13:14–23), prediction of the appearance of the son of man (13:24–27), and final warnings (13:28–37).

13:5–8. As noted above, his answer as to "when these things will take place" begins with a series of general warnings against being misled (13:5) by **many who will "appear in my name, saying, 'I am he!' and will lead many astray"** (13:6). It is questionable whether this refers to messianic claimants masquerading as manifestations of the resurrected Jesus (cf. 13:21–22), or early Christian prophets uttering disturbing oracles in the name of Christ. Another NT document, 2 Thessalonians, is addressed to a church that has received a letter, claiming to be from Paul, containing similar teachings: "As to the coming of our Lord Jesus Christ and our being gathered together to him, we beg you, brothers and sisters, not to be quickly shaken in mind or alarmed, either by spirit or by word or by letter, as though from us, to the effect that the day of the Lord is already here" (2 Thess. 2:1–2). Paul (or pseudo-Paul) goes on to list a series of events that must occur before Jesus appears (2:3–8), and attributes the deceptive working of "power, signs, [and] lying wonders" to "Satan" (2:9). The future events referred to in the next two verses of Mark 13 are the kinds of disasters that are the common lot of humanity: **"wars and reports of wars; . . . nation shall rise up against nation and kingdom against kingdom, there will be earthquakes in places, there will be famines"** (vv. 7–8). While apocalyptic texts roughly contemporaneous with Mark often interpret such events as signs of the end (e.g., 2 Esd. 13:30–32; 2 *Bar.* 70.8; Rev. 6:1–17), Mark's Jesus emphasizes that these things must take place, but they do not mean that the eschaton is imminent (13:7). Rather, these things are only the **beginning of birth pangs** (13:8), a metaphor for the agonies the world must endure before the reign of God is established, found in both prophetic and apocalyptic literature (e.g.,

Isa. 13:8; Jer. 4:31; Hosea 13:13; Mic. 4:9; *Jub.* 23.11–25; 2 Esd. 4:40–43; for further examples, see Boring 2006, 262n54). Similar to 2 Thess. 2:1–8, the tone is cautionary—**"The end is not yet"** (3:7b)—while affirming that these events are indeed divinely ordained precursors of the last days. Possibly the figures who "lead many astray" (13:6) are prophets of the evangelist's time who are preaching that current events are evidence that the day of the Lord is at hand.

13:9–13. The admonitions in 13:9–13 are specifically addressed to the disciples as stand-ins for the missionaries in the Markan audience, addressed in the second-person plural: **"Look out for yourselves!"** (13:9a). The dangers of being handed over to councils ("sanhedrins"), beaten in synagogues, and standing before governors and kings for the sake of Jesus are justified by the testimony to the gospel that they provide, **as a witness to them** (13:9b–c). The verb "they will hand over" (*paradōsousin*) is the same one used to describe the "handing over" of Jesus by Judas (3:19; 14:10–11, 18, 21, 41–42, 44) and the arrest of John the Baptist (1:14), thus placing the audience in continuity with the heroes of the Gospel (cf. 13:11–12). Accounts of the sufferings, arrests, and imprisonments endured by missionaries on behalf of Christ are common in early Christian literature (e.g., Acts 4:1–4; 5:17–21, 27–32; 6:1–8:1; 16:19–24; 1 Cor. 4:11; 2 Cor. 11:23–33; Rev. 2:2–4, 9–10; 3:8) and echo the stories of Jewish martyrs who stood firm in obedience to the law of God (e.g., Dan. 3:1–30; 6:1–28; 2 Macc. 6:1–11, 18–31; 7:1–42). The references to sanhedrins and synagogues on the one hand, and governors and kings on the other, envision persecution by both Jewish and non-Jewish authorities, which is interpreted positively as an opportunity for evangelization throughout the world: **"and to all the nations the good news must first be preached"** (13:10).

Although the reference to the preaching of the good news to "all the nations" seems intrusive (see, e.g., Nineham 1963, 347–48; Hooker 1991, 310–12), it is actually Mark's justification for the persecutions that must be endured by emissaries of the gospel. In the Jewish scriptures is a recognition that though Israel is God's treasured possession, the whole earth belongs to YHWH (Exod. 19:5–6; Deut. 7:6; 14:2; 26:18–19). This notion of God's sovereignty is developed in a universalistic direction in some of the prophetic literature, where it is said that "all the nations" will participate in the worship of the one God when divine rule is established (e.g., Isa. 56:7; Amos 9:11–12; Zech. 14:16; Mal. 3:12; cf. Pss. 82:8; 86:9; Tob. 13:11–14; 14:5–7; cf. Matt. 28:19a; Acts 15:14; Rev. 22:2; see Donaldson 2007, 499–505, 543). Mark's echo of the Great Commission (cf. Matt. 28:18–20) sees "the inclusion of gentiles within the community of Jesus's disciples as having been made possible by the resurrection of the messiah and the inauguration of his universal rule" (Donaldson 2007, 411), and as a divine necessity (*dei*; cf. Mark 8:31; 9:11; 13:7, 10, 14). Thus the difficulties anticipated by those who preach in Jesus's name play a vital role in salvation history, and they will be upheld in their time of trial: **"And when they lead you and hand you over, do not be anxious what you** will say, but it will be given to you in that hour what to say; for it is not you speaking but the Holy Spirit" (13:11). For Mark, the Holy Spirit (*to pneuma to hagion*) is the spirit (Hebrew *rûaḥ*) that inspired the prophets (12:36), and which is an eschatological gift of God to the baptized (1:8; cf. Joel 2:28–29). The prophetic spirit of God will support the faithful when they need it most.

The kinds of events foretold in 13:12 are frequently found in apocalyptic literature: **"And a brother will hand over a brother to death and a father a child, and children will rise up against parents and kill them"** (cf. Collins 2007, 607). *First Enoch* speaks of parents who forsake their infants (99.5), fathers who strike down their children and grandchildren, and brothers who raise their hands against their brothers (100.2; cf. *Sib. Or.* 2.154–76; Ezek. 5:10; Mic. 7:6). The reference to family strife in the end times also echoes Markan passages where Jesus is portrayed as at odds with his own family members (3:21, 31–34; cf. 1:20; 6:1–6; 10:29–30). The next verse shifts to the second-person plural, indicating that the reader/audience is being directly addressed: **"You will be hated by many on account of my name. But the one who perseveres until the end will be saved"** (13:13). The theme of those who bear the name of Christ (cf. 9:41) while enduring affliction patiently (*ho de hypomeinas*) is a feature of early Christian exhortation (Rom. 12:12; 1 Cor. 13:7; 2 Tim. 2:10; Heb. 10:32; 12:2–7; James 1:12; 5:11; 1 Pet. 2:20), as is the virtue of steadfastness (*hypomonē*; e.g., Rom. 2:7; 1 Thess. 1:3; 2 Thess. 1:4; James 1:3; 2 Pet. 1:6), including in an apocalyptic context (Rev. 1:9; 2:2; 3:10; 13:10). The verb *hypomenō* and the noun *hypomenē* have the nuance of waiting patiently for someone (BDAG 1039, 1049), anticipating the arrival of the son of man (13:26–27). The theme of Christians being hated by "many" may be echoed in the famous reference to the *odium humani generis* of Christians in Rome during the Neronian persecution (Tacitus, *Ann.* 14.444); the phrase may refer to the reputation of Christians for harboring "hatred of the human race" or to the hatred of Christians "by the human race" (cf. France 2002, 519).

13:14–23. The discourse turns from the period of the "birth pangs" (13:8) to the signs of the end (13:14–23), which are heralded by events in Judea: **"But when *you* see 'the desolating sacrilege' standing where it must not be—let the reader understand—then let those who are in Judea flee to the mountains, but let the one on the housetop not enter his house to take away anything, and let the one in the field not turn back to take away his garment"** (13:14–16). The phrase "desolating sacrilege" ("abomination of desolation" in the KJV) is found in the Jewish scriptures (Dan. 9:27; 11:31; 12:11) as a cryptic description of some blasphemy committed in Jerusalem during the reign of Antiochus IV Epiphanes (175–164 BC). Although Daniel does not specify the precise nature of the sacrilege, Josephus mentions that the Seleucid king erected a pagan altar over the altar of the temple, and sacrificed pigs on it (*Ant.* 12.5.4 §253; cf. 1 Macc. 1:54; 2 Macc. 6:5). The evangelist interprets the abomination not with reference to events of Maccabean times, but to events of his own time;

the notice to the reader (*ho anaginōskōn*) alerts the person reading the text aloud to the assembled believers that the significance of the allusion may need to be explained (see Beavis 1989, 142–43; cf. Collins 2007, 598).

There has been much speculation regarding the exact nature of the "sacrilege" anticipated in Mark 13:14: possibly it refers to Caligula's attempt to install an image of himself in the temple (AD 40; see Josephus, *Ant.* 18.8.2 §261; Philo, *Embassy* 29 §188; 31 §§207–8) or to the antichrist-like figure of 2 Thess. 2:4 who "opposes and exalts himself above every so-called god or object of worship, so that he takes his seat in the temple of God, declaring himself to be God." More generally, it may allude to the fall of the temple in the evangelist's own time (cf. Donahue and Harrington 2002, 372; Stein 2008, 603). In view of the prophecy of the temple's downfall in 13:2, and the disciples' question ("when will these things be, . . . what will be the sign?" [13:4]), the context of the Jewish War seems most likely. As noted above, it is questionable whether the Markan author had access to detailed accounts of events in Judea. Yet Joel Marcus has suggested that the Zealot Eleazar's occupation of the temple in the winter (rainy season) of AD 67–68 (cf. 13:18), before Vespasian's complete occupation of the area around Jerusalem (Josephus, *J.W.* 4.9.1 §§486–90), fits the situation of 13:14: Judeans could still escape to the mountains while the Jewish rebels defiled the temple with their presence (Marcus 1992a, 454–55). Victoria Balabanski (1997, 133–34), connects the flight to an exodus of Jewish Christians from Jerusalem in 67, some to Pella and other locations in Perea, some to Syria (see also Moloney 2002, 261). The injunctions to the audience to flee without turning back to snatch their possessions may be based on the recollections of such refugees, cast in language reminiscent of the flight of Lot and his family before the destruction of Sodom and Gomorrah (Gen. 19:17; cf. Zech. 14:5).

The "woe" (*ouai*) pronounced on **"those bearing in their wombs and the ones nursing in those days!"** (13:17) echoes Hosea 9:11–14, 16 in portraying the coming judgment as a time of "reproductive tribulation" (Pitre 2001, 70–71), when the children of Israel will be led out to the slaughter: "Ephraim is stricken, their root is dried up, they shall bear no fruit. Even though they give birth, I will kill the cherished offspring of their womb" (Hosea 9:16). The phrase "in those days," which occurs three times in the account of the last things (Mark 13:17, 19, 24; cf. v. 20), signals the prophetic force of the language. The tribulations described in vv. 14–24 are more redolent of the "day of YHWH," a time of doom and disaster for Israel (Isa. 13:6, 9; Ezek. 13:5; 30:3; Joel 1:15; 2:1, 11, 31; 3:14; Amos 5:18, 20; Obad. 15; Zeph. 1:7, 14; Zech. 14:1; Mal. 4:1, 5), than of "those days" of the prophetic literature, which herald salvation (Jer. 3:16, 18; 5:18; 31:29, 33; 33:15–16; 46:26; 50:4, 20; Ezek. 38:17; Joel 2:29; 3:1; Zech. 8:6, 9, 10, 23; however, cf. 2 Esd. 4:51; *1 En.* 80.1). For Mark, "those days" will bring **"affliction such as there has not been since the beginning of creation that was created by God until now and there never will be. And unless**

[the] Lord had shortened the days, no flesh would be saved; but on account of the elect whom he chose, he shortened the days" (13:19–20). Since the war in Judea is envisioned as penultimate to the appearance of the son of man (13:26), it is described as a time of unparalleled tribulation (*thlipsis*), rendered survivable only through divine intervention. The term "elect" (*eklektoi*) is found in Mark only in this chapter (13:20, 22, 27); elsewhere in the NT it refers to the community of the faithful (Rom. 11:7 [*eklogē*]; 1 Tim. 5:21; 2 Tim 2:10; Titus 1:1; 1 Pet. 1:1; cf. Matt. 24:22, 24, 31). Similar usages are found in *1 Enoch*, where "the elect" designates the eschatological community made up of the righteous remnant of Israel (e.g., 1.1, 3, 8; 5.7–8; 93.1, 10), and in the Dead Sea Scrolls (e.g., 1QpHab 5.49; 9.11–12; 10.12–13; Collins 2007, 611–12). Possibly the elect on view here are Jewish-Christian refugees (see comment on 13:14), whose memories of the sufferings in Judea are still traumatic.

The final warning prior to Mark's account of the end (13:24–27) forms an inclusion with the beginning of the discourse:

> Look out lest anyone leads you astray; many will appear in my name, saying, "I am he!" and will lead many astray. (13:5–6)

> And then if someone should say, "Behold, here is the Christ! Behold he is there!" do not believe it. For false christs and false prophets shall rise up and perform signs and wonders to lead astray, if they are able, the elect. But look out; I foretold to you all things in advance. (13:21–22)

The term "false christs" (*pseudochristoi*) is found only here in the NT (par. Matt. 24:24) and is not to be confused with the antichrist of popular apocalyptic thought. In the NT, the term *antichristos* is found only in 1 John 2:18, 22; 4:3; and 2 John 7, and refers simply to one who denies that Jesus is the messiah. The reference is better interpreted as a warning against the kinds of messianic figures who periodically appeared in Palestine throughout the first century: Theudas (Josephus, *Ant.* 20.5.1 §§97–98), an unnamed Egyptian prophet (Josephus, *J.W.* 2.13.5 §§261–63), or the prophet in Jerusalem who preached that the people should gather on the one standing portico of the temple to await "signs of their salvation" even as the sanctuary was burning (*J.W.* 6.5.2 §285). Second Thessalonians 2:1–2 bears witness that rumors about the return of Jesus Christ troubled early Christian communities (see comment on 13:6 above). The *pseudochristoi* are paralleled by *pseudoprophētai* ("false prophets"), also a concern of many other NT authors (e.g., Matt. 7:15; 24:11, 24; Luke 6:26; Acts 13:6; 2 Pet. 2:1; 1 John 4:1; Rev. 16:13; 19:20; 20:10; cf. 1 Cor. 14:29–32; 2 Cor. 11:4–5). The criteria for distinguishing true from false prophets are laid down in Deut. 18:20, 22: a prophet who speaks in the name of another god, or who speaks in the name of YHWH but whose prophecy is not fulfilled—such a prophet is false and should not be feared; nor should

Wikimedia Commons

Figure 12. Roman sestertius, AD 71, celebrating victory in the Jewish War. It is inscribed on the obverse with the image of Vespasian and on the reverse with the inscription "Judea capta" (Judea taken captive).

the audience credit the false prophets of their own time. The reference to the "signs and wonders" performed by impostors to deceive the elect finds its closest NT parallel in the eschatological enemy of 2 Thess. 2:9–10: "The coming of the lawless one is apparent in the working of Satan, who uses all power, signs, lying wonders, and every kind of wicked deception for those who are perishing, because they refused to love the truth and so be saved." The final **"Look out!"** (*blepete*, v. 23a) in Mark's litany of eschatological signs (vv. 14–22) is followed by reassurance: **"I foretold to you all things in advance"** (13:23b). Although cast in the form of warnings, Jesus's words reassure Mark's audience that the end-time events are under God's control, and they have nothing to fear (cf. Boring 2006, 369). The repeated use of the term *dei*, translated as "it is necessary" (13:7, 10, 14), underlines the divine causality of the historical upheavals described in the preceding verses: God is in control.

13:24–27. In the evangelist's worldview, the events of the Jewish War have cosmic implications. The final phase in the eschatological drama is described in vivid apocalyptic language in 13:24–27: **"But in those days after that affliction, the sun will be darkened, and the moon will not give its light, and the stars will be falling from the heaven, and the powers that are in the heavens will be shaken. And then they will see the son of man coming on the clouds with great power and glory. And then he will send the angels, and he will gather the elect from the four winds, from the end of the earth to the end of heaven."** The phrase "in those days after the affliction" refers to the aftermath of the war, when the vindication of the elect will finally be at hand. The account of the shaking of the heavenly bodies (13:24–25) is dense with prophetic language (Isa. 13:10; 34:4; Joel 2:10, 31; 3:15; Amos 8:9; Hag. 2:6, 21). As in other apocalyptic texts, the cosmic upheavals are interpreted as eschatological signs (cf. Dan. 8:10; Rev. 6:12–13; 8:10; *T. Mos.* 10.5; 2 Esd. 5:4; *1 En.* 80.4–7; *Sib. Or.* 3.796–97, 801–3; 5.512–31).

The idea of "powers" (*dynameis*) in the heavens may refer to hostile spiritual beings (cf. esp. Rom. 8:38; Eph. 3:10; 6:12; Col. 1:16; 2:15) vanquished through the power of Christ; these spiritual powers may be the (unspecified) subjects who "will see [*opsontai*] the son of man coming on the clouds with great power and glory." The heavenly portents and the shaking of the powers are the prelude to the arrival of the son of man, described here in language borrowed from the book of Daniel: "I saw one like a human being [son of

---

Signs of the End

"The moon shall alter its order, and will not be seen according to its (normal) cycles. In those days it will appear in the sky and it shall arrive in the evening in the extreme ends of the great lunar path, in the west. And it shall shine (more brightly), exceeding the normal degree of light. Many of the chiefs of the stars shall make errors in respect to the orders given to them; they shall change their courses and functions and not appear during the seasons which have been prescribed for them. All the orders of the stars shall harden (in disposition) against the sinners and the conscience of those that dwell upon the earth. They (the stars) shall err against them (the sinners); and modify all their courses. Then they (the sinners) shall err and take them (the stars) to be gods." (1 En. 80.4–7; second cent. BC–first cent. AD; trans. Isaac, OTP 1:58–59)

---

man] coming with the clouds of heaven" (7:13). Both Richard T. France (2002) and N. T. Wright (2001) have argued that Mark 13:26 is not, as most scholars assume, a parousia prediction, but as in Dan. 7:9–13, an account of the postresurrection exaltation and enthronement of the son of man, who for Mark is Jesus (against this view, see Adams 2005). In its immediate context, the son-of-man prophecy is amenable to this interpretation; as with the "one like a son of man" of Daniel, the appearance of the Markan figure is preceded by the vanquishing of hostile powers (cf. Dan. 7:11–12) in the context of divine judgment (7:9–10). However, since Mark's other references to the coming of the son of man refer to a future appearance that will be seen by people on earth (8:38; 14:62), the traditional interpretation seems justified. Unlike the Danielic son of man, who is presented to God (the "ancient one") and is granted eternal dominion over the nations (Dan. 7:13–14), the Markan figure participates in the judgment of the earth by sending the angels (according to some manuscripts, "his angels") to gather the elect (cf. 13:20, 27; cf. 1 Thess. 4:17). The expressions the "four winds of heaven" and "from the end of the earth to the end of heaven" echo scriptural language, emphasizing the prophetic tone of the discourse (e.g., Jer. 49:36; Ezek. 37:9; Zech. 2:6; Dan. 7:2; 8:8; 11:4; Deut. 33:17; 1 Sam. 2:10; Job 28:24; 37:3; 38:13; Pss. 19:6; 48:10; 59:13; Prov. 30:4; Isa. 26:15; Jer. 10:13; Mic. 5:4; Zech. 9:10).

13:28–37. The concluding verses of the discourse are built around two parables: the parable of the fig tree (13:28) and the parable of the doorkeeper (13:34). The first is cast in the form of a command to the disciples/audience: **"From the fig tree learn the parable; by the time when its branch becomes tender and brings forth leaves, you know that the summer is near"** (13:28). As noted above (see comment on 11:13), the fig was known in antiquity as a species of tree that bore fruit before sprouting leaves; the sight of the tree bringing forth leaves thus shows that the season is well advanced. Here the *parabolē* is a similitude:

"a brief narrative of a typical or recurrent event from real life" (Aune 2003, 444). Like many of the synoptic parables, it is followed by an explanation of the significance of the saying: **"Thus also you, when you behold these things happening, know that he is near the door"** (13:29). "These things"—the words of the discourse—describe the signs of eschatological fulfillment sought by the disciples (cf. 13:4). The events of the Jewish War, especially the realization of Daniel's "desolating sacrilege" prophecy, signify that the advent of the son of man, and the vindication of the elect, are imminent.

Sandwiched between this and the next parable are two sayings that underscore the authority of the discourse. **"Amen I say to you, this generation shall not pass away until these things happen. The heaven and the earth shall be destroyed, but my word shall not be destroyed"** (13:30–31). The first saying (13:30) again refers back to the disciples' initial question ("these things") and reiterates the solemn assurance of imminent judgment appended to the first parousia prediction: "'For whoever is ashamed of me and my words in this adulterous and sinful generation, also the son of man shall be ashamed of that person, when he comes in the glory of his father with the holy angels.' And he was saying to them, 'Amen I say to you that some people are standing here who will not taste death until they see the kingdom of God has come in power'" (8:38–9:1). The second saying (13:31) emphasizes the authority of the discourse; the word (*logos*) of Jesus has the stature of the word of God, which is flawless (e.g., 2 Sam. 22:31; Pss. 12:6; 18:30; Prov. 30:5) and precedes the creation of the heavens and the earth (Gen. 1:1–2:4a).

The next saying is transitional to the second parable: **"But concerning that day or the hour no one knows, neither the angels in heaven nor the son, but only the Father"** (13:32). Consistently with the theocentric perspective of the Gospel, knowledge of the precise date of "that day," "the day of the LORD" (see, e.g., Isa. 13:6, 9; Ezek. 13:5; 30:3; Joel 1:15; Amos 5:18; Mal. 4:5), is reserved to God (cf. Mark 8:38, where the son of man is associated with the divine "Father"; see also 1:1, 11; 9:7; 12:6; 15:29). The parable is punctuated by exhortations to "look out" (*blepete, agrypneite, grēgoreite*; 13:33a, 34b, 35a, 36), beginning with one that explains the theme of the parable: **"Look, watch! For you do not know when the time will be"** (13:33). The parable itself is a vignette from Greco-Roman domestic life, which presupposes a household that includes slaves who are entrusted to attend to their master's interests in his absence: **"It is like a man who left his house and gave his slaves the authority each to do his own work, and he ordered the gatekeeper to keep watch"** (13:34). Possibly the evangelist meant the parable to be interpreted allegorically:

That the man is *apodēmos* ("on a journey") already suggests that his return will not be immediate. The "house" suggests the house churches of Mark's community (cf. 1:29–34; 2:1–2, 15; 3:20–21; 7:24; 9:28–34; 10:28–31). The *douloi* ("servants"/"slaves") are transparent to Christian ministers, especially apostles

201

and prophets (10:44; Acts 4:29; Rom. 1:1; Titus 1:1; Rev. 10:7; 11:18) who have received Christ's authority to represent him in the Christian mission (cf. 3:15; 6:7), and whose ministry is called *ergon* ("work"; cf. Acts 13:2; 15:38; Phil. 1:22; 2 Tim. 4:5). It is a picture of the absent Lord of the church who has assigned it a missionary responsibility involving the whole world. (Boring 2006, 377)

Although this brief parable is generically different from the narrative parables of the sower (4:3–9, 14–20) and of the tenants (12:1–8), and Boring's detailed interpretation seems out of proportion with the brevity of the doorkeeper similitude, Mark's preference for allegorical interpretation gives this suggestion some plausibility (cf. comments on 4:14–20; 12:1–8). The association of the master with the son of man is accentuated by the reference to "the gates" (*thyrais*) in the eschatological warning of 13:29 and the role of the "gatekeeper" (*tō thyrōrō*) of the parable, who keeps watch for the returning householder. There is also an echo of 12:9 ("What will the owner of the vineyard do?"), where the arrival of the landlord presages the destruction of the negligent tenants. The exhortation in 13:35–36 draws out the moral of the parable: **"Keep *watch*, therefore; for you do not know when the master will return to the house, at evening or midnight or cockcrow or morning; let him not come and find you sleeping."** Commentators often relate the time indicators (evening, midnight, cockcrow, morning) to the four Roman night watches; more correctly, they are popular Judean time reckonings used toward the end of the Second Temple period (cf. T. Martin 2001, 701), possibly reflecting the recollections of Judean refugees. The point of the parable is that the lord (*kyrios*), the son of man, may arrive at the gates at any time, and as members of the household of God (cf. 3:34–35), the disciples/audience will be called to account. The final exhortation makes explicit the application of the discourse to both the first- and second-degree audiences: **"But what I say to you I say to all, keep watch!"** (13:37), and echoes the initial warning to "look out" (13:5).

The overall effect of the parables and sayings in 13:28–37 is to promote eschatological vigilance while discouraging attempts to calculate "the day or the hour." If the Markan community believed that their own "generation"— possibly including even a few elderly disciples of Jesus's time—would see the advent of the son of man, surely the war in Judea would have sparked both hope and apprehension that the time of consummation was near. Jesus's words reassure them that "these things" will certainly take place, because his prophetic words have the authority of the word of God (13:31–32). The disciples of Mark's time might have taken comfort from the words of Methodius (d. AD 311), who wrote concerning the "passing away" of heaven and earth:

It is usual for the Scriptures to call the change of the world from its present dire condition to a better and more glorious one by the idiom of "destruction." For its earlier form is thereby lost in the change of all things to a state of greater splendor. This is not a contradiction or absurdity. Paul says that it is not the world as such but the "fashion of this world" that passes away. So it is Scripture's habit to call the passing from worse to better as "destruction." Think of a child who passes from a childish stage to a more mature stage. We sometimes express this as an undoing of outmoded patterns. (*On the Resurrection* 9, trans. Oden and Hall 1998, 180)

The Epistle to the Hebrews expresses a similar idea in Platonic terms: that which is unshakeable and permanent will replace the unstable and impermanent: "Therefore, since we are receiving a kingdom that cannot be shaken, let us give thanks, by which we offer to God an acceptable worship with reverence and awe" (Heb. 12:28).

Theological Issues

Mark's eschatological discourse (sometimes called the "little apocalypse"), with its synoptic parallels (Matt. 24–25; Luke 21:5–36), is the most extensive passage of apocalyptic teaching in the NT outside the book of Revelation. Many scholarly books devoted to the interpretation of Mark 13 have been published since the middle of the twentieth century (Beasley-Murray 1954; 1957; Hartman 1966; Lambrecht 1967; Pesch 1968; Gaston 1970; Geddert 1989; Dyer 1998), and they come to varying conclusions. Some see Mark as teaching that the signs of the end can be recognized, while others see the evangelist as criticizing the idea that signs can be believed. Some see the chapter as an apocalyptic countdown; others take it as repudiating such calculations. Some argue that the evangelist is warning his audience that the second coming may be delayed, while others see him preparing them for an imminent return of Christ (Geddert 1989, 22). Geddert (1989, 22) wryly observes that when it comes to Mark 13, "scholarly diversity on the issue of Mark's agenda can hardly be overestimated."

In contrast to the diversity of academic viewpoints on the meaning of the eschatological discourse, thanks to the influence of popular apocalyptic works like Hal Lindsey's *Late Great Planet Earth* (1970) and the Left Behind series of novels and movies, it is often understood as part of the scriptural evidence for a lurid end-time scenario that includes the premillennial rapture, the "great tribulation," the appearance of the antichrist, and the second coming of Jesus—all of which are expected to take place in the near future. Thus, like the book of Revelation, Mark 13 is an "overdetermined" text: a unitary meaning has been imposed on a complex and multifaceted discourse (see Thompson 2007, 24–25).

The return of Christ, divine judgment, and the establishment of God's eternal reign remain part of Christian hope. As the Nicene Creed (AD 325) affirms, "He will come again in glory to judge the living and the dead, and his kingdom will have no end." However, one thing scholars *do* agree about is that

Christians and the End Times

For the past two thousand years, certain groups of Christians have periodically come to the conclusion that they were living in the end times, based on their own intepretations of Scripture. For example, in the second century a group called the Montanists or the "New Prophecy" fervently believed that the last judgment was imminent, and that the new heaven and new earth prophesied in Rev. 21 would be established in Asia Minor (present-day Turkey). In 1420, an Eastern European sect known as the Taborites gathered on a hill near Prague to await the second coming in the second week of February. Like the Montanists, they were disappointed. In nineteenth-century United States, the followers of William Miller interpreted the Scriptures as teaching that Christ would return on October 22, 1844 (and when he didn't, in April, July, or October 1845—a sequence of events known as "The Great Disappointment").

One of the most contentious passages in Revelation says that after the souls of the martyrs have been judged, they will be raised, and Christ will reign for a thousand years (20:4–5), that is, for a millennium, before the final judgment and the establishment of God's rule. Beginning in the nineteenth century, various Protestant sectarian groups have taught a doctrine called premillennialism, meaning that the thousand-year reign of Christ is a future event, which will happen before the last judgment. However, throughout history the majority Christian interpretation of the millennium is that the "thousand-year" reign of Christ is to be taken not literally but figuratively and that it refers to the millennial reign of the church, through which Christ reigns on earth. That is, the "mainstream" Christian teaching is that the millennium is now, and the people of God are living in it.

ancient apocalyptic writings like Mark 13 and Revelation were not meant for people living thousands of years in the future but for members of their own struggling communities, who needed reassurance that the alarming events unfolding around them were under divine control and that the persecuted faithful were the elect, whom God would soon vindicate. Jesus's message to Mark's church carefully balances confidence that deliverance is near with caution against jumping to the conclusion that contemporary events were signs of the end: "But concerning that day or the hour no one knows, neither the angels nor the son, but only the Father. Look, watch! For you do not know when the time will be" (Mark 13:32–33).

From a contemporary standpoint, Jesus's references to "the elect" (13:20, 22, 27) might imply a sense of exclusivism: the notion that only a select group of chosen faithful will participate in eschatological salvation. However, later theological developments such as the doctrines of election and predestination (see *WDCH* 670–72) should not be read into the Gospel, where the chosen few are not conceptualized as a select group of believers preordained by God for eternal salvation, but as the Jewish-Christian survivors of the Jewish War (AD 66–70). For Mark, the good news must be preached to "all the nations" (13:10; cf. 14:9); Jesus criticizes the temple not in and of itself, but because it is not living up to its divine mandate to be a place of prayer for people of *all* nationalities (11:17; Isa. 56:7). This universalistic outlook is consistent with the Jewish scriptural tradition of the eschatological inclusion of the gentiles in the people of God:

> They will be summoned to Jerusalem "from the coastlands far away" (Isa 66:19) in order to see the glory of the Lord. They stream to Zion to learn God's ways and to be instructed in God's paths (Isa 2:2–4/Mic 4:1–3). "Full of the knowledge of the LORD," they will search out the "root of Jesse" and his glorious dwelling (Isa 11:9–10). "Many peoples and strong nations shall come to seek the LORD of hosts in Jerusalem" (Zech 8:22), where they will participate in a joyous end-time banquet on the "mountain of the LORD of hosts" (Isa 25:6) and where they will offer gifts (Isa 18:7; 60:5–6; Hag 2:6–9) and sacrifices to God in a temple that "shall be called a house of prayer for all peoples" (Isa 56:7). (Donaldson 2007, 500, with references corrected)

This is a perspective that is also widely expressed in early Jewish apocalyptic works (for examples, see Donaldson 2007, 502–3). It is intriguing to speculate whether the Markan evangelist anticipated a new Jerusalem, and even a new temple, to replace the ones destroyed by the Romans, or whether, like other NT authors, he spiritualized these elements of Jewish eschatological hope (e.g., John 4:21–24; 1 Cor. 3:16–20; 8:10; Gal. 4:26; Eph. 2:19–22; Heb. 12:22; cf. Rev. 3:12; 21:1–27):

> I saw no temple in the city, for its temple is the Lord God the Almighty and the Lamb. And the city has no need of sun or moon to shine on it, for the glory of God is its light, and its lamp is the Lamb. The nations will walk by its light, and the kings of the earth will bring their glory into it. Its gates will never be shut by day—and there will be no night there. People will bring into it the glory and the honor of the nations. (Rev. 21:22–26)

Either way, the Markan community has nothing to fear. The reign of God will prevail, and the gentiles will be admitted into the assembly of the righteous because they have heard the good news (Mark 13:10).

Mark 14:1–15:47

Act 5: Passion Narrative

Introductory Matters

Mark 14–15 is the earliest surviving connected account of the events surrounding the arrest and execution of Jesus, the earliest Passion Narrative. Here the term "Passion," from the Latin *patior* (to bear, endure, suffer), refers to the suffering and death of Jesus, a theme foreshadowed as early as the arrest of John the Baptist (1:14) and made explicit at the midpoint of the Gospel (8:31), the first Passion prediction (cf. 9:12; 10:33). The execution of John (6:14–29) foreshadows the crucifixion; John is the eschatological Elijah, who has come before Jesus, the son of man, and whose fate parallels that of his successor, "as it is written" (9:11–13). Throughout this section, Jesus's foreknowledge of his ordeal, and its conformity to Scripture, is repeatedly emphasized: the woman who anoints Jesus at Bethany prepares him for burial (14:8); the house where the Last Supper will take place is furnished and ready (14:12–16); Jesus prophesies that one of the Twelve will hand him over to his opponents (14:18); the disciples' abandonment is foretold by Scripture (14:27, 49–50); Jesus knows beforehand that Peter will deny him (14:30, 72). The account of the crucifixion (15:21–32) is woven out of multiple allusions to Scripture, emphasizing the sense of divine destiny: Jesus is offered wine mixed with myrrh (15:23, 37; cf. Prov. 31:6); the soldiers cast dice for his clothing (15:24; cf. Ps. 22:18); passersby mock Jesus and shake their heads at him as he suffers on the cross (15:29; cf. Ps. 22:7; Lam. 2:15a). Although Jesus anticipates every step on the way to the cross, the theological focus of the Gospel is upheld: it is not Jesus's will but God's will that must prevail (14:36).

Mark's narrative of the Passion and its aftermath takes place over the course of five days: The first is a Wednesday, two days before Passover, when Jesus is anointed at Bethany (14:1–11). The second is Thursday, the day of preparation for the Passover (14:12). This leads to the third day, beginning on Passover evening, when Jesus and his disciples share the Passover meal, and that night he is arrested and tried by the Sanhedrin (14:12–72). The third day, Friday, continues as the first day of the festival, when Jesus is tried by Pilate, crucified, and buried (15:1–47). On the Sabbath (Saturday) all work ceases and Jesus lies dead in his tomb (16:1a). On the first day of the Jewish week (Sunday), three women arrive to find the tomb empty (16:1–8). Theodor Lescow (2005, 93) helpfully structures the Passion Narrative (including the finding of the empty tomb) in five acts, followed by the apotheosis of the protagonist:

Act 1:   Bethany (14:1–11)
Act 2:   The Passover Meal (14:12–26)
Act 3:   Gethsemane (14:27–53a)
Act 4:   The Double Death Sentence (14:53b–15:15)
Act 5:   Golgotha (15:16–47)
         Apotheosis (16:1–8)

Although the apotheosis ("exaltation to divine status") of the hero is not a standard feature of ancient tragedy, heroes often die a "beautiful death" in Greek literature (see Brant 2004, 231–55).

In commentaries on Mark, Martin Kähler's (1964, 80n11) famous comment (originally made in 1896) that the Gospel is "a passion narrative with an extended introduction" is often quoted. Many scholars would agree with Kähler that the evangelist inherited an early Passion tradition that forms the basis of this section of the Gospel. For example, Rudolf Pesch (1976–77, 2:1–27) argues that a historically reliable Passion account developed with the earliest Jewish-Christian community in Jerusalem (similarly, V. Taylor 1935, 44–62; Green 1988). At the opposite end of the spectrum of scholarly opinion are those who attribute Mark with maximum creativity (e.g., Kelber 1976; Crossan 1995). Many scholars would agree with Donald Senior (cf. R. Brown 1994, 5) that a mediating view between the two extremes is justified:

> Given the importance of Jesus's death in early Christian preaching, it is likely that the basic story would have taken shape prior to Mark and would have been known to him as it was to every Christian. However, Mark seems to have boldly retold the story in his own way: . . . the language, tone and message of Mark's passion narrative blends with his entire portrayal of Jesus. The passion does not appear to be grafted on the Gospel but is the integral climax of all that has preceded. (Senior 1984, 11)

Mark 14:1–15:47 in the Narrative Flow

Prologue: John and Jesus (1:1–13)

Transition: Summary of the good news (1:14–15)

Act 1: Jesus in Galilee (1:16–3:35)

Interlude: Teaching in parables (4:1–34)

Act 2: Beyond Galilee (4:35–6:56)

Interlude: Teaching on ritual and moral purity (7:1–23)

Act 3: Mission in gentile regions (7:24–9:29)

Interlude: Teaching on the way to Jerusalem (9:30–10:52)

Act 4: Opposition in Jerusalem (11:1–12:44)

Interlude: Teaching on the end times (13:1–37)

►Act 5: Passion Narrative (14:1–15:47)

    Plotting and anointing (14:1–11)

        Plotting against Jesus (14:1–2)

        The anointing at Bethany (14:3–9)

        A disciple joins the plotting (14:10–11)

    The Last Supper with the disciples (14:12–25)

    Predicting Peter's denial (14:26–31)

    Anguish in Gethsemane (14:32–42)

    The arrest of Jesus (14:43–52)

    Denial and trial (14:53–72)

        Peter's distant following (14:53–54)

        Trial before the Sanhedrin (14:55–65)

        Peter's denial (14:66–72)

    Before Pilate: Jesus on trial, Barabbas freed (15:1–20a)

        Trial before Pilate (15:1–5)

        Barabbas freed (15:6–15a)

        Sentencing by Pilate (15:15b–20a)

    The crucifixion (15:20b–38)

    Three responses to the death of Jesus (15:39–47)

        The centurion's exclamation (15:39)

        The watching women (15:40–41)

        Joseph of Arimathea (15:42–47)

While the Passion Narrative meshes artfully with the rest of the Gospel, there are features that set it apart, giving credence to the view that Mark adapted an earlier tradition. Notably, with the exception of 14:3–9 and 14:22–29, it is a connected account, with little material likely to have circulated independently; unlike in the previous narrative sections of the Gospel, Jesus works no miracles; and the Pharisees disappear from the story (cf. Boring 2006, 379).

**An Outline
of Mark 14:1–11**

**Plotting and
anointing (14:1–11)**

Plotting against
Jesus (14:1–2)

The anointing at
Bethany (14:3–9)

A disciple joins the
plotting (14:10–11)

Tracing the Narrative Flow

Plotting and Anointing (14:1–11)

The story of the woman who anoints Jesus at Bethany (14:3–9) is bracketed by a notice that his opponents are plotting against him (14:1–2) and a report that one of Jesus's disciples has joined them (14:10–11). The woman's "beautiful" act (14:6b) of anointing Jesus is thus implicitly contrasted with the treachery of Judas and the priests. The anointing story, paired with the incident of the poor widow (12:41–44), also serves to frame the eschatological discourse with narratives of women whose acts of devotion are commended by Jesus in superlative terms: the widow "gave all that she had, her entire livelihood" (12:44); the woman at Bethany will be remembered wherever the good news is proclaimed (14:9).

14:1–2. Jesus's opponents are seeking a way to have him arrested and executed without drawing the attention of the crowds: **not on the festival, in case there is agitation among the people.**

14:3–9. Mark's anointing story (paralleled by Matt. 26:6–13) has often been confused with two similar stories in Luke and John. In Luke's version (7:36–50), Jesus is in Capernaum (cf. Luke 7:1), dining at the house of a Pharisee named Simon, and a woman reputed to be "a sinner" enters and tearfully anoints Jesus's feet. For her act of hospitality, Jesus proclaims her sins to be forgiven. John's anointing story (12:1–8), like the one in Mark, takes place in Bethany, but six days, not two days, before the Passover (cf. Mark 14:1); the woman is not an unnamed "sinner" but Mary, sister of Martha and Lazarus; and as in the Lukan story, she anoints Jesus's feet and wipes them with her hair, rather than anointing his head, as in Mark (14:3). The *chreia* that concludes the Johannine story echoes, but does not duplicate, Mark 14:7–8: "Leave her alone. She bought it so that she might keep it for the day of my burial. You always have the poor with you, but you do not always have me" (John 12:7–8). These stories are often conflated so that the woman is misidentified as the repentant Mary Magdalene; yet in no version is the anointing woman identified as Mary Magdalene, nor is there a statement that the woman in any of the stories is a prostitute. Especially Mark's account focuses on the value of the woman's act, obscuring any hint of sexual impropriety that such a story might connote (see Corley 1993, 102–6). Although the word translated as "anoint" (*myrisai*,

14:8) is different from the verb used to describe the "anointing" of a messiah/ *christos* (*chriō*, as in Luke 4:18), the woman is the only human character who actually anoints the anointed one (assuming that 1:10–11 constitutes a divine "anointing").

Mark's version of the story—the earliest written—takes place in the house of **Simon the Leper** (14:3), presumably someone who has recovered from the disease and been readmitted to the community after ritual purification (cf. 1:44). Jesus and his companions are **reclining at table** in Greco-Roman style when the woman comes to him with **an alabaster flask of ointment of costly pure nard** (14:3b); the vessel is literally an *alabastron*, "a vase for holding perfume/ointment, often made of alabaster, . . . with a rather long neck which was broken off when the contents were used" (BDAG 40). Both the flask, made of thin, translucent stone in order to be snapped off (cf. 14:3b), and its contents, nard (or "spikenard"), an aromatic ointment, were luxury items. The woman breaks the flask and pours its contents over Jesus's head; as Schüssler Fiorenza (1983, xiv) notes: "Since the prophet in the Old Testament anointed the head of the Jewish king, the anointing of Jesus's head must have been understood immediately as the prophetic recognition of Jesus, the Anointed, the Messiah, the Christ." The woman's act is thus more than a gesture of hospitality, as in the Lukan and Johannine stories, but a "prophetic sign-action" (cf. 1 Sam. 10:1; 16:13; 1 Kings 1:34, 45; 19:16; 2 Kings 9:5–6).

The indignant reaction of Jesus's dinner companions is reminiscent of other Markan stories where onlookers challenge the validity of his words and deeds (e.g., 2:1–12, 15–17; 3:1–6), or his disciples' activities (e.g., 2:23–28; 7:1–2). In this case, the critics disparage a woman disciple of Jesus, possibly one of his female followers (as in 15:40–41): **"Why has this waste of the ointment taken place? For this ointment could be sold for more than three hundred denarii and given to the poor." And they loudly admonished her** (14:4b–5). In addition to underlining the generosity of the woman's gift—worth about a year's wages for a male day laborer, two years' for a woman (see Maloney 2002, 35)—it sets up a contrast between the woman's insight and the onlookers' wrongheadedness. Jesus answers the censure of the woman's action with his own lengthy admonition, topped off by a prophetic commendation of the woman: **"Leave her be. Why do you give her trouble? She has done a beautiful thing. For you will always have the poor among you, and you can do good for them whenever you wish, but you will not always have me. She has done what she could; she has anointed my body in advance for burial. Amen I say to you, wherever the good news is preached in the whole world, also what she did will be spoken in memory of her"** (14:6b–9). Jesus's famous statement that "you will always have the poor among you" is not a repudiation of concern for the poor but a reference to Deut. 15:11, part of a commandment for Israelites *always* to be generous toward the needy among them: "Since there will never cease to be some in need on the earth, I therefore command you, 'Open your hand to the poor and needy neighbor in your land.'" The second half of Mark 14:7—"You will not always have me"—is prophetic, amounting to a fourth Passion prediction (cf. 8:31; 9:31; 10:33–34; cf. Donahue and Harrington 2002, 387–88). Jesus's reference to the anointing as preparation for burial (14:8) is similarly prophetic; the women who go to the tomb to anoint Jesus's body find it empty (16:1–8), so their ointments go unused. Feminist interpreters have often recognized the irony of the prophecy that the woman's act will be remembered throughout the world (14:9), since her prophetic anointing is not reenacted liturgically during holy week, and her name is not even known (notably, Schüssler Fiorenza 1983, xiii; cf. Beavis 1988, 7; Corley 1993, 105; Kinukawa 1994, 89). Jesus's final comment on the anointing is his longest and most positive pronouncement on the words or deeds of any character in the Gospel.

14:10–11. The solemn amen saying commending the woman starkly contrasts with the terse reference to one of Jesus's own disciples who joined the conspiracy against him (14:10–11): after the anointing, Judas, **one of the Twelve,** went out and plotted with the chief priests to hand Jesus over to them for **money** (14:10–11).

The Last Supper with the Disciples (14:12–25)

The scene shifts to **the beginning of the day of unleavened bread, when they sacrifice the Passover lamb** (14:12), the day of preparation for the Passover (14 Nisan in the Jewish calendar). As in the story of Jesus's entry into Jerusalem (11:1–10), Jesus instructs two disciples to go to the city, predicts what they will find (**"a man carrying a jar of water"**), and tells them how to proceed (**"follow him . . . wherever he enters"**), and what to say (**"the teacher says, 'Where is my guest room where I shall eat the Passover meal with my disciples?'"**; 14:15). When they arrive in Jerusalem, events unfold in accordance with Jesus's words, and they prepare for the festival in the **large furnished upper room** waiting for them (14:15–16). Again, the close correspondence between the instructions and their fulfillment suggests prearrangement, that "Jesus has a contact in Jerusalem whose premises he has arranged to use for this special meal" (France 2002, 564). However, in the context of the Passion Narrative, the incident contributes to the theme of Jesus's prophetic foreknowledge of the events culminating in his death and resurrection.

Jesus and the Twelve join the two disciples in the guest room in the evening, the beginning of the festival (14:17). The instructions for partaking of the Passover meal are found in Exod. 12:1–13: each household is to eat the roasted lamb with unleavened bread and bitter herbs, hurriedly by night, letting nothing remain until morning, commemorating Israel's hasty preparations for the flight from Egypt. Over time, the Passover developed into a family meal where the head of the household would explain the reason for the festival to the children (cf. Exod. 12:25–27; see Gorman 2000, 1012). Although it is usually assumed

Figure 13. *The Last Supper*, by Tintoretto, 1594.

that only Jesus and the Twelve partook in the Last Supper, Mark implies that there were at least fifteen participants: Jesus, the Twelve, and the two disciples who had preceded them. Maurice Casey (1999, 227–28) has argued that since the upper room was "large" (14:15), the celebrants would have included Jesus's other followers, including women and children, reflecting the familial setting of the meal. The progression of the dialogue between Jesus and the others at the table supports this view: he prophesies that *one of those dining with him* will hand him over (14:18); each of them sorrowfully asks, "Not I?" (14:19); and Jesus further specifies that it will be **"one of the Twelve, who dips with me in the dish"** (14:20), thus not a member of the larger circle of disciples (against this view, see, e.g., France 2002, 563; Gundry 1993, 835). The Passion prediction that follows (**"The son of man will go up as it is written about him, but woe to that man by whom the son of man is handed over; it would be well for that man if he had never been born"**; 14:21) zeroes in on the culprit, implicitly contrasting the wicked deed and woeful fate of "that man" with the "beautiful deed" and high repute of the woman who has prepared him for his burial (14:8–9). The formula "as it is written" does not seem to refer to a specific prophecy but reflects the early Christian conviction that the Passion and resurrection were "according to the Scriptures" (1 Cor. 15:3–4 NIV).

Mark's description of the Passover meal does not reflect the traditional blessings, prayers, and customs associated with the festival (cf. France 2002, 563). Possibly there was no reason to remind Mark's audience of the familiar Jewish ritual; the evangelist's attention is on the institution of a new kind of ritual meal. The unleavened bread of the seder, blessed, broken, and shared by the head of the household, becomes **"my body"** (14:22); the wine-cup of the Passover ritual, shared among the disciples after a prayer of thanksgiving, becomes **"my blood of the covenant, which is poured out for many"** (14:23–24; cf. 1 Cor. 11:23–26). The reference to the blood of the covenant poured out "for many" is consistent with other early Christian expressions of the significance of Christ's death (e.g., Rom. 5:8; 8:32; 1 Cor. 11:24; Gal. 1:4; 2:20), but especially with Mark 10:45: "For the son of man has not come to be served but to serve and to give his life a ransom for many." As noted in the comment on that verse, the accent is on the son of man's service to humanity; in the context of the Passover, the reference to the blood of Jesus evokes the blood of the paschal lamb, smeared on the doorposts of the Israelites in preparation for their escape from Egypt (Exod. 12:1–13). Although the Jewish seder ritual and the early Christian sacred meal prefigured in the Gospels ritualize their respective foundation stories, using certain foods to function as more than simply nourishment, they serve different ritual functions: The Passover meal is a ritual of reintegration that emphasizes the continuity between Jews and their Israelite ancestors. The Christian ritual involves both separation and reintegration, "stressing the Christian break with other first-century Jews, as well as the union of contemporary Christians with their ancestors" (Brumberg-Kraus 1999, 165, cf. 168). Thus the "ancestors" of the participants in the Christian meal include both Jews and Christians. Mark portrays the Last Supper as foreshadowing the eschatological banquet, when Jesus concludes his table talk with a solemn prophetic pronouncement: ***"Amen*** **I say to you that never again will I drink of the fruit of the vine *until that day* when I drink it anew in the kingdom of God"** (14:25; cf. Matt. 8:11–12; 22:1–10; Luke 13:28–29; Rev. 2:7; 19:9; see also Isa. 25:6; *1 En.* 62.12–16; *2 Bar.* 29.1–8; 1QS 2.11–22).

Predicting Peter's Denial (14:26–31)

The theme of prophecy and fulfillment continues with Mark 14:26–31. The hymn sung by the disciples before leaving for the Mount of Olives (14:26), a north-south oriented ridge east of Jerusalem, is probably the Hallel (Pss. 113–118), psalms of thanksgiving and praise sung during the Passover meal. When they arrive, Jesus continues to address the theme of discipleship failure begun in the previous pericope, predicting that his companions will all abandon him, **"because it is written, 'Strike the shepherd, and the sheep will be scattered'"** (Mark 14:27b; cf. Zech. 13:7). In its original context, the prophecy from Zechariah is ambiguous; it may refer to either a ruler of Judah or a postexilic high priest whose demise will afflict the people whom he shepherds (Cody 1990, 358). Here it is marshaled to explain the defection of the disciples after Jesus's arrest (14:50). Contrary to expectation, Jesus continues not by chiding the disciples for their inevitable abandonment (cf. 4:40; 6:50), but by reassuring them as to what will happen in the near future: **"After I am raised, I will go before you to Galilee"** (14:28; cf. 16:7).

The famous exchange between Peter and Jesus that follows (14:29–31) ironically echoes Peter's confession at Caesarea Philippi (8:27–33). In both scenes, Peter speaks without comprehension when he rebukes Jesus for speaking of the suffering of the son of man (8:32), as he does when he promises not to stumble even if the other disciples fall away (14:29). In both scenes, Jesus contradicts Peter: "Get behind me, Satan!" (8:33a); **"Amen I say to you that you this very night before the rooster calls twice, you will deny me thrice!"** (14:30). In both scenes, Peter is portrayed as not comprehending Jesus's prophetic speech and as speaking rashly: **"If I must die with you, I will not deny you!"** (14:31a; cf. 8:32b). As they did earlier in the evening, all of Jesus's companions pledge their loyalty (14:31b; cf. 14:19). By the end of the drama, Jesus's prophecies are vindicated, and the disciples' vows are shown to be empty in the face of the divine will.

Anguish in Gethsemane (14:32–42)

The scene in Gethsemane (14:32–42) may be a Markan addition to a preexisting Passion Narrative (for discussion, see Collins 2007, 673–75). The location of the garden is unknown; like the pilgrimage site identified as the garden of Gethsemane in present-day Jerusalem, it was probably at the foot of the Mount of Olives. Jesus instructs the disciples to wait for him while he withdraws to pray (14:32b); as in earlier scenes, he singles out Peter, James, and John to accompany him (14:33a; cf. 5:37; 9:2; 13:3). Although Mark's Jesus is often portrayed as expressing emotion (1:41; 3:5; 6:6, 34; 8:12; 10:21; 11:15–19), here, for the first time, Jesus shows anguish in the face of his impending execution: **He began to be greatly frightened and distressed. And he says to them, "My soul is very sorrowful to death; stay here and keep watch"** (14:33b–34). In view of the conviction expressed in the three Passion predictions that the son of man will rise, his distraught behavior comes as a surprise (cf. 8:31; 9:31; 10:33–34). As Collins (2007, 675) notes, Jesus's obvious distress contrasts with the stoicism expected of martyrs: "The Maccabean heroes and famous Greeks and Romans . . . display composure and bravery."

However, Jesus's words to the three disciples echo Scripture (Pss. 42:5, 11; 43:5; cf. Sir. 37:2; Jon. 4:9) and evoke the tradition of the lament psalm (Dobbs-Allsopp 2000, 785). In the verses that follow, Jesus acts out the abjection expressed by the psalmist: **And he went ahead a little way, and he fell upon the ground and prayed that, if it was possible, the hour might pass him by, and he was saying, "Abba, Father, all things are possible to you; take this cup away from me! Yet not my will but yours"** (Mark 14:35–36). The alternation between misery and steadfast faith echoes the abrupt shifts in mood characteristic of lament psalms (e.g., Pss. 6:8–10; 22:22–31; 31:20–24; cf. Ps. 42:1–11). The appeal to God as "Abba, Father" is an instance of Markan

The Martyrdom of Eleazar

"Eleazar, one of the scribes in high position, a man now advanced in age and of noble presence, was being forced to open his mouth to eat swine's flesh. But he, welcoming death with honor rather than life with pollution, went up to the rack of his own accord, spitting out the flesh, as all ought to go who have the courage to refuse things that it is not right to taste, even for the natural love of life.

"Those who were in charge of that unlawful sacrifice took the man aside because of their long acquaintance with him, and privately urged him to bring meat of his own providing, proper for him to use, and to pretend that he was eating the flesh of the sacrificial meal that had been commanded by the king, so that by doing this he might be saved from death, and be treated kindly on account of his old friendship with them. But making a high resolve, worthy of his years and the dignity of his old age and the gray hairs that he had reached with distinction and his excellent life even from childhood, and moreover according to the holy God-given law, he declared himself quickly, telling them to send him to Hades.

"'Such pretense is not worthy of our time of life,' he said, 'for many of the young might suppose that Eleazar in his ninetieth year had gone over to an alien religion, and through my pretense, for the sake of living a brief moment longer, they would be led astray because of me, while I defile and disgrace my old age. Even if for the present I would avoid the punishment of mortals, yet whether I live or die I shall not escape the hands of the Almighty. Therefore, by bravely giving up my life now, I will show myself worthy of my old age and leave to the young a noble example of how to die a good death willingly and nobly for the revered and holy laws.'

"When he had said this, he went at once to the rack. Those who a little before had acted toward him with goodwill now changed to ill will, because the words he had uttered were in their opinion sheer madness. When he was about to die under the blows, he groaned aloud and said: 'It is clear to the Lord in his holy knowledge that, though I might have been saved from death, I am enduring terrible sufferings in my body under this beating, but in my soul I am glad to suffer these things because I fear him.'

"So in this way he died, leaving in his death an example of nobility and a memorial of courage, not only to the young but [also] to the great body of his nation." (2 Macc. 6:18–31; first cent. BC)

translation of an Aramaic term (cf. 5:41; 7:34; 15:34), reflecting words used by early Christians in prayer (cf. Rom. 8:15; Gal. 4:6). The phrase "all things are possible to you" is Mark's third expression of the theme that "all things are possible with God" (cf. 9:23; 10:27; cf. 11:23–24); the reference to "this cup" recalls the cup of "my blood of the covenant" at the Last Supper (14:23–24). However, in keeping with the sense of prophetic inevitability that pervades the Gospel, Jesus concludes his prayer by acquiescing to God's design (14:36b).

The interchange in 14:37–42 follows from Jesus's charge for the three disciples to keep watch (14:34b) and contrasts Jesus's anguished prayer with his companions' heedlessness. Jesus returns from his solitude to find the three sleeping; he singles out Peter for rebuke; he will be tested and found wanting before the night is over: **"Simon, are you sleeping? Aren't you able to watch for one hour? Watch and pray that you will not be put to the test; the spirit is willing but the flesh is weak"** (14:38; cf. vv. 29–31). Jesus retires to pray twice more; both times he returns to find the disciples asleep, **and they did not know what to answer him** (14:39–41). The threefold repetition of the disciples' failure foreshadows Peter's threefold denial in the high priest's courtyard (14:66–72). It also demonstrates the disciples' failure to grasp the message of the parable of the return of the householder: "Keep watch, therefore; for you do not know when the master will return to the house, at evening or midnight or early at cockcrow; let him not come and find you sleeping. But what I say to you I say to all: Keep watch!" (13:35). Jesus's final rebuke of the three brings together the plot threads of discipleship failure, eschatological watchfulness, and the fulfillment of prophecy in words reminiscent of a stage direction: **"Are you sleeping and taking your rest? Get up! The hour has come; behold the son of man is delivered into the hands of sinners! Get up, let's go—the one who will hand me over is nearby"** (14:42).

The Arrest of Jesus (14:43–52)

On cue, **immediately** Judas—together with some from the chief priests, scribes, and elders—makes his last appearance, this time with a crowd armed **with swords and clubs** (14:43). The crowd (*ochlos*) that accompanies Judas is not to be identified with "the people," who are in danger of rioting if Jesus is arrested and killed (cf. 14:2), but rather a delegation from the Sanhedrin (see R. Brown 1994, 247). In a parenthetical aside (14:44), the evangelist explains, **The deliverer had given them a signal, saying, "The one whom I shall kiss is he, and you shall seize him and lead him away securely."** Since persons close to each other were expected to kiss when they met (Gruber 2000, 776; cf. Gen. 29:11, 13; 33:4; 45:15; 48:10; Exod. 4:27; 1 Sam. 20:41; 2 Sam. 15:5; 19:39; Luke 7:38, 45), Judas's gesture would have been a natural response on meeting his teacher, as would his words of greeting: **And immediately having arrived, coming to him, he says, "Rabbi," and he kissed him warmly** (14:45). The term *rabbi* is applied to Jesus only here and twice on the lips of Peter (9:5; 11:21); thus it is used by the two disciples who fail Jesus most seriously. If, as Donahue and Harrington (2002, 414) suggest, the term was not yet a conventional title of address for a Jewish teacher but rather "a sign of respect or honor" meaning "my great one," its effusive tone is ironic, as is the use of the compound *katephilēsan* ("kissed him warmly") for the "Judas kiss" (cf. the use of the simple *philēsō*, "I will kiss him," in

The Figure of Judas in Scripture and Tradition

Mark's Passion Narrative is the first to introduce the shadowy figure of Judas into Western culture (see Paffenroth 2001; Klassen 1996, 408). The Gospel's portrayal of Judas is minimal; he is identified early on as one of the Twelve (Mark 3:19), the one who "delivered" (*paradidōmi*) Jesus to his opponents, greeting him with a kiss (14:10, 43–45). The other Gospels add the notions that Judas was possessed by Satan (Luke 22:3; cf. John 13:2, 27), that he was a "devil" himself (John 6:70–71), that he was the disciples' treasurer and helped himself to the common funds (John 12:6), that he was paid thirty pieces of silver and remorsefully returned them to the chief priests after the trial (Matt. 26:15; 27:3–5), and that he killed himself by hanging (Matt. 27:5b; for a different account of Judas's death, see Acts 1:18–19). Popular theology and folklore have elaborated on his treachery and wickedness:

> "No one can ever be as evil as Judas was. There are many common forms of evil, but Judas represents an apotheosis of evil. Among the descendants of Adam, Judas remains the only one in whom sin reached its highest peak. He provides a view of sin at its most repulsive and abhorrent manifestation. Faithless, loveless, ungrateful himself, he betrayed with the kiss, the sign of faithfulness, love and gratitude." (Klassen 1996, 5, referring to the theology of Carl Daub, 1816–18, 2–3; cf. Paffenroth 2001, 17–58)

Judas has long served as an excuse for anti-Semitism (Paffenroth 2001, 51–55), the archetypal Jew who rejects Jesus as Israel rejected Christianity, a stereotype perpetuated by such noted twentieth-century theologians as Karl Barth and Dietrich Bonhoeffer. The anti-Jewish excesses of some Christians have led some Jewish scholars to the conclusion that Judas was invented as a cipher for the Jewish religious establishment that opposed Jesus (e.g., Maccoby 2006, 14).

Interest in the figure of Judas has spiked recently with the publication of the *Gospel of Judas*, a gnostic-Christian writing dated to the second century AD (see Ehrman 2006, 91). The *Gospel* is made up mostly of a private discourse of Jesus to Judas, here the most enlightened of the disciples because he is the one who enables Christ to be liberated from the prison of human flesh: "You [Judas] will exceed all of them [i.e., the other disciples]. For you will sacrifice the man that clothes me" (Ehrman 2006, 91). While popular claims that the *Gospel of Judas* revolutionizes our understanding of the Bible are exaggerated, its alternative vision of Judas is a reminder that all of our written traditions about him, including Mark's, are literary constructs, and that if the death of Jesus is seen as intrinsic to the significance of the gospel story, then Judas's role in the Passion Narrative is vital to salvation history.

14:44; cf. Prov. 27:6). From this point on, Judas disappears from the narrative; in fulfillment of prophecy, the crowd lays hands on Jesus and seizes him (14:46; cf. 9:31; 14:41, 48).

An unidentified bystander takes out his sword and cuts off the ear of the high priest's slave (14:47); whether Mark meant the "one standing by" to refer to one of the disciples standing ready to defend Jesus is not explained. In this, earliest version of the arrest story, Jesus does not intervene to heal the wounded slave (cf. Luke 22:50–51) but rather castigates the arresting party: **"Have you come out as against a brigand with swords and clubs to catch me? For days I was before you in the temple, teaching, and you did not seize me; but let the scriptures be fulfilled!"** (14:48–49). The term *lēstēs*, translated here as "brigand," can refer to a robber or bandit, but also to a revolutionary or insurrectionist (BDAG 594); the earlier reference to the fear of the chief priests and scribes that to seize Jesus might cause unrest among the people (cf. 14:2) suggests the kind of political upheaval taking place in Judea in the evangelist's time. Possibly the reproach is meant to contrast Jesus with the rebels who sparked the Jewish war with Rome (cf. Collins 2007, 686). Jesus's words indict his opponents' cowardice in the face of the popular support for him; rather than arresting him in public, they have taken him "by stealth" (cf. 14:1). At one level the reference to the fulfillment of Scripture harks back to 14:27, where Jesus quotes Zech. 13:7 ("Strike the shepherd, and the sheep will be scattered" [NIV]) to foretell the disciples' defection: **And leaving him they all fled** (Mark 14:50). For Mark, however, the whole sequence of events is consistent with "scripture," in that they fulfill the will of God as articulated in Jesus's prophetic utterances. The flight of the disciples is followed by a seemingly random reference to the arresting party's attempt to seize one of them: **A certain young man, clothed in a piece of linen over his nakedness, was following him and they seized him. But leaving behind the linen cloth, he fled naked** (14:51–52). The questions of the identity of this young man, his relation to the youth in the empty tomb (16:5), the similarity of his mode of dress to the linen shroud in which the body of Jesus is wrapped (cf. 15:46), and the possible symbolism of the incident have generated a plethora of explanations (see the survey in Collins 2007, 688–93). In the context of the arrest, the incident belongs to the theme of discipleship failure; rather than being arrested like Jesus, the young man who has been following Jesus flees with the other disciples. The vivid detail of the youth leaving behind his garment in his haste to escape (14:51) is a common motif in Greek art and literature, due to the nature of garments in antiquity. Many of these were sleeveless rectangles of cloth, draped around the body without belts or fasteners, and like the "linen cloth" worn by the boy, apt to slip off the wearer when running (Jackson 1997, 280; cf. Gen. 39:6–20; 2 Kings 2:13; Amos 2:12–16; see also Mark 10:50). Mark's insertion of the shed-garment motif "ensures that the desertion of Jesus is given a hard-hitting climax with a powerful visual of universal personal appeal, a visual . . . that itself so effectively, because so baldly, reports the disciples' flight" (Jackson 1997, 286).

Denial and Trial (14:53–72)

The remainder of the chapter (14:53–72) relates the trial of Jesus before the Sanhedrin (14:55–65), framed by the account of the denial of Peter (14:53–54, 66–72). By intercalating the two stories, the evangelist both represents them as occurring simultaneously and develops the themes of discipleship failure (Peter denies Jesus) and the fulfillment of prophecy; Peter breaks his vow never to fall away, as predicted in 14:29–31.

14:53–54. The opening sentence depicts Jesus being led by the arresting party, including **all the chief priests and the elders and the scribes,** to the high priest (14:53), who is not named in Mark. According to Josephus (*Ant.* 18.2.2 §35; 18.4.3 §95; cf. Matt. 26:3, 57; Luke 3:2; John 11:49; 18:13–14, 24, 28; Acts 4:6), the high priest at the time would have been Caiaphas (ruled AD 18–36), whose family tomb was unearthed in 1990 (see Bond 2004, 2–8; on the distinction between the high priest and the chief priests, see comment on 10:32–34). In the light of Peter's promise never to forsake Jesus (14:31), the note that Peter followed him, albeit **at a distance** and only up to **the courtyard of the high priest** (14:54), sounds promising,

Figure 14. Vase depicting the death of Orpheus, ca. 440 BC, The Louvre. Orpheus flees as his garment slips off (cf. Mark 14:52).

although unlike Jesus, on trial within, Peter sits comfortably, if riskily, with the household servants, **warming himself by the fire.** For an audience unfamiliar with the tale, the question remains open whether Peter will live up to his vow or whether even Peter will fail, as Jesus has predicted.

14:55–65. The account of the trial before the Sanhedrin is the first of two trial narratives in Mark, the first before the Jewish council (14:55–65) and the second before the Roman prefect (15:1–15). Of the two proceedings, only the Roman governor had the legal authority to impose the death penalty. The theme of both trial narratives is that the charges against Jesus are fabricated and that Jesus is unjustly sentenced and executed on the basis of false accusations. It has often been observed that if the mishnaic rules for the conduct of a capital case were already in

**An Outline
of Mark 14:53–72**

Denial and trial (14:53–72)

Peter's distant following
(14:53–54)

Trial before the Sanhedrin
(14:55–65)

Peter's denial (14:66–72)

force in Jesus's time, the hearing before the Sanhedrin would be illegal (Collins 2006, 148; cf. *m. Sanh.* 4.1–5.5). The trial of Jesus is held during the Passover, whereas Jewish trials were forbidden on feast days, including the Sabbath; Jesus is tried at night and in the high priest's house, rather that during the day in the Sanhedrin's official court; the sentence is pronounced immediately after the trial, rather than after a prescribed interval; Mark insists that the testimonies did not agree, while the Mishnah demands full agreement among witnesses; the charge of blasphemy (14:64–65) is not substantiated by anything Jesus says during the interrogation (see Senior 1984, 88). Historical plausibility aside, for Mark, the first trial, in which Jesus, the son of man (14:62), is confronted by the chief priests, scribes, and elders (14:53) and is proclaimed as deserving of death (14:65), is the one that fulfills the Passion predictions that must inevitably come to pass (8:31; 9:31; 10:32–34).

The trial scene begins with the assertion that **the chief priests and the whole Sanhedrin were seeking testimony about Jesus in order to kill him, and they could not find any** (14:55). Rather than Jesus's being brought up on legitimate charges, the council casts about for damaging evidence, but can produce only lies and conflicting testimony: **for many were bearing false witness against him, and their testimonies did not agree** (14:56). According to the Torah, two or three unanimous witnesses are necessary for the death sentence to be imposed (Deut. 17:6; 19:15), and as R. Brown (1994, 435) observes, "Ironically the trial against Jesus has violated the law against false testimony (Exod. 20:16; Deut. 5:20)—one of the Ten Commandments reiterated by Jesus in Mark 10:19." The incriminating speech quoted by the witnesses is placed on the lips of Jesus elsewhere in the NT (John 2:19), but never in the Gospel of Mark: **"I will destroy this sanctuary made with hands and within three days build another not made with hands"** (14:58). From the evangelist's perspective, this is not a saying of Jesus but an invention of false witnesses (14:57). Jesus has indirectly foretold the destruction of the temple in the parable of the tenants (12:1–9) and in the narrative of cursing the fig tree and cleansing the temple (11:1–20), and he has revealed to the disciples (or at least to one of them) that the temple will be destroyed (13:2; cf. 13:14). However, Jesus's words against the temple are not phrased in the first person, as the lying witnesses report ("*I* will destroy," *egō katalysō*); rather, he prophesies God's judgment against its guardians and the corrupt form of worship they have promoted (11:17). The Markan audience knows that Jesus's prophecies against the temple have been fulfilled in their own time by the Romans.

The contrast between that which is made with human hands and that which is not is a conventional opposition between divine and human agency (e.g., Acts 7:41; 17:24; Eph. 2:11; Col. 2:11). It also has an apocalyptic resonance: in Daniel, a rock cut from a mountain "not by human hands" symbolizes the destruction of earthly empires by the power of God (Dan. 2:34, 35, 38). The heavenly sanctuary where God dwells is described as "not made with hands"

(2 Cor. 5:1; Heb. 9:11, 24). The false testimony thus implies that Jesus has arrogated divine powers to himself, but even in this allegation, Mark reiterates, the witnesses did not agree (14:59). Jesus's silence in the face of his accusers is an implicit comment on the illegality of the proceedings; in Jewish law, the accused is not required to answer to confused or conflicting testimony (cf. Deut. 17:6; 19:15). Although at a literal level the temple accusation is false, it may still point to a spiritual reality experienced by the Markan community if, as several scholars have argued, Jesus's followers regarded themselves as the divinely constructed temple (e.g., Donahue 1973, 103–38; Juel 1977, 128–215; Senior 1984, 91–94; Malbon 1986, 120–26). Although the phrase "in three days" (*dia triōn hēmerōn*) resembles the wording of the Passion predictions (*meta treis hēmeras*; 8:31; 9:31; 10:33–34), here it may simply be a conventional expression for a brief time period (e.g., Mark 8:2; cf. Gen. 34:25; Exod. 10:22–23; 15:22; Josh. 2:22; 2 Chron. 10:5, 12; Jon. 1:17; 3:3).

The intense exchange between the high priest and Jesus that follows is dense with christological affirmations: **And the high priest stood up in the midst and questioned Jesus, saying, "Have you no answer to anything of anyone's testimony against you?" But he was silent and didn't answer at all. And he says to him, "Are you the messiah, the Son of the Blessed One?" And Jesus said, "I am—and you will see the son of man sitting at the right hand of the Mighty One and coming with the clouds of heaven"** (14:60–62). After maintaining his silence in the face of false accusations, Jesus answers affirmatively to the high priest's sarcastic question: "Are *you* the messiah?" (14:61a). The reference to the messiah as "the Son of the Blessed One" (synonymous with "Son of God") is consistent with early Jewish traditions that regarded the messiah as the Son of God by adoption (see Dunn 2003, 709–11). Jesus's *egō eimi* is not a claim to divine status (cf. Exod. 3:14 LXX) but an emphatic avowal that the high priest's identification of him as messiah is correct: "*I* am!" (14:62a). The Markan audience already knows that Jesus is the Son of God (1:1, 11; 3:11; 5:7; 9:7; 13:32; 15:39), and that he is the son of man (8:31, 38; 9:31; 10:33–34; 13:26). The image of the son of man seated at the right hand of God ("the Mighty One") "and coming with the clouds of heaven" echoes the language of Dan. 7:13 and Ps. 110:1 (cf. Ps. 80:17), and constitutes a third parousia prediction (cf. 8:38; 13:26).

Jesus's answer provokes a charge of blasphemy, an offense punishable by death: **And the high priest, having torn his tunic, says, "What need do we still have of witnesses? You have heard the blasphemy; what does it look like to you?" And all condemned him as deserving to be put to death** (14:63–64). In rabbinic legislation (*m. Sanh.* 7.5), blasphemy is defined as pronouncing the divine name, something that Jesus pointedly does not do in his reply; both he and the high priest use pious circumlocutions (the Blessed One, the Mighty One). There is no evidence that to claim to be the messiah (or the Danielic "son of man") was considered to be blasphemous by ancient Jews. However, as Collins (2006, 170) states, the definition of blasphemy in the first century "was probably neither universal nor official" and likely broader than that stipulated in the rabbinic law (2006, 169; on the historicity of the blasphemy charge, see R. Brown 1994, 530–47). The Markan audience, unlike the high priest, is aware that Jesus *is* the messiah, Son of God, son of man, and so the accusation of blasphemy is groundless. The scene of Jesus's being attacked and shamed by certain members of the council (14:65a) actualizes the third Passion prediction, that "they will sentence him to death, . . . and they will mock him and spit on him" (10:34), adding a note of bitter irony to their derisive command for Jesus to prophesy (14:65b). Even as they abuse Jesus, his prophecies about them are being fulfilled. The scene ends with the note that **the guards took him with blows** (14:65c).

14:66–72. With near-cinematic technique, the scene shifts back to Peter, **warming himself** (14:67) in the courtyard of the high priest's house (cf. 14:54). As Jesus is interrogated, insulted, and beaten indoors, Peter is questioned by **one of the servant-girls of the high priest,** who remarks that he was **with the Nazarene, Jesus.** Peter not only denies his association with Jesus—**"I neither know nor understand what you say"**—but removes himself spatially from his accuser: **And he went out into the forecourt** (14:68). In fulfillment of Jesus's prophecy (14:30), a rooster crows (14:68c; an element missing in some ancient manuscripts; see Metzger 1994, 97). The servant girl persists, this time telling some bystanders that Peter is **one of them,** which he again denies (14:69–70). Shortly afterward, the bystanders again **were saying to Peter, "Surely you are one of them, for you are a Galilean!"** (14:70). The third time, Peter's denial is more vehement: **He began to curse and swear, "I do not know this man whom you are talking about!"** (14:71). Peter's promise not to deny Jesus, even on pain of death, is nullified while Jesus's prophecy is vindicated; he has denied Jesus three times before the second rooster call (14:72a). Only then does Peter remember Jesus's words (14:30), which are quoted in the last verse of the pericope: **And Peter remembered the word as Jesus had spoken to him, "Before the rooster cries twice, you will deny me three times"** (14:72a). The intercalated stories of the trial before the Sanhedrin and the denial of Peter implicitly contrast the steadfastness of Jesus and the cowardice of Peter. The contrast between Jesus and Peter extends to their faithfulness to Torah. Jesus remains silent in the face of conflicting testimony (cf. Exod. 20:16; Deut. 5:20), speaking only when the charge against him is true (Mark 14:61–62). Peter not only breaks his promise not to deny Jesus, but also readily disavows his relationship with Jesus three times, thus violating the commandment against bearing false witness against one's neighbor (Exod. 20:16).

There is another layer of irony underlying the intercalated stories of the trial before the Sanhedrin and the denial of Peter in the light of the pivotal confession of Peter at Caesarea Philippi (8:27–30):

At Caesarea Philippi Jesus is the questioner, but in Jerusalem he is interrogated. In chap. 8, Jesus is silent in the face of Peter's confession, but he answers the high priest's similarly worded "confession" ["Are you the messiah, the Son of the Blessed One?"] publicly and affirmatively. In Mark 8, the Son of Man saying is a passion prediction [8:31]; in the trial scene, Jesus predicts the exaltation/parousia of the Son of Man. At Caesarea Philippi, Peter is strongly rebuked ("Get behind me, Satan!" in 8:33), while in 14:63–64 Jesus is accused of blasphemy. In the former passage, Peter is eager to confess that Jesus is the Christ; in the latter, Peter is in the background, denying Jesus, while Jesus is openly acknowledging his messianic identity (14:54, 66–73). The presence of Peter in the "frame" of the trial before the Sanhedrin underlines the relation between the two pericopes. (Beavis 1987, 586)

The final notice that Peter **fell down and wept** (14:72c) is characteristically interpreted as meant to evoke empathy (see Herron 1991, 124), a response that would have been particularly poignant for the Markan audience, possibly facing the choice between faithfulness to Jesus and "cowardice and apparent safety" (Donahue and Harrington 2002, 429). In his discussion of the rhetorical device of *pathos* ("pity"), Aristotle wrote that "we feel pity when the danger is near ourselves. Also we pity those who are like us in age, character, disposition, social standing, or birth; for in all these cases it appears more likely that the same misfortune may befall us also. Here too we have to remember the general principle that what we fear for ourselves excites our pity when it happens to others" (Aristotle, *Rhet.* 2.8, trans. Roberts 1984). In contrast, the *pathos* evoked by the trial of Jesus is "most piteous of all . . . when, in such times of trial, the victims are persons of noble character: whenever they are so, our pity is especially excited, because their innocence, as well as the setting of their misfortunes before our eyes, makes their misfortunes seem close to ourselves."

Before Pilate: Jesus on Trial, Barabbas Freed (15:1–20a)

Mark 15:1–15, the trial before Pilate, is often treated as a unit; however, as with 14:54–72, Mark intercalates the story of the trial and sentencing of Jesus (15:1–5, 15b–20a) with the account of the release of Barabbas (15:6–15a) to ironic effect.

15:1–5. The words of the third Passion prediction that the chief priests and scribes will condemn Jesus to death and hand him over to "the gentiles" (10:33) is fulfilled in 15:1: **Immediately early in the morning the chief priests held counsel with the elders and the scribes and the whole Sanhedrin; having bound Jesus they took him and handed him over to Pilate.** The evangelist does not explain who Pilate is, indicating that his

---

An Outline of Mark 15:1–20a

Before Pilate: Jesus on trial, Barabbas freed (15:1–20a)

Trial before Pilate (15:1–5)

Barabbas freed (15:6–15a)

Sentencing by Pilate (15:15b–20a)

Marion Doss, Wikimedia Commons

Figure 15. The Pilate inscription. In 1961 archaeologists discovered this inscription on a limestone block from the amphitheater at Caesarea Maritima. The three lines read "TIBERIEUM / [PON]TIUS PILATUS / [PRAEF]ECTUS IUDA[EAE]," indicating that the structure was commissioned by Pontius Pilate.

audience is already familiar with his role in the execution of Jesus. Scholars have often remarked that the historical Pontius Pilate, prefect of Judea from AD 26 to 36, was much harsher and more ruthless than he is depicted in the Gospels: "as an equitable but weak governor, probably to promote positive relations between the Roman government and Christianity" (Mark 15:1–15 and par.; Cheney 2000, 1058). Ancient writers portray Pilate as deliberately flouting Jewish religious sensibilities (Josephus, *Ant.* 18.3.1 §§55–59; *J.W.* 2.9.2–3 §§169–74; Philo, *Embassy* 38 §§299–305) and provoking a riot by misappropriating funds from the temple to build an aqueduct (*Ant.* 18.3.2 §§60–62; *J.W.* 2.9.4 §§175–77); he was eventually recalled to Rome after a brutal massacre of Samaritans (*Ant.* 18.4.1–2 §§85–89). Luke 13:1 mentions some Galileans "whose blood Pilate had mingled with their sacrifices." Since the Sanhedrin did not have the authority to impose the death sentence, they must persuade the Roman prefect that Jesus has committed a crime worthy of execution.

Contrasting with the lengthy and confused Sanhedrin trial, the exchange between Pilate and Jesus is brief and rather innocuous:

> And Pilate questioned him saying, "Are you the king of the Jews?"
> And answering him, he says, "You say so."
> And the chief priests accused him of many things.
> And again Pilate questioned him, saying, "Have you no answer? Look how they are accusing you!"
> But Jesus answered nothing to anyone, so that Pilate marveled. (15:2–5)

Pilate's initial question echoes the exchange between the high priest and Jesus (14:61–62); the title "king of the Jews" paraphrases the Jewish term "messiah" in terms that would be meaningful to a Roman official. Unlike the religious charge of blasphemy that provokes Jesus's Jewish accusers to pronounce him worthy of death (14:65), the alleged claim to kingship has political implications, placing Jesus in the same category as the "false messiahs" who had arisen in Palestine throughout the first century to liberate Israel from Roman domination (see comment on 13:21–22). Jesus strongly confirms his messianic identity in his reply to the high priest and augments it with a parousia prediction (14:62), but here his curt reply neither affirms nor disavows royal status (*su legeis*, 15:2b). Collins (2007, 713) notes that the deliberate ambiguity of Jesus's answer to Pilate "may be due to the evangelist's, or more likely his source's, recognition of the social reality that provincials needed to be wary when dealing with the representatives of imperial power" (cf. 12:17). Surprisingly, the "false testimony" of the chief priests that Jesus threatened to destroy the temple (14:58) is not repeated before Pilate, although it may be included among the "many things" brought against him by his accusers in 15:3. Despite the priests' allegations (cf. 14:55–59) and Pilate's attempt to provoke him to speak in his own defense, Jesus remains silent (15:5; cf. 14:61). The motif of Jesus's silence before his accusers differs from the usual pattern of Jewish martyrdom accounts, where the heroes facing death make a speech affirming their own faithfulness to the law and expressing opposition to tyranny (Collins 2007, 703; e.g., 2 Macc. 6:18–31; 7:1–42; 4 Macc. 5:15–38; 8:1–17:1; *Acts of the Alexandrian Martyrs*). As noted above, Jesus's silence in the face of false conflicting testimonies is consistent with Torah, but it may also echo the silence of the sufferer in certain lament psalms (Ps. 38:13–14; cf. Pss. 27:12; 35:11) and especially of the suffering servant of Isa. 53:7: "He was oppressed, and he was afflicted, yet he did not open his mouth; like a lamb that is led to the slaughter, and like a sheep that before its shearers is silent, so he did not open his mouth" (cf. Collins 2007, 704, 714). The silence of Jesus in the face of his accusers resonates with the warnings of the eschatological discourse that believers will be delivered to councils and testify before governors and kings (13:9): "Mark presents Jesus as the first in a long line of those who would suffer unjust accusations and be brought to trial for the sake of the gospel" (Senior 1984, 110).

15:6–15a. The Barabbas episode (15:6–15a) breaks the flow between the notice that Pilate wondered at Jesus's silence (15:5) and the scourging of Jesus before he is handed over to the soldiers for crucifixion (15:15b). The evangelist explains that **on account of the festival**, Pilate was accustomed to release a prisoner of the people's choosing (15:6). Although there is no ancient account of such a Roman practice in Judea, there is considerable evidence from ancient societies that prisoners were sometimes released in connection with religious festivals (see Merritt 1985; cf. Collins 2007, 714–17). Senior (1984, 110) notes that the release would fit into the "liberation motif of the Jewish Passover." Similarly, there is no extrabiblical reference to the **insurrection** for which Barabbas was rounded up with **certain rebels who had committed murder** (15:7). Many scholars have speculated on the possible significance of the criminal's name, which in Aramaic, means "son of the father," possibly portraying him as an "evil twin" to the innocent Jesus (e.g., Boring 2006, 420; cf. Matt. 27:16–17, where some manuscripts call the insurrectionist "Jesus Barabbas"). Instead of the name, what is more germane to the significance of Barabbas is his literary-theological role in the narrative. Jennifer K. Berenson Maclean (2007, 313) has drawn attention to the similarity between Pilate's release of Barabbas to the crowd and "curative exit rites" in the Greco-Roman world, "rituals in which an animal or a member of society is exiled and killed in order to achieve purification of the community." The scapegoat ritual of the Day of Atonement (Lev. 16:7–10, 15, 21–22, 26)—in which one goat was sacrificed and the other was driven into the desert, bearing the sins of the people—is an example of such a rite (Maclean 2007, 314). In this light, the juxtaposition of the two prisoners, an innocent person killed and a guilty person loosed to the crowd, takes on a deeper significance:

> The crowd approaches Pilate with the intent of asking for a scapegoat/φαρμακός to be released to them (Mark 15:6, 8). Barabbas, a fitting choice, is already in custody (15:7). Pilate's offer of Jesus (15:9) is rejected by the crowd, which at the instigation of the priests chooses Barabbas (15:11). The narrative then has Pilate turn to the crowd for their judgment on Jesus's fate, a device which allows the crowd's response to designate him as the immolated goat from the Levitical ritual (15:12–14). Indulging the crowd's choice, Pilate releases Barabbas to them as a scapegoat/φαρμακός and dispatches Jesus for crucifixion (15:15). (Maclean 2007, 324)

Although Pilate and the crowd are ultimately complicit in consigning Jesus to the death sentence, the evangelist places more responsibility on the chief priests: Pilate offers to release **the king of the Jews** (15:9); he perceives that the chief priests have handed Jesus over **out of envy** (15:10); the crowd asks for Barabbas rather than Jesus because **the chief priests stirred up the crowd** (15:11); Pilate repeats his offer to release **the king of the Jews** (15:12) and asks what evil he has done (15:14). Only **to satisfy the crowd** does Pilate finally release Barabbas and consign Jesus to execution (15:15). The crowd's repeated chorus of **"Crucify him!"** (15:13–14) echoes the death sentence pronounced on Jesus by the Sanhedrin (14:64b) and points to the fulfillment of the Passion predictions.

15:15b–20a. The frame of 15:15b–20a implicitly contrasts the escape of the guilty Barabbas and the abuse of the innocent Jesus. Pilate does not directly pronounce the death sentence on Jesus but **handed Jesus over for scourging in order to be crucified** (15:15b). The location of the scourging is specified as **inside the courtyard, that is, the praetorium** (15:16a); *praitōrion* is a Latin loanword, referring to the residence of a Roman official, either the Antonia fortress or

Herod's palace in Jerusalem (Mann 1986, 642). Like the Sanhedrin (14:65), the **whole cohort** assembles to mock him, this time not as a blasphemer but as a claimant to kingship: **They clothed him in purple and placed upon him a crown woven out of thorns; and they began to greet him, "Hail, king of the Jews!" and they beat his head with reeds and spit on him and bent the knee in reverence to him** (15:17–18). The soldiers' actions fulfill the third Passion prediction: they mock him, spit on him, and whip him (10:34). The clothing in purple is a color reserved for nobility; Christopher S. Mann (1986, 642) speculates that here *porphyra* refers to "a soldier's red military cloak which had faded"; the crown of thorns is a deliberate parody of the Roman emperor's garb; the greeting echoes the Latin acclamation *Ave Caesar* ("Hail, Caesar"). The reed (*kalamos*) with which the soldiers strike Jesus is often interpreted as a mock scepter (Collins 2007, 727); the soldiers' false show of respect continues with their kneeling in scornful deference (15:18b). Overall the scene is a burlesque of a Roman triumphal procession: "The mocking homage of the soldiers corresponds ironically to the usual shouts of approval received by a triumphator" (Dowd 2000, 158; see also Schmidt 1997). The soldiers' abuse of Jesus evokes the words of Isaiah's servant of the Lord: "I have given my back to scourges and my cheeks to blows, but I did not turn away my face from the shame of spitting" (Isa. 50:6 NETS). In view of the audience's belief that Jesus is the messiah/king of the Jews, the ridicule is deeply ironic: the man they scorn is truly what they derisively say he is. Before he is led off to be crucified, Jesus is stripped of his royal garb and re-dressed in his own clothes (15:20a).

The Crucifixion (15:20b–38)

The crucifixion narrative begins at 15:20b: **And they took him out in order that they might crucify him.** Simon of Cyrene, a Jew who was either visiting Jerusalem for the Passover or had emigrated from the city of Cyrenaica in northern Africa, is pressed into service by the soldiers to **carry his cross** (15:21), following the custom of making the condemned criminal carry the horizontal beam of the cross to the execution site, where the vertical beam was planted (cf. Donahue and Harrington 2002, 441). The next verse states that the soldiers carried Jesus (*pherousin auton*) to the crucifixion site (15:22), implying that the prisoner was too weak to bear the crossbeam himself. There is no indication in the text that Simon had any previous knowledge of Jesus, but the description of him as **the father of Alexander and Rufus** (15:21) suggests that the sons were known to the Markan community. Senior (1984, 116) proposes that Simon may play a symbolic role as one who "takes up his cross" to follow Jesus (cf. 8:34): "Simon, who moves through the passion story without introduction or epilogue, reminds the reader of the cost of discipleship." The name of the crucifixion site, **Golgotha** (15:22b), is translated by the evangelist as **the place of the skull** (Aramaic *gulgultā'*; Hebrew *gulgōlet*), "so named either for its skull-like shape or because it was a customary place of execution" (Mann 1986,

645). The **wine mixed with myrrh** he is given to drink (15:23a) is explained alternatively as an extension of the mockery of the soldiers or as a narcotic to dull the pain of the execution (see Collins 2007, 742–43); Jesus's refusal to take the mixture (15:23b) may reflect back to his promise at the Last Supper: "Never again will I drink of the fruit of the vine *until that day* when I drink it anew in the realm of God" (14:25). The brutal scene of Jesus's being nailed to the crossbeam and hoisted aloft to die slowly of shock or asphyxiation is tersely narrated: **and they crucified him** (15:24a).

The account of Jesus on the cross (15:24–39), punctuated by the phrase "they crucified him" (15:24a, 25, 27; cf. v. 32), is divided into three-hour segments. The narrator explains that it was **the third hour when they crucified him**—the Roman equivalent of 9:00 a.m. Mark's description of the events of Jesus's first three hours on the cross is vivid and packed with details relating to the fulfillment of Scripture:

Old Testament Text	Markan Fulfillment
"They divided my clothes among themselves, and for my clothing they cast lots" (Ps. 22:18 NETS).	"They divided his garments, casting lots for them" (15:24b).
"His soul was given over to death, and he was reckoned among the lawless" (Isa. 53:12 NETS; cf. Mark 10:37).	"And they crucified with him two bandits, one on his right and one on his left" (15:27).
"All who saw me mocked at me; they talked with the lips; they moved the head: 'He hoped in the Lord; let him rescue him; let him save him, because he wanted him'" (Ps. 22:7–8 NETS; cf. Ps. 109:25; Lam. 2:15).	"And those passing by cursed him, shaking their heads (15:29a).... Also the chief priests mocked among themselves with the scribes, saying, 'He saved others; he is not able to save himself! Let the messiah, the king of Israel, come down from the cross now, in order that we might see and believe,' and the ones crucified together with him reviled him" (15:31–32).

The accusations of the Sanhedrin and the Roman court are repeated by his tormentors: **"Ha! The one who was going to destroy the sanctuary and in three days rebuild it! Save yourself and come down from the cross"** (15:29b–30); **"He saved others; he is not able to save himself! Let the messiah, the king of Israel, come down from the cross now, in order that we might see and believe"** (15:31b). At the center of the account (15:26) is a reference to an inscribed placard (*epigraphē*) affixed to the cross, explaining the accusation against Jesus—**THE KING OF THE JEWS**—which, like the other uses of this title by Jesus's detractors (15:2, 9, 12, 18), is unwittingly accurate (cf. Collins 2007, 747–48). The chief priests themselves unknowingly confess his true identity as the messiah and king of Israel (15:32). The priests' use of the title "king of Israel" as opposed to "king of the Jews" reflects an inner-Jewish perspective on Jesus's messianic claims, adding to the irony of the scene: those who should recognize their messiah and king reject and revile him.

Prophecy Historicized or History Remembered?

Mark 14–15 is so dense with scriptural allusions that scholars have raised the question of whether its account of the Passion is "prophecy historicized" rather than history illumined by prophecy. John Dominic Crossan is a proponent of the view that the fulfillment of prophecy, not historical events, underlies the events portrayed in the Passion Narrative. He asserts that the removal of incidents based on the fulfillment of prophecy would leave little but a bare outline of the Passion story (Crossan 1995, 1–13). Raymond E. Brown's magisterial work on the NT Passion Narratives, *The Death of the Messiah* (1984), represents the view that the NT Passion Narratives are ultimately grounded in the recollections of eyewitnesses, underlined by the theme of scriptural fulfillment. Mark Goodacre (2006, 39) observes that the contrast between the two views is overly stark:

> "The reader is presented with a choice: is it history or is it prophecy? Did it happen or is it fictional?... Given these sole alternatives, history remembered or prophecy historicized, and given the undisputed level of scriptural allusion in the Passion Narratives, few critical scholars would be able to resist Crossan's conclusion."

Goodacre (2006, 46) proposes that a more useful way to describe Mark's method of dealing with the daunting and, for the evangelist, unprecedented task of writing a story about a crucified hero is "history scripturalized"—the recasting of traditional materials in the light of the Jewish scriptures, a process that Christians as far back as AD 50 in Corinth—and even AD 30 in Jerusalem—had engaged in, especially in a liturgical setting (cf. 1 Cor. 11:23–26).

The account of the last three hours of Jesus's life, **the sixth hour** (noon) to **the ninth hour** (3:00 p.m.; see 15:33), begins and ends with miraculous and foreboding events. During this period, the evangelist relates, **darkness came over the whole earth** (15:33); after Jesus's death, the temple curtain is torn in half, presumably not by human hands (13:38). In antiquity, prodigious events are often associated with the deaths of famous personages, such as Julius Caesar (Virgil, *Georg.* 1.463–88), Alexander the Great (*Alex. Rom.* 3.33.5), Romulus (Plutarch, *Rom.* 27.6), and the philosopher Carneades (Diogenes Laertius, *Liv. Phil.* 4.64; cf. Collins 2007, 752).

In keeping with the prophetic subtext of the Passion Narrative, the darkening of the earth "at the sixth hour" recalls Amos 8:9: "On that day, says the Lord God, I will make the sun go down at noon, and darken the earth in broad daylight." Here in Mark "the day of the Lord" is interpreted as the day of the death of the messiah, the Son of God: "I will make it like the mourning for an only son, and the end of it like a bitter day" (Amos 8:10b). Of the four evangelists, Mark most unflinchingly portrays the death agony

---

Portents of the Death of Julius Caesar

"Who dare say the Sun is false? He and no other warns us when dark uprisings threaten, when treachery and hidden wars are gathering strength. He and no other was moved to pity Rome on the day that Caesar died, when he veiled his radiance in gloom and darkness, and a godless age feared everlasting night. Yet in this hour Earth also and the plains of Ocean, ill-boding dogs and birds that spell mischief, sent signs which heralded disaster. How oft before our eyes did Etna deluge the fields of the Cyclopes with a torrent from her burst furnaces, hurling thereon balls of fire and molten rocks. Germany heard the noise of battle sweep across the sky and, even without precedent, the Alps rocked with earthquakes. A voice boomed through the silent groves for all to hear, a deafening voice, and phantoms of unearthly pallor were seen in the falling darkness. Horror beyond words, beasts uttered human speech; rivers stood still, the earth gaped . . . ; in the temples ivory images wept for grief, and beads of sweat covered bronze statues. King of waterways, the Po swept forests along in the swirl of his frenzied current, carrying with him over the plain cattle and stalls alike. Nor in that same hour did sinister filaments cease to appear in ominous entrails or blood to flow from wells or our hillside towns to echo all night with the howl of wolves. Never fell more lightning from a cloudless sky; never was comet's alarming glare so often seen." (Virgil, Georg. 1.463–488, trans. Fairclough 1935)

---

of Jesus on the cross: after three hours of darkness, Jesus utters a loud cry in Aramaic, *"Eloi, Eloi, lema sabachthani,"* which, the evangelist explains, means **"My God, my God, why have you abandoned me?"** (15:34). But even this cry of utter abjection signals the inevitable fulfillment of Scripture; Jesus's last words are a quotation of Ps. 22:1 (see comment on Mark 15:24b–32 above). Like the psalm, which begins with despair and ends with the vindication of the sufferer and acclamations of praise and glory (Ps. 22:19–31), the abuse, suffering, and death of Jesus must inexorably be followed by the resurrection, in fulfillment of his prophetic words (Mark 8:31; 9:31; 10:34). As in many instances throughout the Gospel where Jesus's sayings are misunderstood or misconstrued (e.g., 4:13; 7:2–3, 17–18; 8:16–18, 21; 9:10, 32; 14:58, 61–64), the bystanders think that he is calling the prophet Elijah and quickly offer him a **sponge with vinegar, placed on a reed for him to drink,** presumably to revive him long enough for the prophet to appear: **"Let's see if Elijah comes to free him!"** (15:35–36). Again unwittingly, their actions advance the scriptural scenario: "For my thirst they gave me vinegar to drink" (Ps. 69:21b). The astute member of the Markan audience remembers Jesus's words on the way down from the transfiguration mount: "Elijah has come first to restore all things; and how is it written about the son of man that he must suffer many things and be despised? But I say to you, they did to him what they wanted, just as it is written about him" (9:12–13). The crucifixion narrative ends as tersely as it began, with Jesus crying out wordlessly in a loud voice and exhaling his last breath (15:37). As with his portrayal of the crucifixion, Mark's account of the death of Jesus is the starkest—and probably the most realistic—of the Gospel accounts: Matthew says that Jesus "yielded up" his spirit (27:50 ASV); in Luke, he utters the prayer "Father, into your hands I commend my spirit" (23:46); John's Jesus pronounces that "it is finished," bows his head, and "gives up" his spirit (19:30). Mark's Jesus, in keeping with the theme of the suffering of the son of man, dies a painful and anguished death.

Mark's portrayal of Jesus's last moments is both theologically challenging and dramatically effective; it would have resonated with both Jewish and gentile audiences:

> Like a thunderbolt by Zeus in Homeric epic, this cosmic darkness during the most brilliant hours of the day symbolized God's abandonment of Jesus, prompting him to say, "My God, my God, why have you forsaken me?" This utterance obviously cites the first line of Psalm 22, but it also resembles Hector's recognition that Zeus and Apollo had abandoned him. Both heroes soliloquize their dooms. (MacDonald 2000, 138)

The prodigy of the tearing of the temple curtain, like the darkness at noon, is a portent associated with the death of the messiah. The scholarly debate as to whether the **sanctuary curtain** was the veil hung between the holy place and the holy of holies (Exod. 26:33; 2 Chron. 3:14; Josephus, *Ant.* 3.6.4 §§122–23) or the one that hung before the holy place itself (*Ant.* 3.6.4 §§127–29) is less important than its symbolism: it is associated with the inner sanctuary, which was entered only once a year by the high priest on the Day of Atonement (Lev. 16:1–34), a place of divine presence. The curtain is torn (*eschisthē*) **from top to bottom**, in the passive voice (15:38), indicating "God as the source of the rip" (MacDonald 2000, 141). In view of Jesus's prophecies of doom for the temple (13:2, 14; cf. 11:12–21; 12:1–11), the meaning seems clear: in the wake of the death of Jesus, the temple will be destroyed. Perhaps, as MacDonald suggests, the anticipated fall of the temple is linked metonymically with the utter destruction of Jerusalem itself, as Troy is destroyed "from top to bottom" with the death of the Trojan hero Hector (2002, 241; cf. *Iliad* 22.408–11; 14.727–32). However, the symbolism of the torn curtain also has a positive side, pointing to "the release of divine presence into the world" (Dowd 2000, 162).

Three Responses to the Death of Jesus (15:39–47)

Mark relates three human responses to Jesus's death: that of the centurion (15:39), that of a group of women who witnessed the crucifixion (15:40–41) and will also witness the empty tomb, and that of Joseph of Arimathea, who provides for the burial of Jesus (15:42–47).

15:39. First, the centurion standing across from him, seeing how he expired, said, "Truly this man was a son of God!" (15:39). Scholarly opinion varies as to whether the centurion's outburst constitutes a full-blown Christian confession (e.g., V. Taylor 1966, 597), a mistaken identification of Jesus as a hellenistic "divine man" (e.g., Gould 1896, 295; Mann 1986, 654), or a sarcastic sneer like those of Jesus's tormentors throughout the trial and crucifixion narratives (e.g., Fowler 1991, 205–8; Johnson 1987; Dowd 2000, 162). The anarthrous construction of the statement—literally, "Truly this man son of God was"—militates against the first interpretation. Although the syntax of the "confession" does allow the translation of the sentence as "Truly this man was *the* Son of God," Mark always uses the definite article "when Son of God or an equivalent phrase appears as a predicate nominative" (Shiner 2000, 6). The centurion's use of *alēthōs* ("corresponding to what is really so, truly, in truth, really, actually"; BDAG 44) to introduce his statement negates the idea that it is meant to be taken as sarcasm. The use of the imperfect tense of the verb to be (*ēn*) can be taken to refer to the present, but elsewhere in Mark, confessional statements are consistently expressed in the present tense (Johnson 1987, 7); here, after Jesus has died, the centurion's statement that Jesus "was" a son of God makes perfect sense. Several scholars have noted the similarity between the centurion's response to Jesus's death and the admiring reactions of authority figures to martyrdoms or near-martyrdoms (e.g., Dan. 3:28–30; 6:1–3; 3 Macc. 6:18–7:23; *b. ʾAbod. Zar.* 18a; *Gen. Rab.* 65.22; Plato, *Phaedo* 116c; Philostratus, *Vit. Apoll.* 7.16–21, 28; 8.5; see Shiner 2000, 11–14; Collins 2007, 769–71). Whitney T. Shiner (2000, 19) describes the centurion's confession as "reminiscent of the positive but insufficient identifications of Jesus found in 6.14–16 and 8.28, where Jesus is identified as John the baptizer, Elijah, or a prophet." The tone is ironic (the audience knows that Jesus is *the* Son of God [1:1, 11; 3:11; 5:7; 9:7; 13:32] not just *a* son of God) but not sarcastic (the centurion's statement is one of respect for a noble death).

15:40–41. The second set of witnesses to Jesus's death is a group of **women watching from a distance, among them both Mary Magdalene and Mary the mother of James the lesser and of Joses and Salome, who, when he was in Galilee, were following him and serving him, and many others who went up with him to Jerusalem** (15:40–41; cf. 15:47; 16:1–8). Unlike the Twelve, all of whom have failed Jesus in one way or another, the women disciples, who had been with him all along, are portrayed as witnessing the crucifixion and death, albeit from a safe distance. Although this is the first time that women are explicitly mentioned as followers of Jesus, the evangelist clearly identifies them as among the larger circle of disciples who accompanied him on his travels (e.g., 2:15, 16, 18, 23; 3:7, 9, 20; 4:10; 6:1; 7:2, 17; 8:1, 4, 6, 14, 34; 14:12–13); possibly some of them were wives and other family members of the male disciples. Mary Magdalene (from Magdala/Tarichea, a fishing town on the western side of the Sea of Galilee) is the most prominent of the female disciples mentioned in the Gospels (Matt. 27:56, 61; 28:1; Luke 8:2; 24:10; John 19:25; 20:1, 10, 18). The second *Maria* is possibly the mother of Jesus, since his mother's name, along with brothers named James (*Iakōbos*) and Joses (*Iōsēs*), are mentioned in Mark 6:3. The disciple Salome is mentioned in the NT only in Mark (cf. 16:1); Richard Bauckham (2002, 226–33) speculates that she was one of the sisters of Jesus (cf. 6:3), a surmise supported by several early Christian references (Epiphanius, *Pan.* 78.8.1; 78.9; cf. Epiphanius, *Ancor.* 60.1; and Bauckham's [2002, 226–34] discussion of the *Gos. Phil.* 59.6–11; and *Prot. Jas.* 19.3; 20.1, 4; for extracanonical texts where the disciple Salome is given prominence as a disciple, see Bauckham 2002, 234–56).

15:42–47. The third character who responds to the death of Jesus is Joseph of Arimathea (15:42–46), an otherwise unknown location, sometimes identified with the Ramathaim-Zophim of 1 Sam. 1:1, "in the hill country of Ephraim." Joseph is described not as a follower of Jesus but as a man who was an **esteemed councillor, who also was awaiting the kingdom of God** (15:42; cf. Matt. 27:57 and John 19:38, where he is identified as a disciple). As such, he is comparable to the rich man of Mark 10:17–22, who seeks to inherit "eternal life" (cf. 10:23–25), or the "good scribe," whom Jesus pronounces to be "not far from the kingdom of God" (12:28–34). The council (*boulē*) referred to here is the Sanhedrin, which has pronounced Jesus worthy of execution; since the trial narrative states that the councillors all condemned him (14:64), it is unclear whether the evangelist regarded him as sympathetic to Jesus or simply as a pious member of the Sanhedrin concerned with the correct observance of the law. In Mark's time line, the crucifixion takes place on the day of preparation for the Sabbath; Joseph takes on the obligation of seeing that Jesus is properly buried before the Sabbath begins at sunset (14:42a; Deut. 21:22–23; cf. the figure of Tobit, who bravely ensures that his fellow Israelites in Nineveh are properly buried and incurs the wrath of the Assyrian king Sennacherib; Tob. 1:16–22). The evangelist's description of Joseph as **courageously** going to Pilate to ask for the body favors the interpretation of Joseph as a Jesus sympathizer; the participle *tolmēsas* means "to show boldness or resolution in the face of danger, opposition, or a problem" (BDAG 1010; cf. Mark 12:34). As in the trial narrative, Pilate is portrayed as relatively mild and receptive: **Pilate wondered if he was already dead, and he called the centurion and asked him how long ago he had died. And after knowing from the centurion, he gave the corpse to Joseph** (15:44–45). This is a deviation from the usual Roman policy with respect to crucifixion victims, which was simply to leave the corpse on the cross to decompose or be eaten by scavengers as a deterrent

Figure 16. The James ossuary. The ossuary was on display at the Royal Ontario Museum from November 15, 2002, to January 5, 2003.

to would-be criminals (Crossan 1994, 124–27). Burials of crucified criminals were rare (Crossan 1995, 161–62).

Once in possession of the body, Joseph quickly prepares and inters it before sundown: **And he bought a linen cloth and wrapped him in the linen cloth and laid him in a tomb that was cut out of rock and rolled a stone against the door of the tomb** (14:46). Mark has no indication that the tomb in which Jesus was laid belonged to Joseph (cf. Matt. 27:60), or that the tomb was in a garden near the crucifixion site (cf. John 19:41–42). In Jesus's time the normal burial procedure would have been for the body to be placed on a shelf in a tomb cut out of rock and left to decompose for about a year, after which the bones would be gathered and put into a stone ossuary or bone box inscribed with the name of the deceased; the most famous of these is the controversial "James ossuary," purporting to have contained the bones of "James [Jacob], son of Joseph, brother of Jesus." The burial is followed by a brief notice that the burial was witnessed by two of the women named earlier as followers of Jesus: **Mary Magdalene and Mary mother of Joses were watching where he was placed** (15:47; cf. 15:40–41). Since it is the women disciples who will find the tomb empty after the Sabbath (16:1–8), it is important for the evangelist to establish that they did not go to the wrong tomb by mistake. The Markan Passion Narrative is bracketed by the story of the woman who anoints Jesus for his burial (14:3–9) and the women who witness his execution and interment (15:47). Thus the Passion Narrative is framed by stories of women disciples—the anointing woman and the women witnesses to the burial—who, in contrast to the male disciples, recognize that Jesus has to die (14:8) and remain faithful to him throughout his ordeal (cf. Bauckham 2002, 293). Unlike Luke, who denies that the women witnesses were taken seriously by the male disciples (24:10–11), Mark does not imply that the women's testimony should be regarded as inferior to the men's. In view of the framing of the Passion Narrative by stories of women's liturgical acts—the anointing, the witness to the burial, the visit to the tomb, and the finding of the empty tomb (14:3–9; 15:47–16:8)—it is extraordinary that the women disciples' role has not been formally memorialized in Christian liturgy, despite the prophecy of 14:9 (cf. Corley 1993, 105–6; on the omission of these women from the Catholic lectionary, see Fox 1996).

The "Jesus Family Tomb"

In 2007, a documentary and book were released claiming that Jesus's family tomb had been excavated near Jerusalem in 1980, a find that had been covered up by Israeli authorities and Christians for economic and religious reasons—for the Israelis, because it would damage tourism, for Christians, because it would undermine faith in the resurrection (Cameron and Jacobovici 2007; Jacobovici and Pellegrino 2007). The tomb did indeed contain ossuaries (bone boxes) inscribed with names associated with Jesus and his family: Yeshuah (Jesus) son of Yehosef (Joseph), Maryah (Mary), and Yose (Joses; cf. Mark 6:3). Two of the boxes inscribed "Mariamne" and "Yehudah son of Yeshuah" were sensationally identified by the filmmakers as Mary Magdalene, the wife of Jesus, and their son, Judah (Meyers 2006, 116). Although a few scholars have publicly offered some qualified support for these assertions, most notably James Tabor (2007; see also Schaberg 2008), the documentary was immediately followed by a small avalanche of publications discrediting its controversial claims on biblical, historical, archaeological, cultural, and theological grounds (e.g., Bock and Wallace 2007; Burroughs 2007; Habermas 2007; J. White 2007; Sausa 2007; Quarles 2008; López 2008a; 2008b; see also Meyers 2006; S. Gibson 2006; Schram 2006). Whatever the merits of the arguments for and against the identification of the tomb as belonging to Jesus and his relations, it raises some unsettling questions. It is unlikely that a documentary claiming to have discovered the bones of John the Baptist, Martha of Bethany, or the apostle Paul would have met with such automatic skepticism, scorn, and fierce opposition. Another recent find relating to the family of Jesus, the famous "James ossuary," supposed to have contained the bones of James the brother of Jesus, has been interrogated mostly on archaeological grounds (e.g., Puech 2003), although it created consternation among some Catholics due to the perceived threat to the doctrine of the perpetual virginity of Mary (e.g., Akin 2008). In purely historical terms, it is conceivable that at some future date a tomb of Jesus of Nazareth containing his bodily remains could somehow be discovered and authenticated enough to satisfy at least some scholars. While liberal Christians have long questioned the literal historicity of the resurrection (e.g., Spong 1995; Stewart, Crossan, and N. Wright 2006), it is certain that many believers would respond negatively. Others might come to agree with the distinguished biblical scholar and Christian minister James Charlesworth, who opined that such a find would not "undermine belief in the resurrection, only that Jesus rose as a spiritual body, not in the flesh. . . . Christianity is a strong religion, based on faith and experience, and I don't think any discovery by archaeologists will change that" (quoted in McGirk 2008).

Theological Issues

In this section, Jesus the Son of Man suffers, is rejected by Jewish authorities, and is killed, just as he prophesied (8:31; 9:31; 10:32–34). At this point in the narrative, the Markan audience is well prepared to accept the shocking motif of the tormented and executed messiah, since Jesus's words have been proved to be reliable and are supported by the scriptural prophecies woven into the account (see Marcus 1992b, 153–98; Ahearne-Kroll 2007). Nonetheless, these events are under God's control, not Jesus's: "As in the teaching, healings and exorcisms, he does God's will instead of his own" (Dowd 2000, 139). These chapters offer a profoundly human portrait of a messiah who prays for deliverance from death (Mark 14:36); is disappointed, abandoned, and betrayed by his friends (14:10–11, 20–21, 29–31, 37–38, 40–41, 44–45, 50, 66–72); suffers abuse at the hands of his enemies (14:65; 15:16–20, 29–32); and dies in anguish (15:34–37). His faith that "all things are possible" with God (9:23; 10:27; 14:36; cf. 11:24) is confronted by the reality that God's will is for him to suffer and die. Jesus models a faith that is not a facile "You can do miracles if you believe," but a self-surrender to God, an act of free will "bound up with responsibility and love, . . . interested in the preservation of life" (Moltmann-Wendell 2001, 31), a life "poured out for many" (Mark 11:24; cf. 10:45).

In canonical and literary terms, Mark 14–15 is immensely significant as the oldest written Passion Narrative. Many Christians would affirm that it is the most important part of the Gospel since it portrays the saving death of Jesus. The immense significance of the crucifixion in Christian theology is eloquently expressed by Augustine of Hippo:

> In his most compassionate humanity and through his servant form we may now learn what is to be despised in this life and what is to be hoped for in eternity. In that very passion in which his proud enemies seemed most triumphant, he took on the speech of our infirmity, in which "our sinful nature was crucified with him" that the body of sin might be destroyed, and said "My God, my God, why have you forsaken me?" . . . Thus the Psalm begins, which was sung so long ago, in prophecy of his passion and the revelation of the grace which he brought to raise up his faithful and set them free. (*Letter* 140, *To Honoratus*, in Oden and Hall 1998, 222)

In recent times, however, some theologians have questioned the traditional focus on the cross, with its associated doctrines of sacrifice and atonement (e.g., Brock and Parker 2001; Patterson 2004; Finlan 2005; J. Sanders 2006; Reid 2007). They observe that overemphasizing the suffering and death of Jesus can have unhealthy consequences, such as the glorification (or trivialization) of suffering, valuing suffering for its own sake, the fetishization of self-sacrifice, or the deification of violence. At its most extreme, it can portray God as a harsh patriarch who demands the death of his child (Jesus) as the price of his restored favor to humanity (see J. Brown and Bohn 1989, 26–27).

Mark's portrayal of the crucifixion does none of these things. Mark's lead metaphor for the offering of Jesus's body and blood is the Passover sacrifice (14:12), not the Day of Atonement (Lev. 16:8–34; 23:27–32; cf. Dowd and Malbon 2006; Witherington 2001, 243). The emphasis of the Passover ritual is on the liberation of God's people from oppression, not on the suffering of the victim, or even on atonement for sin; although Jesus, like John the Baptist, preaches repentance, offers God's forgiveness, and condemns sin (Mark 1:4–5; 2:5–10; 3:28–29; 8:38; 9:42–47; 11:25), the term appears only once in the Passion Narrative, referring to the "sinners" into whose hands the son of man has been betrayed (14:41). The shedding of the "blood of the covenant" looks forward to the day when God's reign will be definitively established (14:25). In the Markan context, the Passion Narrative is bracketed by Jesus's life and resurrection; the empty tomb, not the cross, is the climax of the story, as Augustine put it, to raise up the faithful and set them free.

A fascinating hypothesis about the origin of the Passion Narrative is that it developed out of early Christian worship. As Sharyn Echols Dowd (2000, 139) observes, the "breathless" narrative pace of the Gospel slows down in chaps. 14–15 to a day-to-day account (Mark 14), culminating in the "agonizing hours of Jesus' tortured death." The careful division of the events surrounding the crucifixion into three-hour intervals (15:25, 33–34) and the chronological references that punctuate the account suggest a twenty-four-hour framework, divided into three-hour segments, with the Last Supper taking place "when it was evening" (14:17), the departure for Gethsemane three hours later (14:32), the arrest at about midnight (14:43–50), and the Jewish trial at 3:00 a.m., cockcrow (14:30, 72; Goodacre 2006, 44). Paul's eucharistic tradition (1 Cor. 11:23–26), known in Corinth in the early AD 50s, points to the likelihood that Mark's community also recalled traditions about the Passion in their worship (Goodacre 2006, 43). Several scholars have argued for the liturgical origin of the passion narratives:

> What is happening, they suggest, is that the early Christians were holding their own annual celebration of the events of the Passion at the Jewish Passover, remembered as roughly the time of Jesus's death. While other Jews were celebrating Passover, Christian Jews held a twenty-four-hour vigil in which they retold and relived the events surrounding Jesus's arrest and death, from sunset on 14/15 Nisan, and for twenty-four hours. Perhaps Mark's account of the Passion, with its heavy referencing of Scripture, its regular time notes, was itself influenced by such a liturgical memory of the Passion. (Goodacre 2006, 45; cf. Carrington 1952; Goulder 1974; Trocmé 1983)

Some scholars go so far as to describe Mark as an early Christian version of the Jewish Passover Haggadah (Bowman 1965; Hanhart 1995; cf. commentary

An Ancient Passover Liturgy

The earliest written version of the Passover ritual is *m. Pesaḥ.* 10 (third cent. AD), which stipulates the essential elements of the meal:

"Rabban Gamaliel says, 'Whosoever does not mention [explain] three things on the Passover, has not fulfilled his duty. These are—the Paschal sacrifice, the unleavened-cakes, and bitter herbs. The Paschal sacrifice is offered because the Lord passed over the houses of our ancestors in Egypt; the unleavened-bread [is eaten] because our ancestors were redeemed from Egypt [before they had time to leaven their dough]; and bitter herbs are eaten, because the Egyptians embittered the lives of our ancestors in Egypt. It is therefore incumbent on every person, in all ages, that he should consider as though he had personally gone forth from Egypt, as it is said, "And thou shalt shew thy son in that day, saying, This is done because of that which the Lord did for me in Egypt" (Exod. xii.27). We are therefore in duty bound to thank, praise, adore, glorify, extol, honour, bless, exalt, and reverence Him, who wrought all these miracles for our ancestors and us; for He brought us forth from bondage to freedom, He changed our sorrow into joy, our mourning into a feast, He led us from darkness into a great light, and from servitude to redemption—let us therefore say in His presence, "Hallelujah!"' [sing the Hallel; cf. Mark 14:26]." (Sola and Raphall 2009, 123–24; see also the sidebar "Four Questions in Mark 12:13–37" in my comments on Mark 11:1–12:44)

on Mark 12:13–37), the liturgy recited at the Passover meal, recalling God's redemption of Israel in the exodus (for the oldest written version of the Passover ritual, see the sidebar of *m. Pesaḥ.* 10) and relating it to the new act of redemption wrought by God in the death and resurrection of Jesus. If the Passion Narrative is indeed grounded in an ancient liturgy practiced by the Markan community, it provides a tantalizing window into the worship of the early church, in addition to its witness to and interpretation of the events surrounding the crucifixion.

Mark 16:1–8

Epilogue: Women at the Empty Tomb

Introductory Matters

If Mark 1:1–13 is the prologue to Mark, then these final verses of the Gospel are its epilogue. However, this does not mean that chap. 16 is a mere afterword. Rather, it is the climax of the story, the fulfillment of the prophecy that Jesus will be raised from the dead (8:31; 9:31; 10:33–34). Like a messenger in an ancient drama, the young man at the empty tomb proclaims that the Jesus who was crucified is risen and that his burial place lies empty (16:6a). As Euripides concluded five of his plays: "There are many shapes of divinity, and many things the gods accomplish against our expectation. What men look for is not brought to pass, but a god finds a way to achieve the unexpected. Such was the outcome of this story" (see Brant 2004, 64). Or as Mark puts it, "All things are possible with God" (10:27; cf. 9:23; 11:22–23; 14:36).

The earliest and most reliable manuscripts of Mark end at 16:8: "And leaving, they fled from the tomb, for fear and astonishment had come upon them. And they said nothing to anyone, for they were afraid" (see Metzger 1994, 102–6). Due to the Gospel's lack of any traditions about postresurrection appearances of Jesus to the disciples, early Christian scribes added endings describing encounters with the risen Jesus, reflecting the vocabulary and theological views of later generations of believers. The best-known of these secondary endings is the so-called longer ending (Mark 16:9–20), probably dating to the early second century (see Stein 2008, 728), which reads like a digest of resurrection accounts from the other Gospels: Jesus appears to Mary Magdalene (cf. Matt. 28:9; John 20:11–18; Luke 8:2); he is seen in another guise by two disciples as they are walking in the country (cf. Luke 24:13–27) and by the Eleven as they are dining, where he reproaches them for their unbelief (cf. John 20:19–29; Luke 24:28–49); he delivers the Great Commission (cf. Matt. 28:19) and is taken up into heaven to sit at the right hand of God (cf. Luke 24:51; Acts 1:9–11; 2:34). These added verses have been regarded as sacred Scripture by many generations of Christians. Even though they are included in many modern translations, the majority of scholars agree that they were not written by Mark. Due to their enduring canonical status, they will be commented on in an appendix at the end of this section.

Another ending, the so-called shorter ending, appears in some manuscripts, usually inserted before the "longer ending." It reads as follows: "And all that had been commanded them they told briefly to those around Peter. And afterward Jesus himself sent out through them, from east to west, the sacred and imperishable proclamation of eternal salvation" (NRSV). The few manuscripts that include this verse date from the seventh to ninth centuries, and the verse is non-Markan in both vocabulary and style (Metzger 1994, 103). An expanded version of the longer ending with additional material inserted after v. 14 is the Freer Logion, which survives only in one fifth-century manuscript, the Codex Washingtonianus:

> And they excused themselves, saying, "This age of lawlessness and unbelief is under Satan, who does not allow the truth and power of God to prevail over the unclean things of the spirits. Therefore reveal your righteousness now"—thus they spoke to Christ. And Christ replied to them, "The term of years of Satan's power has been fulfilled, but other terrible things draw near. And for those who have sinned I was handed over to death, that they may return to the truth and sin no more, that that may inherit the spiritual and imperishable glory of righteousness that is in heaven" (NRSV).

Around the fourth century AD, Jerome (*Against the Pelagians* 2.15) mentions that these verses were found in some manuscripts of his time, although he does not affirm or deny their authenticity. The implications of these secondary endings for the interpretation of Mark will be briefly discussed below, in the section on theological issues.

The structure of the epilogue is simple: The women approach the tomb; in the tomb, a messenger announces the resurrection; the women flee in fear (see the accompanying outline). As with the previous section, the epilogue begins and ends with narratives of women, whose faithfulness is rewarded when they are first to hear the good news that Jesus is risen (cf. Senior 1984, 135).

Tracing the Narrative Flow

Approaching the Tomb (16:1–4)

The same three women disciples mentioned in 15:40–41 (cf. 15:47)—Mary Magdalene, Mary "of James," and Salome—reappear **when the Sabbath was past** (16:1); the verse implies that the women purchased the spices for the anointing of the body in the evening, as soon as the Sabbath was over. Unlike the audience, which knows that Jesus has already been "anointed beforehand for burial" by a woman (14:8), the female disciples are determined to perform the proper burial rites even though Jesus has lain in the tomb two nights and a day. As in other ancient cultures, Jewish women played a central role in preparing corpses for burial, including lamentation (cf. Isa. 32:9–14; Jer. 9:16–20; 31:15; 49:3; Lam. 1:4; Ezek. 32:16; 2 Sam. 1:24; 2 Chron. 35:25), an element missing from Mark's empty tomb narrative (Corley 2002, 114–18). With characteristic wordiness, Mark notes that the women approached the tomb **very early on the first day of the week, . . . at sunrise** (16:2). As in the Passion Narrative, the evangelist's specificity with respect to time references may reflect early Christian worship practices. Pliny the Younger (*Letter to Trajan* 96), governor of Pontus-Bithynia in Asia Minor, mentions in a letter to the emperor Trajan that in the early second century AD, Christians met before dawn on a certain day and sang a hymn to Christ as if he were divine. That "certain day" became the Christian Lord's day, the day of the resurrection, commemorated weekly on Sunday and annually at Easter. Mark may have omitted the expected description of the women's lamentation because it was unbefitting resurrection day.

The women's conversation betrays their anxiety over what will happen when they arrive at the tomb: **They said to each other, "Who will roll the stone away from the door for us?"** (16:3). The reason for their concern is explained by the evangelist only after he has shown that their worry is needless: **and looking up, they saw that the stone was rolled away—for it was very large** (16:4). The use of a "large flat circular stone that could be rolled into a groove cut

241

A Woman's Lament

The following excerpt from a poetic lament attributed to the daughter of Jephthah by Pseudo-Philo (first cent. AD) provides an example of the kinds of lamentations over the dead associated with women in that time:

> "Hear, you mountains, my lamentation;
> and pay attention, you hills, to the tears of my eyes;
> and be witnesses, you rocks, of the weeping of my soul. . . .
> . . . I have not made good on my marriage chamber,
> and I have not retrieved my wedding garlands. . . .
> O Mother, in vain have you borne your only daughter,
> because Sheol has become my bridal chamber,
> and on earth there is only my woman's chamber. . . .
> You trees, bow down your branches and weep over my youth,
> You beasts of the forests, come and bewail my virginity,
> for my years have been cut off
> and the time of my life grown old in darkness."
>
> (L.A.B. 40.5–6, trans. Harrington, OTP 2:354)

---

out of the rock" to prevent tomb-robbing was typical of this kind of burial (Donahue and Harrington 2002, 455). The term *anablepsasai*, here translated "looking up," can also be translated as "to gain sight"; the same verb is used for the healing of Bartimaeus (10:51–52); the women see that the stone has been rolled away, presumably through divine agency.

The Messenger in the Tomb (16:5–7)

Inside the tomb, they are met by another marvel; a young man **sitting on the right wearing a white robe** (16:5). The women's astonishment, the youth's white garb (e.g., Matt. 28:3; John 20:12; Acts 1:10; cf. Dan. 7:9; Mark 9:3), his words of reassurance (e.g., Dan. 8:17–18; 10:10–11; Luke 1:13, 30), and his role as a messenger of miraculous events mark him as an angel: **"Don't be amazed! You seek Jesus the Nazarene, who was crucified; he has been raised, he isn't here. Look, this is the place where they laid him! But go out and tell his disciples and Peter that he is going before you to Galilee. You will see him there, just as he told you"** (16:6–7). Possibly the young man is deliberately portrayed as similar to the risen Jesus:

Just as the risen Jesus is enthroned at the right hand of God, as 12:35–37 implies . . . , so this young man is described as "sitting on the right." . . . Since this

242

Figure 17. A Herodian
tomb at Jerusalem.

description has little or no realistic significance in the narrative, the audiences
are led to reflect on its symbolic import and to recall the citation of Psalm 110:1
(109:1 LXX) earlier in the narrative. (Collins 2007, 795)

The first half of his announcement (16:6) refers back to the Passion and burial,
describing with deliberate precision whose tomb it is (Jesus the Nazarene),
how he died (he was crucified), and where exactly he was laid out (This is the
place!). Since two of the three women had witnessed the burial (15:47), the
messenger does not need to confirm that they are in the right location, but
to verify for the audience that the empty tomb had indeed been occupied by
Jesus. The messenger also confirms the reason that the tomb is empty: Jesus
has been raised, as he prophesied (8:31; 9:31; 10:33–34); here Mark uses the
passive to describe the resurrection (*ēgerthē*), thus indicating the divine origin
of the miracle.

In the second half of the announcement (16:7), the women are commissioned to undertake an important task: to tell the other disciples that the risen
Jesus is going before them to Galilee and that they will meet him there. Peter
is mentioned specifically, indicating that despite his denial of Jesus (14:66–72),
he still belongs in the company of the disciples. The phrase usually translated
as "go before" may also mean "to lead," but the assertion that "you will see
him there" implies that the resurrected Jesus has already departed for Galilee,
where the disciples, both male and female, will meet with him. Unlike Luke
(24:50–52; Acts 1–2), Mark and Matthew (28:16–20) both refer to the meetings between the resurrected Jesus and the disciples taking place in Galilee (cf.
John 21:1–23) rather than Jerusalem. The earliest extant version of Mark does
not contain any accounts of disciples' meetings with the risen Jesus, but the
young man's announcement that "he isn't here" and the direction to witness
the place where the corpse had lain indicates that the evangelist regarded the

resurrection as bodily (on the variety of ancient beliefs about the afterlife and resurrection, see Collins 2007, 782–94). If indeed the young man was meant to be similar to Jesus, the evangelist envisioned the resurrected Christ as existing in an angelified state, like Enoch, Elijah, and Moses (see Segal 1989, 510–11, 464–65), transfigured and clothed in garments of shining white (cf. Mark 9:3).

Flight in Fear (16:8)

The oldest extant version of Mark ends with a brief notice that the **women fled from the tomb, for trembling and astonishment had come upon them. And they said nothing to anyone, for they were afraid** (16:8). The majority of Markan scholars today are of the opinion that this is the original ending of the Gospel; yet before the late twentieth century most thought that Mark originally ended with a resurrection narrative that was lost early on in its transmission, and some contemporary scholars continue to maintain this view (see Croy 2003, 18–32). Scholars who take the latter view do not regard either the shorter or longer endings (see "Introductory Matters" above) as original to Mark, but posit an ending similar to those of the other Gospels; Croy, for example, hypothesizes a narrative where the women go on to report the resurrection to the disciples, and where the disciples, especially Peter (cf. 16:7), meet with the risen Christ in Galilee in obedience to his instructions (Croy 2003, 165). The secondary endings written for Mark by early Christian scribes attest to the discomfort of readers who know the other evangelists' resurrection narratives and are not satisfied with a Gospel that ends abruptly with the faithful women running away from the tomb in fear and remaining silent. In Greek, moreover, Mark 16:8 ends with the conjunction *gar* ("for"), which is rarely used to end a sentence and almost never to end an entire book, thus implying that something is missing. However, Pieter Willem van der Horst (1972, 122) opined that if a Greek sentence could end with *gar*, then so could a book like Mark.

Unlike the ancient scribes who composed what they regarded as more-satisfactory endings for Mark, or like generations of Christians familiar with the "longer ending" and the resurrection narratives of the other Gospels, Mark's first-degree audience, who had never heard a written Gospel before, did not necessarily *expect* the story to conclude with accounts of meetings with the risen Jesus. The Markan Passion predictions (8:31; 9:31; 10:33–34) all foretell that Jesus will rise from the dead, but make no mention of resurrection appearances. The messenger's command to the disciples corresponds with Jesus's prophecy at the Last Supper that he will go before them to Galilee (14:28); since Jesus's prophetic utterances inevitably come to pass in Mark, it is unlikely that the evangelist regarded this prophecy to be unfulfilled. Collins (2007, 797) reports that in ancient writings, it was "standard literary practice . . . to allude to well-known events that occurred after those being narrated in the text, without actually narrating those later events." A prominent example is the account of the death of Oedipus, in the last act of Sophocles's *Oedipus at Colonus*, where a messenger describes the mysterious end of the suffering hero, accompanied by only Theseus of Athens, while Oedipus's daughters stand weeping outside the sacred grove where the death is fated to occur:

> When we had gone a little distance, we turned back. Oedipus was nowhere to be seen; but the King was standing alone holding his hand before his eyes as if he had seen some terrible sight that no one could bear to look upon and soon we saw him salute heaven and the earth with one short prayer. In what manner Oedipus passed from this earth, no one can tell. Only Theseus knows. . . . Certain it is that he was taken without a pang, without grief or agony—a passing more wonderful than that of any other man. What I have said will seem, perhaps, like some wild dream of fancy, beyond belief. If so, then you must disbelieve it. I can say no more. (Sophocles, *Oedipus at Colonus*, lines 1647–66, trans. Watling 1947, 121)

Within the Gospel, Mark 13:1–37 is an example of a series of prophecies whose fulfillment does not take place within the Gospel narrative but are meant to be taken as sure by Mark's audience because of the reliability of the prophet, Jesus, and because some of the events foretold by him were coming to pass in their own time.

In the Oedipus cycle, the daughters, Antigone and Ismene, return to Thebes to prevent bloodshed between their warring brothers, a mission in which they fail. In Mark, the women flee in fear and say nothing to anyone. The anonymous earliest commentator on Mark (seventh cent.) interpreted the women's flight and silence positively:

> "But they went out and fled" (Mark 16:8).
> This refers to the future life. *And sorrow and groaning will flee.* Before the resurrection of all, the women portray what they do after the resurrection—they flee death and terror.
> "And they said nothing to anyone."
> Because they alone see the mystery of the resurrection who themselves have deserved to see it. (Cahill 1998, 129–30)

Some twentieth-century interpreters regard this final verse as part of the theme of discipleship failure (e.g., Weeden 1971, 45–51; Tannehill 1977, 403–4). Elizabeth Struthers Malbon (1983, 44–45) opines that Mark's women characters, like the men, are fallible: their silence and fear portray their human limitations in the face of divinity and point to the fallibility of all disciples, whether male or female, compared to the one they follow, Jesus. More recently, Victoria Philips (2001, 234) protests, "I am disturbed and disappointed that they do not tell the other women with them about what happened at the tomb. . . . I wonder about what they could say: 'We learned that Jesus left us behind?' Or,

'We learned that we should go to Galilee; could that be right?' Either would be a more constructive choice than remaining silent." Many scholars, like Malbon, interpret the women's fear in terms of numinous awe in the face of epiphany: "Now they flee from the tomb on their mission, trembling and 'in ecstasy'" (16:8; e.g., Senior 1984, 137; Collins 2007, 800; Sabin 2006, 155–56). Here the translation of the Greek *ekstasis* in its sense of "a state of being in which consciousness is wholly or partially suspended, . . . associated with divine action, *trance, ecstasy*" (BDAG 309) is key:

> The women are, like Jesus [cf. 3:21], out of their minds at what they have learned from the angel. And like those who witnessed a paralytic rise up from his mat and a child brought back to life, they are in a state of ecstasy at the realization of Jesus's resurrection. The word conveys that they are undergoing some shock of transition. They are experiencing a transformation of consciousness. . . . The wise women follow the example of Jesus and flee from the tomb. (Sabin 2006, 156)

Another possibility is that the women's fear stems from popular beliefs about ghosts (cf. 6:49–50) and fears of the raising of the dead through necromancy (see Corley 2002, 123–28). In any case, the women's fear is a natural response to an experience of the supernatural. Furthermore, the notice that the women "said nothing to anyone" does not necessarily indicate absolute silence. In Mark 1:44, Jesus charges the man healed from leprosy to "say nothing to anyone" but to show himself to a priest, to whom the former leper would presumably speak. Similarly, at the end of Mark, the disciples and Peter are the ones whom the women are authorized to tell and who are equipped to understand their story; the audience is meant to assume that the women tell no one *except the other disciples* (cf. Malbon 1983, 45).

Although the women at the tomb go there to perform tasks of corpse preparation expected of females in ancient cultures, the Gospel women do not conform to stereotyped gender expectations by mourning and lamenting but as "close associates, disciples or friends of the dying hero" (Corley 2002, 107, 139); they follow, they serve (15:41; cf. 10:43–45), and they remain with Jesus to the end. These expectations include the carrying out of the mission entrusted to them at the empty tomb: "Go out and tell his disciples and Peter that he is going before you to Galilee. You will see him there, just as he told you" (16:7).

Appendix: The "Longer Ending" (Mark 16:9–20)

Mark's longer ending falls into four main episodes: (1) the resurrected Jesus appears to Mary Magdalene (16:9–11); (2) Jesus appears to two other disciples (16:12–13); (3) Jesus appears to the Eleven and preaches to them (16:14–18); (4) Jesus ascends to heaven, and the disciples carry out their commission (16:19–20).

Other Biblical Writings with Abrupt Endings

Although the ending of Mark seems unsatisfactory to many modern readers, other biblical books end unexpectedly. For example, the Deuteronomistic History (Joshua–2 Kings) concludes with the notice that the Babylonian king Evil-Merodach released the last Davidic king of Judah, Jehoiachin, from prison in the thirty-seventh year of his exile and treated him respectfully (2 Kings 25:27–30), rather than announcing the fall of Babylon and the return from exile. The book of Jonah ends with God's chastising the resentful prophet for his lack of compassion on the people—and livestock—of Nineveh (4:6–11), rather than portraying Jonah as repenting of his hard-heartedness. Instead of describing the dramatic trial and martyrdom of Paul, Acts ends with the apostle's awaiting his appeal to Caesar in Rome for two years at his own expense (Acts 28:30–31). What happened to Paul afterward is left up to the imagination of the reader/audience. J. Lee Magness (1986, 6–9, 25–85) has shown that many other ancient writings have similarly open endings.

The appearance **first to Mary Magdalene** is somewhat jarring after the women's fearful departure in Mark 16:8, but for a second-century audience familiar with the Gospel of John, it would recall the famous scene of Mary's encounter with the risen Jesus in John 20:11–18. The notice that Mary Magdalene is the one **from whom he had cast seven demons** (16:9b) seems strange in a Gospel that contains no such exorcism story; however, Luke 8:2 refers to Mary in similar terms. As in the other Gospels, Mary tells **those who had been with him** of her experience in the midst of their mourning (16:10; cf. Matt. 28:8; John 20:18; cf. Luke 24:10). The skepticism of the other disciples echoes the scene in Luke where, after finding the empty tomb, Mary Magdalene and other women tell the apostles, who refuse to believe them (Luke 24:10–11; cf. the story of "doubting Thomas" in John 20:24–25). That Mary Magdalene is the only disciple named in the longer ending testifies to her significance as first witness to the resurrection in the early church.

In the next episode (16:12–13), Jesus appears **in another form** (*en hetera morphē*) to two more disciples on the way to the countryside. The two return to Jerusalem and tell the others, but again, they are not believed. The incident seems to be based on Luke 24:13–35, the meeting on the Emmaus road. However, unlike the Lukan story, where the risen Jesus is finally recognized "in the breaking of the bread," the motif of the disciples' unbelief is repeated.

The third appearance is to the Eleven as they are reclining at table; this time, Jesus excoriates them for their hard-heartedness in not believing the previous witnesses to his resurrection (16:14). Jesus then preaches a brief sermon, prophesying the mission of the early church:

Go into all the world and preach the good news to all the creation. Whoever believes and is baptized will be saved, and whoever does not believe will be condemned. And these signs will accompany those who believe; in my name they shall cast out demons, they shall speak in new tongues, and they shall raise serpents in their hands, and if they drink anything deadly, it will not hurt them; upon the sick they will lay hands, and they will be well. (16:15–18)

Once again, the elements of the speech echo other Gospels (Matt. 28:19; cf. Luke 24:47) and especially Acts, with its themes of baptism (e.g., 2:38, 41; 8:12), miraculous signs (e.g., 2:19, 22, 43; 4:30), exorcisms (16:16–18; cf. 19:12–17), speaking in tongues (2:4, 11; 10:46; 19:6), being unharmed by poisonous serpents (28:3–5), and healing by the laying on of hands (9:17; 28:8).

Motifs from Luke-Acts are carried through in the concluding verses, where **the Lord Jesus** is taken up to heaven to sit at the right hand of God (Mark 16:19; cf. Luke 24:51; Acts 1:9; 2:25, 34; 5:31; 7:55–56). Richard T. France (2002, 687) notes that the final verse "is virtually a summary of the whole book of Acts in a nutshell": **And they went out and preached everywhere, with the Lord working with them and the word confirmed through the accompanying signs** (16:20).

There are clear disjunctions between Mark 16:1–8 and the longer ending. The longer ending is obviously derivative of the other Gospels and Acts, but the appended verses extend the Markan theme of the unbelief/hard-heartedness of the disciples to the period after the resurrection. The obduracy of the Eleven is remedied only when the risen Jesus appears to them, rebukes them harshly (the verb *ōneidisen* means to find fault with someone in a demeaning way, or justifiably to reproach another; BDAG 711), and sends them forth with a sermon

Drinking Deadly Poison

Mark 16:18b refers to the ability of believers to drink poison without being harmed, a tradition not paralleled in the book of Acts or any other canonical writing. This deficit is remedied in a story, attributed to Philip, that Justus Barsabbas, one of the candidates for apostleship in Acts 1:23, drank a deadly poison but survived through divine grace, reported by the church historian Eusebius (*Hist. eccl.* 3.39.9). James A. Kelhoffer (2000, 432–66) has shown that early Christian extracanonical writings show considerable fascination with the theme of immunity to poison, including the Barsabbas tradition, the testing of the parents of Jesus in the *Protevangelium of James*, the Eucharist as a preventive for poison in Hippolytus's *Apostolic Tradition* 36, the apostle Matthias surviving a potion administered by cannibals (*Acts of Andrew and Matthias*), and traditions about the apostle John's encounters with poisoners in several apocryphal writings (*The Virtues of John*, *The Passion of John*, *The Acts of John in Rome*; Kelhoffer 2000, 433).

that amounts to a summary of early Christian traditions about the apostolic age. The "original" Mark's emphasis on faith as preceding miracles and the challenge to the reader in Mark 16:8 to believe without seeing that Jesus is risen are negated by the longer ending's representation of the disciples as only believing when they see the Lord Jesus and are exhorted by the resurrected Lord. The message of the new ending—and consequently of the Gospel as a whole—for its second-century audience is twofold. First, the resurrection is verified by eyewitnesses: initially Mary Magdalene, then the two disciples, then the Eleven. Second, the apostolic mission as portrayed in Acts and other early Christian writings is commanded by the risen Jesus, who still works together with them, and whose word is confirmed by powerful signs.

Theological Issues

Although the women's flight from the tomb was likely the original ending of the Gospel, Mark 16:9–20 is the traditional ending, and it continues to be received as Scripture by many present-day Christians. Lectionaries include it as a reading for Ascension Day, forty days after Easter (cf. 16:19). The wording of the Great Commission in Mark 16:15, "Go ye into all the world, and preach the Gospel to every creature" (KJV), is quoted as often as Matthew's "Go ye therefore, and teach all nations, baptizing them in the name of the Father, and of the Son, and of the Holy Ghost" (28:19 KJV). Should Christians be concerned that these verses were not written by the evangelist but by a second-century scribe who wanted to rectify the Gospel's abrupt ending and adapt its message to new circumstances? If those scholars who argue that the original ending was lost are right, can it be possible for inspired Scripture to disappear? Or was the hypothetical Markan ending lost because it wasn't so inspired? What if, like the Nag Hammadi writings, the Dead Sea Scrolls, and the *Gospel of Judas*, Mark's "original ending" was found in modern times? While such a discovery would certainly excite biblical scholars, and the text would make its way into critical editions and new translations of the Bible, it is doubtful that it would displace the traditional ending's status in the church. Perhaps the best way to consider the multiple endings of Mark—including any hypothetical endings that might surface in the future—is that they are snapshots of early churches at various points in their history, struggling to understand the implications of Mark's Gospel for their own times and circumstances (for a fuller account of the second-century context of the longer ending, see Kelhoffer 2000).

Although the alternative endings are evidence of early Christian unease with Mark 16:8, many contemporary interpreters regard the original conclusion as highly effective. For example, Bart Ehrman (2005, 68) speculates that "Mark may well have intended to bring his reader up short with his abrupt ending—a clever way to make the reader stop, take a faltering breath, and ask: What?" Similarly, Norman Petersen (1980, 163) observes,

> The ultimate closure to Mark's story comes in the reader's imaginative positing of a meeting in Galilee—because 16:8 is the bridge between the expectation (re-) generated in 16:7 and the implied satisfaction provided by "Galilee," and because Galilee constitutes the imaginative resolution of the story's plot—in seeing Jesus the eleven come to understand what they had not previously understood.

Such an "imaginative positing" includes the reader's own answer to if and how the messenger's commission was ultimately carried out: to supply their own Markan ending—or continuation. The open ending of Mark compels readers to envision their own sequel to the story, a sequel in which they take part. This is consistent with the rest of the Gospel, which portrays Jesus and his message in bold and demanding terms, for the reader to ponder and take to heart. Jesus is a figure of sharp contrasts: powerful and suffering, angry and compassionate, faithful and desolate, a popular teacher whose message is veiled in mystery and parables. Throughout the Gospel, the reader, like the sometimes recalcitrant disciples, is exhorted to see, hear, perceive, and understand the meaning of Jesus's proclamation of the reign of God through senses illumined by faith. For contemporary Christians, the message of the Gospel that Jesus is both the powerful messiah and the beloved Son of God, the suffering son of man who will vindicate the faithful in the reign of God— all this has been tempered by centuries of familiarity. Mark's first-century audience, however, likely did not easily equate suffering with divine sonship, crucifixion with vindication. Above all, for Mark's audience, unlike many contemporary readers, the threat of persecution and even martyrdom for the sake of the reign of God was a very real cause for fear and anxiety: "If anyone wants to follow after me, let them deny themselves and take up their cross and follow me. For the one who wants to save their life will lose it; but the one who loses their life on my account and of the good news will save it" (8:34–35; cf. 13:9–13). The fear of the women who flee the tomb—panic at finding the unexpected, numinous awe in the presence of the miracle before their eyes, fear of the consequences of delivering the young man's extraordinary message—is well justified. In the face of such fears, Mark challenges the reader/audience to "see" the risen Christ through the lens of faith, to "hear" the words of Jesus relayed by the messenger and obey them, and to follow Jesus's example in proclaiming the good news of God, whatever the cost. The resurrection proclaimed by the messenger is fulfilled not only in the story of Jesus, but also in the faithfulness of his disciples, then and now.

Bibliography

Abrahams, Israel. 1917–24. "The Tannaitic Tradition and the Trial Narratives." In *Studies in Pharisaism and the Gospels*. New York: Ktav.

Achtemeier, Paul J. 1970. "Toward the Isolation of Pre-Marcan Miracle Catenae." *Journal of Biblical Literature* 89:265–91.

———. 1972. "The Origin and Function of the Pre-Marcan Miracle Catenae." *Journal of Biblical Literature* 91:198–221.

———. 1978. "'And He Followed Him': Miracles and Discipleship in Mark 10:46–52." *Semeia* 11:115–45.

Adams, Edward. 2005. "The Coming of the Son of Man in Mark's Gospel." *Tyndale Bulletin* 56:39–61.

Ahearne-Kroll, Stephen P. 2001. "'Who Are My Mother and My Brothers?' Family Relations and Family Language in the Gospel of Mark." *Journal of Religion* 81:1–25.

———. 2007. *The Psalms of Lament in Mark's Passion*. Cambridge: Cambridge University Press.

Akin, Jimmy. 2008. "Bad Aramaic Made Easy." Catholic Answers. http://www.catholic.com/library/Bad_Aramaic_Made_Easy.asp.

Albertz, Martin. 1919. *Die synoptischen Streitgespräche: Ein Beitrag zur Formengeschichte des Urchristentums*. Berlin: Trowitzsch & Sohn.

Alsup, John E. 1979. "Mark 1:14–15." *Interpretation* 33:394–98.

Anderson, Hugh. 1981. *The Gospel of Mark*. New Century Bible. Grand Rapids: Eerdmans; London: Marshall, Morgan & Scott.

Anderson, Janice Capel. 1992. "Feminist Criticism: The Dancing Daughter." In *Mark and Method: New Approaches in Biblical Studies*, edited by Janice Capel Anderson and Stephen D. Moore, 103–34. Minneapolis: Fortress.

Anderson, Janice Capel, and Stephen D. Moore, eds. 1992. *Mark and Method: New Approaches in Biblical Studies*. Minneapolis: Fortress.

Anderson, Robert T. 2000. "Samaritans." In *Eerdmans Dictionary of the Bible*, edited by David Noel Freedman, 1159–60. Grand Rapids: Eerdmans.

Ascherman, Arik W. 2006. "Tisha B'Av [*Tiš'â Bě'Āb*]: Human Rights and Self-Criticism." Rabbis for Human Rights. http://rabbisforhumanrights.org/tisha-bav-human-rights-and-self-criticism.

Atkinson, Kenneth. 2000. "Synagogue." In *Eerdmans Dictionary of the Bible*, edited by David Noel Freedman, 1260–62. Grand Rapids: Eerdmans.

Aune, David. 1991. *Prophets and Prophecy in Early Christianity*. Grand Rapids: Eerdmans.

———. 2003. *Westminster Dictionary of New Testament and Early Christian Literature and Rhetoric*. Louisville: Westminster John Knox.

Avalos, Hector. 2000. "Leprosy." In *Eerdmans Dictionary of the Bible*, edited by David Noel Freedman, 801. Grand Rapids: Eerdmans.

Balabanski, Victoria. 1997. *Eschatology in the Making: Mark, Matthew, and the Didache*. Society for New Testament Studies Monograph Series 28. Cambridge: Cambridge University Press.

———. 2002. "Opening the Closed Door: A Feminist Rereading of the 'Wise and Foolish Virgins' (Matt. 25.1–13)." In *The Lost Coin: Parables of Women, Work and Wisdom*, edited by Mary Ann Beavis, 71–97. London and New York: Sheffield Academic Press.

Barton, Stephen C. 1994. *Discipleship and Family Ties in Mark and Matthew*. Society for New Testament Studies Monograph Series 80. Cambridge: Cambridge University Press.

Bauckham, Richard. 1994a. "The Brothers and Sisters of Jesus: An Epiphanian Response to John P. Meier." *Catholic Biblical Quarterly* 56:686–700.

———. 1994b. "Jesus and the Wild Animals (Mark 1:13): A Christological Image for an Ecological Age." In *Jesus of Nazareth, Lord and Christ: Essays on the Historical Jesus and New Testament Christology*, edited by Joel B. Green and Max Turner, 3–21. Grand Rapids: Eerdmans.

———. 1998. "For Whom Were the Gospels Written?" In *The Gospels for All Christians: Rethinking the Gospel Audiences*, edited by Richard Bauckham, 9–48. Grand Rapids: Eerdmans.

———. 2002. *Gospel Women: Studies of the Named Women in the Gospels*. Grand Rapids: Eerdmans.

Beale, G. K., and D. A. Carson, eds. 2007. *Commentary on the New Testament Use of the Old Testament*. Grand Rapids: Baker Academic.

Beasley-Murray, G. R. 1954. *Jesus and the Future: An Examination of the Criticism of the Eschatological Discourse, Mark 13, with Special Reference to the Little Apocalypse Theory*. London: Macmillan.

———. 1957. *A Commentary on Mark 13*. London: Macmillan.

Beavis, Mary Ann. 1987. "The Trial before the Sanhedrin (Mark 14:53–65): Reader Response and Greco-Roman Readers." *Catholic Biblical Quarterly* 49:581–96.

———. 1988. "Women as Models of Faith in Mark." *Biblical Theology Bulletin* 18:3–9.

———. 1989. *Mark's Audience: The Literary and Social Context of Mark 4:1–34*. Journal for the Study of the New Testament: Supplement Series 33. Sheffield: Sheffield Academic Press.

———. 1998. "From the Margin to the Way: The Story of Bartimaeus." *Journal for the Feminist Study of Religion* 14:19–39.

———. 2006. *Jesus and Utopia: Looking for the Kingdom of God in the Roman World*. Minneapolis: Fortress.

———. 2008. "Feminist (and Other) Reflections on the Woman with Seven Husbands (Mark 12:20–23)." In *Hermeneutik der Gleichnisse Jesu: Methodische Neuansätze zum Verstehen urchristlicher Parabeltexte*, edited by Ruben Zimmerman, 603–17. Wissenschaftliche Untersuchungen zum Neuen Testament 231. Tübingen: Mohr Siebeck.

———. 2010. "The Resurrection of Jephthah's Daughter: Judges 11:34–40 and Mark 5:21–24, 35–43." *Catholic Biblical Quarterly* 72:46–62.

Berger, Klaus. 1973. "Die königlichen Messiastraditionen des Neuen Testaments." *New Testament Studies* 20:1–44.

Best, Ernest. 1981. *Following Jesus: Discipleship in the Gospel of Mark*. Journal for the Study of the New Testament: Supplement Series 4. Sheffield: JSOT Press.

Bilezikian, Gilbert G. 1977. *The Liberated Gospel: A Comparison of the Gospel of Mark and Greek Tragedy*. Grand Rapids: Baker Academic.

Black, C. Clifton. 1993. "Was Mark a Roman Gospel?" *Expository Times* 105:36–40.

———. 2005. *Mark: Images of an Apostolic Interpreter*. Minneapolis: Fortress.

Black, Matthew. 1967. *An Aramaic Approach to the Gospels and Acts: With an Appendix on the Son of Man*. 3rd ed. Oxford: Clarendon.

Blomberg, Craig L. 1990. *Interpreting the Parables*. Leicester, UK: Apollos.

Bock, Darrell L., and Daniel B. Wallace. 2007. *Dethroning Jesus: Exposing Popular Culture's Quest to Unseat the Biblical Christ*. Nashville: Nelson.

Bolt, Peter G. 2003. *Jesus' Defeat of Death: Persuading Mark's Early Readers*. Society for New Testament Studies Monograph Series 125. Cambridge: Cambridge University Press.

Bond, Helen Katharine. 2004. *Caiaphas: Friend of Rome and Judge of Jesus?* Philadelphia: Westminster John Knox.

Boobyer, G. H. 1959–60. "The Secrecy Motif in Mark's Gospel." *New Testament Studies* 6:225–35.

Booker, Stephen. 2004. *The Seven Basic Plots: Why We Tell Stories*. New York: Continuum.

Boomershine, Thomas E. 1981. "Mark 16:8 and the Apostolic Commission." *Journal of Biblical Literature* 100:225–39.

Boring, M. Eugene. 1990. "Mark 1:1–15 and the Beginning of the Gospel." *Semeia* 52:43–81.

———. 1995. "The Gospel of Matthew: Introduction, Commentary, and Reflections." *The New Interpreter's Bible*, edited by Leander E. Keck, 8:87–505. Nashville: Abingdon.

————. 2006. *Mark: A Commentary*. New Testament Library. Minneapolis: Fortress.

Bornkamm, Günther. 1970. "Πνεῦμα Ἄλαλον: Eine Studie zum Markusevangelium." In *Das Altertum und jedes neue Gute: Für Wolfgang Schadewaldt zum 15. März 1970*, edited by Konrad Gaiser. Stuttgart: Kohlhammer.

Borrell, Augustí. 1998. *The Good News of Peter's Denial: A Narrative and Rhetorical Reading of Mark 14:54, 66–72*. Atlanta: Scholars Press.

Boucher, Madeline. 1977. *The Mysterious Parable: A Literary Study*. Catholic Biblical Quarterly Monograph Series. Washington, DC: Catholic Biblical Association.

Bowman, John. 1965. *The Gospel of Mark: A New Jewish-Christian Passover Haggadah*. Leiden: Brill.

Brant, Jo-Ann. 2004. *Dialogue and Drama: Elements of Greek Tragedy in the Fourth Gospel*. Peabody, MA: Hendrickson.

Brock, Rita Nakashima. 1989. "And a Little Child Will Lead Us: Christology and Child Abuse." In *Christianity, Patriarchy and Abuse: A Feminist Critique*, edited by Joanne Carlson Brown and Carole R. Bohn, 42–61. Cleveland: Pilgrim.

Brock, Rita Nakashima, and Rebecca Ann Parker. 2001. *Proverbs of Ashes: Violence, Redemptive Suffering, and the Search for What Saves Us*. Boston: Beacon.

Brown, Joanne Carlson, and Carole R. Bohn, eds. 1989. *Christianity, Patriarchy, and Abuse: A Feminist Critique*. Cleveland: Pilgrim.

Brown, Raymond E. 1971. "Jesus and Elisha." *Perspective* 12:85–104.

————. 1994. *The Death of the Messiah, from Gethsemane to the Grave: A Commentary on the Four Passion Narratives*. Vol. 1. New York: Doubleday.

Brown, Raymond E., and John Meier. 1983. *Antioch and Rome: New Testament Cradles of Catholic Christianity*. Mahwah, NJ: Paulist Press.

Brumberg-Kraus, Jonathan. 1999. "'Not by Bread Alone . . .': The Ritualization of Food and Table Talk in the Passover Seder and in the Last Supper." *Semeia* 86:165–91.

Bryan, Christopher. 1993. *Preface to Mark: Its Literary and Cultural Settings*. New York: Oxford University Press.

Buchanan, George Wesley. 1965. "Some Vow and Oath Formulas in the New Testament." *Harvard Theological Review* 58:319–26.

Bultmann, Rudolf. 1963. *The History of the Synoptic Tradition*. New York: Harper & Row.

Burkitt, F. C. 1910. *The Earliest Sources for the Life of Jesus*. London and Boston: Constable.

Burridge, Richard. 2004, *What Are the Gospels? A Comparison with Greco-Roman Biography*. 2nd ed. Grand Rapids: Eerdmans.

Burroughs, Dillon. 2007. *The Jesus Family Tomb Controversy: How the Evidence Falls Short*. Ann Arbor, MI: Nimble.

Butler, H. E., trans. 1921–33. *Quintilian: Institutio Oratoria*. 4 vols. London: Heinemann.

Butts, James R. 1986a. "The *Chreia* in the Synoptic Gospels." *Biblical Theology Bulletin* 16:132–38.

———. 1986b. "The *Progymnasmata* of Theon: A New Text with Translation and Commentary." PhD diss., Claremont University.

Cahill, Michael, ed. and trans. 1998. *The First Commentary on Mark: An Annotated Translation*. New York and Oxford: Oxford University Press.

Cameron, James, and Simcha Jacobovici, directors. 2007. *The Jesus Family Tomb: The Discovery, the Investigation, and the Evidence That Could Change History*. Discovery Channel.

Carlston, C. E. 1975. *The Parables of the Triple Tradition*. Philadelphia: Fortress.

Carrington, Philip. 1952. *The Primitive Christian Calendar: A Study in the Making of the Marcan Gospel*. Cambridge: Cambridge University Press.

———. 1960. *According to Mark: A Running Commentary on the Oldest Gospel*. Cambridge: Cambridge University Press.

Carroll, Robert P. 1969. "The Elijah-Elisha Sagas: Some Remarks on Prophetic Succession in Ancient Israel." *Vetus Testamentum* 19:400–414.

Casey, Damien. 2002. "The 'Fractio Panis' and the Eucharist as Eschatological Banquet." *McAuley University Electronic Journal* (August 18). http://www.women priests.org/theology/casey_02.asp.

Casey, Maurice. 1999. *Aramaic Sources of Mark's Gospel*. Society for New Testament Studies Monograph Series. Cambridge: Cambridge University Press.

Catchpole, David R. 1974. "The Synoptic Divorce Material as a Traditio-Historical Problem." *Bulletin of the John Rylands Library* 57:92–127.

Charlesworth, James H. 1995. "The Son of David: Solomon and Jesus (Mark 10:47)." In *The New Testament and Hellenistic Judaism*, edited by Peder Borgen and Søren Giversen, 72–87. Peabody, MA: Hendrickson.

Cheney, Emily. 2000. "Synagogue." In *Eerdmans Dictionary of the Bible*, edited by David Noel Freedman, 1058–59. Grand Rapids: Eerdmans.

Chilton, Bruce. 1982. "Jesus *ben David*: Reflections on the *Davidssohnfrage*." *Journal for the Study of the New Testament* 14:88–112.

Clark, Kenneth W. 1962. "Galilee, Sea of." In *The Interpreter's Dictionary of the Bible*, edited by G. A. Buttrick, 2:348–50. New York and Nashville: Abingdon, 1962.

Cody, Aelred. 1990. "Haggai, Zechariah, Malachi." In *The New Jerome Biblical Commentary*, edited by Raymond E. Brown, Joseph A. Fitzmyer, and Roland E. Murphy, 349–61. Englewood Cliffs, NJ: Prentice Hall.

Collins, Adela Yarbro. 1994. "Rulers, Divine Men, and Walking on the Water." In *Religious Propaganda and Missionary Competition in the New Testament World: Essays Honoring Dieter Georgi*, edited by Lukas Bormann et al., 207–28. Novum Testamentum Supplements 74. Leiden: Brill.

———. 2006. "The Charge of Blasphemy in Mark 14:64." In *The Trial and Death of Jesus: Essays on the Passion Narrative in Mark*, edited by Geert Van Oyen and Tom Shepherd, 149–70. Leuven: Peeters.

———. 2007. *Mark*. Hermeneia. Minneapolis: Fortress.

Combs, Jason Robert. 2008. "A Ghost on the Water? Understanding an Absurdity in Mark 6:49–50." *Journal of Biblical Literature* 2:345–58.

Cope, O. Lamar. 1976. *Matthew: A Scribe Trained for the Kingdom of Heaven.* Catholic Biblical Quarterly Monograph Series 5. Washington, DC: Catholic Biblical Association.

Corley, Kathleen. 1993. *Private Women, Public Meals: Social Conflict in the Synoptic Tradition.* Peabody, MA: Hendrickson.

———. 2002. *Women and the Historical Jesus: Feminist Myths of Christian Origins.* Santa Rosa, CA: Polebridge.

Cotter, Wendy. 1986. "For It Was Not the Season for Figs." *Catholic Biblical Quarterly* 48:62–66.

———. 2001. "Mark's Hero of the Twelfth-Year Miracles: The Healing of the Woman with a Hemorrhage and the Raising of Jairus's Daughter (Mark 5:21–43)." In *A Feminist Companion to Mark*, edited by Amy-Jill Levine, 54–78. Sheffield: Sheffield Academic Press.

Cranfield, C. E. B. 1959. *The Gospel according to St. Mark: An Introduction and Commentary.* New York: Cambridge University Press.

Crossan, John Dominic. 1971. "The Parable of the Wicked Husbandmen." *Journal of Biblical Literature* 90:451–65.

———. 1992. *The Historical Jesus: The Life of a Mediterranean Jewish Peasant.* San Francisco: HarperSanFrancisco.

———. 1994. *Jesus: A Revolutionary Biography.* San Francisco: HarperSanFrancisco.

———. 1995. *Who Killed Jesus? Exposing the Roots of Anti-Semitism in the Gospel Story of the Death of Jesus.* San Francisco: HarperSanFrancisco.

Crossley, James G. 2005. "The Damned Rich (Mark 10:17–31)." *Expository Times* 116:397–401.

Croy, N. Clayton. 2001. "Where the Gospel Text Begins: A Non-Theological Interpretation of Mark 1:1." *Novum Testamentum* 43:106–25.

———. 2003. *The Mutilation of Mark's Gospel.* New York and Nashville: Abingdon.

Culpepper, R. Alan. 2007. *Mark.* Smith & Helwys Bible Commentary. Macon, GA: Smith & Helwys.

Cuvillier, Elian. 1993. *Le concept de ΠΑΡΑΒΟΛΗ dans le second évangile.* Études bibliques, n.s., 19. Paris: Gabalda.

Dahood, Mitchell. 1970. *Psalms 101–150.* Anchor Bible. Garden City, NY: Doubleday.

Danby, Herbert. 1919–20. "The Bearing of the Rabbinic Criminal Code on the Jewish Trial Narratives in the Gospels." *Journal of Theological Studies* 21:51–76.

D'Angelo, Mary Rose. 1992. "Re-membering Jesus: Women, Prophecy, and Resistance in the Memory of the Early Churches." *Horizons* 19:199–218.

Daniélou, Jean. 1961. *Primitive Christian Symbols.* London: Burns & Oates.

Daub, Carl. 1816–18. *Judas Ischariot oder das Böse in Verhältnis zum Guten.* Heidelberg: Mohr & Winter.

Daube, David. 1956. *The New Testament and Rabbinic Judaism.* London: Athlone.

———. 1972–73. "Responsibilities of Master and Disciples in the Gospels." *New Testament Studies* 19:1–15.

Deatrick, Eugene P. 1962. "Salt, Soil, Savior." *Biblical Archaeologist* 25:41–48.

Denton-Borhaug, Kelly. 2007. "The Language of 'Sacrifice' in the Buildup to War: A Feminist Rhetorical and Theological Analysis." *Journal of Religion and Popular Culture* 15 (Spring). http://www.usask.ca/relst/jrpc/art15-langsacrifice.html.

Derrett, J. Duncan M. 1979. "Contributions to the Study of the Gerasene Demoniac." *Journal for the Study of the New Testament* 3:2–17.

DeVries, LeMoyne. 2000. "Caesarea Philippi." In *Eerdmans Dictionary of the Bible*, edited by David Noel Freedman, 207. Grand Rapids: Eerdmans.

Dewey, Joanna. 1973. "The Literary Structure of the Controversy Stories in Mark 2:1–3:6." *Journal of Biblical Literature* 92:394–401.

———. 1980. *Marcan Public Debate.* Society of Biblical Literature Dissertation Series 40. Chico, CA: Scholars Press.

———. 1991. "Mark as Interwoven Tapestry: Forecasts and Echoes for a Listening Audience." *Catholic Biblical Quarterly* 53:221–36.

———. 1994. "The Gospel of Mark." In *Searching the Scriptures*, vol. 2, *A Feminist Commentary*, edited by Elisabeth Schüssler Fiorenza, 470–509. New York: Crossroad.

———. 2004. "Sacrifice No More." In *Distant Voices Drawing Near: Essays in Honor of Antoinette Clark Wire*, edited by Holly E. Hearon, 157–90. Collegeville, MN: Liturgical Press.

Dibelius, Martin. 1934. *From Tradition to Gospel.* New York: Scribner.

Dobbs-Allsopp, Frederick William. 2000. "Lament." In *Eerdmans Dictionary of the Bible*, edited by David Noel Freedman, 784–85. Grand Rapids: Eerdmans.

Dodd, C. H. 1961. *The Parables of the Kingdom.* Rev. ed. New York: Scribner's Sons.

Donahue, John R. 1971. "Tax Collectors and Sinners: An Attempt at Identification." *Catholic Biblical Quarterly* 33:39–61.

———. 1973. *Are You the Christ? The Trial Narrative in the Gospel of Mark.* Society of Biblical Literature Dissertation Series 10. Missoula, MT: Society of Biblical Literature.

———. 1982. "A Neglected Factor in the Theology of Mark." *Journal of Biblical Literature* 101:563–94.

———. 1988. *The Gospel in Parable.* Philadelphia: Fortress.

———. 1995. "Windows and Mirrors: The Setting of Mark's Gospel." *Catholic Biblical Quarterly* 57:1–26.

Donahue, John R., and Daniel J. Harrington. 2002. *The Gospel of Mark.* Sacra Pagina 2. Collegeville, MN: Liturgical Press.

Donaldson, Terence L. 2007. *Judaism and the Gentiles: Jewish Patterns of Universalism (to 135 CE).* Waco: Baylor University Press.

Donfried, Karl P. 1980. "The Feeding Narratives and the Marcan Community: Mark 6,30–45 and 8,1–10." In *Kirche: Festschrift für Günther Bornkamm zum 75. Geburtstag*, edited by D. Lührmann and G. Strecker, 95–103. Tübingen: Mohr (Siebeck).

Donin, Hayim Halevy. 1972. *To Be a Jew: A Guide to Jewish Observance in Contemporary Life.* New York: Basic Books.

Dowd, Sharyn Echols. 1988. *Prayer, Power, and the Problem of Suffering: Mark 11:22–25 in the Context of Markan Theology*. Society of Biblical Literature Dissertation Series 105. Atlanta: Scholars Press.

———. 2000. *Reading Mark: A Literary and Theological Commentary on the Second Gospel*. Macon, GA: Smith & Helwys.

Dowd, Sharyn E., and Elizabeth Struthers Malbon. 2006. "The Significance of Jesus's Death in Mark: Narrative Context and Authorial Audience." *Journal of Biblical Literature* 125:271–97.

Driggers, Ira Brent. 2007. *Following God through Mark: Theological Tension in the Second Gospel*. Louisville: Westminster John Knox.

Drury, John. 1973. "Mark 1:1–14: An Interpretation." In *Alternative Approaches to New Testament Study*, edited by A. E. Harvey, 25–36. London: SPCK.

Duling, D. C. 1983. "Testament of Solomon." In *The Old Testament Pseudepigrapha*, edited by James H. Charlesworth, 1:935–59. Garden City, NY: Doubleday.

Dunn, James D. G. 1980. *Christology in the Making: An Inquiry into the Origins of the Doctrine of Incarnation*. London: SCM.

———. 2003. *Jesus Remembered*. Grand Rapids: Eerdmans.

Dyer, Keith D. 1998. *The Prophecy on the Mount: Mark 13 and the Gathering of the New Community*. International Theological Studies 2. Bern: Lang.

Edwards, J. R. 1989. "Markan Sandwiches: The Significance of Interpolations in Markan Narratives." *Novum Testamentum* 31:193–216.

Ehrman, Bart D. 1999. *After the New Testament: A Reader in Early Christianity*. New York and Oxford: Oxford University Press.

———. 2005. *Misquoting Jesus: The Story behind Who Changed the Bible and Why*. San Francisco: HarperSanFrancisco.

———. 2006. "Christianity Turned on Its Head: The Alternative Vision of the Gospel of Judas." In *The Gospel of Judas*, edited by Rodolphe Kasser, Marvin Meyer, and Gregor Wurst, with Bart D. Ehrman, 77–120. Washington, DC: National Geographic.

Elliott, John H. 2002. "Jesus Was Not an Egalitarian: A Critique of an Anachronistic and Idealist Theory." *Biblical Theology Bulletin* 32:75–91.

———. 2003. "The Jesus Movement Was Not Egalitarian but Family-Oriented." *Biblical Interpretation* 11:173–210.

Elliott, Susan. 2000. "Mystery Cults." In *Eerdmans Dictionary of the Bible*, edited by David Noel Freedman, 931–32. Grand Rapids: Eerdmans.

Ernst, J. 1981. *Das Evangelium nach Markus*. Regensburger Neues Testament. Regensburg: Pustet Verlag.

Esler, Philip. 2005. "The Incident of the Withered Fig Tree in Mark 11: A New Source and Redactional Explanation." *Journal for the Study of the New Testament* 28:41–67.

Evans, Craig A. 1989. *To See and Not Perceive: Isaiah 6:9–10 in Early Jewish and Christian Interpretation*. Journal for the Study of the Old Testament: Supplement Series 64. Sheffield: Sheffield Academic Press.

———. 2001. *Mark 8:27–16:20*. Word Biblical Commentary 34B. Nashville: Nelson.

Fairclough, H. Rushton, trans. 1935. *Virgil*. Vol. 1, *Eclogues; Georgics; Aeneid, Books I–VI*. Rev. ed. Loeb Classical Library 63. Cambridge, MA: Harvard University Press.

Fay, G. 1989. "Introduction to Incomprehension: The Literary Structure of Mark 4:1–34." *Catholic Biblical Quarterly* 51:65–81.

Feldman, Louis H., trans. 1965. *Josephus*. Vol. 12, *Jewish Antiquities, Books XVIII–XIX*. Loeb Classical Library 433. Cambridge, MA: Harvard University Press.

Finlan, Stephen. 2005. *Problems with Atonement: The Origins of, and Controversy about, the Atonement Doctrine*. Collegeville, MN: Liturgical Press.

Fowler, Robert. 1981. *Loaves and Fishes: The Function of the Feeding Stories in the Gospel of Mark*. Society of Biblical Literature Dissertation Series 54. Chico, CA: Scholars Press.

———. 1991. *Let the Reader Understand: Reader-Response Criticism and the Gospel of Mark*. Minneapolis: Fortress.

———. 1992. "Reader Response Criticism: Figuring Mark's Reader." In *Mark and Method: New Approaches in Biblical Studies*, edited by Janice Capel Anderson and Stephen D. Moore, 50–83. Minneapolis: Fortress.

Fox, Ruth. 1996. "Women in the Bible and the Lectionary." *Liturgy* 90 (May/June). http://www.cta-usa.org/reprint6-96/fox.html.

France, Richard T. 2002. *The Gospel of Mark*. New International Greek Testament Commentary. Grand Rapids: Eerdmans.

Frank, Jerome. 1973. *Persuasion and Healing*. Baltimore: Johns Hopkins University Press.

Fredriksen, Paula. 1999. *Jesus of Nazareth: King of the Jews*. New York: Vintage Books.

Freyne, Sean. 1988. *Galilee, Jesus, and the Gospels: Literary Approaches and Historical Investigations*. Philadelphia: Fortress.

Funk, Robert W., and the Jesus Seminar. 1998. *The Acts of Jesus: The Search for the Authentic Deeds of Jesus*. San Francisco: HarperSanFrancisco.

Funk, Robert W., Roy W. Hoover, and the Jesus Seminar. 1993. *The Five Gospels: What Did Jesus Really Say?* New York: Scribner.

Garrett, Susan R. 1998. *The Temptations of Jesus in Mark's Gospel*. Grand Rapids: Eerdmans.

Gaston, Lloyd. 1970. *No Stone on Another: Studies in the Significance of the Fall of Jerusalem in the Synoptic Gospels*. Novum Testamentum Supplements 23. Leiden: Brill.

Gathercole, Simon J. 2006. *The Pre-existent Son: Recovering the Christologies of Matthew, Mark, and Luke*. Grand Rapids: Eerdmans.

Geddert, Timothy J. 1989. *Watchwords: Mark 13 in Markan Eschatology*. Sheffield: JSOT Press.

Gero, Stephen. 1976. "The Spirit as a Dove at the Baptism of Jesus." *Novum Testamentum* 18:17–35.

Gibson, Jeffrey. 1990. "Jesus' Refusal to Produce a 'Sign' (Mk 8.11–13)." *Journal for the Study of the New Testament* 38:37–66.

Gibson, Shimon. 2006. "Is the Talpiot Tomb Really the Family Tomb of Jesus?" *Near Eastern Archaeology* 69:118–24.

Gillmann, Florence Morgan. 2003. *Herodias: At Home in the Fox's Den.* Interfaces. Collegeville, MN: Liturgical Press.

Ginzberg, L. 1913. *The Legends of the Jews.* Vol. 4. Philadelphia: Jewish Publication Society.

Gnilka, Joachim. 1978–79. *Das Evangelium nach Markus.* 4th ed. 2 vols. Evangelisch-katholischer Kommentar zum Neuen Testament. Zurich: Benziger Verlag.

———. 1998–99. *Das Evangelium nach Markus.* 5th ed. 2 vols. Evangelisch-katholischer Kommentar zum Neuen Testament. Zurich: Benziger Verlag.

Goodacre, Mark. 2006. "Scripturalization in Mark's Crucifixion Narrative." In *The Trial and Death of Jesus: Essays on the Passion Narrative in Mark,* edited by Geert Van Oyen and Tom Shepherd, 33–47. Leuven: Peeters.

Goodenough, Erwin R. 1958. *Jewish Symbols in the Greco-Roman Period.* Vol. 8, *Pagan Symbols in Judaism.* New York: Pantheon.

Gorman, Frank H. 2000. "Passover, Feast of." In *Eerdmans Dictionary of the Bible,* edited by David Noel Freedman, 1013–14. Grand Rapids: Eerdmans.

Gould, Ezra P. 1896. *A Critical and Exegetical Commentary on the Gospel according to St. Mark.* International Critical Commentary. Edinburgh: T&T Clark; New York: Charles Scribner's Sons.

Goulder, Michael. 1974. *Midrash and Lection in Matthew.* London: SPCK.

Gowler, David. 2000. *What Are They Saying about the Parables?* Mahwah, NJ: Paulist Press.

Grant, Frederick C. 1943. *The Earliest Gospel.* New York and Nashville: Abingdon.

Green, Joel B. 1988. *The Death of Jesus: Tradition and Interpretation in the Passion Narrative.* Tübingen: Mohr Siebeck.

Gruber, Mayer L. 2000. "Kiss." In *Eerdmans Dictionary of the Bible,* edited by David Noel Freedman, 776. Grand Rapids: Eerdmans.

Grundmann, W. 1973. *Das Evangelium nach Markus.* 6th ed. Theologischer Handkommentar zum Neuen Testament 2. Berlin: Evangelische Verlagsanstalt.

Gundry, Robert. 1993. *Mark: A Commentary on His Apology for the Cross.* Grand Rapids: Eerdmans.

———. 1996. "Εὐαγγέλιον: How Soon a Book?" *Journal of Biblical Literature* 115:321–25.

Gunner, R. A. H. 1962. "Number." In *The New Bible Dictionary,* edited by J. D. Douglas, 841–46. 2nd ed. Leicester, UK: Inter-Varsity; Wheaton: Tyndale House.

Gutiérrez, Gustavo. 1991. "Mark 1:14–15." *Review and Expositor* 88:427–31.

Habermas, Gary R. 2007. *The Secret of the Talpiot Tomb: Unraveling the Mystery of the Jesus Family Tomb.* Nashville: Broadman & Holman.

Hagner, Donald. 2000. "Matthew's Parables of the Kingdom." In *The Challenge of Jesus' Parables,* edited by Richard N. Longenecker, 102–24. McMaster New Testament Studies. Grand Rapids: Eerdmans.

Halliwell, Stephen. 1927. *Aristotle.* Vol. 23, *The Poetics.* Loeb Classical Library 199. Cambridge, MA: Harvard University Press; London: Heinemann.

Hanhart, Karel. 1995. *The Open Tomb, A New Approach: Mark's Passover Haggadah.* Collegeville, MN: Liturgical Press/Michael Glazier.

Hanson, K. C., and Douglas E. Oakman. 1998. *Palestine in the Time of Jesus: Social Structures and Social Conflicts.* Minneapolis: Fortress.

Harrington, Daniel J. 1990. "The Gospel according to Mark." In *The New Jerome Biblical Commentary,* edited by Raymond E. Brown, Joseph A. Fitzmyer, and Roland E. Murphy, 596–629. Englewood Cliffs, NJ: Prentice Hall.

———, trans. 1985. "Pseudo-Philo [*L.A.B.*]." In *The Old Testament Pseudepigrapha,* edited by James H. Charlesworth, 2:297–377. Garden City, NY: Doubleday.

Harrison, Everett Falconer. 1971. *Introduction to the New Testament.* Grand Rapids: Eerdmans.

Hartman, Lars. 1966. *Prophecy Interpreted: The Formation of Some Jewish Apocalyptic Texts and of the Eschatological Discourse in Mark 13 par.* Lund: Gleerup.

Hawkin, David J. 1977. "The Symbolism and Structure of the Marcan Redaction." *Evangelical Quarterly* 49:98–110.

Hedrick, Charles W. 1993. "Miracle Stories as Literary Compositions: The Case of Jairus's Daughter." *Perspectives in Religious Studies* 20:217–33.

Heil, John Paul. 1992. "Reader Response and the Narrative Context of the Parables about Growing Seed in Mark 4:1–34." *Catholic Biblical Quarterly* 54:271–86.

———. 1997. "The Narrative Strategy and Pragmatics of the Temple Theme in Mark." *Catholic Biblical Quarterly* 59:76–100.

———. 2006. "Jesus with the Wild Animals in Mark 1:13." *Catholic Biblical Quarterly* 68:63–78.

Hellerman, Joseph H. 2000. "Challenging the Authority of Jesus: Mark 11:27–33 and Mediterranean Notions of Honor and Shame." *Journal of the Evangelical Theological Society* 43:213–28.

Hengel, Martin. 1968. "Das Gleichnis von den Weingärtnern Mc 12.1–12 im Lichte der Zenonpapyri und der rabbinischen Gleichnisse." *Zeitschrift für die neutestamentliche Wissenschaft* 59:1–39.

———. 1985. *Studies in the Gospel of Mark.* London: SCM.

Herron, Robert W. 1982. "Mark's Jesus on Divorce: Mark 10:1–12 Reconsidered." *Journal of the Evangelical Theological Society* 25:273–81.

———. 1991. *Mark's Account of Peter's Denial of Jesus: A History of Its Interpretation.* Lanham, MD: University Press of America.

Hester, J. David. 1995. "Dramatic Inconclusion: Irony and the Narrative Rhetoric of the Ending of Mark." *Journal for the Study of the New Testament* 57:68–86.

Hock, Ronald F., and Edward N. O'Neil. 1986. *The Chreia in Ancient Rhetoric.* Vol. 1, *The Progymnasmata.* Atlanta: Scholars Press.

Hollenbach, Paul W. 1981. "Jesus, Demoniacs, and Public Authorities: A Socio-Historical Study." *Journal of the American Academy of Religion* 49:119–28.

Holmes, Michael W., trans. and ed. 2006. *The Apostolic Fathers in English*. Grand Rapids: Baker Academic.

Hooker, Morna D. 1991. *The Gospel according to St. Mark*. Black's New Testament Commentaries. London: Black.

———. 1997. *Beginnings: Keys That Open the Gospels*. Harrisburg, PA: Trinity.

———. 2000. "Mark's Parables of the Kingdom (Mark 4:1–34)." In *The Challenge of Jesus' Parables*, edited by Richard N. Longenecker, 79–101. McMaster New Testament Studies. Grand Rapids: Eerdmans.

Horsley, Richard A. 2001. *Hearing the Whole Story: The Politics of Plot in Mark's Gospel*. Louisville: Westminster John Knox.

Horst, Pieter Willem van der. 1972. "Can a Book End with γάρ? A Note on Mark xvi.8." *Journal of Theological Studies*, n.s., 23:121–24.

Hultgren, Arland J. 2000. *The Parables of Jesus: A Commentary*. Grand Rapids: Eerdmans.

Humphries-Brooks, Stephenson. 2004. "The Canaanite Woman in Matthew." In *A Feminist Companion to Matthew*, edited by Amy-Jill Levine and Marianne Blickenstaff, 138–56. Cleveland: Pilgrim.

Hurtado, Larry W. 1983. *Mark*. San Francisco: Harper & Row.

Ilan, Tal. 1992. "'Man Born of Woman . . .' (Job 14:1): The Phenomenon of Men Bearing Metronymes at the Time of Jesus." *Novum Testamentum* 34:23–45.

———. 1995. *Jewish Women in Greco-Roman Palestine*. Peabody, MA: Hendrickson.

Incigneri, Brian J. 2003. *The Gospel to the Romans: The Setting and Rhetoric of Mark's Gospel*. Leiden: Brill.

Ingholt, Harald. 1953. "The Surname of Judas Iscariot." In *Studia orientalia Ioanni Pedersen septuagenario A.D. VII id. nov. anno MCMLIII*, edited by students and friends, 152–62. Copenhagen: Munksgaard.

Isaac, E., trans. 1983. "1 (Ethiopic Apocalypse of) Enoch." In *The Old Testament Pseudepigrapha*, edited by James H. Charlesworth, 1:5–90. Garden City, NY: Doubleday.

Ivie, Robert. 1980. "Images of Savagery in American Justifications for War." *Communications Monographs* 47:279–94.

Jackson, Howard M. 1997. "Why the Youth Shed His Cloak and Fled Naked: The Meaning and Purpose of Mark 14:51–52." *Journal of Biblical Literature* 116:273–89.

Jacobovici, Simcha, and Charles R. Pellegrino. 2007. *The Jesus Family Tomb: The Evidence behind the Discovery No One Wanted to Find*. San Francisco: HarperOne.

Jeremias, Joachim. 1972. *The Parables of Jesus*. 3rd, rev. ed. London: SCM.

———. 1978. "Ηλ(ε)ίας." In *Theological Dictionary of the New Testament*, edited by Gerhard Kittel, trans. Geoffrey W. Bromiley, 2:928–41. Grand Rapids: Eerdmans.

Johnson, Earl S., Jr. 1978. "Mark 10:46–52: Blind Bartimaeus." *Catholic Biblical Quarterly* 40:191–204.

———. 1987. "Is Mark 15:39 the Key to Mark's Christology?" *Journal for the Study of the New Testament* 31:3–22.

Juel, Donald. 1977. *Messiah and Temple: The Trial of Jesus in the Gospel of Mark*. Society of Biblical Literature Dissertation Series 31. Missoula, MT: Scholars Press.

———. 1990. *Mark*. Augsburg Commentary on the New Testament. Minneapolis: Augsburg.

———. 2000. "Messiah." In *Eerdmans Dictionary of the Bible*, edited by David Noel Freedman, 889–90. Grand Rapids: Eerdmans.

Jülicher, Adolf. 1910. *Die Gleichnisreden Jesu*. 2 vols. Tübingen: Mohr.

Kähler, Martin. 1964. *The So-Called Historical Jesus and the Historic Biblical Christ*. Translated by C. Braaten. Philadelphia: Fortress.

Kant, Immanuel. 1909–14. *Literary and Philosophical Essays*. Edited by Charles W. Elliot. Harvard Classics. New York: Collier & Son. http://www.bartleby.com/32/602.html.

Keck, Leander E. 1965–66. "The Introduction to Mark's Gospel." *New Testament Studies* 12:352–70.

Kee, Howard Clark. 1977. *Community of the New Age: Studies in Mark's Gospel*. Philadelphia: Fortress.

———, trans. 1983. "Testaments of the Twelve Patriarchs." In *The Old Testament Pseudepigrapha*, edited by James H. Charlesworth, 1:775–828. Garden City, NY: Doubleday.

Kelber, Werner. 1974. *The Kingdom in Mark: A New Place and a New Time*. Philadelphia: Fortress.

———, ed. 1976. *The Passion in Mark: Studies on Mark 14–16*. Philadelphia: Fortress.

Kelhoffer, James A. 2000. *Miracle and Mission: The Authentication of Missionaries and Their Message in the Longer Ending of Mark*. Tübingen: Mohr Siebeck.

Kelly, Geffrey B., and F. Burton Nelson, eds. 1990. *A Testament to Freedom: The Essential Writings of Dietrich Bonhoeffer*. San Francisco: HarperSanFrancisco.

Kelly, Henry Ansgar. 2006. *Satan: A Biography*. Cambridge: Cambridge University Press.

Kertelge, K. 1970. *Die Wunder Jesu im Markusevangelium: Eine redaktionsgeschichtliche Untersuchung*. Munich: Kösel-Verlag.

Kingsbury, Jack Dean. 1983. *The Christology of Mark's Gospel*. Philadelphia: Fortress.

Kinukawa, Hisako. 1994. *Women and Jesus in Mark: A Japanese Feminist Perspective*. Maryknoll, NY: Orbis Books.

Klassen, William. 1996. *Judas: Betrayer or Friend of Jesus?* Minneapolis: Fortress.

Klijn, A. F. J. 1983. "2 Baruch." In *The Old Testament Pseudepigrapha*, edited by James H. Charlesworth, 1:615–52. Garden City, NY: Doubleday.

Krause, Deborah. 2001. "Simon Peter's Mother-in-Law—Disciple or Domestic Servant? Feminist Biblical Hermeneutics and the Interpretation of Mark 1:29–31." In *A Feminist Companion to Mark*, edited by Amy-Jill Levine, 36–53. Sheffield: Sheffield Academic Press.

Lagrange, P. M. G. 1929. *Évangile selon Saint Marc*. Paris: Lecoffre.

Lambrecht, Jan. 1967. *Die Redaktion der Markus-Apokalypse: Literarische Analyse und Strukturuntersuchung*. Analecta biblica 28. Rome: Päpstliches Bibelinstitut.

————. 1981. *Once More Astonished: The Parables of Jesus*. New York: Crossroad.

Lane, William L. 1974. *The Gospel of Mark*. New International Commentary on the New Testament. Grand Rapids: Eerdmans.

Lemcio, Eugene E. 1978. "External Evidence for the Structure and Function of Mark iv.1–20; vii.14–23 and viii.14–21." *Journal of Theological Studies* 29:323–38.

Lescow, Theodor. 2005. "Die Markuspassion: Eine antike Tragödie." *Biblische Notizen* 127:91–104.

Lev, Elizabeth. 2007. "A Modern Saint; Unearthing San Clemente's [Basilica]; Remembering St. Petronilla's Legacy." http://www.elizabethlev.com/Zenit/2007-06-07.htm.

Levine, Amy-Jill. 2004. "Discharging Responsibility: Matthean Jesus, Biblical Law, and Hemorrhaging Woman." In *A Feminist Companion to Matthew*, edited by Amy-Jill Levine and Marianne Blickenstaff, 70–87. Cleveland: Pilgrim.

Levine, L. I. 1992. "Jewish War (66–73 C.E.)." In *Anchor Bible Dictionary*, edited by David Noel Freedman, 3:839–45. Garden City, NY: Doubleday.

Lightfoot, Robert H. 1934. *History and Interpretation in the Gospels*. London: Hodder & Stoughton.

————. 1950. *The Gospel Message of St. Mark*. Oxford: Clarendon.

Lindsay, Hal. 1970. *The Late Great Planet Earth*. Grand Rapids: Zondervan.

Linnemann, Eta. 1966. *Parables of Jesus: Introduction and Exposition*. Translated by John Sturdy. London: SPCK.

Loader, William. 1996. "Challenged at the Boundaries: A Conservative Jesus in Mark's Tradition." *Journal for the Study of the New Testament* 63:45–61.

Lohse, Eduard. 1964. "*Huios Dauid*." In *Theological Dictionary of the New Testament*, edited by Gerhard Kittel and Gerhard Friedrich, translated by Geoffrey W. Bromiley, 8:484–87. Grand Rapids: Eerdmans.

López, René. 2008a. "Does *The Jesus Family Tomb* Disprove His Physical Resurrection?" *Bibliotheca sacra* 165:425–46.

————. 2008b. *The Jesus Family Tomb Examined*. Springfield, MO: 21st Century.

Lövestam, Evald. 1995. *Jesus and "This Generation": A New Testament Study*. Coniectanea biblica: New Testament Series 25. Stockholm: Almqvist & Wiksell.

Maccoby, Hyam. 2006. *Antisemitism and Modernity: Innovation and Continuity*. London: Routledge.

MacDonald, Dennis R. 2000. *The Homeric Epics and the Gospel of Mark*. New Haven: Yale University Press.

Maclean, Jennifer K. Berenson. 2007. "Barabbas, the Scapegoat Ritual, and the Development of the Passion Narrative." *Harvard Theological Review* 100:309–34.

MacMullen, Ramsay. 1966. "Provincial Languages in the Roman Empire." *American Journal of Philology* 87:1–17.

Magness, J. Lee. 1986. *Sense and Absence: Structure and Suspension in the Ending of Mark's Gospel*. Semeia Studies. Atlanta: Scholars Press.

Malbon, Elizabeth Struthers. 1983. "Fallible Followers: Women and Men in Mark's Gospel." *Semeia* 28:29–48.

————. 1984. "The Jesus of Mark and the Sea of Galilee." *Journal of Biblical Literature* 103:363–77.

————. 1986. *Narrative Space and Mythic Meaning in Mark*. San Francisco: Harper & Row.

————. 1991. "The Poor Widow in Mark and Her Poor Rich Readers." *Catholic Biblical Quarterly* 53:589–604.

————. 1992. "Narrative Criticism: How Does the Story Mean?" In *Mark and Method: New Approaches in Biblical Studies*, edited by Janice Capel Anderson and Stephen D. Moore, 23–49. Minneapolis: Fortress.

————. 2002. *Hearing Mark: A Listener's Guide*. Harrisburg, PA: Trinity.

Maloney, Linda. 2002. "'Swept under the Rug': Feminist Homiletical Reflections on the Parable of the Lost Coin (Luke 15:8–9)." In *The Lost Coin: Parables of Women, Work and Wisdom*, edited by Mary Ann Beavis, 34–38. London: Sheffield Academic Press.

Mann, C. S. [Christopher Stephen]. 1986. *Mark: A New Translation with Introduction and Commentary*. Anchor Bible 27. Garden City, NY: Doubleday.

Marcus, Joel. 1984. "Mark 4:10–12 and Apocalyptic Epistemology." *Journal of Biblical Literature* 103:557–74.

————. 1986. *The Mystery of the Kingdom of God*. Society of Biblical Literature Dissertation Series 90. Atlanta: Scholars Press.

————. 1989. "'The Time Has Been Fulfilled!' (Mark 1:15)." In *Apocalyptic and the New Testament: Essays in Honor of J. Louis Martyn*, edited by Joel Marcus and Marion L. Soardes, 49–68. Sheffield: JSOT Press.

————. 1992a. "The Jewish War and the *Sitz im Leben* of Mark." *Journal of Biblical Literature* 103:441–62.

————. 1992b. *The Way of the Lord: Christological Exegesis of the Old Testament in the Gospel of Mark*. Louisville: Westminster/John Knox.

————. 2000. *Mark 1–8: A New Translation with Introduction and Commentary*. Anchor Bible 27. New York: Doubleday.

————. 2009. *Mark 8–16: A New Translation with Introduction and Commentary*. Anchor Bible 27A. New Haven: Yale University Press.

Mare, W. Harold. 2000. "Decapolis." In *Eerdmans Dictionary of the Bible*, edited by David Noel Freedman, 333–34. Grand Rapids: Eerdmans.

Marshall, C. D. 1989. *Faith as a Theme in Mark's Narrative*. Society for New Testament Studies Monograph Series 65. Cambridge: Cambridge University Press.

Martin, Clarice L. 1993. "Womanist Interpretations of the New Testament: The Quest for Inclusive Translation and Interpretation." In *Black Theology: A Documentary History*, edited by James Cone and Gayraud Wilmore, 1:225–44. 2nd, rev. ed. Maryknoll, NY: Orbis Books.

Martin, Troy W. 2001. "Watch during the Watches (Mark 13:35)." *Journal of Biblical Literature* 120:685–701.

Marxsen, Willi. 1969. *Mark the Evangelist: Studies on the Redaction History of the Gospel*. Translated by James Boyce, Donald Juel, and William Poehlmann, with Roy A. Harrisville. Nashville and New York: Abingdon.

Mason, Steve. 2000a. "Pharisees." In *Eerdmans Dictionary of the Bible*, edited by David Noel Freedman, 1043–44. Grand Rapids: Eerdmans.

———. 2000b. "Sadducees." In *Eerdmans Dictionary of the Bible*, edited by David Noel Freedman, 1150–51. Grand Rapids: Eerdmans.

Matera, Frank J. 1988. "The Prologue as the Interpretative Key to Mark's Gospel." *Journal for the Study of the New Testament* 34:3–20.

Mays, James Luther. 1972. "Jesus Came Preaching: A Study and Sermon on Mark 1:14–15." *Interpretation* 26:30–41.

McCurley, Foster R. 1974. "'And after Six Days' (Mark 9:2): A Semitic Literary Device." *Journal of Biblical Literature* 93:67–81.

McGirk, Tim. 2008. "Jesus 'Tomb' Controversy Reopened." *Time*, January 16. http://www.time.com/time/world/article/0,8599,1704299,00.html.

McKenna, Megan. 1994. *Not Counting Women and Children: Neglected Stories from the Bible*. Maryknoll, NY: Orbis Books.

McVey, Kathleen E., trans. 1989. *Ephrem the Syrian: Hymns*. Classics of Western Spirituality. Mahwah, NJ: Paulist Press.

Meier, John P. 2004. "The Historical Jesus and the Plucking of the Grain on the Sabbath." *Catholic Biblical Quarterly* 66:561–81.

Merritt, L. 1985. "Jesus Barabbas and the Paschal Pardon." *Journal of Biblical Literature* 104:57–68.

Metzger, Bruce M. 1975. *A Textual Commentary on the Greek New Testament*. Corrected ed. Stuttgart: United Bible Societies.

———. 1994. *A Textual Commentary on the Greek New Testament*. 2nd ed. Stuttgart: Deutsche Bibelgesellschaft and United Bible Societies.

Meyers, Eric M. 2006. "The Jesus Tomb Controversy: An Overview." *Near Eastern Archaeology* 69:116–18.

Millar, Fergus. 1993. *The Roman Near East, 31 BC–AD 337*. Cambridge, MA: Harvard University Press.

Miller, Robert J., ed. 1994. *The Complete Gospels*. San Francisco: HarperSanFrancisco and Polebridge.

Miller, Susan. 2004. *Women in Mark's Gospel*. Journal for the Study of the New Testament: Supplement Series 259. London: T&T Clark.

Molinari, Andrea Lorenzo. 2000. "Legion." In *Eerdmans Dictionary of the Bible*, edited by David Noel Freedman, 799. Grand Rapids: Eerdmans.

Moloney, Francis J. 2002. *The Gospel of Mark: A Commentary*. Peabody, MA: Hendrickson.

Moltmann-Wendel, Elisabeth. 2001. *Rediscovering Friendship: Awakening to the Promise and Power of Women's Friendships*. Minneapolis: Fortress.

Monbiot, George. 2008. "If You Care about World Hunger, Eat Less Meat." *Prairie Messenger* (April 30), 14. First published in *The Guardian*, April 15, 2008.

Moore, Clifford H., and John Jackson, trans. 1931. *Tacitus: Histories, Books IV–V; Annals, Books I–III*. Cambridge, MA: Harvard University Press.

Moule, C. F. D. 1953. *An Idiom-Book of New Testament Greek*. Cambridge: Cambridge University Press.

Moxnes, Halvor. 1988. *The Economy of the Kingdom*. Philadelphia: Fortress.

Myers, Ched. 1988. *Binding the Strong Man: A Political Reading of Mark's Story of Jesus*. Maryknoll, NY: Orbis Books.

Nardoni, Enrique. 1981. "A Redactional Interpretation of Mark 9:1." *Catholic Biblical Quarterly* 43:365–84.

Neill, Stephen, and [N.] Tom Wright. 1988. *The Interpretation of the New Testament, 1861–1986*. 2nd ed. Oxford and New York: Oxford University Press.

Neusner, Jacob. 1987. *The Talmud of the Land of Israel*. Vol. 21, *Yebamot*. Chicago Studies in the History of Judaism. Chicago: University of Chicago Press.

———. 1989. *Introduction to the Mishnah*. Northvale, NJ: Jason Aronson.

Neyrey, Jerome H. 1986. "The Idea of Purity in Mark's Gospel." *Semeia* 35:91–128.

Nineham, D. E. 1963. *Saint Mark*. Harmondsworth, UK: Penguin.

Oakman, Douglas E. 1986. *Jesus and the Economic Questions of His Day*. Studies in the Bible and Early Christianity. Lewiston, NY: Mellen.

Oden, Thomas C., and Christopher A. Hall. 1998. *Ancient Christian Commentary on Scripture*. Vol. 2, *Mark*. Downers Grove, IL: InterVarsity.

Osiek, Carolyn, and Margaret Y. MacDonald, with Janet H. Tulloch. 2006. *A Woman's Place: House Churches in Earliest Christianity*. Minneapolis: Fortress.

Owen-Ball, David T. 1993. "Rabbinic Rhetoric and the Tribute Passage (Matt. 22:15–22; Mark 12:13–17; Luke 20:20–26)." *Novum Testamentum* 35:1–14.

Paffenroth, Kim. 2001. *Judas: Images of the Lost Disciple*. Louisville: Westminster John Knox.

Parris, David P. 2002. "Imitating the Parables: Allegory, Narrative and the Role of Mimesis." *Journal for the Study of the New Testament* 25:33–53.

Patterson, Stephen. 2004. *Beyond the Passion: Rethinking the Death and Life of Jesus*. Minneapolis: Fortress.

Payne, P. 1978–79. "The Order of Sowing and Ploughing in the Parable of the Sower." *New Testament Studies* 25:123–29.

Perkins, Pheme. 1990. "The Gospel according to John." In *The New Jerome Biblical Commentary*, edited by Raymond E. Brown, Joseph A. Fitzmyer, and Roland E. Murphy, 942–85. Englewood Cliffs, NJ: Prentice Hall.

———. 2002. "Patched Garments and Ruined Wine: Whose Folly? (Mark 2:21–22; Matt. 9:16–17; Luke 5:36–39)." In *The Lost Coin: Parables of Women, Work and Wisdom*, edited by Mary Ann Beavis, 124–35. London and New York: Sheffield Academic Press.

Perrin, Norman, and Dennis C. Duling. 1982. *The New Testament: An Introduction*. 2nd ed. New York: Harcourt Brace Jovanovich.

Pervo, Richard. 1987. *Profit with Delight: The Literary Genre of the Acts of the Apostles*. Philadelphia: Fortress.

———. 1994. "Early Christian Fiction." In *Greek Fiction: The Greek Novel in Context*, edited by J. R. Morgan and Richard Stoneman, 239–54. London: Routledge.

Pesch, Rudolf. 1968. *Naherwartungen: Tradition und Redaktion in Mark 13*. Düsseldorf: Patmos.

———. 1976–77. *Das Markusevangelium*. Herders theologischer Kommentar zum Neuen Testament. 2 vols. Freiberg: Herder.

Petersen, David L. 2005. "Genesis and Family Values." *Journal of Biblical Literature* 124:5–23.

Petersen, Norman. 1980. "When Is the End Not the End? Literary Reflections on the End of Mark's Narrative." *Interpretation* 34:151–66.

Peterson, Dwight N. 2000. *The Origins of Mark: The Markan Community in Current Debate*. Biblical Interpretation Series 48. Leiden: Brill.

Petzke, G. 1976. "Die historische Frage nach den Wundertaten Jesu." *New Testament Studies* 22:180–204.

Philips, Victoria. 2001. "The Failure of the Women Who Followed Jesus in the Gospel of Mark." In *A Feminist Companion to Mark*, edited by Amy-Jill Levine, 222–34. Sheffield: Sheffield Academic Press.

Pitre, Brant James. 2001. "Blessing the Barren and Warning the Fecund: Jesus' Message for Women concerning Pregnancy and Childbirth." *Journal for the Study of the New Testament* 81:59–80.

Powell, Charles E. 2005. "The 'Passivity' of Jesus in Mark 5:25–34." *Bibliotheca sacra* 162:66–75.

Powery, Emerson B. 2007. "The Gospel of Mark." In *True to Our Native Land: An African American New Testament Commentary*, edited by Brian K. Blount, 121–57. Minneapolis: Fortress.

Priest, J. 1992. "A Note on the Messianic Banquet." In *The Messiah: Developments in Earliest Judaism and Christianity*, edited by James H. Charlesworth, 222–38. The First Princeton Symposium on Judaism and Christian Origins. Minneapolis: Fortress.

Puech, Émile. 2003. "James the Just or Just James? The 'James Ossuary' on Trial." *Bulletin of the Anglo-Israel Archaeological Society* 21:45–53.

Quarles, Charles, ed. 2008. *Buried Hope or Risen Savior: The Search for the Jesus Tomb*. Nashville: Broadman & Holman.

Rackham, H., trans. 1932. *Aristotle*. Vol. 21, *Politics*. Loeb Classical Library 264. Cambridge, MA: Harvard University Press.

Räisänen, Heikki. 1990. *The Messianic Secret in Mark's Gospel*. Edinburgh: T&T Clark.

Reed, Jonathan. 2000. "Capernaum." In *Eerdmans Dictionary of the Bible*, edited by David Noel Freedman, 220–21. Grand Rapids: Eerdmans.

Reid, Barbara E. 2007. *Taking Up the Cross: New Testament Interpretations through Latina and Feminist Eyes*. Minneapolis: Fortress.

Rhoads, David, and Donald Michie. 1982. *Mark as Story: An Introduction to the Narrative of a Gospel*. Philadelphia: Fortress.

Richardson, A. 1941. *The Miracle Stories of the Gospels*. London: SCM.

Ringe, Sharon H. 1985. "A Gentile Woman's Story." In *Feminist Interpretation of the Bible*, edited by Letty M. Russell, 65–72. Philadelphia: Westminster.

———. 2001. "A Gentile Woman's Story Revisited: Rereading Mark 7:24–31." In *A Feminist Companion to Mark*, edited by Amy-Jill Levine, 79–100. Sheffield: Sheffield Academic Press.

Robbins, V. K. 1984. *Jesus the Teacher: A Socio-Rhetorical Interpretation of Mark*. Philadelphia: Fortress.

Roberts, W. Rhys, trans. 1984. *Rhetoric*, by Aristotle. In *Rhetoric*, translated by W. Rhys Roberts; *Poetics*, translated by Ingram Bywater. Both by Aristotle. In one volume. New York: Random House.

Robinson, James M. 1957. *The Problem of History in Mark*. Studies in Biblical Theology 21. London: SCM.

Robinson, R. G. 1985. "Ezekiel the Tragedian." In *The Old Testament Pseudepigrapha*, edited by James H. Charlesworth, 2:804–19. Garden City, NY: Doubleday.

Rohrbaugh, Richard L. 1993. "The Social Location of the Markan Audience." *Biblical Theology Bulletin* 23:114–27.

Roth, Wolfgang. 1988. *Hebrew Gospel: Cracking the Code of Mark*. Oak Park, IL: Meyer-Stone Books.

Royster, Dmitri. 1996. *The Parables: Biblical, Patristic, and Liturgical Interpretation*. Yonkers, NY: St. Vladimir's Seminary Press.

Rutgers, Leonard Victor. 1998. "Roman Policy toward the Jews: Expulsions from the City of Rome during the First Century CE." In *Judaism and Christianity in First-Century Rome*, edited by Karl P. Donfried and Peter Richardson, 93–116. Grand Rapids: Eerdmans.

Sabin, Marie Noonan. 2006. *The Gospel according to Mark*. New Collegeville Bible Commentary. Collegeville, MN: Liturgical Press.

Salyer, Gregory. 1993. "Rhetoric, Purity, and Play: Aspects of Mark 7:1–23." *Semeia* 64:139–69.

Sanders, E. P. 1985. *Jesus and Judaism*. Philadelphia: Fortress.

Sanders, John, ed. 2006. *Atonement and Violence: A Theological Conversation*. New York and Nashville: Abingdon.

Sausa, Don. 2007. *The Jesus Family Tomb: Is It Fact or Fiction? The Scholars Chime In*. Fort Myers, FL: Vision.

Schaberg, Jane D. 2008. "Response to Charlesworth." *SBL Forum*, February. http://sbl-site.org/Article.aspx?ArticleID=753.

Scharen, Hans. 1992. "Gehenna in the Synoptics." *Bibliotheca sacra* 149:324–37, 454–69.

Schildgen, Brenda Deen. 1998. *Power and Prejudice: The Reception of the Gospel of Mark*. Detroit: Wayne State University Press.

Schmidt, Thomas. 1997. "Jesus' Triumphal March to Crucifixion: The Sacred Way as Roman Procession." *Bible Review* (February): 30–37.

Schottroff, Luise. 1980. "Frauen in der Nachfolge Jesu in neutestamentlicher Zeit." In *Traditionen der Befreiung*, vol. 2, *Frauen in der Bibel*, edited by W. Schottroff and W. Stegemann, 91–133. Munich: Kaiser.

————. 1993. "Women as Disciples of Jesus in New Testament Times." In *Let the Oppressed Go Free: Feminist Perspectives on the New Testament*, translated by Annemarie S. Kidder, 80–130. Gender and the Biblical Tradition. Louisville: Westminster/John Knox.

————. 1995. *Lydia's Impatient Sisters: A Feminist Social History of Earliest Christianity*. Louisville: Westminster John Knox.

Schram, Sandra. 2006. "Trial by Statistics." *Near Eastern Archaeology* 69:124–26.

Schreiber, Johannes. 1961. "Die Christologie des Markusevangeliums." *Zeitschrift für die neutestamentliche Wissenschaft* 58:154–63.

Schüssler Fiorenza, Elisabeth. 1983. *In Memory of Her: A Feminist Theological Reconstruction of Christian Origins*. New York: Crossroad.

Schwank, B. 1983. "Neue Funde in Nabatäerstädten und ihre Bedeutung für die neutestamentliche Exegese." *New Testament Studies* 29:429–36.

Schweizer, Eduard. 1970. *The Good News according to Mark*. Translated by Donald H. Madvig. Richmond: John Knox.

Scobie, Charles. 2003. *The Ways of Our God: An Approach to Biblical Theology*. Grand Rapids: Eerdmans.

Scott, Bernard Brandon. 1989. *Hear Then the Parable: A Commentary on the Parables of Jesus*. Minneapolis: Augsburg Fortress.

Segal, Alan F. 1989. *Life after Death: A History of the Afterlife in Western Religion*. New York: Doubleday.

Senior, Donald. 1984. *The Passion of Jesus in the Gospel of Mark*. Wilmington, DE: Michael Glazier.

————. 1987. "'With Swords and Clubs . . .'—the Setting of Mark's Community and His Critique of Abusive Power." *Biblical Theology Bulletin* 17:10–20.

Sheeley, Steven M. 2000. "Judas Iscariot." In *Eerdmans Dictionary of the Bible*, edited by David Noel Freedman, 748–49. Grand Rapids: Eerdmans.

Shiner, Whitney T. 2000. "The Ambiguous Saying of the Centurion and the Shrouding of Meaning in Mark." *Journal for the Study of the New Testament* 78:3–22.

————. 2003. *Proclaiming the Gospel: First-Century Performance of Mark*. Harrisburg, PA: Trinity.

Shuler, R. A. 1982. *A Genre for the Gospels: The Biographical Character of Matthew*. Philadelphia: Fortress.

Silva, Moisés. 2007. "Esaias." In *A New English Translation of the Septuagint*, edited by Albert Pietersma and Benjamin G. Wright, 823–75. Oxford: Oxford University Press.

Smith, D. Moody. 1992. *John among the Gospels*. Minneapolis: Fortress.

Smith, Morton. 1973. *The Secret Gospel: The Discovery and Interpretation of the Secret Gospel according to Mark*. New York: Harper & Row.

Smith, Stephen H. 1995. "A Divine Tragedy: Some Observations on the Dramatic Structure of Mark's Gospel." *Novum Testamentum* 37:209–31.

————. 1996. "The Function of the Son of David Tradition in Mark's Gospel." *New Testament Studies* 42:523–39.

Smith-Christopher, Daniel L. 2000. "Fasting." In *Eerdmans Dictionary of the Bible*, edited by David Noel Freedman, 456. Grand Rapids: Eerdmans.

Sola, D. A. de, and M. J. Raphall. 2009. *Eighteen Treatises from the Mishna*. Santa Cruz, CA: Evinity.

Spencer, F. Scott. 2000. "Theudas." In *Eerdmans Dictionary of the Bible*, edited by David Noel Freedman, 1301. Grand Rapids: Eerdmans.

Spong, John Shelby. 1994. *Resurrection: Myth or Reality?* San Francisco: HarperCollins.

Standaert, Benoit. 1978. *L'Évangile selon Marc: Composition et genre littéraire*. Brugge, Belgium: Sint-Andriesabdij.

Stein, Robert H. 1976. "Is the Transfiguration (Mark 9:2–8) a Misplaced Resurrection Account?" *Journal of Biblical Literature* 95:79–96.

———. 2008. *Mark*. Baker Exegetical Commentary on the New Testament. Grand Rapids: Baker Academic.

Steinhauser, Michael G. 1986. "The Form of the Bartimaeus Narrative (Mark 10,46–52)." *New Testament Studies* 32:583–95.

Sterling, Gregory E. 1993. "Jesus as Exorcist: An Analysis of Matthew 17:14–20; Mark 9:14–29; Luke 9:37–43a." *Catholic Biblical Quarterly* 55:467–93.

Stern, David H. 1991. *Parables in Midrash: Narrative Exegesis in Rabbinic Literature*. Cambridge, MA: Harvard University Press.

———. 1992. *Jewish New Testament Commentary*. Clarksville, MD: Jewish New Testament Publications.

Stewart, Robert B., John Dominic Crossan, and N. T. Wright. 2006. *The Resurrection of Jesus: John Dominic Crossan and N. T. Wright in Dialogue*. Minneapolis: Fortress.

Stock, Augustine. 1982. *Call to Discipleship: A Literary Study of Mark's Gospel*. Dublin: Veritas.

———. 1989. *The Method and Message of Mark*. Wilmington, DE: Michael Glazier.

Stookey, Lawrence Hull. 2000. "Baptism." In *Eerdmans Dictionary of the Bible*, edited by David Noel Freedman, 147–48. Grand Rapids: Eerdmans.

Strong, L. Thomas, III. 2000. "Nard." In *Eerdmans Dictionary of the Bible*, edited by David Noel Freedman, 948. Grand Rapids: Eerdmans.

Swete, Henry Barclay. 1908. *The Gospel according to St. Mark: The Greek Text with Introduction, Notes and Indices*. London: Macmillan.

Tabor, James. 2007. "Two Burials of Jesus of Nazareth and the Talpiot Yeshua Tomb." *SBL Forum*, March. http://sbl-site.org/Article.aspx?ArticleID=651.

Talbert, Charles. 1970. *What Is a Gospel? The Genre of the Canonical Gospels*. Philadelphia: Fortress.

Tannehill, Robert C. 1977. "Disciples in Mark: The Function of a Narrative Role." *Journal of Biblical Literature* 57:386–405.

Taylor, Archer. 1970. *Dictionary of World Literary Terms*. Boston: Writer.

Taylor, Charles. 1970. *Sayings of the Jewish Fathers*. Amsterdam: Philo.

Taylor, Michelle Ellis. 2000. "Dog." In *Eerdmans Dictionary of the Bible*, edited by David Noel Freedman, 352. Grand Rapids: Eerdmans.

Taylor, Vincent. 1935. *The Formation of the Gospel Tradition.* 2nd ed. London: Macmillan.

———. 1966. *The Gospel according to St. Mark.* 2nd ed. London: Macmillan.

Telford, George B. 1982. "Mark 1:40–45." *Interpretation* 36:54–58.

Telford, William R. 1980. *The Barren Temple and the Withered Tree: A Redaction-Critical Analysis of the Cursing of the Fig-Tree Pericope in Mark's Gospel and Its Relation to the Cleansing of the Temple Tradition.* Journal for the Study of the New Testament: Supplement Series 1. Sheffield: JSOT Press.

Theissen, Gerd. 1983. *Miracle Stories of the Early Christian Tradition.* Edinburgh: T&T Clark.

———. 1991. *The Gospels in Context: Social and Political History in the Synoptic Tradition.* Translated by Linda M. Maloney. London: T&T Clark.

Thompson, Kirsten Moana. 2007. *Apocalyptic Dread: American Film at the Turn of the Millennium.* Albany: State University of New York Press.

Thrall, Margaret E. 1969–70. "Elijah and Moses in Mark's Account of the Transfiguration." *New Testament Studies* 16:306–17.

Thurston, Bonnie B. 2008. *The Spiritual Landscape of Mark.* Collegeville, MN: Liturgical Press.

Tipson, Baird. 1984. "A Dark Side of Seventeenth-Century English Protestantism: The Sin against the Holy Spirit." *Harvard Theological Review* 77:301–30.

Tolbert, Mary Ann. 1989. *Sowing the Gospel: Mark's World in Literary-Historical Perspective.* Minneapolis: Fortress.

———. 1992. "Mark." In *The Women's Bible Commentary,* edited by Carol A. Newsom and Sharon H. Ringe, 263–74. Louisville: Westminister/John Knox.

Trocmé, Etienne. 1983. *The Passion as Liturgy: A Study in the Origin of the Passion Narratives in the Four Gospels.* London: SCM.

Tucker, W. Dennis. 2000. "Rabbi, Rabboni." In *Eerdmans Dictionary of the Bible,* edited by David Noel Freedman, 1105–6. Grand Rapids: Eerdmans.

Twelftree, Graham H. 2007. *In the Name of Jesus: Exorcism among Early Christians.* Grand Rapids: Baker Academic.

Unterman, Alan. 1991. *Dictionary of Jewish Lore and Legend.* London: Thames & Hudson.

van der Horst, P. W. *See under* Horst, Pieter Willem van der.

Verhey, Allen. 1984. *The Great Reversal: Ethics and the New Testament.* Grand Rapids: Eerdmans.

Vermès, Géza. 1973. *Jesus the Jew: A Historian's Reading of the Gospels.* Reprint, Philadelphia: Fortress, 1981.

———. 1997. *The Complete Dead Sea Scrolls in English.* New York: Penguin.

Vriesen, Theodor Christian, A. S. van der Woulde, and Brian Doyle. 2005. *Ancient Israelite and Early Jewish Literature.* Leiden: Brill.

Walker, Larry L. 2000. "Heart." In *Eerdmans Dictionary of the Bible,* edited by David Noel Freedman, 563. Grand Rapids: Eerdmans.

Walters, James C. 1998. "Romans, Jews, and Christians: The Impact of the Romans on Jewish/Christian Relations in First Century Rome." In *Judaism and Christianity in First-Century Rome*, edited by Karl P. Donfried and Peter Richardson, 175–95. Grand Rapids: Eerdmans.

Watling, E. F. 1947. *Sophocles: The Theban Plays*. Reprint, London and New York: Penguin, 1974.

Watts, Rikki E. 1997. *Isaiah's New Exodus in Mark*. Tübingen: Mohr Siebeck. Reprint, Grand Rapids: Baker Academic, 2000.

Weeden, Theodore J. 1971. *Mark: Traditions in Conflict*. Philadelphia: Fortress.

Wefald, Eric K. 1996. "The Separate Gentile Mission in Mark: A Narrative Explanation of Markan Geography, the Two Feeding Accounts and Exorcisms." *Journal for the Study of the New Testament* 18:3–26.

Westcott, B. F. 1860. *Introduction to the Study of the Gospels*. New York: Macmillan.

Wheller, Mark. 2003. "The Boat and the Storm: A Literary Analysis of the Gospel of Mark's Boat Motif." MA thesis, Department of Religious Studies, University of Saskatchewan.

Whiston, William, trans. 1987. *The Works of Josephus: Complete and Unabridged*. New updated ed. Peabody, MA: Hendrickson.

White, James R. 2007. *From Toronto to Emmaus: The Empty Tomb and the Journey from Skepticism to Faith*. Birmingham, AL: Solid Ground Christian.

White, K. D. 1964. "The Parable of the Sower." *Journal of Theological Studies* 15:301–7.

Wills, Lawrence M. 1994. "The Jewish Novellas." In *Greek Fiction: The Greek Novel in Context*, edited by J. R. Morgan and Richard Stoneman, 223–38. London: Routledge.

Witherington, Ben, III. 1997. *The Jesus Quest: The Third Search for the Jew of Nazareth*. Leicester, UK: Inter-Varsity.

———. 2001. *The Gospel of Mark: A Socio-Rhetorical Commentary*. Grand Rapids: Eerdmans.

Wray, T. J., and Gregory Mobley. 2005. *The Birth of Satan: Tracing the Devil's Biblical Roots*. New York: Palgrave Macmillan.

Wrede, William. 1901. *Das Messiasgeheimnis in den Evangelien: Zugleich ein Beitrag zum Verständnis des Markusevangeliums*. Göttingen: Vandenhoeck & Ruprecht. ET, *The Messianic Secret*. Cambridge and London: James Clarke, 1971.

Wright, R. B., trans. 1985. "Psalms of Solomon." In *The Old Testament Pseudepigrapha*, edited by James H. Charlesworth, 2:639–70. Garden City, NY: Doubleday.

Wright, Tom [Nicholas Thomas]. 2001. *Mark for Everyone*. London: SPCK.

Yang, Jayhoon. 2004. "'One of the Twelve' and Mark's Narrative Strategy." *Expository Times* 115:253–57.

Index of Subjects

Index of Modern Authors

Index of Scripture and Ancient Sources